PORTUGUESE SPINNER
AN AMERICAN STORY

EDITED BY MARSHA L. MCCABE & JOSEPH D. THOMAS

Marsha L. McCabe

Joseph D. Thomas

A limited edition of 1500
of which this is number _556_

PORTUGUESE SPINNER

AN AMERICAN STORY

PORTUGUESE SPINNER

AN AMERICAN STORY

Stories of History, Culture and Life from

Portuguese Americans in Southeastern New England

EDITED BY

Marsha McCabe & Joseph D. Thomas

WITH

Tracy A. Furtado and Jay Avila

Spinner Publications, Inc.

New Bedford, Massachusetts

Cataloging–in–Publication Data

McCabe, Marsha and Thomas, Joseph D.
Portuguese Spinner: An American Story
288 pp., illus., 28 cm

1. History—New England—Portuguese
2. Portugal—Emigration and Immigration—New England
3. New England—Pictorial Works
4. Oral History—Massachusetts, Southeastern
5. Portugal—Social Life and Customs

I. Thomas, Joseph D. II. Title
Library of Congress Catalogue Number: 96-92236

ISBN: 0932027-385 cloth
ISBN: 0932027-393 paper

Image Editing: Jay Avila
Cover Design: John K. Robson & Joseph D. Thomas

PORTUGUESE SPINNER

AN AMERICAN STORY

published in cooperation with

Slade's Ferry Bank

with major support provided by

Massachusetts Cultural Council

Massachusetts Foundation for the Humanities

Center for Portuguese Studies and Culture at UMass Dartmouth

Students of the University of Massachusetts Dartmouth

City of New Bedford

Dartmouth Arts Council

CITY OF NEW BEDFORD

Frederick M. Kalisz, Jr., Mayor of New Bedford

For two hundred years, pilgrims from Portugal and her colonies have brought their culture, customs, work ethic, moral integrity and celebrations of life to our communities. New Bedford is proud to say that we are the beneficiaries. Portuguese culture defines our city's character and enriches our people boundlessly. With hope that this enrichment continues and helps bring together all the communities in New England who share it, we commend Portuguese Spinner.

— Frederick M. Kalisz, Jr.

CITY OF FALL RIVER

Preserving our history and our heritage is crucial to our future. Portuguese Spinner promises to do just that. It will celebrate the Portuguese culture that has been an integral part of the Spindle City for more than a century. I congratulate Spinner Publications for providing our community as well as the many other communities with strong links to the Portuguese culture with this historical publication.

— Edward M. Lambert, Jr.

Edward M. Lambert, Jr., Mayor of Fall River

HENRY THE NAVIGATOR SPONSORS

ACUSHNET RUBBER COMPANY

PECKHAM RENTAL CENTER
144 Dartmouth Street • New Bedford, MA 02740

ST. ANNE'S HOSPITAL ~ FALL RIVER
Caritas Christi • A Catholic Health Care System • Member

PRINCE HENRY SOCIETY ~ NEW BEDFORD

Vasco da Gama Sponsors

American Copy Supply, Inc., New Bedford

Dartmouth Building Supply, Inc.

C. Douglas Fogg, M.D., F.A.C.S.

Lincoln Press Co. Inc., Fall River

Luzo Foodservice Corporation, New Bedford

McDonald's of New Bedford

Whaling Manufacturing Co. Inc., Fall River

James Sears / Donna Huse photograph

Salt of the Earth Sponsors

Albino Dias and Eleanor Joan Smith
Duraclean Craftsmen / Acacio & Dorothy Ferreira
Açoreana Chouriço and Meat Mfg. Co.
Alves Chiropractic Center, New Bedford
Antonio's Restaurant, New Bedford
Bank of Fall River
BankBoston
Candleworks Restaurant, New Bedford
Chas. S. Ashley & Sons, Inc., New Bedford
Cobblestone Restaurant, New Bedford
Compass Bank
Cornish & Co., Inc.
Dartmouth Funeral Home of Sullivan-Waring
Diane's Place & Confectionary Shop, Westport
Dr. & Mrs. L. Michael Gouveia, New Bedford
Ed Sylvia, CPA, New Bedford

First Citizens Federal Credit Union
Furtado's Chouriço and Linguiça, Fall River
Gaspar's Sausage Co., Inc., Dartmouth
MacLean Consulting, Inc., Boston
Neto Insurance Agency
Paul & Dixon Insurance, New Bedford
Portuguese American Export Line, Inc.
Quaker Fabric Corporation, Fall River
Sippican, Inc., Marion
Southeastern Regional Transit Authority
Ronald Joseph Souza
Sylvia & Company Insurance Agency, Inc.
T.A. Restaurant, Fall River
Rodney Metals, an Allegheny Teledyne Co.
Venus de Milo Restaurant, Swansea

American Eagle Motor Coach, Fairhaven
Cape Island Express Lines, Inc.
Cooper Insurance Agency, Inc., New Bedford
Costa's Fish Market, Fall River
deMello's Furniture of New Bedford, Inc.
Don Adams Home Heating Oil, New Bedford
Duro Industries, Inc., Fall River
Fall River Furniture and Gifts, Inc.
Folco Jewelers, New Bedford
Attorney David A. Jorge, New Bedford
Frank Corp., New Bedford
Gilbert J. Costa Insurance Agency, New Bedford
Inner Bay Cafe, New Bedford
Irene's, Inc., Fall River
Jardin & Dawson Partners, Public Accountants

Jeanne Weaver Swiszcz
John George, Jr., Dartmouth
La-Z-Boy Furniture Galleries, Dartmouth
Miguel's American & Portuguese Restaurant
New Bedford Hearing Aid Service
Pacheco Insurance Agency, Fall River
Pencils, Inc., New Bedford
Dr. & Mrs. Ralph Pollack, Dartmouth
Poyant Signs, Inc., New Bedford
Sarah S. Brayton Nursing Home, Fall River
Southcoast Health System
In memory of Christopher Jon Souza
Vasco da Gama Restaurant / The Butcher Shop
White's of Westport / Hampton Inn

Milton Silvia photograph

CREDITS

Editors

Marsha McCabe
Joseph D. Thomas

Associate Editor

Tracy A. Furtado

Layout / Design

Joseph D. Thomas

Image Editor

Jay Avila

Fund Raisers

Ruth J. Caswell
Deborah DeBarros
Tracy A. Furtado
Milton P. George
Christine Krause
John-Paul Patricio

Copy Editors / Proofreaders

Onésimo T. Almeida
Stephen Cabral
Ruth J. Caswell
Manuel A. Ferreira
Milton P. George
Kathryn Grover
Anne J. Thomas
Manuel Vieira
Rev. Joseph Vivieros

Translators / Interpreters

Frank Avila
Susana Coelho
Rita Monteiro
Naomi Parker
Rosa Rão
Clementina Valente
Michelle Valente

Writers

Onésimo T. Almeida
Christopher Arruda
Paula T. Beech
Stephen Cabral
Kenneth Champlin
Christina Connelly
Eva Cordeiro
Bridget Cushing
Rhondalee Davis
Stephen Farrell
Bela Feldman-Bianco
Tracy A. Furtado
Dan Georgianna
Kathy Hackett
Donna Huse
Gavin Hymes
Jason Leary
Yvonne Levesque
Jill Lupachini
Fatima Martin
Marsha McCabe
Miguel Moniz
Emily A. Monteiro
George Monteiro
Maria da Gloria Mulcahy
Beth Negus
Rick Pavao
Chorlette Penlington
Maria Candida Pereira
Paul Pinto
Philip J. Rackley
Penn Reeve
James Sears
Joseph D. Thomas
Mary T. Silvia Vermette
Lynne Wilde

Photography / Art

Ron Caplain
Miguel Côrte-Real
The Herald-News
Donna Huse
John K. Robson
James Sears
Joseph Sousa
The Standard-Times
Milton Silvia
Joseph D. Thomas
Rev. Joseph Viveiros

Photographic Collections

Amaral Family
Associação Académica
Rodney and Manuel Avila
Frank Avilla
Bel-Art Studio
Irene Braga
Cordeiro Family
Miguel Côrte-Real
DeSousa Family
Edwards Family
Fernandez Family
Furtado Family
Gaspar Family
George Family
Gouveia Family
T. M. Holcombe
Library of Congress
Luiz Family
Mandly Family
Martin Family
Eva and Sophie Medeiros
Parsons Family
Tina Ponte
Raposo Family
Rhode Island Hist. Soc.
Santo Christo Club
Sousa Family
Tavares Family
Tomasia Family
Mary T. Silvia Vermette
Thomas Whittaker
Xavier Family

Contributors

Victor António Augusto
Maria José Carvalho
Everett Caswell
Rev. Luis A. Cardosa
The Consulate of Portugal
Rev. Raul Lagoa
Melissa MacLeod
Rev. John C. Martins
Robert L. McCabe
Roberto Medeiros
Daryl Murphy
Rev John J. Oliveira
Darlene Pavao
Alan Silvia
Rebecca Simonin
Jane Thomas
Linus Travers

Interviewees

Alfredo Alves
Nelson Amaral
José B. Avila
Raymond Canto e Castro
Alberto Cordeiro
Miguel Côrte-Real
Maria DeJesus
Fernanda DeSousa
Armando Estudante
John Fernandes
Manny Fernandes
Gilbert Fernandez
Mary Fonseca
Edward, Joseph and Tobias
    Furtado
Robert, Charles, Edward
    and Fernando Gaspar
John George, Jr.
Noe Gouveia
Ethel Lima
Liduina Linhares
Martin Family
John Medeiros
Eula Mendes
Frank Parsons
Jorge Manuel Pereira
Maria Candida Pereira
José C. Pinheiro
Tina Ponte
Emidio Raposo
António and Mary Lou
    dos Santos
Joseph Sousa
Ligia and Basilio Sousa
Dineia Sylvia
Pedro Tavares
Tavares Family
Maria Tomasia
Mary T. Silvia Vermette

Organizations

Casa da Saudade Library
Center for Portuguese
    Studies at UMass
    Dartmouth
The Herald-News
The Prince Henry Society
    of New Bedford
The Portuguese Times
The Standard-Times
UMass Dartmouth

ACKNOWLEDGMENTS

In the process of crafting this book, we made many wonderful friends. People opened up their hearts, relived their personal lives, allowed everyone to share their experience. This was a brave undertaking and we are truly grateful. It will enrich us all.

Many people shared their family albums and generously allowed us to publish their treasured pictures. Our thanks to *The Standard-Times* of New Bedford and *The Herald-News* of Fall River for permission to use photographs from their archives, and to Miguel Côrte-Real for access to his personal collection.

We thank our professional scholars, Donna Huse, Jim Sears, Dan Georgianna, Penn Reeve, Bela Feldman-Bianco, Onésimo T. Almeida, George Monteiro, Mary T. Silvia Vermette, Stephen Cabral, Miguel Moniz and Maria da Gloria Mulcahy for their thoughtful and creative contributions.

There would have been no book without our hard-working local freelance writers: Stephen Farrell, Christina Connelly, Eva Cordeiro, Emily Monteiro and Jason Leary are new names for us while old friend Ken Champlin has worked with Spinner since 1982.

We owe a debt of gratitude to the students at UMass Dartmouth who participated in the Portuguese Oral History Project between 1986 and 1990. They produced most of the oral histories published here, and hundreds we were not able to include.

Copy editors and proofreaders included Manuel A. Ferreira, editor of the *Portuguese Times*, who helped with matters of fact and the Portuguese language. Kathryn Grover, Manuel Vieira, Onésimo T. Almeida, Stephen Cabral, Anne Thomas and Milton George also helped in proofing.

We thank neighborhood people and business owners on Columbia Street in Fall River and Fox Point in Providence; Professor Frank Sousa and Chancellor Peter H. Cressy at the University of Massachusetts Dartmouth; librarians Dineia Sylvia and Maria José Carvalho of the Casa da Saudade Branch Library of the New Bedford Public Library; and all the members of the Portuguese community in southeastern New England who have supported our efforts.

We are especially grateful to the institutions that have funded this project, particularly the Massachusetts Cultural Council, which has supported Spinner Publications every year since our incorporation in 1983. Generous support also comes from the Massachusetts Foundation for the Humanities, the Center for Portuguese Studies and Culture at UMass Dartmouth, the Luso-American Development Foundation, the student body at UMass Dartmouth, the cities of New Bedford and Fall River, and the Dartmouth Arts Council.

STAFF AND PHOTOGRAPHERS

JOSEPH D. THOMAS is publisher, editor, and contributing writer at Spinner and is also responsible for art editing and design. He has published thirteen books and numerous publications about the history and culture of southeastern Massachusetts. Joe is a recent winner of the Commonwealth Award, Massachusetts' highest cultural achievement award.

MARSHA MCCABE, senior editor and writer at Spinner Publications, is a national award-winning columnist for *The Standard Times*. She is the author of *Not Just Anywhere: The Story of WHALE and the Rescue of New Bedford's Waterfront Historic District*. Her novella, "The Woman Behind the Counter," is featured in *Spinner IV*.

TRACY A. FURTADO, a graduate of UMass Dartmouth in the writing/communications program, is director of special projects and associate editor of *Portuguese Spinner*.

JAY AVILA manages the Spinner Collection, an archive of more than 200,000 images. His special skills include computers and image editing.

RUTH J. CASWELL is managing editor and business manager, and brings strong organizational and research skills to every Spinner project.

MILTON P. GEORGE, former president of SEA (Southeastern Advertising Agency), is marketing director at Spinner.

RON CAPLAIN was looking for a "project" when he ran into a Portuguese festival procession on Brightman Street in Fall River. An Arts Lottery grant took him to São Miguel where he photographed the island festivals. His project turned into a work of art: documenting and comparing the Azorean festivals with the American versions here.

When REVEREND JOSEPH VIVEIROS' collection of snapshots from his annual trips to visit relatives in the Azores, Madeira and mainland Portugal began to attract interest, he decided to share his photos with the public.

MILTON SILVIA, now retired from a distinguished career at *The Standard-Times*, visited mainland Portugal, the Azores and Madeira twice on assignment, the first time to promote tourism, the second to cover a New Bedford soccer team. Regarding the Azores, he remembers: "Each island is different. They look different, the people speak differently. São Miguel is the most harried, the others are more laid back. It's all very picturesque."

Among the many hats worn by JOSEPH D. THOMAS is that of photographer at Spinner. His degree is from the Art Institute of Boston in 1980 and his focus is documenting the people, industry and culture of southeastern Massachusetts.

JOHN K. ROBSON is a free-lance photographer and designer who has worked at Spinner since 1985. He also produces digital video documentaries for personal and commercial use.

JIM SEARS and DONNA HUSE, a husband and wife team, visited São Miguel in 1993 to photograph and research Portuguese gardens. Their aim was to show the continuity of gardening culture between the Azores and southeastern Massachusetts. They received a grant from the Massachusetts Cultural Council to transfer the images to video.

INTRODUCTION

The Portuguese culture with its strong work ethic, delicious tastes and colorful traditions gives a distinctly ethnic flavor to many of the cities and towns in southern New England. The American story of the Portuguese—who first trickled in on whaling ships, who arrived by the thousands to work in the cotton mills and needle trades, and who are now an integral part of the regional economy and social structure—has been waiting to be told.

At Spinner Publications, we have wanted to tell this story for a long time. But where to begin? How to select? How to shape? The subject is enormous. Ultimately, we decided to focus on the lives of people who represent the common experience—working people, neighborhood folk, immigrants who struggled to provide for family and integrate into the mainstream of American life.

Who are the Portuguese? Who are these people who arrived from the beautiful Azorean and Madeiran islands, the Iberian Peninsula or the African colonies; who moved from an agrarian society shaped by the land and the sea, into the heart of the Industrial Revolution? How did they make the enormous psychological adjustments required to begin again in such a very foreign land?

Who are these people who landed in Provincetown and turned to the sea to make a living? Who populated the cities and suburbs from Rhode Island to Cape Cod, turning their urban yards, wooded swamps and glacial thickets into magnificent gardens and productive pastures? Who gave us linguiça and saudade? Religious festivals in the streets? Who have names like Sousa, Medeiros and Amaral?

Portuguese Spinner: An American Story began in the mid 1980s when a visiting professor from Brazil, Bela Feldman-Bianco, was invited to teach at UMass Dartmouth. Arriving with an abundance of energy and creativity, she initiated a resource group at UMD of interested professors whose mission was to help gather oral histories from the Portuguese community. She enlisted Donna Huse in Anthropology, Penn Reeve in Political Science, Fred Gifun in History and others. The group was called the Portuguese Oral History Project.

University students, many of Portuguese descent, were trained in the techniques of conducting oral history, then sent out into the cities and suburbs to interview grandmothers and grandfathers, priests and politicians, shopkeepers and factory workers, farmers and teachers. The result is a collection of over 200 oral history accounts, now stored in the Archives at UMass Dartmouth.

The subjects told their stories honestly and movingly and we tried to select the best and most representative for our book. We do confess to falling in love with several accounts of women from the Azores who described their islands as places of enchantment, compared with the gray industrial reality of their new world in the northeastern United States. Their struggles to adapt, to achieve, to sacrifice so their children might become educated makes for dramatic reading.

Many of the oral histories have a common theme: Immigrant women often described themselves as divided selves, with one foot in Portugal and one foot in the United States, torn between the old world and the new; bound by their parents to the "old ways," but enticed by American culture and its freedoms. For some, this conflict goes on for years, sometimes forever.

Another recurring theme centers around the difference between their pre-immigration image of the United States as a place where streets are paved with gold, and the reality they found when they arrived. Culture shock! Nevertheless, the Portuguese endured, triumphing over prejudice, language problems, inner conflict and long hours of work. The resilience and determination of the people comes through in these personal accounts.

Two years ago, we began shaping and editing the materials we had been gathering for over a decade. With the oral histories at the heart of the book, we sought to provide scholarly overviews for each section, from "Azorean Dreams" to "The Construction of Immigrant Identity" to "Assimilation and Future Perspectives." Finally, we sent local free-lance writers, staff and interns out into the field, to visit farms, churches and clubs. After years of work, we finally have our book. We do not claim to tell the whole story here; that would take volumes. But we do believe we have captured a certain Portuguese flavor.

We realize that in doing this form of history, there will be careful examination of the contents and critical argument over the selections. The oral histories were chosen according to the quality of the story and not on the subject's standing in the community. Likewise, we chose to feature certain farms, fishermen, neighborhoods and landmarks because we had ready access to photographs and information, or because writers had an affinity for a particular subject. We hope that future writers and artists will fill in the gaps by publishing works on many of the worthy subjects we may have omitted.

The reader will note that Cape Verdeans are not represented. We made the decision to treat Cape Verdeans as a separate entity. Over the last 25 years, Cape Verdeans have shown that theirs is a rich history, distinctly African with Portuguese influences, and unique to the world. It is our hope to publish several books dealing with Cape Verdean history in the coming years. The prominence of the Azorean people in these pages merely reflects their dominance in the region.

Portuguese Spinner: An American Story is just that—a story. It is not a chronology of events or a "who's who." It is written for both the Portuguese and non-Portuguese reader. It is a story to inform, entertain, stimulate, encourage, and leave for the ages.

We proudly present *Portuguese Spinner: An American Story.*

Marsha L. McCabe
Joseph D. Thomas

CONTENTS

The volcanic summit of Pico can be seen in the distance from Moinhos de Vento on the neighboring island, Faial. The windmills are a reminder of the Flemish influence dating back to the 14th century.

THE HOMELAND

The Standard-Times Library

Azorean Dreams

By Onésimo T. Almeida

Plato's Atlantis may be submerged under the waters of the Atlantic Ocean. The Azoreans, although great lovers of the balmy beauty of their islands, never believed the Azores could be related to that utopian land. Soon after the discovery of the nine islands of the archipelago by the Portuguese in the first half of the fifteenth century, some of its new inhabitants engaged in voyages to the West in search of Antilia (or the Island of Seven Cities). According to some vague information circulating for centuries in the Iberian peninsula, Antilia lay somewhere in the seas beyond the horizon. Fernão Dulmo, for one, was convinced he could find a tenth island named "Island of Happiness." There is no sound historical record of these dreamers and adventurers ever having found any land. Gaspar Côrte-Real did reach and explore Newfoundland in 1498, but no more is known of him after he decided to continue sailing to the West.

When the Portuguese seaborne empire collapsed, Brazil first attracted the mainland Portuguese. A century later, some Azoreans followed them. (It was actually via Brazil that a group of Portuguese Sephardic Jews ended up being the first Portuguese to settle in North America. Their most important colony was in Newport, Rhode Island, where they built the Truro synagogue.)

The islands were no longer a mandatory stopping point for loaded ships returning from India to Lisbon. The Azoreans, tired of being forgotten in the middle of the Atlantic, still looked West. But by then they could only hope that someone would come to their rescue. Hence the whalers.

In the early 1800s the American whaling industry made the Azores attractive again. The seas surrounding the islands were a fertile ground for sperm whales, and they soon became a stopping point on the route to the

Seventeenth century map of the Azores published by P. Mare Vicent Coronelli of Venice, 1696.

Courtesy of Miguel Côrte-Real

South Atlantic and Pacific. Crewmen, "hardy peasants of those rocky shores," were recruited in the islands in no small numbers, Herman Melville tells us in *Moby-Dick*. By the middle of the century, Charles Nordhoff drew a lasting profile of these "Western Island Portuguese," of whom almost every vessel from New Bedford carried lots:

They are quiet, peaceful, inoffensive people, sober and industrious, penurious almost to a fault, and I believe invariably excellent whalemen. They are held in great esteem by ship owners and captains, but are often despised by their shipmates in the forecastle, who seeing them of such different habits to their own choose to decry them as sneaks and talebearers…

The Azoreans, accustomed to volcanic eruptions, earthquakes and violent storms, forgotten in the middle of the Atlantic, at the mercy of the elements, grew deeply in the belief that only God could save them. Thus the whaling ships must have appeared to them as a disguised divine hand, one which the islanders seized in earnest.

Life was tough on board, the reports from the first daring whalers warned, but others followed suit. America was in their horizon, and working in the whaling ships was proving to be a gateway to the emerging Promised Land. Pedro da Silveira, a poet from Fajã Grande, Flores, powerfully captures the drama and hope of the poor islanders in a poem written a century later when the dream of America had reached its zenith. It is entitled simply, "Island."

Só isto:
O céu fechado, uma ganhoa
pairando. Mar. E um barco na distância:
olhos de fome a adivinhar-lhe, à proa,
Califórnias perdidas de abundância.

The Luso-American poet and scholar George Monteiro has successfully captured the density of this gem in English:

Only this:
Closed sky, hovering heron. Open sea.
A distant boat's hungering prow
eyeing forever those bountiful
  Californias.

Thus, it should come as no surprise that the moment an opportunity to work on firm land appeared, they left ship. Plenty of those

opportunities emerged, for the New England whaling industry was fading slowly and the Industrial Revolution was picking up steam in some New England cities. Life in the islands continued to provide little hope for better days. The cotton mills of New Bedford, Fall River, Pawtucket, and Lowell lured the

Facing the sea, in Lisbon, is the monument to Portugal's discoverers.

Below, two fishermen at Vila Franca mend their nets in preparation for a day's work on the sea.

Milton Silvia photograph

Milton Silvia photograph

21

Roving in the card room of the Devon Mill, (also known as Gosnold Mill), 1926. "Francisco Medeiros (fourth from left, front row) spent all of his working years in cotton mills. He came to New Bedford from a small village, Agua de Pau, Azores, and as a teenager went to Fresno, CA to be a rancher. After a year, he returned to visit his aunt and sister, liked what he saw and stayed. He met Maria L. Pinheiro, from Vila Franca de Campo, who worked as a winder in the mill. They married and raised 10 children— three were weavers at Gosnold and Page Mills," – Eva & Sophie Medeiros (daughters).

Azoreans not only from the whaling ships but also directly from the islands, as the need for manpower increased. The few who remained attached to the sea settled in small fishing communities on Cape Cod, particularly Provincetown, also Nantucket, Martha's Vineyard and Gloucester.

By the second decade of the 1900s, a massive wave of immigrants came from the Azores and, in smaller numbers, from the other archipelagos of Madeira and Cape Verde, as well as mainland Portugal.

Mary Heaton Vorse, one of the founders of *The Provincetown Players*, the theater group that staged the first plays of Eugene O'Neill, wrote in one of her chronicles entitled, *The Portuguese of Provincetown*:

…the immigration of the Portuguese to Provincetown and other fishing ports was unlike any other immigration. They were invited here. What sort of people they are, I have shown in my mention of the Avellars.

This family is unusual and outstanding, yet among the other people from the islands, the same dignity and courage and beauty abound. The gifts which they have brought to this country are incalculable.

Vorse describes the town as mainly Portuguese. "The tax list of Provincetown shows more Portuguese names than it does those of the Americans." On the three-mile-long Commercial Street there were "perpetual little crowds of brilliantly colored Portuguese children." Near Railroad Wharf were "always knots of fisherman—handsome, strong-looking fellows," and as one went toward the West End, one seemed to be "in a foreign community altogether," the names on the shops being "Coreas, Silvas, Cabrals, Mantas… The very language of the street was foreign." Vorse wrote a chronicle entitled *Clan Avellar* which opens with the following lines:

Besides my own family I had another, the Avellars. Our two families were so close

Photograph donated to the New Bedford Textile Museum, courtesy of Eva and Sophie Medeiros

we scarcely knew where the Vorse-O'Briens left off and the Avellars began. Vorses and Avellars are interchangeable in either home. They often slept in each other's houses... All the Avellar children called me "Mother Vorse" and mine called Mrs. Avellar "Ma."

In New Bedford and Fall River the proportions were never as high, but the number of Portuguese immigrants was quite significant. In the first two decades of this century 160,000 Portuguese immigrated to the United States and distributed themselves through paths opened by their predecessors, with higher concentrations in southeastern New England and California.

The Depression caught them by surprise and shattered their American dream. The future was no longer what it used to be. Many returned to the islands, and stories circulated about many dead accounts left in New England banks. Years later, the children of many returned. World War II ended and the United States emerged a giant—a Phoenix reborn. The immigration laws were severe, and the quotas for Portugal were limited. A tragedy in the Azores, the Capelinhos suboceanic volcanic eruption in Faial in 1957, left thousands of Azoreans homeless. Portuguese-Americans initiated the legislation necessary to permit more to come. It attracted

Portuguese fishermen and their families salt codfish in their backyards in Provincetown, MA, circa 1900.

Spinner Collection

23

the attention and empathy of Rhode Island Senator John Pastore and Massachusetts Senator John F. Kennedy.

The new regulations came at the right time, since Portugal and the Azores were experiencing yet another economic crisis with extremely high unemployment. Besides, the African liberation movements reached the colonies and Portugal was maintaining a war on three fronts—Angola, Mozambique, and Guinea-Bissau. Families with adolescents were eager to leave to avoid the draft.

The number of people who took advantage of the opportunity surpassed those of fifty years earlier. Between 1960 and 1970 more than 180,000 Portuguese immigrated to the United States, again replenishing the older communities with Portuguese life that, by then, was slowly fading into the mainstream.

During the first half of this century, tens of thousands of Portuguese assimilated leaving no trace, not even their names. Ferreira was transformed into Smith, Martins into Martin, Pereira into Perry, Morais into Morris. This endless list of acculturated names reflected a desire to blend in externally, yet such people often maintained at deeper levels plenty of ties with the culture of the Old World. That is why Esthelie Smith, a half-Portuguese-American anthropologist, called the Portuguese an "invisible minority."

The Portuguese do not seem to be invisible any longer. Still subdued and going about their business in low profile, they are everywhere in southeastern New England and form a country which I have called the L(USA)land. Because it continues to be heavily Azorean, I have also called it

"Flash light photo of John Sousa, his mother and his brothers and sister." *—Lewis W. Hine, January 1912.*

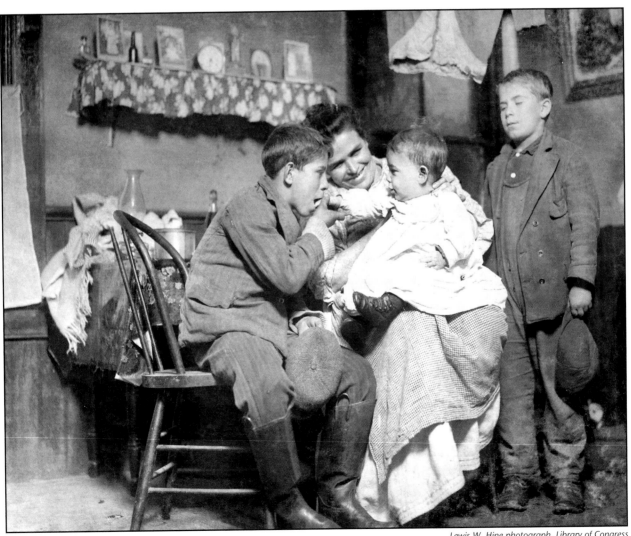

Lewis W. Hine photograph, Library of Congress

the Tenth Island, which suggests that, in fact, for the Azoreans, Atlantis is farther to the west. It is here—the sought-after Island of Happiness of Fernão Dulmo. The America they found had rocky social and cultural shores; and they faced the hardships of a new life, a foreign language and an often hostile culture.

The Azores often reemerge as a Paradise Lost, whereas the new land appears as the punishment that comes with the loss of innocence. Most islanders remain divided between two worlds. They appreciate the many advantages and opportunities in the new world but long for the serene, bucolic atmosphere of their sealand where one can still sense timelessness. To complicate their feelings, Portugal and the Azores have gone through a remarkable transformation in the quarter-century following the overthrow of a long-lasting, backwards political regime.

The immigrants visit their islands, many of them with the feeling that they came to America at the wrong time and thinking to themselves that had they known what was ahead, as well as what was going to happen to the country they left

behind, they would never have ventured out. Most of them, however, have made peace with themselves and feel part of two countries, of two worlds, and try to reap the benefits of both.

Community garden, August 1948. Popularized during the depression years to utilize vacant urban lots and provide people the opportunity to grow food, community gardens were a huge hit in New Bedford and were carried on into the 1950s. Here, Tony Texeira of South Second Street poses beside one of his flourishing pepper plants and displays samples of his cucumbers. His garden was at the Acushnet Mill lot.

Spinner Collection

The Herald-News Library

Fall River's favorite son, Cardinal Humberto Medeiros is surrounded by relatives and friends, including his brother Manuel Medeiros, his sister Mrs. Natalie Souza, brother-in-law Antone S. Souza, and nieces Deborah Souza and Jeanne Medeiros, during the reception at North American College following his elevation as Cardinal in Rome. March 11, 1973.

The islands of the Azores have an impressively rich literature documenting the islands' history of struggles to stay afloat above the often rough high Atlantic seas. One of the registrars of those dramas and tragedies is *Dias de Melo*. In a novel written in the early '60s, Francisco Marroco, a brave whaleman from Pico, arrives in America and tries to do what

Left: Photographer Lewis W. Hine working for the National Child Labor Committee, wrote: "New Bedford. Joe Mello of 62 Grinnell Street. Plays in the mill yard with the other children while waiting for the 6AM bell to signal the start of the workday." August 1911.

Right: Hine wrote: "Fall River. Gertrude Pereira of 99 Stowe Street, 14 years old. 6th grade, Wiley School. At the work certificate office. Applying for work paper, first time. To be a ring spinner in Borden City Mill. Learned to spin during school vacation. Would rather go to work." June 1916.

Lewis W. Hine photograph, Library of Congress

Lewis W. Hine photograph, Library of Congress

Hine notes: "Fall River June 21, 1916. Evening recreation of the 'Young Holy Ghosters.' Ages 15-25, average is 18—all mill workers. All Portuguese. Whole house on George Street. Great need of leadership."

Lewis W. Hine photograph, Library of Congress

many have done—jump off ship and seek his fortune in the great land of opportunity. Here is a glimpse of an emblematic scene in the history of the emigration from the Azores:

"Land ho!" yelled the lookouts.
The whalers all ran to the railing, looked and saw, shrouded in mist, out beyond the bow of the Queen of the Seas—*the land of America!*

Spinner Collection

Courtesy of Joseph Sousa

Early portraits of life in America: A wedding portrait, circa 1900; Maria Purificação Jorge playing the mandolin 1907; and Mr. Nascimento (below) and friends in theatrical garb, circa 1920s.

"My maternal grandfather immigrated to the United States, lived here for three years and then returned disappointed. I grew up listening to his stories of struggles and the misery he saw everywhere. I remember him vividly telling me when I was a child that America was an illusion, a big lie, and he had seen it with his own eyes. Years later I learned from my grandmother that the years he spent here were 1927–30. No wonder."—O. Almeida

Courtesy of Joseph Sousa

27

Standing next to Tony, overwhelmed by the grief he felt inside for the death of João Peixe-Rei, Francisco Marroco also looked and saw—the land of America.

"I know it's none of my business," Tony said to him, with some hesitation, "but do you have any money with you?"

"Any money?"

"Yes."

"How much money do you expect I'd have from home?"

"And where are you going to look for work?"

"California."

"It's a long way to California." And Tony's eyes turned away from Francisco Marroco's eyes. "It's on the other side of the country. To get there, you'll have to go all the way across the country. I don't know how many days by train. It's not cheap."

"Won't my share be enough?"

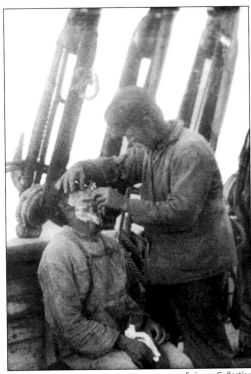

At right, whalemen grooming at sea, 1920s.

Amid barrels of whale oil, lumber and other cargo, Portuguese and Cape Verdean immigrants are taken off the Portuguese steamship Evelyn *at a city pier in New Bedford in 1912.*

"You don't know that..." And Tony was silent.

"I don't know what?"

"That you are not getting a share."

"I'm not getting a share!?"

"No. I thought you knew."

"And the money from my work?"

"The captain's hanging on to it, payment for dropping you off in America."

"That's not fair!" Francisco Marroco felt as if he'd been stabbed in the heart. "Nobody who ever left the Island the way I did even sent a word back that that's the way things work!"

"And there're many other things they never sent back word about. No word back and they won't tell if they return. And you'll wind up doing the same thing."

No, many never told, but, when they did, that seldom acted as a deterrent (well, just think of what I did with my grandfather's advice). They came because the islands, as beautiful as they are, don't have space for them all—"Lots of sea, little land" as the Azorean writer João de Melo put it. They came because, despite all the blood, sweat, and tears of *saudades*, they hoped there would be, above all, a larger land for their children. And now, in a shrinking world, the Atlantic is looking more and more like a river—with Portugal on the other margin. In the heart of the river, for us, lies the lost Atlantis—the Azores.

About the Author

Onésimo T. Almeida is professor and chairman of Portuguese and Brazilian studies at Brown University. A native of the Azores, he received his Ph.D. in philosophy at Brown in 1980. Besides scholarly books and articles, he has also written books of fiction dealing with the Portuguese-American experience.

Spinner Collection

Azorean immigrants land in New Bedford, 1908.

The shores of Rabo do Peixe, São Miguel.

Rev. Joseph Viveiros photograph

THE LONG JOURNEY

INTERVIEW WITH MARIA DE JESUS

BY PAUL PINTO

Maria de Jesus and her family took the long way to the U.S., from Portugal to Africa, back to Portugal, then to America. This "transmigration" from place to place was not uncommon for Portuguese immigrants, but for Maria, who was from a small village in Portugal, it had its adventure. After traveling alone on a boat with her infant son to join her husband in Mozambique, the family got caught up in that country's revolution. They fled for their lives, leaving their belongings behind, and returned to Portugal. In 1980, they journeyed to America, settled in Taunton, worked hard in the Nabisco factory and saw their two children, Paul and Elizabeth, go to college.

· · · · · · · · · · · · · · · · · ·

A Spirit Untouched by Poverty

I was born at home in a small village (*aldeia*) called Jou in the north of Portugal. In that time, women gave birth at home. My aunt Celeste knew a lot about this, and when women were about to give birth she would be called to help. When I was two years old, my mother died giving birth.

I was brought up by my godmother because my father got married again and my stepmother wasn't very nice to her stepchildren. It's not that she was mean. It's just that when she had something special like candy, she would keep it for her own children. She didn't love us. She only loved her own children, and sometimes, when my sister asked my father for money to buy a skirt or sweater or notebook, she would tell my father my sister didn't need it. Sometimes my father would give us the money, even though my stepmother said no.

My godmother had lived with my parents before my mother died, but she didn't want to be in the way when my father remarried. She was 45 years old when she got married herself, and I went to live with her. She used to say, if my father had not married again, she would never have married either. I used to sleep in her bed and I remember the night they got married, I cried so much—I wanted to be with her. They never had any kids so she took care of me. My older brother and sister lived with my father.

My godmother, Maria Ferreira, was like a mother to me. I loved her more than my father. She would keep good things like cheese, linguiça, chouriço or candy and give them to me instead of eating them herself. She always took care of me when I was sick. She gave me lots of love and I loved her too. She died in 1982 and she still lives in my heart. I had a brother, a sister, a stepbrother and two stepsisters, but we didn't share the same table. Though I saw them all the time, at the end of the day we went different ways.

When I went to school in the winter, it rained a lot and the streets were mud. We didn't even have shoes. We had *soquinhas*, a kind of sandal, closed in the front and open in the back with a little heel. Sometimes we would get stuck in the mud and the others would help pull us out. The school was four or five miles from our houses because we had to go down across the valley to the other village.

Traditional outfits found in the northern province Minho, 1962. The hat is called a pampilho. *The dress is* trajo douriense.

The Standard-Times Library

Our hands sometimes were so cold we couldn't even untie our clothes and underwear and go to the bathroom along the way. You see, our underwear didn't have elastic, so we had buttons or a little cloth cord to hold them up. Sometimes our hands were so cold we had to untie the cord of each other's underwear with our teeth. We were all little girls and good friends and we laughed so much, we forgot how cold it was. The kids who lived close to the school brought wood to make a fire. We would dry our clothes and heat our hands and feet. Sometimes we had to dry our socks on our own feet.

In those times we wore little dresses that came up over the knees. We wore long socks but our legs were so cold! We had little pink vests and the boys had blue vests to wear over our clothes. Over the vests we had little coats. The first and second grades were together in one classroom, the third and fourth in another.

I remember one teacher, Miss Saudade, was real nice and people called her *"Maria dos beijos"*—Maria with kisses, because she took care of us when we were sick and she didn't hit us. The people would give her potatoes, vegetables, linguiça and other things because she was not from there and lived in a rented house with her mother. I remember another teacher who was real bad. He would hit the kids with a metal ruler, pull their hair and sometimes kick them because they didn't know how to do the exercises.

I lived in a village of about 300 to 400 people. We lived from the land and life was busy but happy. I would sometimes go get water with some of my girlfriends from a spring well, a little outside the village. There was no water at home. I had to get it with *cântaros*—big plastic jars. I would carry the big one on top of my head and the smaller ones in each hand so I didn't have to go too many times.

Usually I went with Celeste, Adelaide, Helena, Gracinda and Rosa. All of us made a feast of it. We talked about boys, our boyfriends and when the next time we would meet each other again was. Usually our boyfriends would come and meet us on the road. Sometimes one couple would go in front and the other couple a little behind so we could talk more privately. My first boyfriend's name was Norberto. My husband was my second boyfriend. I never kissed Norberto because, in those days, that was unthinkable. When he and his family left for Brazil, I never saw him again.

On Saturday, I would clean the house and wash all the floors. I would pick roses or Marias (white flowers with a yellow center) and beautiful red and white carnations from our garden and I'd put them in a jar or two in the house. Sometimes I also had to help my godmother and uncle get food for the pigs, two cows and a donkey. We brought corn plants that were still green, grass and lots of kale for the pigs. We usually had six or seven pigs, the mother and the little ones.

Portrait of Village Life

On Sundays I would get up and feed the pigs and chickens if my godmother had not done it already. My uncle would take care of the oxen team and the donkey. Then I would wash myself and eat breakfast—coffee, linguiça cooked in the fireplace, homemade butter and black bread, made from

Doing laundry at a rural laundromat near Lisbon, 1967.

Milton Silvia photograph

31

grain we grew. I would then get dressed in my best Sunday clothes—a nice skirt, stockings that came over the knee, black shoes, a shirt and a coat or shawl, then I would go to ten o'clock Mass. Then we'd have lunch—meat or fish and I would help wash the dishes.

In the afternoon, my friends and I would get together, usually on the street outside my house. We talked and laughed and then went for a walk. During grape time, we would pass by our grape-vines and cut some grapes. Sometimes we passed by the little stream that ran out of the spring well and we washed the grapes. Our boyfriends, or just friends, would come and we'd laugh, tease each other about getting married or anything just to laugh. It was the best time because we were all very good friends.

Village life was so full of happiness, everybody knew each other. Sometimes I would be in the window looking at the street and when people passed, we'd talk and laugh. Here in the city (Taunton), I'm always inside the house. When I go out, most of the time I don't see anybody I know. In the village, when people passed by, they would ask

me if I wanted to go with them to the village grocery or to the fields to get fruits and vegetables. There was always so much to do. The time went by very fast. There were no televisions back then, but we didn't need them. People really talked. Some-times it was just gossip, but it was fun to listen to.

In the winter, nights were very long and cold so mostly every night families from two or three nearby houses, or friends and close family, would get together, usually at my godmother's or my father's house, for the *serão*, to pass the night. While the women did their crochet, everybody talked because they all had a lot to say.

They told beautiful stories. I was just a young girl and I remember I would just want to stare at the person telling the story and picture what they were saying. Sometimes I got so involved I'd forget that my back was freezing or my socks were burning because I always had my feet next to the fire. Then I would remove my feet fast. I can't remember any story because it's been such a long time, but I do remember they were very beautiful, entertaining and simple, usually telling or teaching a lesson to us younger children. It was the best.

Pilgrims on the road to Fatima, 1952.

Marriage in Mozambique

Raul Pinto was from the village where the school was. Though I knew who he was and who his family was, I never talked to him except to say, "How are you?" when we passed each other. He was good looking and I think I was too. He asked me to marry him at a feast. In those days, when a boy asked a girl to marry him, it was with the intention of getting married soon.

I didn't want to get married yet, and he kept on asking me whenever he saw me. After I finally said yes, we saw each other more often and danced when we went to feasts. Of course, we never thought of doing anything else but talking. I just knew I wasn't supposed to do something with a boy though nobody ever told me that. All my girlfriends knew too.

Two years after he asked me, we got married, but first he asked my father and godmother for permission and they said yes because they liked him. I was 27 and Raul was 33. It was a small wedding because we did something different from the others. We went away to get married. When we came back, everybody was at my house with lots of food to give us a party.

A month and a half after we got married, my husband left for Africa. His brother was there and called for him. I stayed behind, already pregnant. He had bought his ticket before we got married. He wanted to make a life there, then send for me to give me a better life. He wanted to take me away from the agrarian way of life of the small village. When he left, I lived with my godmother, the same as when I was single.

When I left for Africa, my son Paul was already nine months old. He was so cute. He had a little white hat and had already started talking. We got on the boat in Lisbon. At night, it looked like a big city in the middle of the ocean. One night, the ocean got so bad I could feel the ship move over the waves. Everybody was called to the top deck to get ready for an emergency. The baby was sick because his teeth hurt, and I thought it was going to be the end. The baby was screaming, I was crying and everybody else was screaming too. But in the morning the ocean was so calm, it seemed to be asleep. From then on, the baby got better and we had a nice trip. The trip took 18 days and we arrived in Mozambique on April 18, 1967.

My husband was waiting with his sister and brother-in-law. It was a feast because neither my husband nor the rest of the family had seen the baby. The biggest difference in Africa from Portugal was the climate. It was so hot there. When it's winter in Portugal, it's summer in Africa. And in Africa it's *always* like summer. There was also a fruit I came to like very much called *papaia*. It looked like a big pumpkin and people ate it as if it were a melon. There were other differences such as the way people dressed. The women wore dresses very short and fresh and men wore shorts because it was so hot. I liked Africa very much.

We lived in Africa for seven years. Nine or ten months after I arrived, I had my daughter Elizabeth. Mozambique had been a Portuguese colony and was now fighting for independence. I took care of my son and daughter and the house, and my husband was part owner of a trucking company. Because of the fighting, we had to leave the house and business and all our belongings behind and leave. We couldn't even bring all of our money because the government of Mozambique wanted to keep the money in their banks. We just wanted to leave alive because people we knew and people we had heard of were being killed.

Off to America

I don't remember much about the war. I left for Portugal with my two children, and my husband stayed behind to see if he could do something with the house and business. He planned to meet us in Portugal in one or two months. Then things got worse and he waited to see what would happen. One year later, he was forced to return to Portugal because the houses in Mozambique were going up in flames. In 1975, it became an independent nation.

After my husband returned, we opened a little grocery and gift store in our village with the little money we brought from Africa. The store was on the side of my godmother's house, which she had given to me. We lived there for five years.

In 1980, we came to America in search of a better way of life. Not so much for me and my husband but to be able to give my kids an education that we were never able to have. When I was young, I had heard of America and thought that when people came here, they would become rich. I found out I didn't get rich, but we are able to eat meat everyday, if we wanted to, and give my kids a good education. I love Portugal and I'm always eager to go back and visit loved ones and old customs.

Two Women

Conversation with Mrs. Linhares & Mrs. Pereira

by Maria Candida Pereira

Mrs. Liduina Linhares and Mrs. Maria Candida Pereira talk about life on the island of Pico in the Azores—their youth, working in the fields, courtship and rituals and the expectation of marriage as their only destiny.

. . . .

MRS. LINHARES: We islanders live surrounded by nature. On Pico, in São Caetano village, the majesty of the big mountain stands behind us, spreading itself with valleys, hills and rocks toward the sea. Facing us is the sea and its different moods which shape our lives—making us happy and dreamy when it is calm and blue, filling us with dread when the angry waves invade the land.

MRS. PEREIRA: Looking at the line that separates the sea from the sky, we wonder what is beyond it. We dreamed about a family, a career and a better life. We were dreaming about America. The Islands did not offer much opportunity, only the hope of having a family. We found that better life in America but we still remember life in the Islands with longing. Something is missing: the island dreams, the dances and movies when friends got together; the summer afternoons when we crocheted and laughed; the fountain where we met our boyfriends on the run; the picking up of the grapes and the white church of the village.

MRS. LINHARES: Life on the island of Pico is peaceful and full of joy, a quiet, delightful place where nature, plants and animals seem to live in harmony. You need only experience the beginning of a new day and hear the birds singing, smell the aroma of wet grass and watch the hurry of people going to work to understand this. We loved the mountain, the fields and the sea but wanted more, a better life for ourselves and our children.

Windmills overlook a man and his plow on Santa Maria, circa 1960.

Courtesy of Miguel Côrte-Real

Pico seen from a Faial village, since destroyed by a volcano, 1920s.

Spinner Collection

Figs and Long Skirts

MRS. PEREIRA: All the girls dreamed of being teachers, but the possibilities were few. We had to move to another island to do that, which meant economic expenses and separation from the family. We ended up doing housework and working in the fields. Then we waited until we were 20 or 21 to get married and start our own lives. But the new beginning was nothing new. Once married, life was just the continuation of the life we had when living with our parents—washing clothes, cooking, cleaning the house, feeding the chickens and pigs and working in the fields.

MRS. LINHARES: I liked most working in the fields. We would get up very early, no later than 6:30AM in winter, but even earlier in summer, when we went to the vineyards to pick up figs to make *aguardente,* a kind of brandy. We wore big hats, long skirts and large shirts with long sleeves. Women did not dress in pants in those days, only skirts and dresses.

On the way to work in the fields with the men, we had to be careful about crossing fences. The men were the first to go over, then the women. We also had to be careful about the way we sat. We couldn't cross our legs and we made sure our skirts were covering up our feet. During the season of seeding corn, a man walked in front with a plow, tilling the ground. We walked behind sowing the seeds with a stake. We took precautions when bending over so we would not show our legs.

Picking up figs was painful too. Besides wearing all those clothes, we wore leather sandals called *albarcas,* which were very thin. Every time we walked over the dry rocks of the vineyard, it felt like the rocks were drilling the sandals. The sandals also had leather straps that crossed behind our ankles and tied in the front. When we walked, those straps went up and down and hurt so much. After picking up the figs, we carried them in baskets on top of our heads. We felt so tired by the end, our necks were wobbling and our legs trembling.

MRS. PEREIRA: Working in the fields was especially fun if we worked with a group of girls. Sometimes we sang and told jokes. Other times we just laughed about everything—about a person who passed by and the way she dressed, or a single but old man who looked at us, and we would start laughing and say, "Look at his eyes, he still thinks he is young!" Life was happier at that time. We were closed in our little world because there was no radio or TV. There were films, old films, and we liked the songs from those films so much that on our way home, we sang the songs.

The next day, we could also hear the young people singing or whistling the songs while they were working in the fields. That was the sound of the new day: people singing, along with the noise of the hoes digging and cutting the fields. We used to get up very early to pick apples, potatoes, corn and more. We were poor and had to work hard, but I miss those walks in the morning and the smell of that pure air—a mixture of wet grass, beech and incense.

MRS. LINHARES: We liked working in the fields in summer because of the picking of the grapes, a

Traditional island dress, 1930s—the hat is lenço, *the scarf* carapuça.

Courtesy of Miguel Côrte-Real

task that went from dawn to night. Early in the morning, the women filled baskets with food and carried them on their heads to the vineyards. We took fish and potatoes already cooked or to be cooked at the vineyard to eat all day. First we made a fire for the potatoes, then stuck the fish on a spit for roasting. That food had a different smell, maybe because we ate it next to the vines and the smell of the grapes made the food tastier.

In the fields, the family always worked together, the father, mother, children and sometimes the neighbors. Men would go first with the animals to prepare the land to be cultivated. Then the women went, taking the food and helping with the planting. Once I took a big basket of food on my head and a can of four liters of coffee in my hand. Because the field was far away and the can was very heavy, it started cutting my hand. When we got to the fields, the men ate and then we started working together.

The men had already made the trenches and the women put in the fertilizer—cow, sheep or poultry manure. The men followed us, covering the potatoes or planting the *inhames*. April was a busy month. Besides the *inhames*, we had the sowing of the corn, which involved the whole family. Some were in front pulling up the lupine which was planted before. Others were plowing the soil with the help of the cows. Others were sowing the corn by digging a hole with a stake or putting seeds in the trenches.

MRS. PEREIRA: In the afternoon, we even sat on the sides of the street doing crochet and looking at the young men who were coming from work.

MRS. LINHARES: Some of the girls of our village got married that way, by looks and glances. Men just looked at them when they were passing by in the truck, and they would come on Sundays just to look at them, smile or say how pretty they were. We did not have any entertainment like you have here. We could not say we were going to work hard during the day and have a good time in the evening. In winter, we could not go outside because of the weather and life became a little sad. In winter the temperatures are mild but those islands are desolated by strong winds and rain.

One happy time in winter was the feast. If Mrs. Pereira's pig was going to be slaughtered, the day

The family works together separating grain from the wheat using an old-time harvester called lagoínhas, *Santa Maria, Azores, circa 1900.*

Courtesy of Miguel Côrte-Real

before we would bake the cornbread, scrape the *inhames* and cook them on the wood stove. In the evening my husband would go help Mr. Pereira cut the onions for the blood pudding. While the men were chopping the onions, they were also drinking little glasses of *aguardente*.

The next morning I would go to her house early and take the *inhames* from the wood stove, peel and put them on the dishes. She would be preparing the fish. The men brought us the pig's liver so we could start seasoning it. The onions were mixed with the blood, garlic, pepper and seasoning and we cleaned the intestines to make the linguiça and blood pudding.

MRS. PEREIRA: I also liked the *serões* in winter. We'd get together in one of our friends' houses. The men sat around the kitchen table playing cards and talking about the sowing. The women sat on the floor or in chairs making crochet. When one was almost done with her crochet, we helped her so she could finish it earlier and sell it.

We also told jokes and did crazy things. One night, I and one of my friends—now my sister-in-law—told everybody we were going to the balcony. We were very young and crazy. Instead of going there, we went to pick up pears from my uncle's pear tree. It was far away so we ran fast before they could miss us. We picked up the pears, the leaves and even some branches. There was a full moon that night. On the way home, we started thinking about ghosts and the souls of dead people. We ran home so fast you could see our ankles touching our backs.

MRS. LINHARES: We believed in spirits. We heard stories from our parents and grandparents about things that had happened. In winter at night, the island was very dreadful. We lived right at the bottom of that big mountain next to the sea. In every corner we thought we saw the shadows of people who had died. At night the darkness was so strong, it became more dreadful when the strong wind from the south and the rain would hit the rocks and trees. On those nights we were scared of the noise of a straw scratching the window, a seagull that flew over us or a loose animal that walked on the streets with the chain dragging.

I remember people talking about what happened to a man who was walking by the cemetery. When he left home, he put some straws of corn in his back pants pocket to make cigarettes, then forgot about them. He heard a strange scratching noise with every step he took. Nearing the cemetery, the noise grew louder. He started running.

The noise followed him and grew even stronger. He was terrified. Then something fell to the ground and there it was. Straws of corn!

I also remember somebody had died recently and my mother needed to go to my uncle's house. It was night. She put a coat on her shoulders and left our house. But when she closed the door, a sleeve got stuck in the door. Holding the coat, she felt that something was holding her back and she started screaming. She thought it was the soul of a dead person holding her back.

MRS. LINHARES: In those winter serões, we sometimes started dancing. My father-in-law played the *chamarrita* and we danced. One of the men shouted the steps for us to follow, according to the music. Sometimes we even planned bigger dances, inviting neighbors and friends who lived in other villages. It was one more opportunity for seeing and dancing with our boyfriends.

Courtship

MRS. LINHARES: Courtship was very different then from what it is today. A girl could only talk with a young man during the day and in front of everybody. If by any chance she met a boyfriend and talked with him away from the public eye,

In the Azores, embroidery is a pastime and a cottage industry. This woman babysits, does her work and taps available light.

Rev. Joseph Viveiros photograph

people started talking. They said she was not decent and her mother would be ashamed of not being able to keep her daughters at home.

MRS. PEREIRA: We all had tanks with enough water for the whole year. But in some years, the dry season was longer and we had to get water from a public tank. One day, my boyfriend—who is my husband today—knew I was going to get water, and he went there to talk with me. My mother suspected that and came to watch me. When she saw us talking, she took me home by my arm and beat me up.

MRS. LINHARES: Going to church was one way of seeing our boyfriends. Men always stayed outside in the church yard until the Mass started. The front benches were reserved for the women and the back ones for the men. They were the last to enter and the first to leave. We looked and smiled at them as we were entering or leaving. Just smiling or looking was a way of showing we cared about them. We also went to church on weekdays at special times such as Lent. They knew we were going and they waited just to talk and take us back to our homes.

A young girl laden with fresh supplies, including a garrafão of wine, pauses for a moment on the road home in Santa Maria, 1945.

Courtesy of Miguel Côrte-Real

Courtesy of Miguel Côrte-Real

The Foliões, in traditional costumes on São Miguel in the 1890s, are the musicians who lead the Holy Ghost procession.

Games and Holidays

MRS. LINHARES: *Belamêndoa* was a game we played during Lent with another person. In the weeks before Easter, we said the word *belamêndoa* to our partners, everyday. The one who says it first, gets a point. The one who has less points has to give the other a package of almonds on Easter Sunday. We always chose our boyfriends to be our partners. That was a popular game, and our mothers let us play it, but we used it as an excuse to see them.

MRS. PEREIRA: St. John's Day is very important in a girl's life. The night before, we would write the names of several young men, each on a small piece of paper. Then we wrapped them and placed them under a rose bush. The next morning we went to see which one was opened—that would be the name of our husband-to-be.

On St. John's Day, we got up very early. My grandmother said if we stared at the sky, we could see a cloud with the shape of a sword and King Sebastian, or a new island in the sea. I never saw either one. We also got up early to swim as it was the first day of summer. Sometimes we just sat where the sea could reach us. We did not have bathing suits. We could not afford them and they were considered indecent. We put on old skirts and blouses to take a swim and took other clothes to wear after the swim.

MRS. LINHARES: We would swim very early in the morning so nobody could see us. We'd sit in a big splash of water and wait for the waves to come, then start screaming and laughing when they came stronger and stronger. Then we could only see a mixture of water and girls and hear our screams and the waves throwing us to the rocks. Also, if any seaweed touched our legs, or even our skirts, we would start screaming, "it's an octopus, an octopus!"

MRS. PEREIRA: After taking the bath, we would catch grottos on the rocks and go to the *adega* (wine cellar) to spend the day. There we talked, ate the grottos with cornbread and drank wine. In the evening we made a fire in the streets, then jumped over it or just stayed around and waited for people to approach. This was also a chance to see our boyfriends. If a young man liked us, he would come to see the fire and look at us.

Parents were opposed to courtship, especially for their daughters. They did not want us to do anything that made people start talking. We knew that marriage was going to be our future. I remember, when I was still a child and doing crochet with my mother on our balcony, people from other villages passed by and talked with my mother. They would say, "You have a beautiful girl there. One of these days, she is almost ready for marriage."

MRS. LINHARES: I was always afraid of my parents. When we went to the movies, we went in groups, supervised by a married lady. On the way, we had the opportunity of talking with our boyfriends, but we never sat together. We were afraid somebody would see us and tell our parents. We always dressed up very well to go to the movies because we knew we would see our boyfriends or other young men. At the time, the fashion was pleated skirts and blouses with long sleeves and buttons in the front. I had one of those blouses with the neck the color of the skirt.

MRS. PEREIRA: I also liked to tie my hair with a black barrette covered with a bright stone, sent from America by my godmother. I thought it was beautiful because it shone at night.

MRS. LINHARES: Life in the islands was wonderful but we wanted to have a better life. The ones who left for America had a different future.

MRS. PEREIRA: Coming to America was very good. My children will have the future I wanted and never had. I wanted to be a teacher, but I didn't have the opportunities. Now, I would like my daughter to be the teacher I couldn't be. America gave me the things I wanted when I was young, but now I am missing the happiness I had when I was living on the islands. I don't think I am going to have it again.

MRS. LINHARES: No, never again.

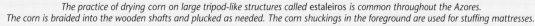

The practice of drying corn on large tripod-like structures called estaleiros *is common throughout the Azores.*
The corn is braided into the wooden shafts and plucked as needed. The corn shuckings in the foreground are used for stuffing mattresses.

Courtesy of Miguel Côrte-Real

SUMMER VACATIONS

by Chorlette Penlington

Though Nelson Amaral was born in America, he found his paradise on the island of São Miguel where he spends summers visiting his uncle's farm: "When walking through the woods, I hear everything, especially the high pitched-sound of birds chirping back and forth to each other. Most of the time you don't see them, but you can hear the fluttering of their wings as they fly from one tree branch to another."

. . . .

As the plane descends on this tiny island in the middle of the Atlantic, the view is breathtaking. The land looks so neat, divided into squares that cover the entire countryside. I land in Ponta Delgada and take a bus to my uncle's farm, located in the village of Lomba de São Pedro on the other side of the island. On my journey I like to picture the farm the way it was the last time I was here. My uncle has acres and acres of land so trying to remember everything occupies the hour ride.

The roads are narrow, winding and dangerous. From my bus window, I can see the ocean at the bottom of high cliffs and jagged rocks below. I freeze in my seat thinking about how far down the water is. I am petrified that the bus might tip over. I turn away from the window and focus my eyes on the flowers along the roadside, hydrangeas and roses. Seeing things growing everywhere is always such a wonderful sight.

Aerial view of Faial.

Milton Silvia photograph

View of Lagoa, São Miguel from Agua de Pau.

James Sears / Donna Huse photograph

I usually arrive at dusk and everyone is there to greet me. My aunt cooks up a big meal. Their house is a typical farmhouse of brick and wood. Outside there are chicken and pig pens, cows in the pasture, hay stacks—lots of hay stacks, and feed scattered all around for the animals and birds passing by.

The twins help me unpack, and we try to catch up on the past eight months. Though I get along well with all five kids, I tend to hang around with the twins, mostly because they are closer to my age. We talk about the latest music in America and the latest happenings with girls. I teach them English, they teach me more Portuguese. They treat me as another brother.

The oldest son is in Rome studying for the priesthood, and the second son works in construction with my uncle—construction is my uncle's second job. The twins work on the land as herders, taking care of the cows. The only girl helps her mother in the house. Anyone who earns money on jobs outside of the family contributes their earnings to the household. But the kids can have what they want, within reason, from the family pot.

The family gets up early and they work all day. I don't help in the fields because I would be completely lost, sort of like a skinny kid trying to lift a 500 pound weight. By the time they taught me the basics, summer would be over. My uncle grows corn, potatoes, vegetables and beans of all kinds. The squares of land are called plateaus, and they shimmer in different shades of green, indicating the different vegetation. The colors are beautiful—lots of green, dark green, light green, green and brown combined, some blends of yellow.

Observing the land, you see hills over hills, going up and down, up and down. The colors of the sunset blend beautifully with the land—pink, an odd color of red and, of course, blue and white from the sky. It is so colorful, unlike any sunset I have ever seen. To the farmers and herders, however, it just means the end of another day of hard work and, soon, the start of another.

My aunt wakes up at 5:30AM, then gets my uncle up. They have been doing this for years. My uncle and cousins head out to the fields to feed the animals, milk the cows, check the vegetation, then return home for breakfast. My aunt and her daughter wash the dishes and begin the house chores—scrubbing the clothes by hand, sewing and stitching, cooking and baking. My cousin is engaged to be married so she must be well-prepared to take care of her husband and children. The girls at a young age are taught how to treat their future husbands and the duties of motherhood.

My uncle and his oldest son then head off to do their construction work, a government job. They do roadwork such as tarring the road and maintaining the beautiful flowers I so admire. The twins usually work the land until dusk. Some days they go into the village to sell milk. With these outside sources of income, the family is pretty well off; the women do not need to work outside of the home.

Bringing home the day's milk supply, São Miguel.

Rev. Joseph Viveiros photograph

Mountain view of coastal farmlands and village on the island of Graçiosa.

Milton Silvia photograph

41

I usually wake up around 8AM or 9, and the family is finished with breakfast and out working. Fresh milk is left on the table for me, and my aunt makes me some breakfast. Then I like to go outside, walk the land and, at some point, meet up with the twins while they are herding. Sometimes if they finish early we head for the beach. The younger one never hesitates.

The beaches are great. With the high cliffs, the jagged rocks and the clear blue water, it's paradise.

Farm boy follows his herd to pasture on São Miguel, 1985.

Rev. Joseph Viveiros photograph

The waves are huge, at least six feet high, and there is a strong undertow. The rocks are sharp and dangerous, and some are life-threatening. My favorite place to swim is a little lake near the farm house. It's small but it's fresh water, very clear and clean, and flows to the ocean. The waterfall is fascinating. We love to swim under it and watch the black tadpoles flying by, but they're too fast to catch.

We eat dinner together (no one eats separately or whenever they feel like it), and it usually takes over an hour. It is respectful to eat slowly and show how much you enjoy the meal because the mother and daughter have been preparing the meal all day. Everything tastes like it was slowly sautéed. And there's no getting away from the table until you have finished everything on your plate. The Portuguese custom is to be plump. A skinny person is often considered to be from a poor family. You are supposed to eat even when you are full. I am always ten pounds heavier when I return home. There is an abundance of seafood because of fishing off the coast. One of my favorite dishes is octopus. A common fish is lodfish, a squid-like fish with a hard shell. There is also lobster, crab, sardines and cod.

Tourists, perhaps, posing as dairy maids in Bretanha take a rest along the milk route, 1988.

Rev. Joseph Viveiros photograph

We sit around and talk at night. My aunt and uncle love telling us stories about growing up in Portugal, and my cousins fill in the gaps with their point of view. Some are made up as they go along, which adds a bit of mystery and fascination. We don't sing or dance like so many other families, I guess because everyone is too grown up.

Sometimes at night my cousins and I go into the city and visit the discos, but not often because the ride is too long. The city of Ponta Delgada is somewhat like a modern city, with several high-rises. The sidewalks are made of cobblestones, sometimes in different colors, but usually black or white. Some roads are dirt and create a lot of dust. When the villagers clean their houses, they throw the excess water into the road to keep the dust down. There are many churches. I am always amazed by the size of the them. From the outside they look very big, but inside they are tiny. Most are painted in gold wreaths and flowers inside and out. The priests dress in white and gold.

Many townspeople have cars, which amazes tourists. Some of the younger people drive sporty-looking Nissans and Volkswagens. Buses and taxis constantly shuttle people back and forth from the city to the village. Groups of elderly people usually occupy all the city benches and parks.

Images of the Azores and those summer vacations will be with me forever—my paradise. I'll always remember life on the farm with "my family"—the good food, the friendship of cousins, walking, hiking, swimming and being swept away by the colors of land, sea and sunset. Even if I can't be there, the Azores are in me.

In Sete Cidades, packed with grain and tools, ready to go planting.

Ronald Caplain photograph

Ponta Delgada, circa 1960.

Courtesy of Miguel Côrte-Real

Folk Tales from the Village

Hanging out with the Family

by Paul Pinto

Sesta *falls between noon and 5PM in the blazing summer, in the small agricultural villages in Portugal. It is a time for rest and socializing. People leave early in the morning to work in the fields and return home at noon to avoid the burning sun. Although some have chores to do, like taking care of the animals or repairing things at home, most take advantage of the sesta. People eat, take a short nap, then get together in small groups to socialize.*

Sometimes the sesta takes place in the street or in somebody's house on the veranda, *but not by invitation; people know they are welcome because everybody likes to spend these few hours talking and laughing. At the same time, people learn the news, which travels by word of mouth. When sesta time ends, they return to the fields until sunset.*

The following are stories I heard from a group of people gathered on my veranda, in a hot summer sesta of 1986, in Jou, Murça, Trás-os-Montes, Portugal. You can see these people are trying to top each other with their stories, and one rapidly follows another.

· · · · · · · · · · · · · · ·

The Old Man and the Donkey

A soldier passed through our village on his way home. As he was crossing the valley between the two villages, he passed an old man on top of a tree. The old man was cutting a branch and sitting on the wrong side of the tree.

John, the soldier, saw this and said, "Excuse me, sir, you are going to fall out of the tree."

The old man said, *"Vá com Deus"* (Go with God). "I know what I'm doing."

The soldier left, and five minutes later, the old man fell out of the tree. He then ran towards the soldier, and when he caught up with him he said,

"Mr. soldier, since you knew I was going to fall out of the tree, could you please tell me when I'm going to die."

The soldier said, "Sure. You are going to die when your donkey makes 'boom' three times."

The old man said, *"Meu Deus."* (My God). "My donkey does that so much." Well, he went back and loaded the donkey. But the road was too uphill, the donkey was weak and the load was very heavy—so the donkey made his first *boom*.

The old man got behind the donkey to see if he made anymore and a few minutes later, he made his second boom. Then the old man got a stick from the load and made a cork with his knife. He stuck it up the donkey's behind and said, "Now I feel safe."

A few minutes later, the donkey made this third and biggest boom and hit the old man on the forehead with the cork. The old man fell backwards on the road and started screaming. "Ai, Ai, I'm dying." And so he died.

Goat-power is the preferred mode of transport for this gentleman roadster, 1967.

Milton Silvia photograph

My First Shoes

I remember when I bought my first pair of shoes—poor shoes. They were black and white and opened in the back. What a pair of funny-looking shoes! But in those days, I liked them. I bought them myself. Poor *mãe* (mother), she gave me the money and I went on the bus to the *feira* (market) in Carrazedo Montenegro, all by myself. I wasn't scared. I wanted those shoes for the *festa*. We couldn't afford to pay another bus ticket so somebody could go with me. We needed the money for other things. I was so happy when I bought them, and I couldn't wait until the day of the feast. Then when I got home, I put them in my room, inside their little box.

But, poor shoes, because everytime nobody was around and my mother was busy doing something—there I went, running to my bedroom to try the shoes on again. I always waited until I was alone because if someone saw me with the shoes on, they would make fun of me and I would be screamed at by my mother. My father had died when I was young, so my only worries were that my mother would scream at me. She had given me money we probably needed to buy other things so, of course, she wanted the shoes to last a long time.

But all I cared about was they looked pretty. I walked around the house from room to room. They felt so good. At the end, I took the shoes off and put them in the box again. I did this so many times that when the feast day came, the poor shoes looked old already. But I had a great time, and that's all I cared about. I was lucky too. It seems that my mother had a similar experience with a dress my father had bought for her—so I didn't get in trouble. They laughed, and then told me to never do it again. I never did.

The Poet and the Boots

Once there was a man called Bocage who lived in our village, and he was a poet. He could never sell his poems so he was very poor. He always wore an old brown jacket that had holes in it, a brown hat that looked like it had been in a fire, and his toes were showing through the holes of his boots.

One cold morning he was in the village shoe store admiring all those warm boots, but admire was all he could do. He got so upset, went back out into the cold air of the winter morning, hoping it would be so cold he would freeze instantly and die. He got outside but it was taking too long for him to freeze. Again, he started thinking of those warm boots and how his toes would feel inside them.

At the dairy, a family apportions their milk into measured containers set for delivery, 1967.
Note the sandals on the man pouring—they are made from auto tires. This was typical in rural areas of Portugal before the 1970s.

Milton Silvia photograph

45

"Well," he said to himself, "I have to get those boots somehow because this cold is painful and I hate pain." A young boy passed by and started making fun of his funny looking toes. The boy was at the end of the street when the poet had a great idea. He screamed for the young boy to come to him. The boy came and the poet told him he would give him his last five *centavos*, if he helped him get a pair of boots. The boy, laughing, said, "A pair of boots costs a lot more cents."

The poet replied, "I know but we're not going to pay for them."

"What?" said the young boy.

The poet said, "We're going to go inside the shoe store and I'm going to make believe I'm trying on a pair of boots. When I have one on my foot and one in my hand, you come next to me and slap me in the face. I will make believe I'm real mad and run out of the store after you—with the boots."

It sounded like fun, and the boy agreed. They went inside and when the poet had one boot on and one in his hand, the young boy ran towards the old poet and slapped him. The poet got up and started screaming, "I'll catch you, you little *macaco* (monkey)."

He ran out of the store with one boot in his hand and another on his foot. When he was far enough away, where nobody could see him, the old poet stopped, looked at his foot and smiled:
"With one boot in my hand
and one on my foot,
what warm land
Now that I have a warm boot."

The Shoe Fixer and The Fisherman

A long time ago, a man lived in a city and fixed shoes. During the day he walked through the city, and at night he worked. He lived on the second floor, and he made a lot of noise at night fixing shoes. The couple upstairs couldn't sleep. The man who lived on the third floor was a fisherman and needed to sleep because he had to get up early. One night he went to have a talk with the man downstairs.

Mr. F. told Mr. S., "Have some consideration for other people, and instead of working at night, work during the day and sleep at night."

Mr. S., the shoe fixer, said, "I am my own boss. This is my apartment and I can do anything I want. If you're not happy, leave."

A thriving profession throughout Portugal is shoemaking, as demonstrated by this young shoemaker/cobbler making boots in Madeira, 1989.

Rev. Joseph Viveiros photograph

46

Mr. F., the fisherman, slammed the door behind him and left. When he got to his apartment, the shoe fixer was already hammering away. After returning from fishing the next day, he thought, "What he needs is a lesson and if he can do his work at night, so can I."

Mr. F. closed all the doors and windows in the kitchen, then called two women to carry water into his apartment because, back then, he didn't have water at home. The women dumped water in the kitchen until it came to the level of the windows. Then Mr. F. got inside his canoe.

Mr. S. was busy fixing shoes when water started dripping on top of his head. The floor was made of wood that had little openings that leaked. He waited until he could not take it anymore and went upstairs to see what was going on.

When he saw Mr. F. inside of the canoe, he said, "You can't do this. It's raining downstairs and I can't work."

Mr. F. said, "I can do anything I want. I'm my own boss. This is my apartment. TRRRR-RRR (making believe he was fishing). This is my job and I am fishing."

Without saying anything, Mr. S. left and thought to himself, "I just received a taste of my own medicine."

From then on, the shoe fixer worked during the day and slept at night.

Mrs. Ana: Too Much Money

When I was a young girl, an old man lived at the end of the *aldeia* (village) and he was very poor. One summer he worked for Mr. António picking potatoes, and he made some money. To him, oh boy, that was a lot of money! He couldn't even sleep thinking about all the money he had under his bed—he never had so much. He didn't know what to do with it.

One night he was so restless, he got the money from under his bed and threw it out the window. He returned back to bed and said, "Hahhh—I'm poor again. Now I can sleep."

Grandmother Rosária and the Ultimate Style

About 20 years ago, a daughter of a very rich family from the village called Rio was getting married, and her family planned a big wedding. An older guy in the village, Joe, was a little off mentally, and the father of the bride invited him to the wedding. The bride's father told him he wanted him to look nice in front of his rich friends and gave him material so a tailor could make a suit in the latest style. The intentions of the bride's father were not good. He just wanted to have some jokes at the poor guy's expense.

Joe always thought the best of everyone and kept the material. He had heard the styles from Paris were always changing, so he waited until the last minute to have the suit made. The day of the wedding came, and the suit was not made. He put his shoes and hat on, took the material, wrapped it around himself and went to the wedding.

When he arrived, everybody was dressed in the latest style. The father of the bride started laughing at Joe. But Joe said, "I waited until the last minute so I could go in the very latest style." All the rich friends felt embarrassed by how they were dressed—not in the latest style. They didn't know that Joe was a little off.

The friends said to each other, "I guess that's the ultimate style," and Joe had a great time at the wedding.

Man with his own "ultimate style," Ribeira Grande, 1991.

Ronald Caplain photograph

47

THE MAN FROM SANTA MARIA

INTERVIEW WITH MIGUEL DE FIGUEIREDO CÔRTE-REAL

BY JOSEPH D. THOMAS

When I first met Senhor Côrte-Real, 30 years ago, he lived upstairs on the third floor of my parents' apartment building on Rivet Street. From where I stood, at 16, he was a large, bellicose man, whose impassioned temper rattled the walls. What I thought was rage had more to do with the passion and intensity of his persona. He had a large family, many lovely daughters, and he seemed to govern with a power that thundered from deep inside his being. When I learned that he was an relative of the great Portuguese explorers Gaspar and Miguel Côrte-Real, I reinterpreted his stern demeanor as intense pride, sharpened by his new New World position as laborer, immigrant and apartment-dweller.

As I have come to know the man, I now marvel at his childlike enthusiasm over history and culture, his thirst for knowledge, his fine intellect, and the valuable contribution he has made in documenting his people's history. At 76, and coming from a wealthy family, he seems to be cognizant of his privileges in life, and wants to return the knowledge and other gifts acquired during his quiet journey through life.

Senhor Côrte-Real is a man that cannot possibly be interviewed in two or three sittings—especially by someone who doesn't speak Portuguese, like myself. Yet, I boldly present this banter. The man is a connoisseur of thought and conversation. If he were French, he may have spent his days sipping cafe au lait at Place de Notre Dame and arguing the merits of existentialism with Camus. But he is all Azorean—and proud of it. It is my recommendation that anyone seeking to learn Azorean history, with perhaps a twist of controversy and a side of joie de vivre, engage the Man from Santa Maria.

· · · · · · · · · · · · · · · · ·

The region of São Lourenço, Santa Maria, Azores, 1960.

Courtesy of Miguel Côrte-Real

A Lifelong Student

My occupation is a student. I want to learn everyday, everyday! I like reading and learning. It is not just genealogy, it is everything! If you ask me how rockets go to the moon, I have no idea. But I get newspapers from the Azores and the Continent everyday. I receive books from the Azores. Yesterday, I was clipping newspapers. I like to have biographies from people, you see? I like to learn. I have a passion.

I try to go back to Santa Maria every two years, and I head straight for the library. I record family histories. What makes each family special? I write personal histories, not kings and queens. But I also like to write about "discoveries"—like how Christopher Columbus was taken prisoner on Santa Maria. I record transactions and land deals. I have hundreds of documents from hundreds of years ago. Someday I will donate all my work to the University of the Azores. For stimulating conversation, I talk with lots of people. I promise myself I will try to work on my research everyday.

In Santa Maria, until 1947, all I wanted was the girls and horses. I loved horses, my car was a horse, and what I liked was the girls. In that year, a cousin of mine called Armando Pacheco de Canto e Castro opened a new world to me. I didn't know why I called him cousin. His name was Pacheco de Canto e Castro and mine was Figueiredo. He was known by his bad temper. So one day I asked him, "Hey cousin Armando, how on earth are we cousins?"

"Oh, you don't know? Come here!" he said. And he went to get a book. "Look at this: this is your father... so many cousins on this side, other cousins on the other side."

"Oh! I didn't know that! That's funny!" And very shyly I asked him, "Do you mind if I come here on Sundays, to copy this?"

"Come, come, whenever you want... it will be my pleasure."

And so I did. I started going there on Sundays when I didn't have much to do, and I would copy some things. One fine day I got there, I knocked on the door, and the maid came downstairs to welcome me, "Please, come in." I went to the living room, one of those old rooms with heavy velvet curtains, heavy red chairs, some old paintings from the walls. Then cousin Úrsula showed up.

"Oh, how are you, cousin?" We kissed as usual and she said, "Do you know Mr. Armando is sick? He has a problem in his kidneys."

"If cousin Armando is sick, I'm going to leave!" I said, because I knew about his temper...

"No, no, no, God forbid! If he knew you were here and didn't speak to him, he would be furious! Wait, because I'm going to ask him if he wants to see you." She went to the third floor and yelled down, "Please, come up. Armando wants to talk to you!"

He was lying in bed, a strong man, with steel hands. He had a rope tied to his bed so he could get up. He grabbed the rope, pulled it and sat up. He had on his woolen sweater from Santa Maria with long sleeves, and we started to talk. "Cousin Armando, I heard you were sick, so I'm not going to study the book this week. I will be back next week."

"No, no, no... Listen, tell Úrsula to come here." I called her and he said, "Listen, Úrsula, we don't have any kids. Well, we have a daughter, but she is crazy, completely crazy. We have several nephews. None of them cares about genealogy. We

A Santa Maria farmer directs his corn-filled ox-cart to Vila do Porto, circa 1930s. Visible at far left are large ovens used to fire clay for roofing shingles.

Ox-cart loaded with wheat is ready to be ground, Santa Maria, circa 1930s.

Stone gate and close-up showing embossed crest of the Figueiredo de Lemos family in Lugar dos Pontes, São Pedro County, Santa Maria.

have no one. Do you know something? The only person who cares about all this is Miguel. So, if you don't mind, we give him the book."

So they gave me the book and I was radiant with joy! A book of mine. It is right here. I have kept it religiously, and I couldn't wait to get home so I could run through it at my will. At their home, I had to be very careful so it wouldn't get ruined.

I was all happy. When I left, I thanked my cousin and ran home. I went to my bedroom on the third floor, took my coat and tie off, made myself comfortable. I put the book on the desk and started running through it. I was all excited about seeing all those old relatives. I had no idea who they were.

Someone knocked on my door. It was cousin Armando's maid. The maid? Oh my God! He's already sorry for having given me the book! He was always a little bit crazy! What does she want? I went downstairs and said, "So, what's going on?"

"Senhora Úrsula told me to let you know Mr. Armando died. After you left, he started not feeling good. We called the doctor, the priest, but he was already dead." That shocked me. It touched me. He gave me the book because he felt he was going to die. It was about an hour between the time I left his house and the time he died. Even when I talk about this, I feel a chill down my back.

From that point on I started to get interested in genealogy. Then I had a friend, Dr. Manuel Monteiro Velho Arruda, an historian with an international reputation and an expert in genealogy.

He would tell me many stories. He would scream; he spoke very loud. He would grab my arm and would squeeze it sometimes. He was short, fat, with a funny face, but he was very educated, very, very educated. So, he told me, for instance, the story of Inês who was kicked out of the house by her father. And he would say, "Miguel Figueiredo Lemos was a mean man."

But he never said why. I found out from my genealogy books the reason he kicked his daughter out of the house was because she had married the son of a Jewish woman.

Family Origins:

Miguel de Figueiredo de Lemos settled in Santa Maria in 1540. He married there, and had his children there. One died in Madeira, a bishop who had a chapel built to São Luís, bishop of Tolosa. He

Two views from opposite ends of the town of Vila do Porto, Santa Maria, 1940s.

Courtesy of Miguel Côrte-Real

Courtesy of Miguel Côrte-Real

50

was buried there in the chapel. In 1908, the bishop of Madeira, D. Agostinho Barreto, exhumed the bishop's bones because the chapel was abandoned, and they are now in the cathedral, near the main door, marked by a big white marble memorial stone.

I was born in São Miguel for political reasons. My father was the head of the Regenerador Party in Santa Maria. On February 1, 1908, King D. Carlos was killed. D. Manuel was king for some time, and on October 5, 1910, he was exiled to England and the monarchy was ended.

I was six when we moved back to Santa Maria in 1931. My father, who was ill, felt he was going to die and wanted to go back. I returned to São Miguel every year. It's only 52 miles. You don't realize what life in the Azores was like back in 1930s. When it was time for you to go to fourth grade—books? There were no books for sale anywhere! We would go from door to door to ask the boys who had just finished elementary school to buy used books. It wasn't a matter of money; the thing is there were no books. There was no place to buy the books!

My father was a judge, and I'm my father's son. When I was little, my best friends had no shoes, their pants had patches, but money was never important to me. What's important is what is inside. It used to be—if you had a chicken, you could trade eggs for sugar, for salt, for everything. Corn, corn... There was no money, no money...

Do you know where people kept the little money they had? They would keep it in a belt they would tie around their waist. It had a lot of small pockets, and as soon as they had a dollar, a gold eagle, they would put it inside one of the pockets and close it, and sleep every night and every day close to it. This was the bank.

My mother was very intelligent, very proper, but she could only read a religious book. When she was little, they didn't let her go to school. They only taught her how to read religious books, and she didn't need to know how to write. She could read print but not cursive. Do you want to write love letters? No ma'am! It was only religious books! I still have the book she used to read, and the book my father would read, and I even have my father's spelling-book. She could read the newspaper, but she couldn't read a letter. You see?

There were only three high schools in the Azores—São Miguel, Terceira and Faial. None in Santa Maria. I went four years to the industrial school and completed the commercial program. When I was 20, I went to the military service for 16 months. After the war was over, I went back to industrial school.

There were no universities in the Azores at the time. My father left me money to go to a university on the Continent, but everything changed so fast after the war the money wouldn't have been enough. All my brothers studied and attended S. Féil School in mainland Portugal. My sister went to the S. Patrício School in Lisbon, too.

Courtesy of Miguel Côrte-Real

Miguel's father, Luis de Figueiredo de Lemos do Canto Côrte-Real, as a young man in his hunting outfit, 1890.

I'm going to tell you something. When I was in elementary school, I learned more than what kids know when they graduate from a university today. Back then, we had to learn! If a certain number of the students the teacher brought to the exam failed, the teacher might lose his job. The school Inspector would kick him out!

Hunting has been a passion of the Côrte-Real family for generations. Here, Miguel, Manuel Carvalho (Carvalhinho) and Manuel Inácio de Melo (Mim), display their kill in São Miguel, 1940s.

Courtesy of Miguel Côrte-Real

Thoughts on This and That

On Salazar: He was a serious man. His temperament was not to forget what others did against him. He had always to seek revenge against these people. He only saw what he wanted to see.

I never talked to Salazar even though I had opportunities to do so. A friend of mine, Maria Margarida da Câmara Medeiros, knew him, and one day she asked me to go with her to see Salazar. But I didn't. What was he going to tell me? "Who are you? Are you from the Azores?" Salazar wanted to live surrounded by the people like him.

On coming to America. Why did I come? No special reason. My former wife's mother was here in America, that's all. I had a good job, the assistant manager of Moaçor, the ration factory. I belonged to the Azorean ploughmen group, and I was earning more money than Salazar himself. But I came to America and I kept on learning.

On vocations: If someone has a vocation to be a doctor, and he is a shoemaker, he will never be a good shoemaker. This is natural. This is my own vocation (to be a student). I was born with it. I enjoy it. I'm happy.

How immigration changed: In the old days, a man would come to America but not with his wife. He would make some money and go back to his country and buy a piece of land, so he could organize his life, work for himself, have his own house, have his own piece of land. Only after this, did families begin to emigrate—the husband, the wife, and everybody else—but not in the old days.

Looking down on Azoreans? I have never felt that people in the Continent think that people in the Azores are inferior. I lived in the Continent for a long time, you know. I attended the best societies of Lisbon. And I have never felt diminished. They (the Azoreans) were the ones who felt diminished because the education they had was limited.

On wealth and poverty in the Azores: In the Azores, although there were social differences, I never felt that. A fisherman, a shoemaker, I don't care, if someone has the brain, he's my friend.

What is saudade? I'm going to tell you. Your father dies. You have *saudades* from remembering his death. I have *saudades* of my country, of the place where I was born, *saudade* of the birds I used to see when I was little, *saudade* of the spinning of the hula-hoop, from spinning the top. I am a man of this age, and I bought a top in Fall River the other day. This is *saudade*.

On mother's cooking: My mother could cook excellent food—food I will never taste again in my life. She would make this crab soup I will always miss. One of my friends said he never had anything like it anywhere! When I was little, we wouldn't go in the kitchen because of the maids. If I saw them cooking, what would happen to me? I can cook some things today I learned from talking to my mother. She would say, "You do this like this, you do that like that…"

On the Portuguese Community Today

It is a divided community, unfortunately. If our community would get together, not just the Azoreans but the whole Portuguese community, we could have some power here. We don't have any power because this person is jealous of that person, because he bought new furniture for his living-room so the other one has to buy the same one, but at a better price! And they live on this. They live on jealousy.

Do you remember Mr. António Alberto Costa? I was talking to him one day and I said, "This is so sad! There is no unity among soccer clubs here… Why don't they get them all together?" He said, "Yeah! Let's go!" We went to the radio station

A traditional rural outfit, Santa Maria, 1940s.

Courtesy of Miguel Côrte-Real

which was on the air one hour each day. But we had to give up the idea, because they poke our eyes out! What we got ourselves into! The headaches! Soon someone suggested we put several soccer teams together, WHAT? And we gave up!

Do you see what happened to the Portuguese club *O Ateneu*? It was so good, had such good members, but it's over! Do you see the problem with the *Casa dos Açores*? The problem they are having just because someone gave them some money? You see?

Our community is developing slowly. Thirty years ago, it was almost a zero. When I got here, I didn't know anyone, and I had a lot of difficulties. I was going to work with Dr. Francis M. Rogers at Harvard University. But my sister-in-law, who lived here, didn't know how to go to Cambridge. I had already been to Brazil, Africa, France, Spain, and everything. I had never been here before. I only had my wife's family here. No one could bring me there! So Rogers was mad at me for twelve years.

I am proud of many people. (He points to a photograph on the wall). Manuel das Neves Xavier ran away from Pico, a man who couldn't read and write, and he published the first Portuguese newspaper on the East Coast of the United States. He published four newspapers, one after the other. It was not easy to sell newspapers to Portuguese people at that time, so he failed. Cardinal Medeiros is another man who was self-made.

Courtesy of Miguel Côrte-Real

Above, students and friends gather to discuss events of the day at the Bar Avião, *in Vila do Porto, Santa Maria, 1945. Left to right are: Freitas (the manager), Miguel de Figueiredo Côrte-Real, Floriano Manuel do Rego Silva, Manuel Vieira Viula, Eduardo Pereira, unknown, and Passos Faria. Below, town gentlemen enjoy a stroll, circa 1918. Left to right are: Dr. Manuel Rebelo do Canto Pereira, António Monteiro Velho Arruda, António Monteiro Leandres, José Leandres de Chaves, Manuel Valeriano, Henrique Pais, Capitão Joaquim Monteiro Velho Arruda, José Monteiro Velho Arruda, Luís de Figueiredo Lemos do Canto Côrte-Real, José Inácio Gago, Bernardo do Canto and António Xavier da Câmara Falcão*

Courtesy of Miguel Côrte-Real

Portuguese people are beginning to get more involved in education. We have come a long way and will continue, but our ancestral roots may weaken. People tend to forget their origins. A lot of people say the Portuguese put too much emphasis on work instead of education. But these people are forgetting where people came from and the difficulties they had on the islands. It was not that they wanted the kids to work. They just couldn't afford to keep them in school. When they came to the United States, they went to work in the factory, thinking they could make all the money they wanted, get set up, and go back. But today, that is not happening anymore. Today people think the first thing is education.

My Life as a Pro Soccer Player

Interview with Pedro Tavares

By Jill Lupachini

Pedro Tavares of New Bedford showed great promise playing soccer as a youth in Portugal, and, at 14, he was groomed to become a professional soccer player. Though he tells his story modestly, Pedro was a star who traveled the world with his professional team. His account, given in 1986, gives us an understanding of the life of a soccer player and of the importance of soccer in Portugal.

. . . .

Soccer Dreams

In Portugal, we started playing soccer real young, when we were only five and six years old. When a kid is young and others see he plays well, they push him to play. That's what happened to me. When I was very young, everyone influenced me to try as a professional. So you grew up with ideas. At 14, I started to play semiprofessional on juvenile teams, then I became a junior player and, at 18, a senior player. The professional teams have nothing to do with the schools. Soccer is your work. It's your full-time job.

In Portugal, soccer is the king sport, as it is in many European countries. It has never caught on quite as strong in the United States. I was born and grew up in Portugal, Setúbal, about 30 miles from Lisbon. I lived in a three-room house with my mother, father and five brothers. Though it was poor, it was nice and clean. We are still very close. Each time I go back, we get together, eat, joke and play. It is very good, very good! My father is a foreman who works with big boats and steamboats loading and unloading like at the New York docks. My mother worked for a couple of years in a factory making sardine cans, then she stayed home.

I did not have many hobbies when I was young because I played soccer. When I began playing professional, I started to travel. Each country has three or four teams, and you play against them. We played against France, England, Germany, Yugoslavia, Brazil, Argentina, Columbia, Venezuela and Canada. We'd play two games and whoever won kept going, then you'd go to another country and

the winners kept moving on. This is how I saw much of the world.

Sometimes we played exhibition games before the season starts. As I was a young player in 1966, I got to come to America and play in exhibition games in Boston, San Francisco, New Jersey and Chicago.

At 20, I served in the Army but still went to practices and played professional soccer. At the time, Portugal was at war with Africa, Angola and Mozambique. Professional soccer players did not have to leave the country. I went to the post for a couple of hours early in the morning—I worked with air guns. While in the service, I got a medal for soccer! That was when we won our championship season.

Money Matters

The team is financially supported by associates. Some 50,000 to 60,000 people may be associated, and they pay so much each month. We also get the money that people pay to get in the game. In my time, we didn't make as much as they do today, but it was enough to make a good life. A professional soccer player's pay was better than other occupations. In my time, we made double or possibly triple a normal worker's pay. Today soccer players make pretty good money as professionals.

High school soccer players compete in Faial, 1979.

Milton Silvia photograph

Not all players make the same salary. It's like here. Seniority and the best players make more. The substitutes make the same pay. They worked like us all year long. They would practice and "concentrate" on weekends and get ready to play just in case. My team never had a strike. These were the days of Salazar. You couldn't afford to be arrested and put in jail. Now, since the '74 Revolution, the players can strike.

The name of my team was V.F.C. (Vitória Futebol Clube). Two big teams in Portugal are Benfica and Belenenses. In '69, Benfica wanted to buy me but my team didn't want to sell me. I think I was a good player. My team contracted with me, and I was with them for 13 years. You are not a free agent. If a team is interested in a player, they offer so much, but if your team doesn't want to sell you, you cannot go. Sometimes the smaller teams will sell because they need the money, but otherwise they just don't sell.

Not Just a Game; It's a Job

The whole team meets for practice on Tuesday, 16 players, the coach and trainers. Weekday afternoons are spent with soccer, the last three days of the weeks are soccer and not much else. You get a free day on Monday after the Sunday game, then you start right in on Tuesday again. Some teams make you practice twice a day, others just once. Whatever the team wants, the coach wants, we have to do.

On weekends the practice was called "concentration." We would get rest and special kinds of foods to prepare for Sunday's game. Just the players, no wives, no kids. We'd practice in the morning, have lunch, rest, then practice in the afternoon again. We went to the movies on Saturday nights to relax. We would do all this to be in real good shape for the Sunday game. The game was always at 3PM or 4PM and sometimes 70,000 to 80,000 people attended the game. Normally, it was 30,000 to 40,000.

When I married at 22, my wife already knew I played soccer all the time so she accepted it. Sometimes I would be gone for weeks. You may go to France and play, then to Italy, then back to France, then home. Sometimes it takes 20 to 30 days.

Soccer is year-round, but you get a couple weeks in summer to vacation. That's it. In Portugal, the season starts in July and ends in June. Normally Portugal is warm, which is why you can play all year. Sometimes January or February gets a little cold but not like here. The temperature may drop to 40-45 degrees, not that bad.

In winter, in the Scandinavian countries and sometimes Germany, we played a few times in the snow. If they didn't cancel, they would clear the field before the game, and you would keep playing. It rains a lot in Portugal in the winter, but it doesn't snow. January and February are the cold months over there. We would practice and play in the rain, though there was a lot of water on the field. It would have to be a big thing to cancel the game. The weather definitely affected the game; it became a different kind of game. We had no turf. It was always natural grass.

The temperaments of the teammates varies. Usually the members of the team were friends. We would joke, play games and try to be as happy as we could. But sometimes we would get together and fight as a team. I still have many friends from soccer, a few in New Bedford, six or seven in

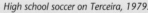
High school soccer on Terceira, 1979.

Milton Silvia photograph

Canada and a couple in New York. I see them a lot. Two former teammates live in New York, two brothers from Africa, and they usually come twice a year to my home.

The Game

Normally we knew the starting players before the game and what was going to happen because everyone has a position. The 11 players the coach feels are the best are the ones that start. I played midfield. I could play all the positions, center forward, wing, left side and right side. I was an assistant and played midfield normally. I would get the ball to the front.

Every teammate is at the game. If something happens to you before the game, there must be someone to replace you. I could replace the injured person, and someone could replace me. It was important to play a couple of positions. That's why you don't need so many teammates. But if someone was injured during a game, you couldn't replace him. We would sometimes play with ten or even nine. Now they've changed the rules. We can have three substitutions, so if someone gets an injury we can replace them.

Everybody tries their best to make the team. The big teams have 28 to 30 players. We had 18, but only 11 players started so there's a lot of competition in the practice. It is sport competition, not physical fighting. We also have lower divisions so if you don't make the team, you can try out for a second division team. You have the teams that fight for the championship, and you have the teams that fight not to be moved down to the second division. The good ones pay more and get better players.

You tried to get the team picked ahead so you practiced a couple of months before the season starts. We practiced twice a day so the coach could see the 11 best players. Of course, there were always injuries or people out of shape so you needed replacements. I was a tough player. Even being skinny, I was a tough player! A couple of very small things happened to me, but I never left a game because of an injury. I know a lot of guys that broke legs, knees, hands or anything. I was lucky. If someone was injured, they would stop the game, and doctors and trainers would come and take care of them or take them to a hospital if needed.

I played in a few championships and won the Portuguese cup twice. There are two different kinds of games, the regular championship and the cup. After I finished playing soccer in Portugal, I played two seasons in Canada (winning the championship in '74) and two years in New York, where I won the championship in '75. I was also an all-star in '75.

I officially moved to the United States in '75 because of soccer. Soccer was starting to grow here. All I needed to stay in the United States was a certificate from the European Soccer Association saying I had been a professional since 1962. This country needed professional soccer players. Even now I am a permanent resident but not a citizen.

Family Life When Dad is a Professional

ANGELA (PEDRO'S DAUGHTER): I did not have to pay to go to the games. People would recognize me because my father was a professional. Sometimes we would go to cookouts and family events and award ceremonies with the players.

What I remember most was my daddy not being home. My mom, brother and I would eat supper together. My mother was like a mommy and daddy all in one. When daddy did come home, he took us places and brought home presents. I have dolls from Switzerland and a doll I called a china doll because it was Chinese. He would bring us clothes too. My mom would get jewelry, also gorgeous silk material because she loved to sew.

PEDRO: My son became interested in soccer when he came with me every day to the stadium to the practices. When he was three or four years old, he would play all day long. Now he has a coach. Sometimes I give advice when I go to the games and tell him what he does good or bad. I try to teach him, but I am not the kind to push him. I don't tell him as much anymore because he may get mixed up. I may see something a different way from his coach. He could get messed up and say to the coach, "Hey, my father says it isn't this way. My father was a big Portuguese star."

He loves to play soccer. He could go back to Portugal and play for a few years as a professional and live the rest of his life with the money he can make. It depends on him. I am not going to push him into anything.

I still play sometimes in the summer. I played recently in Toronto. My agent and a team of soccer stars came from Portugal, and we played an exhibition game. It was really nice with all the guys that used to play together. We played, then went out to eat and talked. Soccer is the most popular sport in Europe, Portugal, South America and Brazil but not in the States. I think soccer is one of the best sports in the world.

The Feast of Santo Christo, 1992. This three-day celebration held on the last Sunday of June, culminates in a solemn Mass at Santo Christo Church on Columbia Street. For the 40,000 visitors, this is a feast of lights and color as well as food. Hundreds of colored bulbs form patterns similar to those on the front of the Convent of Hope at Ponta Delgada, São Miguel where the feast originated in the 1700s. The statue of Christ (Ecce Homo), carried through the neighborhood, is a replica of one kept at the Convent of Hope in Ponta Delgada. While feastgoers parade in color and pageantry, cameras click and the smell of Portuguese food fills the evening air.

THE NEW WORLD

Ronald Caplain Photograph

THE CONSTRUCTION OF IMMIGRANT IDENTITY

BY BELA FELDMAN-BIANCO AND DONNA HUSE

Saudade: Memory and Identity

The Portuguese are a world people, the discoverers and colonizers of new lands; they are also immigrants who settled in different parts of the world. This wanderlust, marked by the great age of discoveries and subsequent labor immigration, has been constitutive of the Portuguese experience.

Saudade, a word that originated in the sixteenth century, has been associated with the Portuguese unending wanderlust. While loosely translated as "longing" or "nostalgia," *saudade* is in fact a dynamic cultural construct that defines Portuguese identity in the context of multiple representations of space and (past) time.

Saudade, on the level of the self or the person, has been viewed as "the uprooted experience located between the desire of the future and the memories of the past" or simply as "the memories which touch a soul—not only longing, it is also belonging," as one New Bedford young immigrant put it. These memories are associated with the layers of time and space prior to emigration, that is to say, with *saudade da terra*, or *saudade* for the homeland. Symbolic representations and social practices of the homeland's everyday life further shapes differentiated Portuguese regional identities.

Saudade, as the collective memory of Portugal, has been narrated as the basis of the Portuguese imagined national community. Temporally, this collective national imagination dates back to the discovery era and to the history of immigration; encompassing, spatially, the maritime explorations and the long separations from relatives around the world.

Popular immigrant poetry, as well as philosophy and literature, often portrays *saudade* as central to the Portuguese collective experience. Consider this poem by the late poet João Teixeira de Medeiros of Fall River:

> the word saudade
> who felt it who made it
> made it fit the Portuguese heart at large
> saudade *has happiness and sadness*
> *feeling and voice*
> saudade *is very Portuguese*
> *it is an offspring of all of us*
> saudade *gives flavour to entire nations*
> *it is part of our daily life*
> saudade *will be present*
> *in any place where there are Portuguese flags*
> saudade *travelled with us in the sea*
> *as well as in the thousands of hinterland*
> saudade *traveled with us on the air*
> *it is with us in the airplanes*
> saudade *god help us*
> *has such a deep power*
> *it is like a hurricane spreading us*
> *in the little corners of the world*

The dynamic cultural construction of *saudade* is certainly a constitutive part of the everyday life in southeastern Massachusetts, one of the oldest Portuguese "little corners of the world." Portuguese immigration began in the whaling era with mostly Azorean

Ronald Caplain photograph

60

males. Mass immigration of Portuguese families from the Azores, the continent and Madeira, and the formation of Portuguese neighborhoods in a network of New England towns began at the turn of the twentieth century. At that time, the Portuguese were among several immigrant groups, including English, French-Canadian, Irish, Polish and Italians, which settled in the region as a result of the demand for cheap labor in the flourishing cotton mill economy. Since the 1920s, the Portuguese have become the predominant ethnic group of the area. Later, between the late 1950s and the mid 1980s, with the arrival of new immigrant contingents from the Azores, continental Portugal and Portuguese Africa, the Portuguese neighborhoods of southeastern Massachusetts were renewed and expanded.

Immigration to southeastern Massachusetts has changed the rhythms and the ways of life of Portuguese women and men. In contrast to their experiences in an agrarian world, the majority of these immigrants were confronted, for the first time, with the time-discipline and the physical confinement of industrial work; first, as workers in the mills and later in the needle trades or garment assembly, as well as in fishing and other types of industries.

What are the meanings of the cultural construction of *saudade* in the lives of Portuguese immigrants? We present the voices of fifteen women who have narrated their life experiences at the intersection of Portuguese and American cultural borders, in the context of three dramatic events: the decision to leave Portugal; the first years of settlement and work in southeastern Massachusetts; and the decision (with its accompanying ambivalence) to stay in the United States. These moments, epically narrated, bring to the fore the juxtaposition of lyric and realistic narratives, interposed by the endless search and construction of utopias.

These women were born in the Azores and came to the United States in the course of the second major Portuguese mass immigration to southeastern Massachusetts, from the late 1960s to the mid 1980s. Their ages range from their 20s to 70s. Most of them came from rural settings and, despite their varied social backgrounds prior to emigration, most started their lives in southeastern Massachusetts as factory workers. A number of them became professionals in later years and have since served as cultural brokers between Portuguese immigrants and American institutions.

Saudade in the Immigrant Neighborhoods

While dramatic experiences have marked the lives of immigrants, in the Portuguese enclaves of southeastern Massachusetts, there is a sense of a certain immutability of time; different representations of time and space seem to unfold into the present. *Saudade*, as the collective historical memory of Portugal, has been reconstructed as part of political mobilization by community leaders through community rituals and the ethnic media.

Opposite page: A Fall River woman observes the procession during the Feast of Santo Christo.

Azorean man in Ponta Delgada, São Miguel.

Ronald Caplain photograph

61

Home interior, São Miguel, 1990.

Symbols of earlier layers of Portuguese time include the many *caravelles* (the sailing ships of the discoverers) displayed in storefronts and homes, the Prince Henry Monument in Fall River, the fifteenth century costumes of the regional Prince Henry Society (a type of Portuguese Rotary Club, formed in the 1980s) and the Dighton Rock in Taunton, the inscriptions on which suggest that Portuguese explorers arrived in America before Columbus. The annual celebrations of the "Day of Portugal, Camões and the Portuguese Communities" invariably bring the memory of the great age of the discoveries back into the present.

Other layers of time and space refer to the ways in which immigrants have reelaborated symbolic representations and social practices of their past prior to emigration as a way of resisting total submersion in industrial America. These are reflected in the spatial organization of homes, with an American upstairs (represented by the symbols of consumption in the United States), a Portuguese downstairs filled with

Backyard in Fall River, 1988.

Portuguese artifacts and photographs of relatives living in different parts of the world (which is the major setting of everyday interaction and of social practices associated with the homeland) and the yard reproduction of Portuguese gardens, indicating how immigrants adapt their rural traditions to an industrial setting. In the neighborhood outside the house are Portuguese stores.

Leisure-time activities include the continuance of the serões, storytelling and musical gatherings out of a strong oral tradition. The use of time and seasons may also place immigrants within a Portuguese world. Industrial work shapes the lives of many during the entire year but, during the summer, immigrants continue to ritualize their collective memories of the homeland in a succession of regional folk-religious festivals, reminiscent of the harvest season in rural Portugal. Discussions between family members, neighbors, and coworkers are filled with stories from the ethnic media (newspapers, radio, television), bringing the homeland into the everyday life of immigrants.

The incorporation of the past into the present is characteristic of immigrant enclaves. In a way, these neighborhoods resemble still photographs of a past that was already lived and does not exist anymore in the homeland. Yet, these multiple layers of Portuguese time and space are dynamic representations of the ways in which immigrants cope with changing conditions of existence.

America as Utopia

While the multiple representations and symbols of Portuguese past seem immutable, personal testimonies reveal dramatic changes—the movement from the known to the unknown, the encounter with new cultural codes and values and the process of living at the intersection of Portuguese and American cultural borders.

America is present in the everyday life of the Azores just as the Azores is present in the everyday life in America. Immigrant women narrated histories of chain migration and the constant movement of people back and forth between the United States and the Azores; relatives living in America who helped them to emigrate and so forth. The experience of living in the Azores was marked by the constant emigration of relatives, friends and neighbors to the United States (as well as to Brazil, Canada and elsewhere) and encompassed the ever-present possibility of their own emigration. "Hello…Goodbye…my time to leave has come," is the beginning sentence of a song that narrates how emigration was constitutive of daily life in the Azores. From the perspective of constant emigration, an abstract image of America as the land of opportunity emerged as a promise for the future. America will solve all problems, but no picture of the future came to mind. The formulas were simple—better opportunities, jobs, money, schools. But America was still unseen, yet to be manifest.

Almost invariably there was one terse announcement pronouncing sentence on the old country. One disabled factory worker said, "I decided to come to America because there was no future for me in the Azores." A young

In a graveyard in São Miguel, a montage of images of the deceased is placed on or around the tombstone. "The graveyard keeper wanted me to only photograph the remains of his parents, and he wanted to open the tomb." – Ron Caplain

Azorean woman, tending her family's laundry, 1990.

social worker elaborated about life before emigration: "In one way…I think it was easier (in the Azores). It was easier because there were no options!"

Images of "no future" and "no options" set limits to life in the Azores. For some, the limits were set by extreme poverty—two-room houses with dirt floors, no electricity, no bath or toilet, no matches to light fires, plenty of food only some of the time, shoes maybe if you were lucky. The one-room schoolhouse had no pens and little paper; the child had to leave school early to work in the fields or as maids to help the family survive. But the volcanic nature of the islands was also experienced as a limit to building a future, as when a woman remarked, "There is something of life there being so uncertain that it doesn't matter where you are… If there was a hurricane, we'd accept that. I think that being a child and living with this, you were so powerless toward nature."

Since women's reminiscences tend to be intertwined with their female conditions, this "lack of options" may also be linked to the rigid construction of gender roles. The younger women, particularly those who

At right, A young woman and her children in São Miguel watch a procession pass by their door, 1989. In the towns, street residences often have the top door panels cut away so that people can interact more easily with street events of the day.

Household chores in the Azores usually include taking care of livestock as well as family.

Ronald Caplain photograph

pursued professional careers in the United States and became cultural brokers between immigrants and the American institutions, perceived gender roles in the Azores as being fixed by inflexible limits:

All the girls always dreamed of being teachers…but the possibilities were few…and we ended up doing housework and working the fields. Then we waited…to get married and start our own lives. That starting was nothing new; it was just an impression of starting something new. Once married, life was the continuation of the life we had living with our parents."

Given these multiple limits for a future in the Azores, these women turned their hopes for a future in America. And America burned brightly with a promise both material and spiritual, yet completely abstract.

The Homeland turns into Utopia

Just as a great new event such as a conquest, a revolution, a new leader can rewrite the history, so the great event of leaving and arriving often rewrites the history of the immigrant. Initial reactions to America varied, but almost no one reported that reality met their dreams. Contrasting with the Azorean paradise, industrial America appeared shockingly gray! "The houses were all gray," remarked one woman. "I didn't like that." Another said, "I got to…Boston and all

Ronald Caplain photograph

Ronald Caplain photograph

I see is gray! Gray smog, gray buildings, everything was gray! And I'm like, 'What is this? Limbo?"

The move from the Azores to southeastern New England was particularly dramatic because it was from the countryside and village to the heart of old industrial cities and from agricultural work, cottage labor and domestic chores to the factory. Although in the Azores these immigrant women had learned from childhood to work hard, sometimes from dawn to dusk, their work followed the rhythms of agriculture.

In America these women were immediately confronted with the rigid time discipline of industrial work. Work dominated life and the images that unfolded were "gray." Women reported starting to work in the factory a day or so after arrival. The day started as early as 4:30AM, getting breakfast for the family members that made the 7AM shift. Some family members made a second shift as well. Wives and husbands worked in different shifts. One woman remarked that for the winter months she never saw the light of day, and another said, "My life in America has been constantly to work."

A characteristic chronicle of the first years in America followed: they did not speak the language; they moved from tenement to tenement; they got a car or made do without; they worked in this factory or that at so much

a week; they encountered prejudice both outside and within the Portuguese community. To describe the opening years, realistic stories were told in the spare language of survival:

Our first decision was to look for work...we found jobs quickly at Columbia Cable...my husband and I found jobs there in different shifts...my husband worked during the day; I worked nights. Then I enrolled my children in school and at church, and I started to learn English, five days a week from 9 to 12. With all those chores, life was not easy and I am not ashamed to tell you that I used to cry a lot, that I was disappointed, nervous because life was so difficult and I had to make so many sacrifices to take care of four children, cook, attend English classes and work from 3:30PM to midnight.

In reaction to their specific experiences of life and work in the depressed industrial towns of America, immigrant women reconstruct utopian images of the Azores. The new images bring to light a romantic nostalgia or *saudade da terra* for a timeless time of childhood or youth of non-industrial labor. A woman whose immigration experience is marked by her fragmented life between Brazil (where her Italian husband, who did not adapt to life in the United States, lives) and the

Woman from São Miguel, 1988.

Stitcher working "piece work" at Calvin Clothing in New Bedford, 1982.

Joseph D. Thomas photograph

65

United States (where she was a factory worker before retiring and where her children reside) elaborated upon the meaning of *saudade da terra* in her life:

I left São Miguel forty years ago, immigrating in 1949 to Brazil and, later, in 1972, to Fall River. I always remember the farewell… I had the feeling I never would return and in fact I never went back. Then I try to remember my childhood, bringing to my memory everything that happened as if it were an image writ large on a screen.

The center of this image writ large or, in the words of Bachelard, the poetic "space of memory and imagination" may be simply the childhood house.

If I were to describe my home to you, it's…a dream or a paradise. It's set in such a way that I would wake up in the morning with the sun rising in the east. We had a verandah which was very high, and we could actually look across and see a little island…the view was just absolutely gorgeous. The ocean was right in front of my house, so I could see it all the time. And to the north of the house were the mountains.

In these nostalgic recollections of a timeless time of childhood or youth spent in

The village of Furnas, São Miguel.

Milton Silvia photograph

the farms or small villages of the Azores, the abstractions on America and the terseness of the descriptions of Azorean working life and poverty disappeared and the females' autobiographic memories expanded and pulsed in a lyric fashion. The island appeared on those women's memories to be seen, felt and touched, and some narratives sounded like a poem dictated by sensations. A social worker who immigrated to the U.S at 14 remembered:

What I loved most was looking through the grapevines at the pretty designs the leaves would make with the sky. I used to say, "My God, that is absolutely fantastic…" the beautiful colors, the blue sky with the white puffy clouds and the green from the green leaves…" I would try to peak through the leaves to catch a ray of sun, trying to see just how much sun I could catch.

For some, but not for all, these new images emerged from a romantic nostalgia for "a time when time did not count." Women (as well as men) whose migration history includes the transition from pre-industrial task-oriented activities in the Azores to industrial work in the United States, developed a romantic nostalgia, or *saudade da terra*, for their immediate past of non-industrial work. This *saudade da terra* tended to be absent from the testimonies of those who either experienced conditions of extreme poverty in the homeland or managed to leave industrial work and become businesswomen in the United States. Accordingly, the most lyric reconstructions of the past prior to emigration were present in the narratives of female factory workers of rural backgrounds who worked and liked to work on their family's farms. In an explosion of sensory memories, these women recalled how agricultural work was intermingled with sociability and aesthetic dimensions of life. "It was fun

Planting on São Miguel, 1979.

Milton Silvia photograph

working the fields, especially if we were a group of girls. Sometimes we sang. Other times we laughed about anything. Life was happier."

These new images hardly ever mentioned the collective historical memory of Portugal. Even for women involved in community affairs, the images of Portugal that came to mind reflected mainly their everyday life prior to emigration. Their *saudade* was for the pleasure, the colors, the sensuality of the community life they left behind when work was part of, rather than separated from, life. "But I miss those walks in the morning and the smell of that pure air which was the mixture of wet grass, beech and incense." Weaving a tapestry of sensory memories, these women recalled the rhythms of non-industrial work: "We could hear the young people singing or whistling…while they were working in the

fields. That was the sound of the new day, people singing along with the noise of the hoes digging and cutting the fields."

From the intercrossing of these multiple memories on their experiences of immigration and confrontation with industrial America, there emerged a shared memory which brings to the fore the human dimension of a time of non-industrial labor. More than a romanticization of the past of a mere fragmented operation of remembering, this collective memory is directly related to their struggles in the United States. As they recalled their first and hard times in the depressed industrial towns of southeastern Massachusetts, they tended to remember, in a lyric and sensorial fashion, only those beneficial aspects of the homeland they would like to see restored.

This lyrical reconstruction of the homeland represents a strategy to resist total immersion in industrial time and, at the same time, provides the basis for the reconstruction of the self. *Saudade da terra* made them forget the multiple and fixed limits of life in the Azores which made them emigrate in search of the American utopia.

Below, two women make preparations for chicken dinner.

At right, a young boy heads out for morning chores. His friend is a unique animal bred for herding cattle, called cão de fila *or* cão de vacas.

Ronald Caplain photograph

Ronald Caplain photograph

Living in-between Utopias

In the process of living in-between the Azores and the United States, immigrants continue to pursue their share of the American Dream which in most cases is symbolized by house ownership, American consumer goods and the possibility of providing a "future" for their children. The ownership of a house allows them to juxtapose symbolically America and the Azores as utopias. Invariably, in these immigrant dwellings, the *upstairs* tends to concentrate symbols of American consumer goods, representing the attainment of at least a share of the American dream. In contrast, the *downstairs*, including the yard, represents the (utopian) reconstruction of the communal life lived once upon a time in the homeland.

This dual organization of time and space in the immigrant dwellings often masks changing relations between women and men, as well as between generations. These changing relations are a result of women's entrance into the industrial labor force as well as the increasing dependence of non-English speaking parents on their bilingual children. The reinvention of Azorean times and spaces allows women and men to recreate, in somewhat exacerbated fashion, cultural values associated with the construction of gender which were transmitted to them through generations. Older women, in particular, functioned as the extremist arbitrators of the moral values constantly reaffirmed by the traditional Catholic Church which (at least until the 1974 revolution and subsequent acceleration of social change in the Azores), were recurrently passed on from mothers to daughters.

Younger women are dramatically confronted with changing roles and power relations in the domestic sphere. These experiences are particularly painful for those who act as translators for parents who do not speak English. As a woman recalled, "When you came here, as the oldest, you were literally the spokesperson for the family. You went to doctors when you had privileged information that you shouldn't have heard or known. You had to translate for financial matters, for all types of problems that were not really meant to be, as a teenager or as a young girl, to be worried about…"

On the parapet of Castelo de São Jorge, the old fort overlooking Lisbon, 1967.

Milton Silvia photograph

But while delegating responsibilities to their daughters, parents continued to demand from them gender behavior that limits their insertion in the American milieu. The same woman remembered, "My parents were very strict. I could not date. I couldn't go to evening events at the school. That was a no-no. And I couldn't do this and I couldn't do that. That was America, but they were bringing me up the way they knew, especially my father…

Women who were still children or teenagers when they came to the United States, and whose life experiences were marked by simultaneous exposure to diverging cultural codes, dramatically remembered their confrontation with the "clash of cultures." A woman who emigrated at 12, recalled her intense feelings of loss of identity and sense of fragmentation of the self: "If you come (to the U.S) at an age when you already had quite an understanding of your culture, and now you have to learn a whole new set of rules, and a totally new language. It sometimes gets to the point when you don't know who you are."

These younger generations of women tended to make diverse choices. Some opted to break free from family traditions and to live only in the American milieu. Others adjusted to family pressure and to the traditions transmitted to them through generations. Bilingual and bicultural women, in particular, who play brokerage and translation roles for their parents tend to live double and parallel lives—one in the Portuguese domestic and communitarian sphere, another as members of American society. This duality of lives, which magnifies self-fragmentation, comes to the fore in personal memories and poetry:

> The world that we discover
> Cannot be revealed just by chance
> It is made of electrifying contradictions
> The continuous reconstruction of identity
>   in America

The meanings created by the immigrants for both their Portuguese and American experiences continued to unfold as they became established in the United States. As more of the conditions of the American dream were fulfilled—the language learned, the house purchased, the children educated, the career advanced, older immigrant women began to give voice to a new contentment, phrased in a realistic style:

> My sons already completed military service (in the United States)…they are married to wonderful girls…I have a granddaughter who is a gem. We are already teaching her to speak Portuguese. We are now preparing the wedding of my daughter who is about to finish college. And I will pray to God at the altar for her to be a good wife and mother for her children…I think, today, that my mission as a mother is more or less complete since I did everything I could for them.

Extended family, São Miguel, 1990.

Ronald Caplain photograph

Young immigrant family in New Bedford, 1980. He is a fisherman. She works in an office.

Joseph D. Thomas photograph

Other women began to assess the meaning of their achievement in America in a new vocabulary which defines success not so much in material terms as in terms of the evolution of the self—independence, a sense of competence and self-determination. One professional woman with a family commented that her life in the United States has always been a continuous rush and strenuous labor. However great the price, she embraced her passage between cultures:

I wouldn't change my life right now. I've learned too much in this country. I've learned a lot about myself. I like working and I learned to be independent. This is one thing it took a while for my husband to accept. I learned a woman has a lot of rights…I've got more self-confidence. I speak more openly, especially because I was in the union. I spoke at conferences, at a lot of meetings and with the media. I learned how to have confidence in myself.

Those who worked hard, founded families, made homes and sometimes rose to positions of authority in business, labor or politics enjoyed this new sense of empowered self. As the same woman put it, "You learn how to make your own world…in this country." The individual power to make a world is for some sufficient compensation for the loss of a soulful connection to nature and community.

Other women, however, continue to live in-between cultural codes and values:

Fall River women view the procession along Columbia Street, 1992.

Bottom, peeling onions in the late afternoon sun, 1988.

Ronald Caplain photograph

James Sears / Donna Huse photograph

Living in between cultures, I try to maintain a balance…I can grow in different directions…It is not easy! There was a time when I did not know which direction I should follow. I do not have problems now.

For many of the younger immigrants who became cultural brokers between the immigrants and the American institutions, the reconstruction of their personal identities resides precisely in the junction of their Portuguese and American experiences. For them, as Manoela da Costa sings in *Os sonhos de Dona Dores (The Dreams of Dona Dores)*, biculturalism and bilingualism became the basis of their individual growth:

I have two cultures
and two languages
two paths to choose
a woman's virtue is in her growth

An intense feeling of belonging to Portugal can be resolved by returning. What is the fate of those who tried to go home again? The statement of a well-known community leader traced out several stages in perception of her experience in the homeland, all evolving after a 16-year conviction that she belonged in Portugal and not in the United States.

I felt I belonged in Portugal. I mean that was where I was brought up. I had all my friends I'd grown up with there…But actually when I went back in 1976,…things were just the same as they were. My friends were still there…married now with their own children, and we tried to carry on conversations…but it was a very strange and superficial relationship. They could not comprehend where I was coming from, what I had experienced…It made me realize that I didn't belong there either. So I was like a child without a country, you know.

This woman was confronted with the stereotyped images of America which prompted most immigrants to come, and she realized that these stereotypes were completely inadequate to encompass the complexity of her own long voyage in the United States—the initial hardships, the struggles with bosses, priests, husband and father, the increasingly

Below, as is the custom, spectators along the route of the procession adorn their perch with their best blankets, tablecloths, rugs, linens, etc., Fall River, 1992.

At right, keeping the street clean for the public, São Miguel, 1990.

Ronald Caplain photograph

Ronald Caplain photograph

responsible positions of authority which she accepted and developed. Her old friends were unable to fathom her hard-won maturity and her real achievement was hidden behind the old slogans.

However beautiful her islands, however dear the old community, there was no one there who could understand the self she had become. The old country had not provided avenues for the particular kinds of growth which had made her the person she is. Her conclusion was that she belongs to both countries. She is born of two mothers:

Portugal is the mother that gave me my birth and America is the mother that adopted me and nurtured me and brought me up to what I am today. And I love them both dearly. Very dearly.

About the Authors:

Bela Feldman-Bianco teaches anthropology at UNICAMP, Brasil, where she also directs the Center for the Study of International Migration (CEMI). She is a research associate at University of Coimbra's Center of Social Studies (CES), Portugal. She earned her Ph.D. in anthropology from Columbia University and was a Fulbright Scholar at Yale University. For five years, she lived in New Bedford's South End and worked as visiting Professor of Portuguese Studies at Southeastern Massachusetts University (now UMassDartmouth), where she founded and directed the Portuguese Oral History Project (1987-1991). As one of the outcomes of her projects, she produced and co-directed an ethnographic video documentary, entitled Saudade, *distributed by Documentary Educational Resources, Watertown, MA, and CES, University of Coimbra, Portugal.*

Donna Huse is Professor of Sociology at UMass Dartmouth and earned her Ph.D. in Sociology from Brandeis University. She helped organize the Portuguese Oral History Project at UMD in which her students were sent into the community to record the stories of immigrants. An expert on the Portuguese gardens of southeastern Massachusetts, she is a co-founder, editor and consultant with Spinner Publications.

Women and children on São Miguel, 1990s.

Ronald Caplain photograph

Ronald Caplain photograph

COMING TO AMERICA

INTERVIEW WITH MARIA TOMASIA

BY PAULA T. BEECH

Maria Tomasia's journey to America is one of struggle and triumph. It is also a journey of great beauty. She left her island paradise, São Miguel, at age 12 and found only hardship in her new country. She was humiliated by being put in the third grade because she didn't speak English. She graduated from high school at age 20. "I don't know where I got my determination," she says. Later, she began to feel her power when she became involved in public service.

Today Maria says: "Portugal was the country, the mother, that gave me birth and America is the mother that adopted me and nurtured me and brought me up to what I am today. And I love them both dearly."

. . . .

Island Paradise

My mother tells me it was exactly 12 noon, February 15, 1948, when I was born because the bells were ringing during the ceremony in church. She remembers the time specifically because it was so vivid in her mind—the bells, and at the same time, I started screaming myself! That was a good start for me—Maria do Anjos Silva Souza Couto.

Oh, I remember everything. I lived in a small town in São Miguel called Ribeira Chã, between Agua d'Alto and Agua de Pau. Most people just pass it by because you have to go up a steep hill on both sides of the village. It's better known now because it has the second most modern church on the island, built with funds from immigrants in Canada, Bermuda and the United States. It's very beautiful.

Ribeira Cha.

Bel-Art Studios, New Bedford

When I lived there, the population was 600. It is now down to 350, the result of emigration, not only to the United States but to Canada and Bermuda. A lot of outsiders have come in and established residency there. When I went back, I felt like a stranger because the majority of the people I knew just don't live there anymore.

If I were to describe my home to you, it's…a dream or a paradise. I would wake up with the sun rising in the east. We had a verandah that was very high and we could actually look across and see a little island off the ocean and see practically the next town. The view was just absolutely gorgeous. A little to the east, on the other side of the house, the ocean was right in front of my house so I could see it all the time. To the north were the mountains. So I had everything, just looking out from this balcony.

From the back of the house, I could see the sunset and the fields and it was beautiful. To this day, I can close my eyes and picture myself in my house, looking at this blue ocean, blue sky, green mountains and the scenery. When I went back, I just stood there for half an hour and looked. Everything was the same except for scale. As a child, I envisioned these streets as huge or very wide and in fact they were tiny. I was disappointed. It was very small compared to being in the United States.

When I was eight, I began embroidering small things like napkins for about 25 escudos a month. The Madeira Embroideries representatives would bring the work to the villages and one responsible individual would distribute it to different people. As long as you could do the work well and neatly and within the deadline, you could earn a specific price. As time went on, I was given more work. Though the work was tedious and tiring—you'd just sit there, I enjoyed it and worked at it until I was ten. Then I went to the liceu, comparable to a junior high and I didn't have time to do embroidery.

I was 11 when my mother decided to emigrate. She was born in the United States and went back to the Azores when she was 11. My grandfather, who lived in the States for quite a few years, would not allow my mother to return while he was alive. When he died around 1955, my mother decided she wanted a better future for her children. She wanted to return to the area she grew up at Coffin Avenue, New Bedford.

Out of a Child's Eyes

My mother emigrated in April 1960. She left before the rest of the family because our documents weren't ready. We were separated for five months and it was horrible. I thought I would never see her again. Looking back, I think my father had quite a few reservations about us going. He was born in

Looking toward Vila Franca from Ribeira Cha.

Milton Silvia photograph

75

Maria and her father's prize watermelon.

São Miguel and, except for being in the service, had never been off of the island. I think he worried about my mother being by herself, even though she came to family.

The first letter my mother sent back made me cry. She was at the airport in Boston and no one was waiting for her. A lady was waiting for a plane that had been delayed and saw her standing there alone for four hours. She asked my mother her name and where she was going. Fortunately, my mother spoke a little bit of English and said a family member was supposed to be there to take her to New Bedford. Incredibly, this lady was also from New Bedford and offered to take her. It was late at night when they arrived and called my mother's cousin. They had gotten the dates mixed up!

During those four hours, my mother said she died a thousand times. She was in a foreign country with no one to turn to. She didn't even knew her cousin's phone number, just the address. When I got that letter I thought—do I really want to go to this country? But everyone was like: Oh, America, that's the place with streets paved with gold and golden opportunities and you can have everything you ever wanted. It was everybody's dream to go to the United States.

Why Are We Here?

We arrived in America on September 13, 1960 and it was a nightmare. We left this very lush green place, blue skies, green ocean. I mean, it was beautiful but you don't know what's beautiful until you leave it. And then I get off the plane in Boston and all I see is gray! Gray smog, gray buildings, everything was gray! And I'm like, What is this? Limbo? Then I'd think, well, maybe this is just the airport—things are going to get better. Little did I know. Things got worse!

My mother was waiting for us and it was a joyful reunion. Portuguese parents don't really show that much affection but, at that point, we were just so glad to see each other. I think it was the first time

I actually saw my parents kiss! We made several stops on the way to New Bedford because they were clearing the roads from a hurricane the night before. And I thought, what the hell have I got myself into? This is America? I don't want to stay here! I was petrified. A hurricane? I've been through an earth-quake in my village before but never a hurricane! In New Bedford branches were everywhere and windows were taped.

My mother had an apartment ready for us at 33 Nelson Street. Nice beds, a couch and tables. My village in the Azores was so remote, we didn't have electricity so it was strange to actually have a lighting switch to just turn on. For the first few days, we stayed in the house and did nothing. During a thunder storm, the noise sounded like it was rattling inside of a can and I thought it was the end of the world.

Nightmare at School

We were here a week before we actually went to school. Though some old friends from my village were there, as well as other Portuguese kids, I was the newcomer and literally an outsider, even to them. They didn't want to associate with me. I was a greenhorn. Even more humiliating, at age 12, I was put into a third grade class. Can you imagine a 12-year-old with third graders? It was a small room with small desks and I could hardly fit in the chair. I'd learned the material they were covering eight years ago. But I didn't know English. After three months, I was put in the fourth grade, then got a double promotion.

When I was ready for Roosevelt Junior High School, they told me I still could not be with my age group so I attended Mt. Carmel, a Catholic school. Here they took us out of class each day for an hour to teach us English, which benefitted me quite a bit. The center of our world was the Mt. Carmel church and school. My only outlet was the church. The nuns asked me to help record the funds that were donated to the church every week. I used to go once or twice a week to record it in the books. I was allowed to teach CCD. Then I made friends who had the same interests and I participated in school plays. I also got involved in a religious debating team.

Though the school was helpful, they did not prepare me or other Portuguese kids for public school. About 13 of us transferred in September from the Catholic school to the public. By December there were only four or five of us left. The rest dropped out. Portuguese kids with accents were considered intruders into their system. They made fun of us. If you brought a linguiça sandwich or something, they would make fun of you. They laughed at the way we dressed. For a long trime, only my mother was working because my father's job didn't work out until later. New clothes were a luxury. The public school kids were already into designer stuff.

All they had to do was go to school; they had few responsibilities at home. I was more mature. I had to clean house, iron and help my mother. We didn't get a car or TV for five years. When we went shopping, we pushed one of those little carts from the store to the house. On Sunday, the entire family walked around Fort Rodman and got ice cream! This was our big day. I began to go into a shell. I didn't have that many friends. If you were not into the same things they were, they did not want to associate with you. My other Portuguese friends decided to embrace the system. Eventually I did too. It was a matter of survival.

During the 60s, when federal programs were helping minority students, I had a counselor in high school, a woman yet, who said she didn't think it's advisable for me to take the college course considering my background. At the time, I didn't question her and just took the business course. I really wanted the college course but thought, hey, she's a person of authority, she knows. Now I know better.

I was determined to get my high school diploma. Don't ask me where I got the determination. I was 20 when I left high school, one of the oldest in the class. If I had my way, if my parents could have afforded it, I would have gone to college right after that, but I didn't. That would come later.

Coming of Age in America

I could not date—my parents were strict about that. I couldn't go to evening events at the school. This was a foreign country to my parents. Something could happen to me. I was not allowed to learn how to ride a bike—it was not ladylike. I wasn't allowed to wear pants. They were for men and not becoming to a young

lady. I couldn't wear lipstick for a while. I couldn't do this, I couldn't do that. My parents were literally living in two worlds. This was America but they were

Maria with her mother, Hilda, and sister, Maria de Lourdes, 1960s.

bringing me up the way they knew, especially my father who was the man of the house.

Everything had to be the way he said. Though my mother was more understanding, he was the one that ruled. Naturally, trying to be a good daughter, I obeyed. I should have been more rebellious. My sister was totally different. She went out even though they told her not to. They had a lot of fights. Then my brother came along and he was really bad. He did everything he wanted. But, of course, he was a boy and that's a different story.

As the oldest child, I was literally the spokesperson for the family. I had to go to the doctor and the bank with my parents and translate for them. I was uncomfortable knowing so much about family problems but I just dealt with it. I was the only one my parents had to depend on. I was literally in control and could have gotten away with murder, or lied, if I wanted to, but I didn't. I was honest. I didn't know how much I resented taking on adult responsibility as a child until much later in life.

Maria, (first left, second row) with 9th graders at Roosevelt Junior High, 1963.

I met my husband in 1966 or '67. I was walking home from my after-school job at Homlyke Bakery carrying my books and wearing my white uniform. He thought I was a nurse! I said, "No, I work in a bakery. You want to walk me home? You can if you want to." He could only walk me to the corner of my street because if my father had seen me, I would have received a beating. But John was very stubborn. He didn't care. Word got around that John walked me home and had been seeing me. One day when he came by the house, my father said to me, "Get upstairs and stay upstairs." John was furious. He just took the car, put on the brakes and accelerator at the same time and shhhhhh! That didn't stay well in my dad's mind.

Maria's dad, João Couto.

Courtesy of Tomasia family

My husband has always been a very up-front person. He tells you what he feels and he tells it to your face. Though he is from the Azores, he was not your typical Portuguese boy. But when he came to the house to tell my father we were getting married, my father had never even spoken to him, and we had been seeing each other for over a year. My father did not speak to him until I was at the altar.

My father picked somebody for me to marry at one point, somebody from the islands who had seen my photograph and decided he loved me. I did not say yes and he didn't speak to me for a year and a half. I was only 15. I said, No, I am not going to be somebody's passport. I wrote back this very nice letter and said I was not ready. I had a commitment, which was to finish high school. I think my father still hadn't forgiven me but that's tough. He had to understand I'm the one who's getting married. It's going to be my choice. And it was like, "Hmph."

When I got married, I assumed I would be able to go to college but my husband didn't agree at first. He said, "Hon, now you've got to settle down." So I didn't do anything for a while, then began taking evening courses at Bristol Community College and UMass Dartmouth. I got very disillusioned with the classroom atmosphere. There was little respect for the teachers and the students were there to converse. I went back again two years later and it was the same thing. I didn't feel I was benefitting from it. Even if I'm 60, I'm eventually going to do it. But I really think experience in life is the best teacher.

Traditional Grandparents

My father was a farmer and a good winemaker. He would make it, age it, sell it and people would come in to appraise it. He was already a sick man with asthma and bronchitis when he came to America. He had a problem with smoking and I remember him coughing at the edge of his bed for hours. He couldn't give up that cigarette.

It was a hard adjustment for my dad to go from farming to a factory. His first job in America was in a fish factory and his hands would swell from the icy cold water. He then worked in a pocketbook factory for 21 years and was finally forced to leave because of his emphysema. When we had been here for five years, he became seriously ill and his doctor said if he didn't give up smoking, he would die. His kidneys were shattered from constant coughing. I must give him credit. He gave up smoking, cold turkey, but he already had emphysema and it just got worse.

One day he looked awful and was losing weight. I said, Dad, are you all right? He said, "Oh, I'm fine." The doctor told him it was just nerves. I know my dad. He's not nervous. He was so pale, his lips were almost purplish and his feet were swelling up badly. I looked at the pills the doctor had given him and called a nurse friend to ask what they were. She said they were tranquilizers. Tranquilizers? For emphysema? I'm a firm believer in ESP. During my lunch house, I decided to go see my dad. He looked worse than ever and was gasping for breath.

The regular doctor wasn't there so they gave me an appointment with another doctor that afternoon. They took x-rays and his history and we got a call two hours later. "Take him to the hospital right away," said the doctor. My father actually had a collapsed lung and the tranquilizers were making it worse. He was literally purple by the time we got to the hospital. Later I got angry with his regular doctor for giving my father tranquilizers for a collapsed lung. I made sure he never went back to that physician. If I wasn't there, I feel he would have died.

After struggling for 21 years in the pocketbook factory, he had to quit. He was very determined to provide for his family. He was a very proud man and, to this day, refuses to go for any help. When he stopped working, we figured it might be helpful for him to get SSI. I'll never forget how humiliated he was when they asked him questions like how much money he has in the bank, does he hide money, how much money does he have in his wallet? My father was like, "Do I have to go through this?" I had to translate for him and could see the hurt on his face. He's a great man as far as I'm concerned and I'm very proud of him.

My father is the only one who has not returned to the Azores. Right now he is on oxygen 24 hours a day. When we go back we take videos so he can see the old country. He doesn't regret coming here. The toil is much more difficult there. He feels if he'd remained there, he probably would not have survived this long. When my parents moved from Nelson Street and bought a house, my dad took great pride in designing his flower and vegetable gardens. He can grow anything! He's even grown figs. Even though he's very sick and he's on oxygen, he was out there last week for two hours. It's in him to be close to the land.

I learned my mother's story only recently by digging and asking her questions. My grandparents came to this country in 1901 or 1902. After my grandmother had a miscarriage and then became pregnant again, the doctor told her to go back to Portugal, have this child and relax. So she went back and stayed for two years. Though the child was well, my grandmother returned to America alone. My grandfather expected she'd bring their daughter! But, no. She said she wanted to see how *she* adjusted to life here first. Eventually my grandmother got pregnant again (with my mother) and she wanted to return to Portugal—again. My grandfather said, "No. This one is going to be born here with me." He kept thinking they would go back but it was eleven years before they returned.

My mother tells me my grandfather was not a typical immigrant. He adjusted very well to the American lifestyle and was always out, either at the circus, a concert or something. He was a lively gentleman. They might have thought he was Irish because he had reddish hair and a red moustache. We don't know where he got it from. He was very distinguished looking. To this day, when I look at his photos, I say—oh, very handsome. He was proud and always wore a suit when he wasn't working.

He worked at the Wamsutta Mills in New Bedford and I think that's what made him ill. He had lung problems, bad asthma and bronchitis, which they call brown lung. Eventually he was not able to work at all.

They returned to São Miguel in '32 after the stock market crash. There was no work and things were bad here. He had a lot of property in the

Azores so he had men working it for him. He was never able to work again. My mother was 11 when they returned. About ten years later, she wanted to go back to America to continue her education but my grandfather said— America is no place for a woman alone. It was a place for men. After he passed away, she decided to come to America.

High School in the '60s

Like most of the women in the Azores, my mother worked full-time at home. She also pre-pared meals and delivered them to my father during the day. Everything was done by hand. There was no electricity. She'd get up early, the bread had to be done by hand, it had to rise in the oven, she had to get wood to warm the oven. She had to wash everything by hand. She also had a vegetable garden in the backyard that she was responsible for.

When she came to New Bedford, she went to work in a factory as a floor girl. Later she worked for about 15 years in the same factory my dad worked in—as a stitcher. They both retired from the same shop. My mother did not have difficulty adapting to the United States. She lived here until she was 11 and remembered her old house vividly. She spoke English but not well. My father never sold the property they had in the Azores. Though we urged him to sell it and keep a few choice pieces for himself, he would not listen. He feels it's something he wants to keep, to pass on to his children and grandchildren.

A Career in Public Service

After my husband and I were married, we started to get involved in organizations. I was working at the Portuguese radio station and became active in the group that started the Immi-grants Assistance Center. My husband joined at a later point. There was no organization to defend the immigrants or help them work out their problems so the need was there.

After the birth of my daughter in '73, I got a job with Congressman Gerry Studds. When I went for the interview, I was seven months pregnant and didn't think I would get the job. However, they called me again at the end of January and asked if I was still interested. They wanted somebody who was Portuguese, who had a little bit of immigration experience and who understood the problems of immigrants. It was a part-time position and I was able to nurse my daughter in the morning, go to work and still go home for a second feeding at 2PM. After four years, I increased my hours. When my son was born, I was working full-time so things were more difficult.

I stayed with it and I think this job opened my eyes to the American system. I was not really familiar with city, state and federal government. When my friend Mrs. Rosa and I got this job (it was an office of two and one supervisor), it was either sink or swim. We had to learn fast and we did. Even though I had been through the immigration experience, actually dealing with it was a totally different thing.

The Immigration and Naturalization Department is extremely slow and inefficient. But people began to discover there was somebody who could speak the language, help them with forms, guide them, tell them what to do and where to go. The demand was high and the problems were great and the people were very appreciative for any help. Though the Portuguese were the majority, we dealt with other nationalities too. And the laws were constantly changing. I stayed with it for 13 years.

As time went on, I developed an interest in politics and volunteered for John Bullard's first mayoral campaign. He lost. When he ran the second time, he asked me to help out again and we did everything we could. This time he won. Later he asked me if I would be interested in being an Assistant to the Mayor in Constituent Services. Though I loved my job with Congressman Studds, I thought it might be time for a change.

Working for the city, I am constantly called to different departments to do translating. The job is not as demanding as in Studds' office but these are daily questions: My sewer's backed up. What am I going to do? Or, I got this bill. It comes from this department, but I don't know what it's about. I have this letter from the nurse at the Health Department and I don't know what it's for. You have to give them proper information, transfer their calls, you name it.

New Bedford has a Sister City Project with Tellica in Nicaragua. My world grew bigger when I went to Nicaragua as part of a delegation. We took medicine, papers and pencils for school children. The poverty was so great and they appreciated everything. They were so anxious to make friends with the American people.

Portuguese Politics:

The Portuguese have been in this area longer than most other national groups. Though we've made some strides, they've been very small. We have a habit of looking for a leader to come forward and taking a pacifist attitude toward what goes on. I also have a problem with the Portuguese radio station. Though they bring entertainment, we need educational programs to give our community information and knowledge.

I like to be involved in community action, however small it is. I served on the board of Onboard, an anti-poverty agency, for six years and went on to join other boards, including the Women's Center. I believe there is great potential in our Portuguese community but we're a little disorganized and disunited. We need to make people understand: You are taxpayers of this city. You are residents.

The Portuguese contribute immensely to this community but they have to participate in the government by voting and voicing their views and opinions. We all should be leaders not just amongst ourselves but with our own lives and in the community.

Greeting Japanese students at "sister city," Tosashimizu, 1986.

Courtesy of Tomasia family

THE NEW IMMIGRANT

INTERVIEW WITH JORGE MANUEL PEREIRA

BY PHILIP J. RACKLEY

"For people like us who have gone through a Revolution, we saw Portugal come out of the dark ages into the twentieth century. We have brought that to America. The early immigrants lived most of their lives under fascism. Though they are exposed to American democracy, few participate. The new immigrants are trying to change that and make a difference."

. . . .

The Revolution: View from the Azores

When I was 11, I learned there are certain things you should not talk about. My family was always opinionated politically. My maternal grandfather was once arrested and sent to jail for a month because he said something bad about the dictator, Salazar. And my aunt's husband was arrested in the student revolt. This caused a big commotion in the family.

On my mother's side, they didn't see my grandfather's point of view. They despised the republic completely and wanted the monarchy, which ended in 1910. Salazar was in power from 1932 to 1968, when he fell off his chair, literally. He had a stroke and fell off the chair and was basically kicked out of the government. He was never officially told he was no longer prime minister so he died believing he was still in charge.

Before the '74 Revolution, some neighbors at our house in Ribeira Grande, São Miguel, were talking about prices and food being too expensive and I just turned around and said, "Oh, it's all the government's fault." My mother looked at me and said, "Well, there are certain things you cannot talk about and blaming the government is one." You see, there were secret police who would arrest, torture and kill people. They did this on the orders of Salazar and later on Caetano. My father worked at the airport and knew a lot of people on the police force.

Before the Revolution, we also had to live with the war in Africa. It started in the early 60s with the sea-jacking or high-jacking of a Portuguese ship, the Santa Maria. Young men were drafted and they had to go fight in the provinces. One of my uncles went to Angola, another to Mozambique, and a cousin went to Guinea-Bissau. Prior to and during the war, they were called "overseas colonies," then Salazar began calling them "overseas provinces." This change in language now made them "internal problems," of no interest to the world communities. Salazar would say, "We are proudly alone," which means everybody is against us. The United Nations did not support Portugal in its wars but the Americans, who often support dictators, sided with Portugal.

We had a neighbor, this old lady, her son was sent to Mozambique and we lived through it like he was a member of our family. She and her husband could not read or write so my mother used to read his letters to them and write letters back. She would come once or twice a week and dictate.

Salazar's Republican Guard on duty in Santa Maria, 1946.

Courtesy of Miguel Côrte-Real

Many soldiers died. It was always a big party when the soldiers returned. When I was growing up, I knew I had to go and fight in these wars. Unless you were smart enough or had some godfather help you get out of it, you had to go. I thought I would probably be killed by a land mine or something. I should also say that while the fighting was going on, the Portuguese were also building beautiful cities in Africa like Luanda, the capital of Angola, and Maputo, the capital of Mozambique.

In March, 1974, there was mutiny in the Army barracks on the mainland but that was crushed. On April 25, we noticed the national radio only played classical music all day. We didn't know what was going on. We switched to a private station from another island and learned there was a coup on the mainland. Remember, we lived in the Azores, the forgotten part of Portugal, and we were always left in the dark. With the Revolution, we began a very big change.

People could talk freely on the streets and on May 1, International Workers Day, officials of the socialist and communist party came back from exile and they had this big rally in Lisbon with thousands of people, something never seen in Portugal. These juntas began forming and we wondered—What's going to hapen next? Then they named a civilian prime minister and parties started to organize with different ideologies and ideas. Leninists, Maoists, Marxists. My grandfather, reacting against the Revolution, became more fascist than ever. We knew the war in Africa would stop, the colonies would gain their independence and the soldiers were going to come home.

The Experiment in Democracy

I was now 13 or 14 and began moving in a socialist direction, equality for everybody. People became more involved in decision-making. One year after the Revolution, we had the first election. Deputies were elected to write a new constitution so everyone was very involved in that. After it was revised a couple of times, it took a socialist turn. All the old establishment was thrown out and new people came forward and took over. As people became politically conscious, there was a movement for the independence of the Azores. Everybody in my family was against it except my aunt. After a while, it was like a counter-revolution and all the pro-independence people went after the communists. That soon stopped.

Many of my family members became involved in politics. A cousin was eventually elected to the city council of my home town, then when the

"Viva Otelo." A woman in São Miguel seems unmindful of the grafitti praising one of the charismatic (now imprisoned) leaders of the '74 Revolution.

Stephen Cabral photograph

82

mayor resigned, he became the new mayor. Now he is an assemblyman for the local parliament in the Azores. There were clashes within the family because everybody believed in a different party. We had some pretty big arguments and discussions at night. Some family members even wanted Salazar's ideas to come back because things didn't go that well for them after the Revolution.

Thirteen years of war in Africa had drained the economy of Portugal and that reality hit everybody. The cost of living began to go up very rapidly and salaries did not. Sometimes we went without basic goods like sugar and propane gas. People had to find alternative ways of cooking. The new right to strike, now guaranteed by the constitution, affected my family and psychologically it was a big thing. My grandfather, almost 70, had to go on strike for the first time, which put a financial strain on my parents and grandparents.

Portugal had been very stratified by classes— the rich, middle-class and poor. Everybody now had opportunity to go for the same jobs. The "godfather" system was eliminated. The Revolution was also good for the church because it gave them freedom to say whatever they wanted. Salazar had been in close touch with the church. The priests were pressured to preach against the communists, socialists and everybody else.

People wanted the war in Africa to end, which it did, but they didn't want to see the colonies go. Everybody said they were given away the wrong way. Portugal pulled out her troops and the three different parties in Angola began fighting among themselves for control. And it's still going on. Portuguese people who had settled in Africa started coming back. My uncle who fought in Angola, then began a business there, stayed until the last minute, then had to leave.

In education, I feel that my generation was used as guinea pigs with all the experiments. There was chaos in the school the year of the Revolution and nobody flunked. It was

a free ride. In Lisbon, they looked abroad to America and Europe to see which systems worked best. I went to school and never knew what was going to happen. They created all these new subjects of study and schooling became mandatory to ninth grade, or age 16.

Another thing we felt was the opening to Eastern Europe, the Soviet Union and China. People started learning about Russia, and Portugal established diplomatic relations with Cuba and China. Portugal became a showcase for democracy and freedom and became respected in the United Nations. We felt good about that.

The Revolution brought dramatic changes to the Azores. Previously, the only thing we were good for was the American Air Force base in Terceira, especially its importance during the '73 Israeli-Arab War. Now there was not just a political awakening but also a cultural awakening. Things became more available like music and different newspapers. People learned more and became better educated. Only the rich could attain that before. TV came in 1975 and changed everybody's life. Every household in the Azores bought a TV set and people became TV addicts including me.

Also, this might seem strange but one of the big things was the free access to pornography. After so many years of repression, films were coming into the country and shown in major theaters. And there was now access to certain books and authors.

Immigrant teenages in Fall River, 1989.

Ronald Caplain photograph

Exodus and New Experience

My parents started thinking about emigrating back in '74 when they visited Rhode Island to see my cousin ordained as a priest. In 1980, we made the trip. The whole family was excited but me. Immigration always seemed to be the wrong thing to do. I didn't think it was right. You should stay in your country and you know…it's very tough to leave everybody, pick up and start all over. The time was bad for me. I was close to graduating from high school in Portugal. The house wasn't ours but we watched it being closed down and our furniture sold. It was tough to see your things going out the door.

It was very cold day in February when we arrived at Logan, gray with snow on the ground. It was pretty scary. We had 13 suitcases, and everybody had two handbags except me. I had three of them. I always have to carry more. In a huge plastic bag, I carried a little wooden chair I had since I was little. I still have it.

We drove to New Bedford where a friend of my mother owned a three-decker. This would be our new home. Everything was very strange. We just had to wait and see what was going to happen. We lived on Rockland Street, down by St. James Church, and soon started school. My sisters and I were sent to high school. I was in the bilingual program, except for English class.

That same week we went to the Portuguese Library to get cards so we could start taking out books. Right next door is the Immigrants Assistance Center and the director was from my mother's home town. He told my parents I should go to CETA and they could probably get me a job. I worked at the Portuguese Library until I graduated from high school a year and a half later.

Every time I was exposed to something great in the United States, I found some way to compare it to Portugal and told everybody it was better over there. It's the attitude—my country, Portugal, is better than any other country.

At first the feeling of isolation here is overwhelming. You don't know anybody, you don't know the city, you don't know how to get anywhere. You're basically left on your own and have to make the best of it. As I look back, the word that comes to me is "difficult." In Portugal, we were middle-class. It took a while here for my father to get a job and we had very little money. My mother got a job sooner. Also, it was the first time I experienced discrimination. You see, in my country, I was the master. Then, in the U.S., I was just an immigrant.

Young patrons of a Portuguese club on Columbia Street in Fall River, 1989.

Ronald Caplain photograph

Life Changes in America

Coming to America was most difficult for my father. He had never worked in a factory, he had an office job in the Azores and a very large group of friends. Over there we were part of the middle-class. In the American factory, he could not find people at his intellectual level. He still reads a lot. We have books everywhere. And reading helps him cope with the difficulties of being here. He has made some friends but not like the friends he left. He got used to watching a lot of TV which he never did in the old country. He had other things to do.

It was easier for my mother because a lot of her relatives were here. My father had nobody. My mother still had a hard time and became very defensive about everything. She had to fight for the things she needed. For her, adapting to this country was like a great battle, at least in the beginning. She never worked outside the home and had to go to work in the factory. It was difficult for her to learn the language and tough when she had to go to the Immigrants Assistance Center. My father understands English and can speak a little but not much. My mother does better. For my parents, language is the toughest thing.

My parents worked alongside mostly Portuguese but their bosses and supervisors were usually American. Sometimes they were Portuguese but, believe it or not, Portuguese in positions of power in a factory sometimes make life difficult for the newer Portuguese. Those who have been here for a while and know the ins and outs of the country and how things run make life difficult for new immigrants. I think it's because this new group of immigrants arriving in the 1980s were people with more education, people who wanted to do different things, not work in factories but get educated and get better jobs. So there was a lot of resentment in the community.

My mother once told me that Portuguese women who work with her don't understand why the four of us, my brother and two sisters, went to college instead of going to work and buying a house. I think people came here to find the American Dream, to make money, get the material stuff, buy the house, get the car and go back to the old country to visit. They don't understand the new people who want to do more with their lives.

In the beginning, my parents relied a lot on their kids. We would translate for them, fill out their papers, take care of bills, go to the doctor, go places with them when they needed somebody to speak the language. When I was working part-time in high school, I gave my paycheck to my father and that was the end of it. It was needed to help support the family. After I graduated from college, I still felt obligated to live at home a couple more years and help out. When you get to the U.S., you don't find the gold mine and you have to work a lot. It's a sobering thought that things are not easy in America.

In Portugal, my father was the decision-maker but here, decision-making is a family process. We all talk about how things are going to be done. When my father had to buy a car, we all decided. It would be a family car and everybody was going to help pay for it. Moving from one house to another was another joint decision. And so it was when my parents went to Montreal to visit my uncle.

We were American on the outside, but as soon as you stepped into our house, you were in Portugal. We spoke only Portuguese. Everything in the house breathed Portuguese, the food, the smells, the knick-knacks, the books. We watched Portuguese TV, listened to Portuguese radio. The house was like little Portugal. And very Azorean! We talked a lot about the people who were still there.

Icons, idols and artifacts, 1989.

Ronald Caplain photograph

Certain forces out there want you to erase everything, all your customs, your culture and become part of this melting pot. All these ethnic groups are trying to keep their customs. One of my professors called it cultural pluralism and I think he's right. At the house, we try to keep the traditions very alive.

Another New World: College

The main reason my parents wanted us to emigrate was so we could have a college education. In September '81, 18 months after I arrived, I was accepted at UMass Amherst in a minority program. That was the only way I could go. My SAT scores were very low because of my English. I could speak it but very imperfectly. Those four years in college are probably what made me get into the culture of American society. My roommate was a real jerk. He said that since my parents were working in factories, why wasn't I working in a factory too? I probably blocked my reaction because it was not an easy thing to deal with.

It was very important for me to be accepted by other students at school. You're different. You speak with an accent and have a European point of view. I also didn't understand American humor at all and couldn't relate to certain conversations. The other guys thought I was dumb, a jerk. The most frustrating thing is when nobody knows what you're saying because you're not pronouncing the words right. I remember I was trying to tell this woman something to do with cooking and I couldn't find the word for "pan." It took half an hour to come up with something she could understand, which was frustrating and embarrassing. Eventually things got better.

I grew in those four years and made some very good friends. Some Americans are very cold, they're not open and don't like to get close to people. In Portuguese culture, Latin culture, there's very close contact, a lot of touching. People stay very close to each other. That doesn't happen in American culture. There is a lot of space between two people and that makes it difficult to build a relationship. It seems like people are afraid of getting close.

In college, I thought I was going to major in sociology and even took some courses. But then, I got that American idea that I needed to make money and be somebody. I said, well, sociology will not take me there so I decided to major in business administration. But then, I wanted something a little more creative so I took marketing. It's business but it's creative. I always liked history but society is designed in such a way that money is everything. I thought at the time the most important thing was to get a degree so I could get lots of money. Now I realize I was wrong.

At UMass Amherst I developed a sensibility for art, especially classical music, mostly through public radio, and I got a job working for a nonprofit arts organization. Money was always a problem. I got some scholarships, some grants and I had to work. In my senior year I was working 60 hours a week besides my school work and that was crazy. Saturdays I was a bum and couldn't get up until 5PM. So I understood what it meant to always struggle for money.

Between Two Cultures

Sometimes I have the feeling I just got off the plane yesterday and it's mind-boggling that ten years have gone by. I have been exposed to so many things I would have missed in Portugal. That has been very good. Over the years, we have become more Americanized. We watch American television. I like sit-coms and American music but not rock and roll. In ways, we've become like every American family, ordering things from catalogues, having a check book, using credit cards. So I'm very Portuguese and at the same time I'm very American.

I don't like to divide Portuguese friends and American friends but sometimes I do. With Americans there are certain things you cannot say because they would not understand, it's very Portuguese. But when I'm among Portuguese people, I can act American. They understand perfectly because they are part of the understanding.

My brother is an American, he's not Portuguese anymore. He came when he was 12 and he's become part of this culture. He doesn't remember the people and places back there. My sisters and I still remember a lot. So much depends on the age you come. My brother also speaks better English and has almost no accent compared to me and my sisters. He doesn't like Portuguese music, he likes rock and roll. He doesn't read any books in Portuguese as my sisters and I do. Every time there is some Portuguese event, we have to drag him.

If you listen to all the ideas at my house, you might think that together we could make a very good socialist party with all these liberal ideas. But my father actually became more conservative in response to the difficulties of living in the country.

And you know, that's funny, the dynamics of the family—we are more open to certain things. I call myself, my sisters and brother Kennedy liberals.

At this moment, I would not go back to Portugal—I like to be in America. I'm also fascinated by American stuff, by Americans. Not American history, that's 200 years old, not enough time. But by the people dynamics in this culture. It's my home even though I'm still an outsider.

Empowering the Portuguese Community

New Bedford and Fall River are old industrial towns that have seen better days, and they have a lot of immigrants. I think "Americans" see the Portuguese as the source of many problems. On the other hand, the Portuguese community doesn't help itself. It's made up of people from all different parts of Portugal so they're divided and they fight among themselves.

The earlier immigrants are so Americanized, they have become very selfish and do not treat the new people well. They think the newcomers should suffer (as they did) before they get somewhere. Immigrants are very jealous of other immigrants who make something of themselves. They don't understand that having an education is probably more important than anything else.

Many who came to this country 30, 40, 50 years ago stagnated. They didn't improve with the times and they still think Portugal was like it was in 1955 or 1960 and that's not true anymore. For people like us who have gone through a revolution, we saw Portugal come out of the dark ages into the twentieth century and we have brought that over and tried to evolve with the times.

People around here don't see big and they need to. The Portuguese have a responsibility to make better things for this community. Getting involved with Portuguese things is a way of keeping in touch with the culture of the Old Country. It's like an umbilical cord, keeping the connection.

The early immigrants lived most of their lives under fascism in Portugal. They got exposed to democracy in America but didn't participate because they didn't know the language. Now we need to get politically involved instead of being a passive community and taking what comes. We need more officials of Portuguese descent and more representation on community agencies.

I think the Salazar influence, "We are proudly alone" still lives in many older immigrants and we lack the feeling of building a community together. The new immigrants are trying to change that and make a difference.

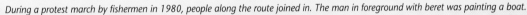

During a protest march by fishermen in 1980, people along the route joined in. The man in foreground with beret was painting a boat.

Joseph D. Thomas photograph

Two Worlds

Interview with Dineia Sylvia

by Kathy Hackett

Dineia Sylvia lived between two worlds, the beautiful Azores she left behind as a small child and the new world where things are grim and gray. Her father speaks of his storybook courtship with her mother; he fills the house with poetry and music. At the same time, he suffers greatly in an alien culture. Her mother cries herself to sleep but spiritedly brings home a paycheck, raises her children and learns the ways of the new world.

Dineia Sylvia is the observant daughter, noticing everything, feeling everything, commenting on all that comes her way, even sizing up that most difficult conflict: the clash between Portuguese parents and their "American" children.

. . . .

Child Memories

When I left São Miguel, Azores, with my parents and settled in New Bedford, I was two-years-old. I cried myself to sleep for years. You would figure a child of two doesn't really know what's going on but that's just not true. I missed the family members we had left behind so badly— That's how real everyone was to me. They were constantly with us in our hearts, yet they were so far away. I missed all my cousins, aunts, uncles and grandparents. You can see that even if adults are not aware of it, children do know these things, they do remember.

We stayed with my grandmother's brother and wife who lived on Nash Road in the North End. They were our only family here except for my father's cousin, who lived on Sagamore Street in the South End. Everything in America seemed very dark and gray, cold and stony. The houses were dark. Cold countries have darker buildings, sunny countries have white and pastel buildings. Also, there are many wooden houses here, but in Portugal and the Azores, a wooden house is for those who cannot afford a regular house. Wood is for the very poor! New immigrants are confused with all this wood.

I had to learn both languages, Portuguese and English, at the same time. Young children pick up languages quickly and easily. However, I was confused when I asked my friends if they wanted to eat *laranja* and they didn't understand! What's the matter with them, I would think, and why are they laughing at me?

When I started school, the teacher suggested I speak more English. It wasn't terrible that I spoke Portuguese—I was a kind of a celebrity at school. Kids would come up to me and say, "Wow, you're not from this country? Oh, tell us about it!" This was before the Americans were complaining the Portuguese were taking jobs away and everything else.

I was lucky I did well in school, but I didn't feel like a success. When I went to high school, I would have conversations with children who used vocabulary that was not very familiar to me. I remember the first time I heard the word "catharsis." What on earth is a catharsis? I was too embarrassed to say, "I don't know what you're talking about." I tried very hard to put the rest of the conversation together without telling the teacher I was not familiar with it. I would think, Oh, my God, they're going to say "She's stupid!" It was really frightening and very difficult.

The word "prejudice" didn't enter my reality. It probably existed but I didn't see it because I felt warm and had hope. Now it is much more complicated than it was then.

Dineia with mother Amelia and father Carlos. Passport photo 1950.

Courtesy of Amaral family

I had to translate for my parents at times, though they went for private English lessons. My mother had picked up English pretty well and my father to a certain degree. He never spoke English in front of me, however. Some people pick up a language in a very natural way but others cannot pick it up no matter how hard they try. My father was one who never quite picked it up.

For years, my mother was a stitcher at Justin Clothing in the Wamsutta Mills complex. She enjoyed work but she always said she should have gone to school when she came here. My father also worked in the Wamsutta Mills as a weaver and, after work, he would do door-to-door sales. I don't understand how he could do so well as a salesman with a limited English vocabulary but somehow he did it.

There was some Portuguese spoken among the workers in the mills but not like it is now. They were very helpful but not too friendly. It was just understood that you learn to get by and stand on your own two feet. You got advice from those who had been here longer, but you go right ahead with your work. It was amazing what the Portuguese immigrants could do.

My parents had a much more difficult time than I had, of course. My mother used to cry at night because she found things to be quite difficult. She didn't want to worry my father about the culture shock because it was her idea to come here. One time she got on the bus and tried to go to the mill where she worked. Well, she ended up in Fairhaven! Having to admit she was lost was very hard for her but she was a fighter, a go-getter and soon she began to adapt very well, better than my father.

Before my brother was born, there was a very nice lady in the North End who used to take care of me while my parents worked, an elderly lady I thought of as a second grandmother. I knew she was a "baby-sitter" because she would sit in that chair all the time and wouldn't move. Once in a while I'd get carried away and start to sing, but then I would realize this was not my home and I would stop.

When my brother came along, my parents had to work different shifts. My father would go to work in the morning and my mother in the afternoon. There was always somebody with us. Friday nights were exciting when my mother came home from work around ten or eleven and we'd have a party We'd put on costumes and sit and wait for her.

Storybook Family Life

My father often told me about his courtship with my mother in the Azores. My mother's village was on the other side of the mountain from his village and he would walk to her village all the time to see her. They met when he saw my mother and two sisters on the verandah of their house. He said he had heard about the lovely daughters of this town and was enchanted at the sight of my mother. At this time, it was admiration from afar. One day by "chance," my father happened to go to the same Mass as my mother. They looked over at each other and that was it. It worked out well for them because my grandparents thought my father liked the oldest daughter and they hid her. They never hid my mother from him.

Much of my parents' life together was a storybook. My father always thought of it as such a romance. He didn't forget one little thing about Ma. He spoke of it so often—how she would look sitting at the verandah and the sound of her voice. He wrote poetry to her and someone in the town would deliver it. This is how they exchanged letters. My grandparents finally caught on but it took a long time.

Family jam session: Little brother Carlos Adolfo Amaral on vocals, Dineia plays piano and father Carlos Amaral plays violin, 1958.

Courtesy of Amaral family

Music was very important in our lives. My father played the mandolin and I played the piano. For a very short time, I studied the violin. Music was something my family loved. When anyone had a birthday, we'd celebrate with the whole family. We alternated between here and Taunton where my cousins now lived. When the celebration was at Dad's house, you were liable to hear the pots and pans being played. I would sit at the piano and everyone would gather around, some with *maracás* and some with pots and pans. We'd use anything that made noise.

At Christmas time, we'd go to a relative's house and have that person join in the musical group. Then the group would move on to the next house. That person would join in and so on. They would take all the instruments except the mandolin. My father wouldn't take it to anyone's house. He was a little shy about it because he felt it had been too long since he had performed in front of others. Our Christmas manger was very Portuguese and different from the American manger. It was under the tree but with lots of boxes around it for the mountains and valleys. There was also a little lake and a little church with little houses all around it. Ours did not have fresh moss in it like those in Portugal. We used a white cotton material that was more American. We were American enough for some things, Portuguese enough for others.

My father also wrote poetry about many of the things he thought about— the seasons, love and the mysteries of life. It was very nice but we were terribly unfair to him. Dad was just dying for us to read his poetry out loud to him and we would always think, Oh, no! Dad's got the poetry book out. We'd try to get out of reading it. But when I sit down now and open those books, it's as if they were different books. They mean so much more. I know wherever my father is, he's got a smile on his face saying, "You couldn't have done that sooner?"

I was not the kind of child that played with dolls. I liked to read and draw. My mother, on the other hand, had been a very active child. In the Azores she was always crossing the streams and jumping over the brook. Every once in a while someone from the family would have to go out and call her to come back in. She was very alive and I was very quiet, different from what she expected a child to be. She would buy me dolls, sit down with them and say—"Come and play." She'd be there with the dolls and I would be thinking, Oh, this poor lady. She tried so hard to get me to play and I didn't quite understand it all.

My parents were both very loving. I think if you have a family that is loving, that's all that matters. They were not like many of today's parents you see embracing one another. A few times we'd see Mom give Dad a quick kiss and we'd go "Oh, wow!" But they were very loving to us. They embraced us and we'd embrace them back. It was a very good feeling.

At a certain point, my father said, "Gee, it's time for us to go back. I want to go back." My

At far right, holding the American flag, is grandfather Adolfo Medeiros; next is his wife Maria. Adolfo's brother and sister-in-law are at left, circa 1900. Maria and Adolfo lived in New Bedford and returned to Portugal in 1925.

Courtesy of Amaral family

90

father had done very well in the Azores and he had been very happy there. I guess eventually you start missing people you knew and the lifestyle you had. By this time my brother and I didn't want to go back. We were comfortable with the school system and had our friends here.

Twice a year our family in the Azores would send us linguiça and morcela. Oh, how we looked forward to that. It was like a big feast. I remember my mother opening it up and crying at the same time. It was like a little bit of home in a package. I have never found anything that tasted quite like it.

First Trip to the Azores

When my brother was small we'd talk about the family in the Azores. He couldn't wait to meet them and he'd dream and fantasize about them all the time. Sometimes he'd knock on the door and he'd come in and say, "Now what if this had been grandpa, what would you have done?" or "Gee, what if we answer the door someday and they're all standing there!" He would go on and on about this. We loved pictures and we had many of our family in the Azores. My brother knew everyone because of the pictures and stories. The family was always with us.

When I was 12, we went to the Azores for a visit. My brother loved it so much he didn't want to come back to America. He was able to run around and have a pet goat. The family over there was so big, it was like a dream to him. In the Azores, you see a lot of greenery. There is natural beauty there like the flowers, lakes and brooks. It is everything you'd dream paradise to be. All the houses in the Azores are white or pastel colors, everything is light and sunny. Of course, there are the poor white cottages but to some they are beautiful. A lovely white cottage to me is absolutely wonderful.

The poverty in the Azores is a different kind of poverty from what you see in America. It's the kind that won't leave you dying in the street with the temperature close to zero and no one cares. Even the poor in the Azores have a sense of celebration and festivity. They feel, "Yeah, we're going to make it." What I found in the Azores was the real life! There was a sense of freedom there. You didn't have to fit into a compartment. It was not synthetic but wholesome and natural. I thought of it as stepping into Heidi. I'd climb up the pathway to a lovely little steeple on top of one of the mountains.

My father's village is Vila da Povoacão in São Miguel and my mother grew up in Faial da Terra,

Faial da Terra, São Miguel, the village of Dineia's mother, Amelia Furtado Amaral, circa 1920.

Courtesy of Amaral family

91

just the other side of the mountain. A brook ran right in front of the house where I was born and it lulled me to sleep at night. I could hear the water rushing over the stones. The beach was at the end of our street. There you would see the beautiful waves. The ocean is raw there. It has really good surf in that area, almost like California, but other parts are like New England.

In the Azores you can go for coffee anytime. If you're from the city, you know things are going on all night. There is no social life in America, it seems. Many immigrants think America is going to be like they see it in the movies. They come here to work, then go back to live the lifestyle they want. But when they return to the Azores, they find it is not quite the way they remembered it because it is changing too. School has changed, attitudes have changed and the methods have changed. They feel there is something missing on both sides.

Pulling a bull near Santa Ana Church, Vila de Capelo, Faial, 1979.

Milton Silvia photograph

Cheese delivery, Ribeira Grande, 1967.

Milton Silvia photograph

My Grandparents

My grandfather came to America before my grandmother. He wanted to get an apartment and start a life for her to come to. When my grandmother came over, she was very upset by the way my grandfather met her. He didn't like the way she was dressed and he wanted her to change her hair, her clothes, even her glasses. Everything was very different and very difficult for her now.

My mother was born here, but when she was an infant, my grandparents decided to return to their homeland because my grandfather's parents were elderly and needed care. They remained in São Miguel for the rest of their lives. At this point, getting my grandmother to leave America was almost as hard as getting her here. She didn't want to go back for anything. She cried so much! When she found out they were going back, she ran to the neighbor's house and cried, "What am I going to do? I don't want to go back!"

With the money my grandparents made in America, they built a house that was larger than all the others in the village. It had a store on the bottom. Upstairs there were two floors the family lived in. This is where they took care of their parents until they passed away. My grandmother's unmarried sister also moved in. The family grew. My mother grew up in the Azores but she always wondered about America. She thought America would give her children better opportunities and one day my father caught on to the idea and said, "Yeah, let's go for it!"

My grandparents would never return to America but they were still an important part of our lives. They used to send us children's books, many of which were translations of English or American stories such as "Cinderella" and "Snow White." There were also Portuguese stories but they thought we'd be more interested in these translations.

Religion and Change

We were very Catholic and always said the rosary together. I didn't always feel like it but it was very important. We were at Mass every Sunday and also on holy days. One Good Friday, I remember playing the Veronica, when I was about ten years old. I had to dress up and lift my veil in front of the people. It was horror of horrors when I realized I had picked up the veil upside down. I was so ashamed, I thought about it for months. It was the end of the world for me.

Religion became a problem when I grew older. I got married and began to take more interest in metaphysics. My brother did also. My mother would say, "What are you talking about?" and she'd listen to us. We'd buy books and follow each other around while one of us read. This really worried my father. I wasn't into anything extreme. I just had a general interest. I wanted to do a comparative study of philosophy and religion. My father got upset when I spoke of reincarnation. "You know the danger of false prophets. I don't want you to lose your soul."

It was an awful struggle because the Catholic Church was so important and religion was the most important thing in your life. Sometimes I think it was the people's form of entertainment. There was nothing much to do so everyone went to church. We heard lots of funny stories about what happened in church. One lady used to fall asleep all the time. She would be asleep and everyone would be getting up and kneeling and the bench would shake. One time, she jumped up and yelled, "Oh, my God, it's a big one!" She thought it was an earthquake.

Adult Reflections

When my parents came over, there weren't many immigrants so they had to adapt. Later on, many Portuguese came and didn't adapt—They created a world within a world. The children, who would grow up American, would become very embarrassed if their parents spoke Portuguese to

In Ponta Delgada, during the Santo Christo procession, it is customary for people to follow the "mundança da imagem," on their knees, fulfilling their pledge to Christ for answering a prayer.

Ronald Caplain photograph

them in a store or restaurant. They would say, "Shhhhh. Don't say that!" They didn't want their parents to speak in Portuguese and the parents couldn't communicate with them in English. Today, there is a better feeling than there used to be but there are still problems between parents and children. Many children are expected to translate everything for their parents. If the parent goes to the doctor, the child has to be there. If the parents go to the bank, they expect the child to take care of their transactions.

Some children develop an attitude that says, "They can't manage without me," and they begin to look down on their parents. Others become so protective of their parents, they become very nervous children. The parents are not able to keep up with all the changes and the children get so frustrated because they are trying to tell them there is a different world out there.

In the house it is one world, and when they leave the house it's a different world. Parents are being kept out of this other life and they don't understand why. Why aren't their children telling them everything? They worry that the children are not obeying once they leave the house, so they try to keep them from going out. The only control they have is inside that house. Outside of the home, they are no longer in control.

My husband Kenneth's family came from the island of São Miguel. In America, his parents held on to Portuguese traditions, but the children lost many of them through time. My husband learned many of these traditions through me.

Today, many new immigrants are more aware and better educated. They're proving they're going to make it and they're more alert and more prepared for change. Americans often aren't ready for today's immigrant. Who do they think they are? They're coming to take our jobs. And why don't they speak English? Today, however, many immigrants come here already speaking English. And sometimes they exploit each other. The Americans don't give the Portuguese as much difficulty as the Portuguese give to each other.

Those who have been here a few years and have become successful often don't want to see the next person reach the same level. They do not want to help each other. You would hope that a successful person would feel an obligation to help someone else knowing that for each person who makes it, it's a better life and it's a better world we all live in.

THE LETTER

INTERVIEW WITH FERNANDA DESOUSA

BY FATIMA MARTIN

For nine-year-old Fernanda DeSousa, the thought of leaving her beloved homeland, her grandmother and aunt, and settling in America is so traumatic, she tries to prevent it by intercepting a "letter." In Portugal, her life is full of small pleasures but in Fall River, life is hard. The image of the family moving from one apartment to another, walking under the Braga Bridge with their meager belongings is wrenching but, after many years, Fernanda begins to understand the significance of their larger journey.

. . . .

One night we were at dinner in Portugal, and I heard that my family was thinking of coming to the United States. My dad had been here twice before and he loved this country. He thought it was the land of opportunity. He kept mentioning that one of these days my uncle might write us a letter notifying us to come to the States.

So everyday I would be on the lookout for the mailman. I knew, more or less, what time he would come by. One day I noticed one of the letters he gave me was from America. I was only nine at the time, but as soon as I saw it, I couldn't help but cry because I knew what it was about. So I read it, and I hid the letter for three weeks.

One night at dinner dad mentioned it was funny how his brothers and sisters had received their letters and he wondered why he hadn't. That's when I began to cry, and my aunt who lived with us, started to cry too. I told my father the truth. He didn't spank me or anything but he wasn't too happy about it.

Every night I used to pray and cry because I didn't want to leave. I loved my surroundings, everything was so familiar to me and a part of me. To leave all that behind to come to a strange country, not knowing what to expect, of course, as a child you don't know and you're scared.

We come from a very small *freguesia* (village) called São Roque. It was well-known for its beaches, one called Praia do Pópulo and the other Praia Grande. There were many kids in our neighborhood and we used to get together and play games like jumping rope and hide and seek.

In the morning my aunt would call my sister and me to do our hair. Our hair was long and we would sit there for what seemed a lifetime, then she would pull strand by strand, braid it and twirl it on top of our heads. That was the most painful thing early in the morning. My sister and I would fight to see who would go last.

Sundays we used to get up real early, have breakfast together and put on our best shoes and clothes. I had this favorite pink dress with a little white collar, trimmed with tiny pink and blue flowers. It had a big pink bow on the back. My sister and I always dressed alike in the same style or color. After church, we changed our clothes, packed a picnic basket and headed for the beach.

My yard was my favorite place, so big and beautiful. There was this big tree in the back and my father made a swing. On a hot summer day I would swing back and forth, feeling the cool air hitting against my skin until I lost the concept of time.

João, Fernanda, Isabel, and father Leonildo enjoy Praia Grande in São Rogue. circa 1967.

Courtesy of DeSousa family

My aunt did the cooking. All the greens came from a vegetable plantation in our yard. I only watched my aunt cook when she made the sweet rice, one of my favorites. Every time she turned around, I'd dip my finger in the pan. She always saved the pan for me. I would add lots of cinnamon, sit on the kitchen floor with the pan between my legs and eat away. I loved when she made sweets.

My bedroom was spacious and my mattress was made out of feathers. Every morning we would shake it to reshape it. My aunt, sister and I would sleep on that bed and my grandmother on a separate bed. Every morning the sun would beam through the big window in my room and I would wake up with its warmth on my face.

My grandmother was so frail and almost blind and she recognized us by our voices. I remember putting my head on her lap and she told me stories of her youth, of how it used to be. She always wore black. One day she was sitting in front of the house crying. She said she was old and she was never going to see me again. I ran through the yard to the back room where my mother washed clothes in these big tanks. She was there with my aunt. I was screaming and my mother asked what was wrong. When they heard, they began to cry too. My grandmother had never expressed how she felt until that day. It was almost like she was saying good bye, not only to me, but to life as well.

When the time was near for us to come to leave, we sat at the table and my grandmother didn't join us. Nobody knew what to say that would comfort her. We immigrated on August 10, 1974—my mother, father, 16-year old sister, 14-year-old brother, and seven-year-old kid brother. I was ten years old. The day we left I didn't even say goodbye. Everybody was saying goodbye to everybody else but I just left.

When we first came here, we lived with my uncle for four days, then moved to this big seven-room apartment in Fall River. My back yard was very small. I had lost the sense of freedom of being

Leonildo as a bus driver in Ribeira Grande. Below, Fernanda, with mother Fernanda, brother João and sister Isabel in São Miguel. Bottom, the classic studio potrait that many families had taken before leaving for America, 1974. Left to right: João, Fernanda (mother), Isabel, Leonildo Jr., Leonildo Sr. and Fernanda.

Photographs courtesy of DeSousa family

able to call it my own. I had totally lost the privacy of being able to call it my own. I had totally lost the privacy of being myself as I was restricted by the landlord's rules. In our apartment, we had only one chair and dad was the only one who sat on that chair. The rest of us sat on the floor. We had a few utensils, two plates and three cups. We lived like this for a good month or so. No one had a job and we lived on the money we brought from Portugal. We had very little clothes because we thought it would be easier to buy them in America.

Dad met someone whose wife worked at Shelburne Shirt in Fall River and that's where mom got her first job. My mother wasn't used to working in a factory. In Portugal, she stayed at home and took care of us. Soon after, my sister went to work with my mother. Mom cried almost every night because she didn't like working all day in the factory, then coming home and having to put dinner on the table. It also began to get very expensive to keep up with the apartment. By this time, we had accumulated a little money and dad bought two new mattresses. Mom and dad slept on one and the four kids slept on the other.

The family moved to their new "luxury" apartment upstairs from Costa's Fish Market, formerly Paiva's, on Columbia Street.

Joseph D. Thomas / Spinner Collection

From there, we moved to this little place above Paiva's Fish Market on Columbia Street. We packed our little belongings inside these two blankets and a spread we brought from Portugal. And one night we headed on foot from Danford Street, crossing underneath the Braga Bridge to Columbia Street. My older sister and brother carried one blanket, my mother and father carried the other one. I and my kid brother carried smaller ones and that's how we transported ourselves. It was beginning to drizzle and all I can remember is my father saying—"We'll get there, we're going to make it." And we did.

Fernanda, as an angel, with her dad at Holy Ghost feast in São Miguel.

After my father got a job, we began saving and buying furniture. We stayed here for a year, then moved to another apartment on Globe Street. And this is where we started to build a little nest. My father had faith that things would be alright and, thanks to him, things are OK.

The first two years I kept having these dreams. I couldn't accept the fact we were in a totally different country with different customs. I wondered: Why did dad want to come here? And why this and why that? There were so many questions and no answers.

Many years have gone by and now I understand why we are here. We have all achieved the "American Dream." We've grown to be what we wanted to be. My oldest brother John graduated from Southern Connecticut College. My kid brother is now at Salem State College and I also go to college. I feel bad for my sister who didn't have the opportunity to go to school. When we came, she was old enought to work and my parents needed her help. Although today she is happily married and content with her life.

The greatest lesson that I have learned through my ordeals is to appreciate everything, not to take anything for granted. Even though I've assimilated into this culture, Portugal will always have a special place in my heart. It will always be "my home."

IMMIGRANT SONG

BY LEONILDO DESOUSA

TRANSLATION BY FATIMA MARTIN

In verse, Fernanda's father, describes the trauma of the family's immigration experience. We have called it "Immigrant Song."
. . . .

It is difficult to immigrate
   to a distant country
and have to confront
   the difficulties of immigrants.

There, I have left my belongings
   and came with an illusion.
Here, I arrived and
   had to sleep on the cold floor.

My children and my wife
   slept the same way.
We shared one spoon,
   and only one chair.

I went one day to live
   in an apartment
and had to bear everything
   against the wind.

My wife and my children
   helped me, and so did God.
But, they too went through
   what is not wished upon anyone.

Isabel, John,
   Fernanda and Leonildo
suffered disillusion
   each in their own way.

They didn't beg.
   My wife and I cared for them,
but not knowing the language
   they all wept.

There goes thirteen years
   and so much has gone by.
Hopes and despairs.
   But, God has helped us.

Now, everything is better
   in the company of mine.
But, if it goes for worse,
   let it be God's will.

É difícil emigrar
   para um país distante
e ter que enfrentar
   as dificuldades de imigrante

Meus haveres lá deichei
   e venho nesta iluzão
e quando aqui cheguei
   tive que dormir no chão

Meus filhos e mulher
   dormiram da mesma maneira
so tinham uma colher
   e apenas uma cadeira

Fui um dia morar
   para um apartamento
e tivemos que acartar
   tudo ao regar do vento

Mulher e filhos me ajudaram
   E Deus do céu tambem
mas eles tambem passaram
   o que se não dezeja a nínguem

Isabel e João
   Fernanda e Leonildo
sofreram tanta dizelusão
   cada qual em seu sentido

Eles não andavam a míngua
   eu e mulher, deles cuidavam
mas como não sabía a língua
   todos eles choravam

Ja lá vão treze anos
   e tanto que se passou
esperança e dezenganos
   e Deus nos ajudou

Agora ja vai melhor
   na compania dos meus
mas se for para pior
   seja a vontade de Deus

The DeSousa family and friends in their backyard on São Miguel, 1970.

Courtesy of DeSousa family

LUSO POETRY

POEMS BY GEORGE MONTEIRO, EMILY A. MONTEIRO, JASON LEARY
AND QUATRAINS BY JOÃO TEIXEIRA DE MEDEIROS

WHO WAS JOÃO TEIXEIRA DE MEDEIROS!

by Onésimo T. Almeida

Poems translated by George Monteiro

Lagoa do Fogo, São Miguel, circa 1965.

João Teixeira de Medeiros (1901-1995) was born in Fall River where he lived most of his life, except for the years 1910-1930, which he spent in Pedeira do Nordeste, a small town in São Miguel, Azores. From his early years he was a poet. He wrote quatrains, mostly in the popular vein, but also sonnets that he was too shy to publish. Only in 1966 did his poems start to appear in the Azores and in the Portuguese-American press. His first book, *Do Tempo e de Mim*, (Of Time and of Myself), dates from 1982, when he was "discovered" by Professor Onésimo T. Almeida at Brown University. The book, published by Gávea-Brown, received high praise in the press and in literary journals. In 1992, a second volume of his poetry *Ilha em Terra*, (Island in Land) followed. A third is planned.

His main themes are the lives of common people, their struggle and hardships, the fragility of material goods, the nostalgia of a life one passes through so fast, the humble facing of one's imminent death. The land and the sea of his beloved Azores were also frequent themes. He writes beautiful love poems as well.

Reviewers have praised the common touch of his poetry, the soul in his quintessential human voice and the pure and earthy quality of his lyrical style. José Saramago, the best known Portuguese writer outside Portugal, dedicates a full page of the third volume of his journal to Medeiros' poetry.

J. T. de Medeiros confessed to his close friends many times that he never expected his final years would be his happiest. He was showered with affection by his readers. and received numerous awards in the United States and Portugal. This humble, humane, sweet, youthful man who walked with dignity and a child's smile on his face, and who, at 94, still walked up to the third floor of his Fall River triple-decker tenement, became the pride of the Portuguese-American community of Southern New England. After his death, he is more alive than ever amongst us.

The two quatrains published here are translated by Professor George Monteiro of Brown University.

São Miguel

Se fosses, ó ilha bela,
Flor que eu pudesse colher,
Pendurava-te á lapela,
Pra todo o mundo te ver.

Sou...Não Sou

Não sou moço nem criança,
Já vou tocando no fim.
Sou cinza duma esperança
Que morreu dentro de mim.

St. Michael

Were you a flower to
Pluck for my boutonniere,
O lovely isle, I'd set you
There for the world to see.

I am...I'm not

Neither boy nor child am I,
Closing in on my death.
I am the ashes of a breath
That within me did die.

Courtesy of Miguel Côrte-Real

Selected Poems

by George and Emily A. Monteiro

Both father and daughter share a passion for poetry. The following poems are taken from their personal collections. "The Finger Legacy," written by Emily independently of her father, complements George's poem "Double Weaver's Knot," by extending the Portuguese connection over three generations.

George Monteiro is author of The Coffee Exchange *(1982),* Double Weaver's Knot *(1990), and* The Presence of Pessoa *(1998). Emily A. Monteiro was born in São Paulo, Brazil in 1969. She has been published in* Grecourt Review, Northeast Journal, Dickinson Studies, *and* James River Review.

. . . .

Milton Silvia photograph

Francisco Monteiro

My grandfather died
after a two-year stint
at the Institute of Mental Health
in Warwick, Rhode Island,
way before I was born.

But I found him
one summer in Lisbon,
where I learned I
was a failure at my father's language.
Instead of going to my
summer classes, I rode the city
looking for something to
fuse me to that place,
and I found him.

I found him over and over,
and there were many of him,
although I could not
speak his language I
found him
wandering crazy in the winding
underground tunnels of the Marquês de Pombal station.
Each time
he came to me arms out,
resting a hand on my warm
head, saying "A Carinha!"
I knew it was him,
just as I imagined,
in a grey hat with low-crotched
black pants, white shirt.

Portuguese, animal-dirty with pigeon dung,
sick, crazy, loving me,
driven underground
where the roots of trees live.

—Emily A. Monteiro

Aftermath

Cutting down the dense
growth beyond the fence

and down to the tracks,
hair pulled back and

almost out of sight
under a red and black

and white kerchief,
sweeping aside grass

harvested with a stone-
edged sickle she kept

on the shelf in the
cellar, she sings to

please herself.
Moved by the task,

she has no mind for
notions when fist and

eye and curved blade
work swiftly to debride

the slope. Easily
she moves, rising in

the rhythm of her
falling once again

within the mercy
of her father's gaze.

—George Monteiro

A Fish Head

to be sold
at weight
centers the
display at
O Polícia.
Everyday
delicacy,
this thing
of no body
is not for
me.   My
mother,
who comes
to mind,
took care
of that.
She just
sat there,
eating her
way through
the head
bones and
brains of
a fish,
while I,
exonerated
by her
sacrifice,
picked at
flakes of
white flesh.

—George Monteiro

100

The Finger Legacy

He, at the loom of his desk, slipped knots
across to me, the youngest of three.

She was a thirty-year-old Portuguese woman,
second marriage, thick calves and tightly
pulled back black hair that spread
webs down around her jaw, sitting in the
factory, weaving. Slipping knots
while her nine-year-old, my father,
passed out pies on a bakery truck.

When I was little, my dad sat at night
in his study, black hair a moon's gem,
dark arm hair pulling his thin shirt,
a pen diving into a Steno.
While we slept, he set
his bloodline stories straight.

Lately my hair has grown dark and
I stay up late at night,
doing things with my hands.
It's a legacy of fingers,
able and fat, weaving and writing;
the need for slipping knots
slipped into the genes of the
hand that weaves.
                              –Emily A. Monteiro

Double Weaver's Knot

In their time her fingers pieced
together the endless ends of a

string. At the kitchen table
once, she displays a whole rush

of intricate knots, fingers turning
over broken thread faster than mere

eyes can follow. This is personal
work, which will not survive in the

museums it serves to authenticate.
                              –George Monteiro

*Opposite page:
Elderly Azorean
woman chops wood
for kindling, 1979.*

*Below, needlework
in Madeira being
done by skilled
professionals.*

*Bottom, while
fishermen in Nazaré
tend their boats and
gear, the women
and young girls
pass the time doing
their needlework.*

Milton Silvia photograph

Milton Silvia photograph

101

BODY OF PORTUGAL

BY JASON LEARY

Jason Leary received his master's degree in professional writing from UMass, Dartmouth in 1998. Living in Fall River, he wrote "Body of Portugal" as a student at UMass. "This mysterious, traditional, enchanting culture was just asking to be written about, and I was lucky enough to hear the call." "Body of Portugal" is one sequential poem from a 30-page unpublished anthology entitled Quequechan. *The following are selected chapters from "Body of Portugal."*

. . . .

West

The earth sways under the steady boat.
João and Luisa, two years apart, look east,
their island sinking paralyzed into the sea.
They remember the American from the mills
talking to their father and the others.
They think of Carolina's letters from the United States.
—first Carolina and Pedro, then Roberto and Jorge,
and now us—Luisa says in her mind.
João, softly, speaks out loud—
"With all the weight gone, our home can leap from the water!"

Watching the Santo Christo Feast from the Window with Vovó

Ronald Caplain photograph

"Vovó, vovó!" the grandchildren plead,
tugging at the rustic skirt, but vovó
—grandmother—is traveling alone,
the flowers and music and
spirit of Columbia Street
sending her back to
her source—

Ronald Caplain photograph

Milton Silvia photograph

The Azores: Formations

From the sky
nine blossoms
fell from Angel's hands
into the melancholy sea
and the sea's prayer was answered.

Temperamental Atlantic,
unsophisticated and mysterious,
you pound against your borders
but for your beads, you give special praise
whispering thanks
as with rough fingers
you rub Santa Maria
     São Miguel
     Terceira
     Graciosa
     São Jorge
     Pico
     Faial
     Flores
     Corvo
     following
     the string
     to the tenth
     in the sky

Opposite page:
Top, elderly celebrant at the Santo Christo Feast, Fall River, 1992. Middle, children and adults vie for position while watching the procession. Bottom, departing view of the Madeiran waterfront, 1987.

Below, solitary farmer plows his fields in the Azores, 1967. Bottom, sunset over Pico, as seen from Faial, 1979.

Milton Silvia photograph

Milton Silvia photograph

THE IMMIGRANTS ASSISTANCE CENTER

BY MARIA DA GLORIA MULCAHY

The Immigrants Assistance Center in New Bedford's South End is abuzz with activity. The staff is busy fingerprinting, distributing food, translating letters, providing information, referring people for services and answering phone calls. A group of animated senior citizens just finished a citizenship preparation class. Another group is expected this afternoon.

Throughout the morning, people stream into the cramped quarters at 58 Crapo Street. Some have come from Cape Cod, others live just around the corner. Some like Gilberto de Almeida arrived in the United States more than thirty years ago; others like Maria Camara came more recently. Most were born in Portugal, but not all. Some are not even immigrants. A man named William said an outreach worker told him to come in for help. "I was born in this country, but my grandparents were immigrants from Germany," he said.

For many, this is their first visit to the Center, but others rely regularly on the staff as interpreters, purveyors of information and advocates. "I've been coming here since I arrived twelve years ago, mainly for help with language," said Maria Albano, a native of Água de Pau on the island of São Miguel. "I don't want to bother my in-laws; they are busy with their own lives."

A man waiting for assistance offers high praise to the staff. "Some of my relatives speak English and I could ask them for help, but they don't know the laws and the ways of this country like these ladies," he said. "We are lucky to have a place like this." Indeed. But help was not always so readily available for those arriving in this area.

Refugees from Faial

Manuel Fernando Neto immigrated to New Bedford in 1960 when the Capelinhos eruption of 1957 forced his family to leave their native Faial. Manuel was 15. The eruption, which destroyed the lives of many, led to the passage of the Azorean Refugee Acts of 1958–1960, which eased immigration for victims. The young Fernando and his family were sponsored by Ana Morais, an American-born woman of Portuguese ancestry.

The eruption of the volcano of the Capelinhos, November 13, 1960.

"They were not related to us," states Mr. Neto with gratitude. "This lady must have sponsored 50 or 60 families." The sponsors took responsibility for finding the newcomers a home and jobs, enrolling the children in school and integrating them into the community. The 4,811 people from Faial admitted under the Azorean Refugee Acts were soon followed by others from various parts of Portugal.

The Immigration Act of 1965 ended the restrictive immigration quotas of the previous four decades, allowing 20,000 immigrants per year from each country. Although Portugal never reached that ceiling, in 1969, some 16,528 Portuguese immigrants entered the United States and 40 percent intended to live in New Bedford and Fall River.

Mr. Almeida Applies for Citizenship

Mr. Gilberto de Almeida was one of the first Portuguese immigrants to come under that law. He arrived in 1966 from the town of Espinhal. "My mother was born in New Bedford and my father came from Portugal in 1922," he said. "They got married, worked in local mills and lost their jobs in the 'Big Strike.' They returned to Portugal to live in 1932. When things got better after the War, they wanted to come back to America, but my father was not a citizen and my mother did not want to go without him."

Mr. Almeida applied for a United States passport to come and live with his grandmother, but was told that those born before 1934 could not get an American passport unless they were the children of male American citizens. According to Mr. Almeida, this law changed in 1934, granting citizenship to children of both male and female Americans. His siblings, who were born after 1934, came to the United States in the '50s. They later sponsored Mr. Almeida.

"The United States Government sent me a letter to serve in the Korean War, but they did not want me to live here," said an incredulous Mr. Almeida, who waited until now to apply for citizenship. "It was out of silly spite." Although he felt spurned by the system, Mr. Almeida was able to rely on his relatives to buffer his adjustment to the new country. Others with less resourceful sponsors had to seek help outside of the family.

The Migrant Education Project

Post-war prosperity and the liberal thinking of the sixties gave rise to social programs aimed at improving the lives of the needy. Among those operating in New Bedford was The Migrant Education Project directed by Jack Custodio. He saw no reason to discriminate between internal and international migrants and reached out to offer services to all newcomers. The program, housed at the Regina Pacis Center on Rivet Street, hired Portuguese bilingual staff, thus providing opportunity for immigrants who arrived with more than elementary education into the white collar sector.

Many of the workers who passed through the doors of the Migrant Education Project later distinguished themselves by their contributions to the immigrant community. People like Paulo Andrade, Manuel Adelino Ferreira, Helena Fraga, Laurindo Machado, Albertina Mendes, Tobias Paulo and others guided immigrants through the maze of the American Way. The agency also gave some immigrants the opportunity to participate in the democratic process as members of the board of directors. Manuel Fernando Neto became chairman of the board in 1970. Two years later, he was elected to the City Council, the first city councilor of Portuguese birth in New Bedford.

Immigrants arriving at Logan Airport in Boston, 1971.

Milton Silvia Collection

A young Azorean immigrant, her luggage intact, smiles for the camera as she awaits processing through customs at Logan Airport, 1971.

Soon after his appointment as chairman of the board, however, Mr. Neto witnessed its demise. Washington officials assessed the program and concluded it was not doing what it was intended to do. Funding was terminated and the immigrant community quickly felt the vacuum. The sponsors of those who came after 1965 were, for the most part, family members who were themselves immigrants and limited in the kinds of help they could provide. Something needed to be done.

The Struggle Begins Again

Radio personality Antonio Alberto Costa was a driving force behind a movement to create a new agency. The issue was discussed over the Portuguese radio station and a planning meeting arranged. Mr. Giordano, a local clothing manufacturer, offered space for the meeting in a building on Orchard Street (now Club União Faialense).

With the help of State Senator George Rogers, the group succeeded in getting Mayor John Markey to agree to start a program to "ease and dissolve the cultural, social and economic barriers faced by people of any nationality who immigrate to the United States, particularly Southeastern Massachusetts." In August 1971, the program began operating out of a building on Tallman Street under the umbrella of Onboard, Inc., an antipoverty program. Three months later, it became a legal corporation under the name Immigrants Assistance Center, Inc.

Although it had official status and a home, the Immigrants Assistance Center did not have money to hire employees. For a year, it was staffed entirely by volunteers. In August, 1972, Heldo Braga and Tobias Paulo were welcomed as the first official staff, public service employees hired through the Emergency Employment Program.

A year later, the building that housed the Center burned down and the agency found itself homeless. Board member Abel Fidalgo sought help from Father Branco of the Immaculate Conception Church who allowed the center to operate out of the cellar of the Church's rectory on Davis Street. But the Center's condition was still precarious. The agency had no budget and no sources of funding besides client donations. Relying on the immigrant

community for support was not feasible because of their humble economic condition.

Board members lobbied politicians and private organization such as the United Way for funding but met with resistance. "The people served by the Center—the immigrants, the non-English speakers, came from that sector of the population that has the least power. It was easy for those in a position to help to ignore their requests," explained Tobias Paulo who left his job at the Immigrants Assistance Center in December, 1975, but joined its board of directors.

One of the few immigrants who had achieved political clout was City Councilor Neto. He approached then Mayor John Markey with a proposal to create a Portuguese Community Center at the vacant Thompson Street School. The idea was to bring newly formed organizations like the Casa da Saudade Library, the Luso American Soccer Association and the Immigrants Assistance Center under the same roof. The city accepted the proposal and in November 1976, the Immigrants Assistance Center moved rent-free to its present location at 58 Crapo Street. However, its funding difficulties continued.

Domingos Paiva

Mr. Domingos Paiva began work at the Immigrants Assistance Center in November of 1976. Like his predecessors, he was a public service employee hired through CEP (Concentrated Employment Program) and his period of service was due to end twelve months later. The work was well-suited to Mr. Paiva, who was familiar with the pre- and post-migration experiences of the Center's predominantly Portuguese clientele. And besides, he owed one of the founders, Laurindo Machado, a debt of gratitude.

Born on the island of São Miguel, Mr. Paiva had trained for the priesthood. While a seminarian, he lived in Madeira and mainland Portugal where he did various kinds of social work. After finishing his seminary studies, at 23, he was eligible for the draft and should have been on a plane heading for Angola or Mozambique to serve his military duty in the Portuguese Colonial War. But instead of flying to Angola, he was flying to New York City to begin a new life. "What time plane starts to Boston?" he recalls asking a Kennedy Airport staffer. He could hardly believe the miracle of being on American soil. It all happened so fast. Two people were responsible for redirecting the course of his life—his mother and Mr. Machado.

Six months before he immigrated, his mother, fearful that she would never see him alive again, had gone crying to Mr. Laurindo Machado of the Regina Pacis Center, pleading for help in getting her son into this country. Mr. Machado, a former Catholic priest and chaplain in the Portuguese Air Force, was able to use his connections to get the Portuguese authorities to grant Mr. Paiva an exit visa.

Once in America, Mr. Paiva followed the general immigrant path to the factory floors, then became a junior accountant and insurance salesman. While pursuing a degree at Southeastern Massachusetts University (SMU), he became a member of the board of directors at the Center. In November of 1976, he resigned his board post to become an employee. He was well aware not only of the needs of the immigrant community and the regional backgrounds of its members, but also of the struggles and workings of the Center.

Mr. Paiva attributes the Center's early difficulties in getting funding to prejudice on the part of funding sources and the political naiveté of the board of directors. For years, the United Way denied the Center's requests for funding on the pretext that the Center only served Portuguese immigrants. While the Center always served anyone who walked through its doors, the demographic reality of New Bedford was sufficient reason to account for the fact that the overwhelming majority of the center's clients were Portuguese. Surprisingly, the negative reactions frequently came from persons of Portuguese background.

Mr. Paiva recalls approaching an important elderly services agency for funding and being told, "If you want to help the immigrant elders; teach them to speak English." To which Mr. Paiva replied, "Since all the people you serve already speak English, there should be no need for your agency." He also remembers that the Center had similar experiences with Community Development money during Mayor Markey's reign.

Before ESL (English as a Second Language) was instituted through the IAC, students learned in "non-English" classrooms, like this one in the Thompson Street School, 1968 (3 photos).

Milton Silvia photographs

107

Money Finds the Center

Eventually, things began to change. In 1978, through the efforts of labor leaders Manuel Fernandes and George Lima, the Center received its first United Way grant for $12,000. The money was used to hire the Center's first director, Mr. Domingos Paiva. "I started to understand politics," he explained, and he and board members reached out and began networking.

That same year, through the efforts of board member Uriel Maranhas, the Center received a CETA grant for $70,000 and could now employ 13 persons. In 1980, the Center began cooperating with the Center for Human Services, offering counseling services to Portuguese-speaking individuals and families. This was followed in the mid-eighties by contracts with the Departments of Social Services and Mental Health. Even City Hall began to cooperate.

In 1983, under Mayor Brian Lawler, the Center received its first Community Development grant for $28,000. Under Lawler, the Center enjoyed a period of expansion and, in November of 1984, opened a second office on Acushnet Avenue in the North End. Three years later, a grant from the Gateway Cities Program for $137, 500 swelled the Center's budget to $235,500 and allowed the expansion of existing services and the creation of new ones.

Immigration Declines

After 11 years of service, Mr. Paiva left the Center to become a guidance counselor with the New Bedford Schools. A period of instability followed. By the late 1980s, immigration from Portugal became a trickle. At the same time, the size of the Spanish-speaking community continued to increase but despite efforts, the Center was never successful attracting them either as clients, staff or board members. Funding declined and so did the number of those seeking help.

The North End office was closed in 1989. From the end of 1987 until the beginning of 1996, the Center had seven different directors, including this writer. In June 1996, executive director John Anjos left amidst a flurry of public and acrimonious controversy and the board of directors found it difficult to attract a substitute. Helena Marques, the Center's executive secretary since 1984, who had provided continuity through the many transitions, was asked to become interim executive director.

New Mission: Citizenship Preparation

Today, under the direction of Helena Marques, the Center has experienced a renaissance despite the lull in Portuguese immigration and alternative centers to serve the growing Hispanic community. Ironically, this rebirth is, at least in part, due to the anti-immigrant sentiment that led to the passage

Domingos Paiva, director of the Immigrants Assistance Center, helps Maria and Francisco Marreiros, November 1982.

Joseph D. Thomas photograph

of the Welfare Reform laws in August of 1996. The elderly, the disabled and the working poor, who in the '70s and '80s had relied on the Center to help them access entitlements, began receiving letters telling them their entitlements were in jeopardy. Legal immigrants saw their SSI, Food Stamps, Medicaid and other welfare benefits threatened. Although the law was changed, many immigrants became aware of their precarious status as noncitizens.

Almost overnight, the immigrant community woke up to their need to become American citizens. In hordes, they turned to the Center which has responded with citizenship preparation, including classes, filling out forms, fingerprinting and testing; ESL (English as a Second Language) and basic literacy classes; also assistance with food and utilities for the needy. To assist those facing deportation, the Center recently entered into a partnership with the office of the District Attorney to offer outreach services to inmates of the Dartmouth House of Correction.

The Center has also become active in the health education and prevention fields. In addition to blood pressure screenings, the Center offers health and nutrition services, and provides HIV/AIDS and substance abuse prevention education. Helena Marques estimates that the Center has served over 10,000 persons in the last twelve months. Currently, the Center has an operating budget of about $175,000 and employs eight persons.

But what about the future? With Portuguese immigration at a standstill and with other ethnic and linguistic groups forming their own centers and programs, what will become of the Immigrants Assistance Center?

Some see a role for the Center in providing services to ethnic rather than linguistic minorities and promoting and defending ethnic cultures and interest. Longtime board member Henry Carreiro, would like the Center to become involved in creating a museum of immigration and a genealogical research library.

"The Center's leadership never looked beyond the Taprobana," said Domingos Paiva in an allusion to the Portuguese epic, *The Lusiadas.* In Mr. Paiva's, opinion the Center could become a mainstream social services provider. Others disagree, stating that it was never the intention of the founders to create a parallel social services system. For most of those providing and seeking services at the Immigrants Assistance Center, the present is too urgent to allow speculation about the future. As immigrants they know that the only certainty is uncertainty and they are experts at adapting.

Author Maria da Gloria Mulcahy grew up in Coimbra, Portugal and in 1971, at 17, visited the United States with her family, then settled here in 1973. She graduated from UMass Dartmouth in 1982 and received her master's degree from Brown University, where she is now working on her Ph.D. Maria Da Gloria is employed as a social worker for the Dept. of Mental Health in New Bedford.

Sandra Brown of the Immigrants Assistance Center receives goods for food drive, 1998.

At left, the old Thompson Street School is the home of Immigrants Assistance Center and Casa da Saudade, 1998.

Workers at IAC discuss strategy during their "Cidadão 2000 Citizens" Naturalization drive. Left to right, Mindy Konior, Maria Maré, Julieta Arruda, Virginia Aguiar, and Helena Marques.

Joseph D. Thomas photographs

The Furtado family of Furtado's Chouriço & Linguiça in Fall River began their American Dream in the late 1800s when Caetano and his wife immigrated to the United States. Family portrait, 1900: Back row, Manuel and John; front row, Joseph, Maria E.S. (mom), Edward, Caetano (dad), Tobias ,Vovó, and young Caetano (a.k.a. Sammy). Not pictured are daughters Deolinda and Mary.

AMERICAN DREAMS

Courtesy of Furtado family

Portuguese Sausage Makers

The Stories of Furtado and Gaspar Linguiça Companies

by Tracy A. Furtado

In the days of the ice man, the rag man and the coal man, when most Portuguese immigrants were working in the mills, the Furtados of Fall River, and the Gaspars of New Bedford, took a different direction: With a strong will and strong hands, they went into the business of sausage-making. The Furtados began in the backyard; the Gaspars in the family garage. Today both families operate out of large buildings, and their small family businesses have become thriving industries.

These spicy sausages—chouriço, linguiça, and morsela were made on farms in Portugal, a tradition with a long history (perhaps introduced by the Moors when they invaded the Iberian peninsula, before Portugal was Portugal). When these Portuguese families immigrated to the United States, they brought with them their longing for the spicy sausage along with the recipe and skills to produce it. Though many made it for their own use, a few began making it and selling it to the public. The Furtados and Gaspars are prominent examples.

The Furtados of Fall River

Furtado's Chouriço and Linguiça Manufacturing Company was founded in 1903 when Caetano M. Furtado first started the North End Provision Company, the forerunner of today's operation. The retail outlet and smoke house located at 544 North Underwood Street is currently headed by Caetano's grandson, Joseph Furtado. Caetano's sons, Edward and Tobias, remember the first days of sausage-making.

Tobias, the eldest of the Furtado children, recalls that Caetano and his wife Maria E.S. came to Fall River in the late 1800s. His first job was selling insurance until he began working for the North End Provision Company. At that time Caetano and his wife, using her recipe from home, would make chouriço for the small corner store on the corner of Stewart and North Underwood Street.

Sausage-making was a family event with many steps. Though some families would kill their own pigs, the Furtados bought their pork in barrels shipped from the West. Edward remembers what it was like when he came home from school. "The chouriço was in 300 lb. barrels. I would take the meat and cut it with a knife, take the bones out, put it in 100 lb. tubs, put in mixer, then we would stuff. We would scoop the meat, 50 lbs., then use the crank. There was no refrigeration. The ice man would come around selling ice." While telling the story, his hands are reliving the moment. He's back 70 years, making chouriço for his family.

Tobias also remembers those early days. "After school I would have to work in the shop. I didn't do too

Edward M., John M., and Tobias M., sons of Caetano Furtado, ready to hit the road for delivery, 1940s.

Courtesy of Furtado family

112

CAETANO M. FURTADO

Manufactor de Linguiça e Chouriço

PARTECIPA ao publico que os sèus pro-
ductos são incontestavelmente os melhores
e mais bem saberosos que se encontram á
venda nos estabelecimentos portuguezes
de varias cidades, devendo por isso ser
proferidos.
Emprega na sua manipulação excellente
carne de porco e magnificos adubos.
Todos os pedidos devem ser feitos a

Caetano M. Furtado,

544 Underwood St.
FALL RIVER, MASS.

many play activities. I would clean the utensils and get the fires going. I was young. I had to enjoy it and I'd probably do it all over again. You were told to do something, you did it. Life is altogether different today."

As time passed, the Furtados got the chance to expand. In 1920 Caetano bought the property on North Underwood Street and they began building and remodeling in the back lot. Today there are two smoke houses and two stuffing tables. Edward wags his finger, "We didn't have that stuff years ago. We would smoke the sausage in the back yard. Then we sold them in the corner store."

During World War II, meat was scarce and business slowed. Edward went to war and some of the Furtado sons took other jobs. Edward remembers a time during the war when he introduced chouriço to his southern comrade. "My family would put the chouriço in a can with lard to preserve it and ship it to me. I would have to melt the lard in order to eat it. I tried to share some with my friend from Kentucky. 'No, I don't want it,' he said. So I get my slice of bread and start eating it. The aroma from cooking makes him want it. He gets bread, eats it, and tells them to send more to us." He laughs as he remembers his friend eating the chouriço.

After the war, business went back to normal. Those who left returned and meat was easier to get. In time, technology took over in the form of modern equipment and vacuum-packed bags. Today when you walk into the shop on North Underwood Street, the smell of fresh meat fills the air. The large metal machines fill the room and the process of mixing, stuffing, smoking, and packaging is completed by workers and machines.

Joseph Furtado is now in charge of his family's business. The pride of being a Furtado is important to him. "This business is very special to me. I worked in insurance for many years, but I was very honored to take over the family business." Joseph believes it's not just a business; it's an important part of the tradition of the Portuguese community.

Edward M. Furtado recalls the history of the Furtado family, 1998.

At left, Caetano's first advertisement in one of the early local papers, circa 1900. The ad claims "his products are incontestably the best and most tasty that are found on sale in the Portuguese stores in various cities and for that reason they should be the preferred ones…"

Emily Nunes (mother) and Emily Nunes (daughter), nieces of Caetano M. Furtado, in front of one of the company's first delivery trucks when they were known as the North End Provision Co., 1920s.

113

The Gaspars of Dartmouth

At right, Manuel A. Gaspar, the founder of Gaspars, admires his work before the chouriço is packaged and sold, 1930s.

Manuel A. Gaspar, flanked by his sons Tobias (right) and Charles (left), use early stuffing techniques, 1930s.

After mixing and stuffing, linguiça is hung on racks for smoking, showering, storing or transporting.

Gaspar's Sausage Company, Inc. on Faunce Corner Road in Dartmouth is overwhelming as you walk in. A deli is to the left and further back are the offices. Walk to the right and you can see the process of sausage-making, but you must put on a hair net and white deli coat while touring. The sound of machines turning fills the air. First we see the mixing machines—two men are artfully adding spices as the huge mixer blends them into the meat.

We move on to the stuffing area where the stuffer pushes the meat into the intestine casing while two men spin the casing around the meat. As we walk into the next room, two ten-foot doors are opened to expose the

chouriço being smoked. Through two more doors, we see hundreds of chouriço being showered. Two more doors and you see the cooler, then the packaging area where five employees cut the chouriço and run it through a machine that creates a vacuum-packed package, ready to be brought to the supermarket.

This modern day sausage-making takes place almost every day, but it's definitely the "old days" that still burn in the hearts of Tobias and Fernando Gaspar, the last two sons of Manuel Gaspar. Their love for the business shines brightly in their eyes as they remember when it all began.

The American success story began in 1912 when Manuel G. Gaspar emigrated from Lisbon. Manuel sent for his future wife, Justina Da Silva, soon after he arrived. Justina brought the chouriço and linguiça recipe with her from Portugal. In America, they had five sons. "Because they knew they were going to go into business!" laughs Tobias, 73 years later. Soon after, Manuel became a partner in the Hendricks Linguiça Company of East Providence.

In a small grocery store in Providence, Manuel and Justina began making linguiça-to-order for their customers. Gaspar left Providence in 1927 and relocated to Circuit Street in New Bedford's south end. Recognizing the demand for tastes from the old country, Manuel began his own linguiça company in the family garage. In 1954, he moved to bigger quarters in South Dartmouth.

Fernando and Tobias remember well what life was like in the early days. For the Gaspar boys, it was lots of work. "We had to

Photographs courtesy of Gaspar family

114

José Ventura pours seasoning into mixer, giving the zesty flavor to the chouriço, 1998.

Left, George Holland cuts chouriço before it is placed in vacuum-packed packages, 1998.

Today Bob and Charles Gaspar run the business. Charles believes that keeping the Gaspar tradition going is one of the most important aspects of his job. "I want to uphold what we've done through the years." Bob is proud of the product. He says, "It is a symbol, the traditional sausage carried on for four generations. More than a way of living, it is a legacy, part of our Portuguese heritage."

Tracy A. Furtado of Fall River graduated from UMass Dartmouth with a B.A. in English, writing, and communications in 1997. Tracy works as the Special Projects Director for Spinner Publications. She is not related to the Furtado family of Furtado's Chouriço and Linguiça Company.

go to school, then come home and help out," Fernando remembers, shaking his head. Even though they had lots of work to do, the parents insisted they stay in school. "After school, we helped them out. Many times our friends were out playing, but we knew the work needed to get done. In those days my parents couldn't afford to hire help."

When they were younger, they would do things like cut the garlic, hang the product, or chop wood for the smoke house. The smoke house consisted of cages placed on rails with fire boxes underneath the rails. "When we got older we could go into the business," said Tobias. Joe and Alfred, the oldest boys, went on the road. Fernando eventually went on the road himself. He remembers how they would bring the chouriço in baskets and put it on the scale to weigh it. He also remembers how the meat came in barrels. "We would hang the linguiça on sticks in the trucks and then they'd weigh it on the scale."

The process looks much different today with all the modern equipment and the vacuum-packed bags. In 1955, the business began to progress when vacuum-packed bags allowed the linguiça to go into the supermarkets. After that "we grew with the supermarkets," said Fernando. This was also the year Manuel died.

When the volume continued to grow, in 1981, they decided to relocate to their present site on 384 Faunce Corner Road in North Dartmouth. The spacious 36,000-square-foot plant is now a second home to Fernando and Tobias who remember their beginnings in a garage, and how their parents chose linguiça-making to working in the mills.

Being careful not to lose pace with the machine, John Xavier and José Martins stuff and twist the meat into an intestinal casing, 1998.

Fernando (left) and Tobias Gaspar at the deli counter. Both men still take part in daily activities, 1998.

Joseph D. Thomas photographs

75 CENTS IN MY POCKET

INTERVIEW WITH ALFREDO ALVES

BY RICK PAVAO

Alfredo Alves arrived in America as a teen-ager with 75 cents in his pocket. Hardworking, thrifty and intuitive about where to put his money, this onetime factory worker now owns a million-dollar business. In 1989, he was named Fall River's Small Business Man of the Year. He is also a Fall River City Councilor.

. . . .

Every person who goes through immigration goes through a revolution. To immigrate is to be a revolutionary. You change your perspective on life. You meet all kinds of new challenges you wouldn't encounter if you had stayed in your place of birth.

I arrived in the United States at age 15, by myself, with 75 cents in my pocket. It was very funny, I'll never forget it. On August 27, 1962, I went from São Miguel, where I lived, to Santa Maria and had to wait four days for the Pan American flight. I stayed in a little *pensão* and blew all my money like a good teenager does. You know, I had a wonderful time. It was the first time I was away from home, all on my own. I went to the movies every day, two, three times a day and ate out in restaurants. I thought the money would never end. Then I had to get through the airport hassle and pay for excess luggage. When I arrived in Boston, I had 75 cents.

In the Azores, I was basically a student and always politically active. As you know, Portugal was under dictatorship at that time and war was raging in Africa. My godfather was a very politically active person and one of the leaders of the revolution in 1931. He had a very big impact on my life. I was a member of a group of students who opposed the war and I started getting into trouble with the secret police. My grandmother in the United States sent me some money to come and visit.

I arrived on a Friday, and on Sunday, my grandmother had a little party for me with some relatives. One gave me a dollar, another two dollars and on Monday my aunt forced me to open a bank account in the Fall River Trust Company, which was nearby. I have kept my money there ever since.

Though I came as a visitor, only planning to stay for about three months, I never went back. I met an old gentleman named Freitas who ran a grocery store and he gave me a copy of the Constitution of the United States, published in Portuguese. It was the first time I was faced with a democratic Constitution and that had quite an impact in my mind. This was one of the reasons I decided to stay.

I changed my visitor status to student and went to Durfee High School for three years until I graduated. I did all kinds of odd jobs like cutting grass and throwing the trash out for the ladies down the street. I also helped my uncle and worked in Mr. Freitas's little grocery store.

I've always been very financially conscious, you know. After I graduated, I worked at the Aluminum Processing Company on Marteen Street, just before they moved into the Industrial Park. I was married for a couple of years and it didn't work out.

Then my grandfather left me $4,000 but I could only collect it after I was 21. I had accumulated some money of my own so when I was 21, I bought a house for $15,000. It was a two-family house on a very nice piece of land. Then the value of the property grew so I sold the house and bought another. I continued to work in factories. I was the shop steward for my union and getting involved in the politics of the union.

On weekends, I started a little business on the side doing tours. I ran bus tours to New York, Washington, Toronto and Montreal. I called them the Alves Tours. I didn't have a license. I made up a little flyer and got the people I knew in the factories to go on the tours. I was their tour guide. I made some money and it was nice. I applied for a license at the Interstate Commerce Commission and was denied three times. The fourth time I got it, then I never used it.

My father came to the United States seven years after me and opened a coffee shop in Fall River. I had started working with him. My mother was on a visa waiting to come here but it took a few years. My father got involved in the coffee shop because he used to go to this place called Cinderella Coffee Shop, which still exists on Columbia Street. And he was hard of hearing. He had a hearing aid. As a result, he used to scream and yell when he talked and everybody would tell him to shut up. He always said that someday he was going to build a place where he could yell and scream so he got together with this other friend, Eddie Botelho. They put together $160 and decided to open a little coffee shop.

They opened it in a little store that had closed. The place was such a mess, the guy gave my father four months of free rent if he would fix the store up. It needed new paneling, new floors, everything. My father had a lot of friends and they all donated panels of sheet rock so the walls were different colors. The chairs and tables were donated. He wanted to have a small place where people could talk, drink coffee and read the newspaper from the old country. It was basically a men's club, men who were working construction. They would come in and drink expresso coffee. My father was the first one to bring expresso coffee to Fall River.

The coffee shop became extremely successful but then my father died of a heart attack. His partner didn't want the business though he wanted it to continue. So I bought him out for $3000. I continued to work in the factory, then the coffee shop. My father had an old guy who was helping him out. So between us, we each worked a few hours and the business was growing very fast. Then I applied for a liquor license and, to my surprise, I got it very easy and I could do more business. My sister became my partner and we decided to buy the building and run a restaurant. In those days, property was very low in this area. Downtown Fall River was full of boarded-up buildings so we bought it for $66,000.

We decided to go slowly building the restaurant so we built half of what you see today and without going to the bank. Then we opened the second phase, then the third phase and now we have a restaurant that seats about 350 people. It also has a function room for 150 people. We fixed the building upstairs and created 17 office spaces and we have another grocery store next door and a beauty parlor. So with the value of the business and restaurant today, we have over a million-dollar operation. Plus it's a lot of hard work.

I've also been very active in community affairs. I was one of the founding members of the Portuguese-American Business Association and past president for the last two years. I am a member of the Mayor's Focus Group for Economic Development and a member of the Chamber of Commerce. I was one of the cofounders of the Downtown Business Association. In 1989, they named me the Small Business Man of the year.

I love America. I've left the Azores but the island never leaves me. I joined the Azorean Independence Movement and became a very strong supporter. Because the economy of the Azores is strictly controlled by the mainland and because Portugal joined the Common Market, it's a mess. The Azores needs to become totally self-supporting. That's what I think. What else do you want to know?

Alfredo Alves' T.A. Restaurant on South Main Street in Fall River, 1998.

Joseph D. Thomas photograph

THE SMELL OF INK

INTERVIEW WITH RAYMOND CANTO E CASTRO

BY BETH NEGUS

In 1947, Raymond Canto e Castro, 14, arrived in America from Pico, the Azores. On the islands, his mother was a linguist and teacher; his father a journalist and poet. In America, however, his father could barely cope as he didn't speak English. As Raymond grew up, he saw the need to bridge the cultural and linguistic gap felt by many immigrants. He became the publisher and editor of O Jornal.

. . . .

Starting Over

Mine was a typical immigrant family—one member comes and then sends for the others. My mother came first, in 1945, at the end of the Second World War. She had been a teacher and writer in Portugal and was able to get a job teaching French and Spanish at Mills College near San Francisco. She was by herself, making contacts and enjoying life until the rest of the group came over. When she sent for my father, my oldest brother and me, her life changed.

She quickly became pregnant with my younger sister and had to give up her job. At her age, I think it was somewhat of a traumatic experience. Nonetheless, my sister was a beautiful child. And then my younger sisters came from the islands two years later.

We came for economic and educational reasons. At this time, high school in Portugal was not free. It was an expensive proposition for a large family of four children. The first three would be going to high school at the same time.

My father had started a newspaper on one of the islands and it failed miserably. He lost a lot of money. He was just not a businessman. It's very difficult to make ends meet there, never mind pay large bills. But as a kid, I was interested in the newspaper. I knew the print shop where the paper was put together. Each letter was an individual entity in lead and these guys were working very hard and fast with their hands, putting letter upon letter, very small letters together to make words and sentences.

Even then I'd go home and put together my own little newspapers with silly names like *Echo* or *Zambumba*, you know, silly things children do. I would write all sorts of news about my family, what my sisters and brother had done, visits of relatives. I suppose it was the family newspaper. And there's the smell of ink. I've heard since then that the smell of ink gets into your blood or something. I do remember being fascinated and loving every minute of my father's newspaper. I don't know why, because of the machines working or the people working—I just loved it.

Getting in the Door

In America, I joined the Air Force, and that was my career for a long time. But I was always looking for part-time jobs in print shops. I wanted to know how they worked. Eventually in Apple Valley, California, I found a small weekly paper but they had no work. Then some guy who did the worst of all the jobs got sick. He swept the floor and melted the lead to be recast to make other things—pigs I think they were called—for the linotype machine. That's the worst job you can have.

I took the job because I wanted to learn the trade. When you want to learn, you do things normal people wouldn't do. And it was really terrible. In this small room, very hot, you had to melt the lead and turn so as to clean it. From there, I went on to learn other things. I was sharp.

Fall River Dreams

There were a couple of Portuguese language newspapers in New Jersey and one of them, *The Portuguese Times*, was read in New Bedford. It didn't penetrate Fall River which had a very large Portuguese community. At that time, such newspapers were very much tuned to Portugal and what was happening there. They ran canned copy from Portugal that came through the consulates. That was never my idea of what a newspaper should be.

I felt that, well, I've gone through the experience of my father coming to this country, a grown man with children in school. In Portugal, he was an educated man but here, he didn't know what the heck was going on around him. He didn't know where to shop, what was going on in school, nothing about social life or about artists or art—all because he didn't know English. For a grown man to be in a place and not know what was going on must be really frightening, especially if he is responsible for his family.

This is why I wanted to be involved in a newspaper that could bridge the two communities, communicate to the immigrant community in its own language what was happening around them in the schools, city hall, the department of public works, where the trash was supposed to be collected, or if there's a storm coming, things like that.

The Birth of *O Jornal*

Today (1980s) I publish *O Jornal*, distributed free throughout the area, with a large circulation. None of the other Portuguese-language newspapers come close! I'm more in competition with *The Herald-News* and *The Standard-Times* but we're reaching a market they don't reach. We're in a lot of factories, almost every supermarket and in the small neighborhood stores.

The Portuguese community is interested in the same news others are interested in. If there's something important going on the world, they're concerned about that. So we provide the national and international news. In the Azores, most of the poetry is published in newspapers. They're very big on that. At times, I have problems with people who want me to publish more poetry than news. My father and mother published some poems in *O Jornal*.

The people are also interested in what their social clubs are doing—the Azorean Cultural Society or the Portuguese-American Cultural Society. There's an interesting group here—the Furnas Alérn Fronteiras (Furnas Beyond Borders). Furnas is a village in the Azores and immigrants have formed a social/cultural club. If a Portuguese artist is coming to perform, we'll cover it. I've seen American television reports on soccer results in Britain and Ireland but not on the scores from Portugal. That's fine with me 'cause we'll have them.

Censorship and the Electricity of Love

In Portugal, my father wrote articles on political analysis. There was censorship then. So many things he wrote would come back crossed out. Generally, he wrote social criticism or just regular news, but I think he preferred writing poetry. That was his big thing. In America and everywhere, there is a degree of self-imposed censorship for economic or political reasons. In the military, there is censorship. The government puts out press releases of what they want you to know. You have to dig to find the rest of the story.

People comment at times that certain things shouldn't be published, maybe because they are a little too risque. We listen, but if we feel it's important to publish certain things, we always will. We published an article by a doctor who wrote "The Electricity of Love," a series of articles in which he explained the physical process

In 1984, O Jornal *editors and owners Kathy and Ray Castro inspect film.*

of love. He was rather descriptive, but it was useful and those articles were very good. I did get calls and one I'll never forget. Some lady was telling me the Portuguese don't need to be taught anything about sex—they already know plenty.

We are a very religious community and sometimes we publish articles that are outside of the traditional religious beliefs and, yes, people do get upset. It's good to have an open mind and hear different views. If you really believe in something, it helps you solidify those beliefs.

Reflections

Some people get upset when people come to this country—work, save money, then go back to Portugal. The number of immigrants who do that is very, very small. The majority come over and the country sort of takes over. They have children here, their children marry here and then they have grandchildren. The grandchildren are going to school here. They're really staying and becoming part of the whole fabric.

Many times the reason they do return is economic. You can work all your life here and towards the end collect Social Security, but it is really not enough to live on in this country. So they find somewhere else and, of course, the natural thing is to go to a country where you know the customs and language and can make ends meet.

My family is close but I'd rather think in terms of preparing children to go into the world and make a mark themselves. Parents' jobs are to be there but not beholden. I see families that are very close. They can't do without each other. That's nice but not realistic. What I'd like to see is my children do better than I did and their children do better than they did.

THE SENATOR

INTERVIEW WITH MARY FONSECA

BY YVONNE LEVESQUE

"There are only two bachelors and three women in the Massachusetts Senate. That means out of 40 senators, 35 of you are going to have to make a determination as to whether or not your wives became less competent the day they married you. When a male teacher gets married, his pay is not lowered, nor are his annual leave and pension rights taken from him. Yet, there is a double standard where women are concerned on this issue. Why? What makes us so different?"

— Senator Mary Fonseca, Maiden Speech, Oct. 19, 1955

Mary Leite Fonseca grew up in a large family in Fall River in the darkest days of the Depression. She began her career as a volunteer in the Public Welfare office and worked her way up to the State Senate, where she became the first woman to be promoted to a leadership position. Even the Senate President admitted at a celebration dinner in her honor, "Mary Fonseca knows the rules better than anyone else in the Senate." Mary tells her story simply and from the heart.

· · · · · · · · · · · · · · · · · ·

I was the second eldest of 12 children, and the oldest girl in our family. Born in 1915, I came of age during the Great Depression when work was scarce and you had to give up dreams. We lived in a very old-fashioned house. When you walked in the door, you had to speak "the language." In that way, you would retain the Portuguese language and culture. My parents, José Leite and Mary Botelho Leite, emigrated from São Miguel, my mother when she was a year old, my father at 16.

We slept three in a bed. There was no running hot water, no steam heat. Usually a big wood-burning Franklin stove that heated the house and also doubled as a cooking stove. We didn't have a modern bathtub, only a folding canvas tub that came from the Sears Roebuck catalogue. If you wanted hot water for the bath, you had to heat it yourself. We dressed behind that stove to keep warm, in shifts, because there were so many of us, the girls first, then the boys.

My father opened a small grocery store, that later became a variety store, located on the corner of Webster and Alden Street. The two eldest children helped by carrying orders out for him before school. There were many immigrant families who would charge their groceries, but this never dampened his community spirit. If someone came into his store asking for help to raise funds for a

Sen. Mary Fonseca, 1960s.

community program, he would always say—"My daughter will do it." So I would go door-to-door soliciting funds. It was like today's fund-raising experience.

As a child, I went to the Samuel Watson School, on Eastern Avenue. Later I was enrolled in the office practice program at B.M.C. Durfee High because my father was not going to be able to afford college. This program trained young girls for secretarial work. The school could not afford to buy books for all the students so material had to be mimeographed. Every day after school, I would stay with Miss Hilda Smolensky and run off copies for economics, physics and other courses. Even the paper we used was scarce so we used margins, backsides, everything. As bad as things were, I prayed the Depression would continue for one more year so I would not be forced to go to work. You see, I had to finish my high school because I wanted to be a lawyer.

After graduation in 1932, however, I put my ambition aside because I had to help support my family, which consisted of six boys and six girls. I was the second oldest. I looked for jobs in the sewing factories but the few left were for skilled power machine operators and I had no experience. Then one day I received a phone call from the City Manager, Alexander C. Murray who asked me to stop by his office. He had received the names of the three highest-ranking students from the Durfee office practice program and wanted us to volunteer for the public welfare office as interpreters. The city of Fall River was experiencing financial difficulties and was headed by a three-man finance board who was appointed by the governor.

I took the job for the experience and worked from 9 to 5 everyday, interpreting for the Portuguese and typing and filing. Every day I went all the way up Pleasant Street, in and out of all the factories, from downtown to Plymouth Avenue trying to get a paying job. The other girls quit in the public welfare office after the first month because they needed paid work because their families couldn't afford to live without their income.

At the public welfare office, the needy heads of large households would come and wait in long lines to see if they were eligible for assistance. If you owned a home, you were never eligible. If you owned a car, you would have to take the registration plates into the welfare office and you couldn't get them back until you went off assistance. The eligible ones would get their rent and a food ticket. I volunteered for 11 months, then Alice Amesworth, the secretary, introduced me to Grace Hartley Howe, who was in charge of federal WPA programs in Fall River.

She asked me what I could do and I said "typing and filing—or anything." "Can you sew?" she asked. Since I had been making my own clothes since I was 15, I began sewing clothes for the young children in a nursery in the Baptist Temple on So. Main Street. Then the city assigned some workers to type and recatalogue books in the public library, which I did for almost a year. I loved to read books and was very proud to be part of a federal program.

From there, I was assigned to the Homeowners Loan Corporation, a Civil Defense agency. I had been keeping company with John C. Fonseca Jr. for a while and he became my husband in '38. For the next seven years, I worked in a Portuguese bank, the Luso Corporation. Our son John was born in 1940, our daughter in 1941. I worked for a lady attorney, Anna Flynn McManus, for 13 months, then had to quit when my son became ill with pneumonia. When he recovered, I went back to that job for the next six years.

Moving into Politics

One of my first political involvements was the Portuguese-American Civic League, a statewide fund-raising organization formed to help promote the cultural, social and educational advancement of the Portuguese-American community. My mother Mary Botelho Leite was a woman ahead of her time. She wanted to go to the meetings but my father José Leite wouldn't let her go out alone at night. She asked me to go with her and my father let her go. I was 16. I became involved in any civic or community drive they held.

Shortly after I was married in 1938, I organized a Junior Council of the P.A.C.L. for boys and girls under 16. Milton Silva who later became a judge, was the first president. The boy who grew up to become Cardinal Medeiros was the treasurer. My husband helped organize the Swansea and Dartmouth chapters. Eventually, there were 28 such organizations statewide.

I was first asked to run for school committee in an unexpected way. My husband and I went downtown to see a movie and I was stopped by a group of men from the Fall River Taxpayers Association. Mr. Gagnon, an officer, said, "Mrs. Fonseca, you're just the one I want to see! We want you to run for School Committee." I turned to my husband and said—"Why don't you ask him?" Mr. Gagnon said, "No, it's got to be a woman. My wife is on the committee and she needs another woman to second her motions. Besides, everyone knows you. You're active." At that point, I shrugged it off but my husband encouraged me to run and so did many of my friends.

We had the first campaign meeting in one of the Franco-American halls in the Flint. There were quite a few people running for School Committee so I was surprised to find the place jammed. More than half the people there were elderly Portuguese-Americans I'd interpreted for when I worked for the public welfare department. I served on the School Committee for four years, then was overwhelmingly reelected for another term.

During my eight years on the School Committee 1945-53, my main victory was getting legislation passed forbidding the exploitation of married women teachers. You see, in those days, the Massachusetts law stated that when a woman teacher got married, she would lose her pension rights, paid leave and earn only a substitute teacher's pay. Yet, when the men got married, they lost nothing. This was clearly discrimination. In Fall

River, we changed that but in most of the remaining 351 towns, the practice continued.

When I was elected to the State Senate my maiden speech was about married women teachers. Up to this time, no Democratic woman had ever been elected to the State Senate. Now there was Elizabeth Stanton and me, both firsts. There was also one Republican woman, Leslie Kubloch. I knew I had their votes but you need one-fifth of the members in order to get a roll call vote. All we needed were five men! I went to one senator whose wife was a doctor, another senator who was the mayor of Chelsea, another who was an attorney. Altogether, I got five. The moment had come.

I stood up on the Senate floor and said, "Mr. President, you recognize me." Not too many did that, but I learned the rules because the men did not talk too much to me. I had defeated an incumbent and that was not a popular thing to do. I ended up saying, "Mr. President, I ask that when the vote be taken, it be taken by a call of the A's." He said one fifth of the members would have to stand with me. The other two women and five men promptly stood up. "I said thank you. We have the necessary one-fifth members." Many men in that body must have been shocked. I proceeded to give my speech:

There are only two bachelors and three women in the Massachusetts State Senate. That means out of 40 senators, 35 of you are going to have to make a determination before we leave here today as to whether or not your wives become less competent the day they married you. When a male teacher gets married, his pay is not lowered, nor are his annual leave and pension rights taken from him, yet there is a double standard where women are concerned. Why? What makes us so different?

We won! Leslie Kubloch, a Republican, who was the first woman elected to the Senate, had been trying to get that bill through for years, but she couldn't get a roll call vote. We got that through the first year. We also accomplished many other things in education. We lowered the school age to 4½. We improved the junior high system and increased the minimum salary for teachers. I also worked for equal pay for men and women teachers. Sometimes their job classification had a different title than the same job for men but the work was identical.

I served in the Massachusetts Senate for 32 years, the last 12 as the Assistant Majority Floor Leader or Majority Whip. When I was promoted to that position, they had a big banquet for me at the Venus de Milo with 1200 people. The Senate President came down to speak and said, "Your Senator has done an excellent job. She taught me the rules. She knows more about the Senate rules than anybody else."

When I was first elected to the Senate, the Republicans were in control and they appointed the chairmen. I had been there a few years when the Democrats took over and we appointed a Democratic president. I became the chairwoman of the Committee on Education and enjoyed it tremendously.

When I was growing up, you were lucky if you could get through high school so I've always believed in the importance of education.

Among my accomplishments, we were able to get increased funding for the construction of Diman Regional Vocational High School. Originally, Fall River received less than a quarter of the cost. With my urging and the helpful support of Senator William Saltonstall, who served with me, Fall River was granted 65 percent of the cost. Durfee High School was also a beneficiary of the new formula. I worked hard for the creation of Southeastern Massachusetts University and the establishment of the community college system.

I believe my career really began when I worked for the Public Welfare office for 11 months without salary and gained experience. Portuguese immigrants, in times of stress, had gone to the Public Welfare office for aid and, years later, they had not forgotten me. There were 57 precincts in Fall River and every one was covered by somebody handing out my cards. I believe I was the first Portuguese-American woman in the United States to be elected to any legislative seat in the country. I know for certain I was the first woman in Massachusetts history to be appointed to a leadership position. I held the position of Assistant Majority Leader for Kevin Harrington from Salem for 12 years until I was defeated by people who "thought I'd been there too long."

The Senate president then offered me a position as his special assistant, assigned to the Committee on Rules. The offer was based on my knowledge of the rules. You see, the male senators wouldn't talk to the women so I studied the rules hard and learned them myself. That's why I know so much about Senate rules and was able to get so many bills passed.

Looking Back With Gratitude

First, I could not have done all this without my mother. I lived on the tenement floor above her and she took care of my son and daughter when necessary. She would feed my husband supper if I worked late. Most of all, she was a friend and she and I were very close. I always felt I could tell her anything.

Second, no woman can hold public office without her husband's support and approval. The same holds true for a man, but it's harder for a woman because the public thinks you are the head of the household. I always made it very clear to my public that my husband was the head of my household. He was so supportive. He circulated my petitions and helped me write my campaign statements. He had a remarkable ability for speaking because his sentence structure was excellent.

Sometimes he'd say, "I'm not going to let you run anymore. It takes too much time. You wear yourself out. You're worrying too much. You're doing this, you're doing that," but he'd be the first one to pick up my nomination papers and have them filled out again. He loved politics with a passion and was able to enjoy it through me. He worked hard all his life and was a district manager of John Hancock. He wanted us to own our home so he built a house on David Street and we lived there only a year before he had a massive coronary and died 17 years ago. I've missed him greatly.

During my career, I was very aware that I was representing the Portuguese people and was always careful to be a positive reflection on my ethnic group. The general public also accepted me and I got a good vote throughout the city. I'm still asked to speak before various clubs and groups and I always say to them—"This gives me another opportunity to say thank you for allowing me to serve you. Everything I did, I did for the district, no other way."

The Massachusetts House and Senate at a Joint Session to hear Governor Volpe. In a sea of male politicians, Senator Fonseca is at far right, 196 5.

Spinner Collection

FROM MELVILLE TO DOS PASSOS

NOTES ON THE PORTUGUESE PRESENCE IN AMERICAN LITERATURE

BY GEORGE MONTEIRO

The commonplace observation that the Portuguese in America constitute a silent minority should not deflect us from recognizing those instances in which they have achieved visibility and sometimes a voice. One should not set aside the historical importance, for instance, of the 23 Portuguese Sephardic Jews who were settled (against their will, to be sure) in New Amsterdam in the 17th century and whose descendants include the jurist Benjamin Cardozo, or that of Aaron Lopez, whose commercial successes in Newport in the 18th century rivaled those of the more celebrated Brown family of Providence.

My subject here, however, is not the presence of the Portuguese immigrant and his descendants in American history, but rather his presence in American literature. It should be noted, first, that his presence in the literature is greater than is recognized.

The Portuguese appear significantly in the work of Nathaniel Hawthorne and Herman Melville. Hawthorne, whose father was a sea-captain who made voyages to the Azores and whose uncle was lost at sea on his return from Faial, introduces a mysterious Azorean woman in the story "Drowne's Wooden Image" (1844). While Melville, a whaler himself (on the *Acushnet* out of Fairhaven) and an avid reader of the Portuguese epic poet Luis Vaz de Camões, introduces Azoreans into the crew of the *Pequod* in his great whaling novel *Moby-Dick* (1851) and meditates on the Portuguese from Brava in the whaling crews out of Nantucket in "The 'Gees" (1856).

In *Innocents Abroad* (1869) Mark Twain levels his famous charge against those "poor shiftless lazy Azoreans" and later makes considerable sport (and deservedly so) at the expense of the pseudonymous Pedro Carolino in an introduction to a translation of his

The Bark Azor, *sailing for the Faial-Boston Packet Trade, brought news, friends, money and goods from America. During the 1866 Azorean famine, New England residents raised and shipped 10,000 bushels of grain on the* Azor.

Photograph from Old Shipping Days in Boston

unintentionally hilarious *New Guide of the Conversation in Portuguese and English*, originally published in Portugal in 1855. A Portuguese "man-cook" ("Joe's the cook," says Eunice "all Portuguese cooks are Joe") makes a brief appearance in William Dean Howells' novel *April Hopes* (1888). An Azorean family plays a more substantial role, providing the mystery and the solution to that mystery, in Thomas Wentworth Higginson's story "The Haunted Window" (1867); and, as a group (or, more accurately, as part of a small mob) the Portuguese appear as bloodthirsty rabbit hunters in Frank Norris's *The Octopus* (1901).

Frank T. Bullen, an Englishman whose books depicted Americans, cast a villainous Portuguese as his captain in *A Whaleman's Wife* (1902), while Rudyard Kipling, another British writer who lived in New Hampshire for a time, celebrates Manuel, a "Portygee" on the *We're Here* out of Gloucester in the popular novel *Captains Courageous* (1897). Jack London wrote (almost sociologically) about the Portuguese in California, especially well in *The Valley of the Moon* (1913), and so did the Nobel-prize winning John Steinbeck, whose treatment of Big Joe Portagee and the promiscuous Rosa Martin ("that Portagee girl") in *Tortilla Flat* (1935) is less congenial than one might have expected from the author sympathetic to migrant fruit-pickers and Okies duped by dreams of California.

Steinbeck's East Coast contemporary, the once much-honored (but now unjustly) neglected short story writer Wilbur Daniel Steele, wrote appreciatively and insightfully about the Portuguese in stories such as "A Life," "The Thinker," "What Do You Mean—Americans?," "For Where is Your Fortune Now?" and "Footfalls"(1920), which is surely his strongest story about the Portuguese on Cape Cod and one of his best stories over all. Erskine Caldwell, the author of *Tobacco Road*, throws in references to the Portuguese in the story "Country Full of Swedes" (1933). And in Doran Hurley's *The Old Parish* (1938) which focuses on Irish-Americans, one encounters an accolade to the "gentle Portuguese who came to us [in Fall River] from the Azores" and, in particular, to

the saintly Father Silva. A somewhat different view of the Portuguese, as exploited cranberry workers, is presented in Edward Garside's avowedly leftist novel *Cranberry Red* (1938), which, it was said at the time, "portrays New England serfdom in a feudal empire."

On the other hand, Edward McSorley, an Irish-American novelist, offers in *The Young McDermott* (1949) an unparalleled portrait of the Portuguese in the Fox Point section of Providence during the early years of the twentieth century. In *Look to the Mountain* (1942), a historical novel about colonial America, LeGrand Cannon creates a memorable "Portygee" villain in Joe Felipe. In *The Haunted*, the last play in the *Mourning Becomes Electra* trilogy (1931), the Nobel Prize winner Eugene O'Neill, who had lived and worked in Provincetown in the 1910s, includes among the townsmen one Joe Silva, whom he describes: "Silva's Portuguese fishing captain—a fat, boisterous man, with a hoarse bass voice. He has matted gray hair and a big grizzled mustache. He is 60." When most of the Provincetown Players moved away, Mary Heaton Vorse stayed. Some of her magazine pieces in later years centered on the Portuguese.

The Portuguese artisan is sketched favorably by William Carlos Williams in the Fifth Book of his epic poem *Paterson* (1958). John Casey's *Spartina*, which won the National Book Award for 1989, offers us a Captain Teixeira in this novel about a Rhode Island Fisherman named Dick Pierce. In "The Summer People" (1969), a literary ballad, James Merrill offers a striking portrait of Stonington, Connecticut, in which figure Azorean immigrants.

Although the Portuguese in America do not number among them as large a group of prominent writers as do, say, the Irish or the Italians, they do possess a handful of prominent names. Two of them bear the name of John dos Passos, father and son whose antecedents are from the island of Madeira. The son, coeval in contemporary fame and

Maria dos Pés Sujos (Maria with the dirty feet), from Agua de Pau, 1987. A folk-legend in her village, her simple, devout look typifies the stereotype that much of the American literati used in portraying the Portuguese over the last two centuries— that is, as a peasant people tied to archaic Old World religious customs.

Milton Silvia photograph

125

certainly in output to F. Scott Fitzgerald and Ernest Hemingway, is famous for such works of fiction as *Three Soldiers*, the first of American World War I novels, and *U.S.A.*, a magisterial trilogy.

The elder Dos Passos deserves to be rediscovered for *The Anglo-Saxon Century* (1903), a work of politics and history that he

The Standard-Times Library

subtitled—prophetically, he hoped—"The Unification of the English-Speaking People." The younger Dos Passos, who for a long time had difficulty accepting his Portuguese heritage, did toward the end of his life make gestures of reconciliation, following up his *Brazil on the Move* (1963) with *The Portugal Story* (1969), an unabashedly admiring and shamelessly "official" account of Portuguese history. It is not widely known that John Philip Sousa, the American March King known almost exclusively for his music, was the author of three novels. *The Fifth String* (1902), a charming novella about music, was followed by two novels. *Pipetown Sandy* (1905) sugarcoats boyhood memories in a way that is only superficially reminiscent of better books in the same vein by Mark Twain and Thomas Bailey Aldrich, and *The Transit of Venus* (1919) is an ambitious try that resulted in a rather conventional shipboard romance. There are no Portuguese characters in Sousa's fiction. But that is not surprising, since there is barely a mention of his Portuguese heritage in his autobiography *Marching Along* (1941).

More recently Katherine Vaz, a descendant of Azoreans, has published *Saudade* (1994), a novel celebrating Azorean-ness. There is a certain suffusing wonderment in the style that fits right in with the author's sense of discovering not only her people but, almost anthropologically, "a people" who can

serve as the substance for her own brand of magic realism. Alfred Lewis, a Portuguese immigrant from the island of Flores, published at least two stories about American Hispanics that could just as easily have been about Portuguese immigrants and one romanticized autobiographical novel *Home is an Island* (1951).

Among the Portuguese-Americans a handful of poets warrants mention. Art Cuelho, a Westerner by inclination and a Whitmanian "rough" by choice, has in recent years published a good deal of first-person expansive verse documenting his self-discoveries while searching out his Azorean ancestry. He also edits a journal entitled *The Azorean Express*. The daughter of Portuguese parents, Olga Cabral was born in 1909 in the British West Indies. She moved as a child to Winnipeg, Canada, and later to New York City. *Voice/Over: Selected Poems* (1993), offers a sample of the distinguished poetry she has been publishing in book form since the 1950s.

The author of *The Marriage of the Portuguese* (1978), Sam Pereira, is, I believe, a Californian. Among his other publications is *Brittle Water*, a second collection of poems, published in 1987. Frank X. Gaspar, another Californian (though he hails originally from Provincetown), is the author of two collections of poems. *The Holyoke* (1988) won the Morse Poetry Prize and *Mass for the Grace of a Happy Death* (1994) won the Anhinga Prize for Poetry. This poetry is of high order by any contemporary standards. But, it is Gaspar's virtue as a premier Portuguese-American poet that I would extol here. He returns to his memories of Cape Cod repeatedly with a reverence and awe that sacralizes, not the original experiences but the poetry-making that sets them down for posterity.

Thomas Braga, a native of Fall River, also writes Portuguese-American poems that are prayers of praise. The author of poems in Portuguese and French, as well as English, Braga has published widely, including collections entitled *Litotes* (1997), *Borderland* (1994), *Crickers' Feet* (1992), *Coffee In The Woodwinds* (1990), in addition to his quite remarkable first collection, *Portingales* (1981).

My own collections are *The Coffee Exchange* (1982) and *Double Weaver's Knot* (1989).

I consider some of the literature written by Portuguese immigrants in Portuguese to be part of American literature. I shall only mention some highlights. There are excellent stories by José Rodrigues Miguéis, who spent most of the last 45 years of his life in Manhattan. Among the best of those stories are, in English translation, "The Stowaway's Christmas," "The Inauguration," and "Cosme," along with *A Man smiles at Death—With half a Face* (1958), a compelling account of the author's stay in Bellevue Hospital. Of all the work published by Jorge de Sena after he immigrated to the United States from Portugal by way of Brazil, I would call attention to a major work by the highest standards *Over This Shore…Eight Meditations on the Coast of the Pacific* (1977), as it is called in translation.

Portuguese immigrant characters, on the other hand, can be found in the stories, chronicles, and poems of José Brites, especially in collection such as *Imigramantes* (1984) and *Coisas e Loisas das Nossas Terras* (1996). Laura Bulger's *Vai-Vem* (1987) retitled *Paradise on Hold* in the English translation, offers a wealth of perspectives on the Portuguese in Canada. The most striking portrayals of Portuguese immigrants in America, however, are in *Ah! Mónim dum Corisco!* (1978) a suite of thematically related dramatic pieces, and *(Sapa)teia Americana* (1983), a collection of short stories—both by Onésimo T. Almeida.

By way of conclusion, let me return to William Carlos Williams' tribute in the long poem *Paterson* to the Portuguese mason working for hire. His own boss "in the new country" who is building a wall for me, moved by old world knowledge of what is "virtuous." "That stuff they sell you in the stores nowadays, no good, break in your hands. That manufactured stuff, from the factory, break in your hands, no care what they turn out…" Williams offers an outsider's commonplace, if approving, view of the Portuguese in America. For an insider's harder, deeper look into the character of the Portuguese immigrant, I direct you to "Adrian," a story by Onésimo T. Almeida that appears elsewhere in this book.

George Monteiro is a teacher, scholar, poet, and translator. His books include The Presence of Camões *(1996),* Conversations with Elizabeth Bishop *(1996),* Robert Frost & the New England Renaissance *(1988), and a translation of José Rodrigues Miguéis',* A Man Smiles at Death—With Half a Face *(1991). Forthcoming are* The Presence of Pessoa *and* The Blue Badge of Courage; Stephen Crane's Working Imaginary. *He is currently Professor of English and of Portuguese and Brazilian Studies at Brown University.*

Watercolor by well-known Azorean artist, Victor Câmara, 1954.

Courtesy of Miguel Côrte-Real

IN SEARCH OF MY FATHER

INTERVIEW WITH JOSEPH SOUSA

BY MARSHA MCCABE

Joseph Sousa's love affair with Madeira began when his immigrant father told him how big everything was on that small island—big vegetables, big flowers, big mountains. His father, who died at 51, never got the chance to return to the island. "Right then, I promised myself I would visit my father's birthplace," says Joe. "My heart and soul wanted to go there. The island was like a magnet, pulling me toward it."

Joe Sousa didn't just find his father's house, he found his heritage. Today Joe Sousa is the guiding spirit behind the creation of a Madeiran museum in New Bedford, featuring art, photographs, family history, textiles, embroidery and other delights. "My father was a farmer and factory worker in America. But he was also a poet, singer and story teller, traditions he brought with him from Madeira. Why should they be lost?"

. . . .

In Search of My Father's House

I promised myself I would visit my father's birthplace when he died, but it still took a long time to get there. We had six children and I was spending long days; sometimes nights and weekends, working as a commercial artist so it wasn't easy to get away. Finally my wife Dolores and I made the trip on New Year's Day, 1980.

Tears came to our eyes in the plane when we looked down and saw the island. Then, whew, we saw we were going to land on top of the mountain—the runway begins at one edge and ends at the other. Some of the passengers started blessing themselves!

The island is a dream, a regular Shangrila. It's only 35 miles long and 14 miles wide, but it's amazing what the island holds. You're in a different world. You can smell the flowers. People will give

Câmara dos Lobos, Madeira Island, 1960.

you anything. I went to the archives and was able to locate my mother's house in Santa Cruz. But my father's house was more of a problem. I went to his village, Gaula, and asked to see the oldest person there. Several old ladies came out of their houses, curious to know who I was.

I said I'm looking for the family of the Sousas. She says there's a lot of them and she tells me different Sousa stories but none are the right Sousa. Then I take my sunglasses off and walk toward her, and she points her finger. 'You have the face of Virginia Sousa,' she says. Well, that's my father's sister, Virginia! "Where is my father's house?" I asked her. She points and says—"It's the last house on top of the mountain." I know it's going to take a day-and-a-half for us to get there and we don't have the time. I swore I'd come back soon.

In 1983, I returned with three of my children, June, John and Rosemary. Before leaving the U.S., I had corresponded with an old Madeiran in Oakland, California, a man who came from the same village as my father, and I asked him for directions. They read, "Go to the church, go down the path, pass by the Vieira house, pass the banana plantation, go along the *levada* (canal), and so forth."

A taxi took us part way, then we began climbing. At the top of the mountain, we found my father's house. It was all broken down, open windows and door, dirt floor, pieces of a bed. But that didn't matter. I was swept away by the beauty of the place, and I bawled. Then I got mad at my father for ever leaving Madeira. No matter how poor he was, he had it all already!

My Father in America:

My father left his beautiful island at 18. His mother died when he was 12 and his grandfather was left to raise seven children. When they grew up, some of these kids went to Brazil, a sister went to France and my father Joe came to the U.S., where he settled in New Bedford.

Joe saw the woman who would become my mother from a distance and liked her. She (Maria) would go to church with her family and he would go too, just to see her. He would wink at her and he knew she knew. Gradually, he inserted himself into her family, but he could never be alone with her. Even when my father went to get the engagement ring, he had to take one of her sisters. After they married, they settled in Central Falls, Rhode Island, where they both worked in a cotton mill. Madeirans stick together no matter what the locale,

The Sousa family (Joe at left) in Central Falls, RI, 1930.

and there were lots of Madeirans in Central Falls. But my neighborhood was like the U.N. with Syrians, Polish, Irish and Italians as well as Portuguese. My parents spoke to us in English.

During the Depression, nobody had anything and my father made moonshine to survive. We lived in a six-tenement house and he made moonshine in the cellar. He figured he would rather work than collect, right? He sold it in five-gallon cans to clubs, bars and homes. The other families in the tenement house would not complain because he was paying their rent too and providing liquor and beer for celebrations like confirmation. My father was like the banker.

The police loved my father but when the federals came in, that was a different story. My father was always tipped off. It worked like this: A guy would stop traffic manually for the trains coming into town. When this individual saw the feds on the other side of the train, he'd tip off the kids playing baseball near the tracks and they would run home and warn their parents. I was one of those kids.

My father and mother returned to New Bedford in 1940 when I was 16 and my dad bought a farm in Acushnet. He also worked as a longshoreman at Quonset Point. During World War II, we raised pigs and chickens. My father wanted me to continue my education, but I joined the Navy and served three-and-a-half years. The day I got home, my father asked me to leave on my uniform and go with him to Central Falls. He needed to pick up some citizenship papers and thought the uniform would impress people so he'd have no problem getting the papers.

Family portrait of Johnny, mom, dad, David and dog Mondigo (star in window represents Joe), while Joe was in the service during WWII.

Photographs courtesy of Sousa family

When we walked inside the police station, the chief beamed. He said—'Jeez, Joe. Good to see you. You making moonshine in New Bedford?' Nobody even noticed me in my uniform.

My father always talked a lot about Madeira and how big everything was—big flowers, big vegetables, big mountains. He talked about running along the *levadas...* Even today I picture him running. When I saw his house, I realized how far he had to go to school. He had to go *miles* and *miles* every single day and he ran all the way. After school, he worked cutting sugar cane. But incredibly, he was a poet, a singer and a songwriter and I thought he must have had some amazing teachers. He could meet you and make up a song about you, just like that. He was extraordinary.

I would ask myself: How does he do that? Where does this come from? When I visited the island, I knew it came from Madeira, where singing and storytelling is an important part of life. The people brought these traditions with them to America and I don't want them to be lost. That's why I'm working to create a Madeiran museum in New Bedford.

We already have a building on Hope Street near Madeira Field. On my trips to Madeira now, I return with more information on the culture and history of the island. I have lots and lots of family histories. We plan to keep the story of Madeira alive through art, photographs and family histories. The museum will display Madeiran tapestries and embroidery. Trees and plants will be planted around the building, even a grapevine. I'm writing grants now and learning how hard it is to build a museum. But the thought of my mother and father keeps me going. They came here with a rich tradition. Why should these people be forgotten?

Joseph Sousa was honored by the Club Madeirense in a celebration at the Century House in January 1998. His engraved gold plaque reads: Lifetime Achievement Award. Joe Sousa. In keeping alive the heritage, culture, religious beliefs of all Madeirans.

Author Marsha McCabe is senior editor and writer at Spinner Publications and an award winning columnist at The Standard-Times.

"Estrada Monumental, Reid's Hotel, Funchal, Madeira," watercolor by Joseph Sousa.

Courtesy of Joseph Sousa

At left, Joe Sousa painted this portrait from memory of a woman he met in Madeira. He used egg-white and gouche and a brush with only one bristle to achieve the crisp, white detail of the hair and face.

Below, the watercolor "Cruzinhas do Faial, Madeira Island."

Courtesy of Joseph Sousa

Donna Maria Carlota Luiz Pereira de Menezes e Agrela Gonsalves

In creating his Madeiran Museum, Joe Sousa has unearthed thousands of precious cultural gems in the form of photographs, artifacts, folktales and information. Among them is the story of Donna Gonsalves and the Portuguese School. Donna was a well-educated woman from an upper-class home on Madeira. She married a commoner, against her family's wishes, a man who promised her the world. After they had six children, he took off for Rio. She was too proud to ask for help from her family. A friend said, "Why don't you go to America and start a new life?" She did. Maria Gonsalves settled in New Bedford and founded the city's first Portuguese school, Club Sé Patria, on April 27, 1927 and operated through 1980. The first school was located on a rented first floor on Earle and N. Front Streets. The school moved to Nash Road and Madeira Avenue, then to 27 Hope Street, and finally to Belleville Avenue in 1980. The first teacher was Donna Conceicão Santos and the first first graduation class was in 1936 (on Hope Street).

Courtesy of Joseph Sousa

CELEBRATION

Grupo Folclórico do Santíssimo Sacramento, the Madeiran Folkloric Dancers, in their traditional costumes, march down Madeira Avenue in New Bedford en route to Madeira Field and the opening celebrations of the Feast of the Blessed Sacrament, 1995. The dancers are wearing striped saias or skirts and embroidered caps known as carapuchos. Flowers, one of the Island's primary exports, decorate the streets and are featured in floats and carried in baskets. The three day festival will draw more than a half million celebrants.

URBAN COTTAGE GARDENS

PHOTOGRAPHS AND TEXT BY DONNA HUSE AND JIM SEARS

Every region and community develops its own "spirit of the place," its own distinctive character, from the interplay of the people who live there and their surroundings. Here in southeastern Massachusetts, where more than half of the population are of Portuguese heritage, Portuguese gardeners have brought certain neighborhoods to life with the colorful and productive gardens which surround their homes.

Vegetable gardens and fruit trees are restricted to the back yard in typical suburban neighborhoods in the U. S., but in these Portuguese gardens in southeastern Massachusetts they are visible from the street and contribute to the neighborhood's identity as well as family economy. Flowers, fruits and vegetables are mixed together in colorful, productive and biologically diverse landscapes all around the house. This is the style

of cottage gardens throughout the world, and because these are in an urban setting in New Bedford, we refer to them as urban cottage gardens.

These gardens represent a way of life, of engaging with nature and working the land, that is directly continuous with a way of life in the Azores and mainland Portugal. The horticultural skills and tools, the ways of harvesting and planting, the inspiration and hard work, and the plants themselves, are a direct legacy of life in Portugal. The continuities between the material culture of Portugal and that of the Portuguese communities in the U.S. are apparent in the patterns and functions of the gardens, the uses of their bountiful produce, and the techniques used by the gardeners.

The traditional patterns seen in these gardens are similar to those in the cottage gardens of England made

This garden, viewed from the street, belongs to Nelson Correia's family on Princeton Street in New Bedford's North End. Seldom has urban land been brought to a higher pitch of fertility, biological diversity and aesthetic charm than in these Portuguese urban cottage gardens in southeastern Massachusetts. The gardens are designed, tended and harvested by their owners for their pleasure and use.

popular in the 18th and 19th centuries. This similarity between the English cottage garden and the urban Portuguese gardens of New England has been noted by garden historian Eleanor Perenyi (1983). While the two are similar in their mixture of flowers and vegetables, the English garden developed its present form during the 18th and 19th centuries and was romantically contrived by the well-to-do or intellectuals out of an increasingly industrialized society. By contrast the Portuguese garden has its roots in a traditional agrarian culture. The urban cottage gardens of New Bedford have an authenticity reflecting a long tradition of gardeners and farmers working their land and producing their own food.

Whether in English villages (top) or Portuguese neighborhoods (bottom), the cottage garden typically combines an interest in utility and beauty. Hollyhocks and roses grace the English cottage, while white and green foliage of Euphorbia marginata *summer icicles, joins yellow and pink dahlias and cosmos in the Mello's garden.*

In seeking the source of the traditions for these gardens, we visited the Azores and mainland Portugal. In Ponta Delgada, São Miguel, we found the views from the street were mostly of high walls rather than of the vines, vegetables and flowers seen in the New Bedford urban landscape. Closely set buildings were walled almost to the street after the traditional pattern of European towns. The only flowers we saw from the street were those in civic squares and parks, of which there were many. Not until we reached the rural villages of São Miguel, along country roads, did we see gardens resembling those in

Portuguese neighborhoods in New England. The landscape opened up along the road to Feteiras and Candelária where low walls and fences replaced high city walls and provided views of various kinds of densely packed gardens.

The kitchen garden, or *horta*, as it is called in Portugal, is often to the side of the house and filled with herbs and vegetables. The residential flower garden, or *jardim*, with its vivid play of flowers brightening the landscape, is usually in front of the house in the cottage garden tradition, sometimes with vegetation right up to the house. One front yard garden

was planted with a crop of *Nicotiana tabacum,* tobacco, behind a rose-covered wall of local stone; we had seen its counterpart in New Bedford. However, these roadside views of house gardens were too infrequent to be considered as a convincing model for the abundant and ubiquitous Portuguese cottage gardens in the United States.

In this rural São Miguel garden, rambling red roses and a yard of tobacco replace what would be a lawn in a typical suburban yard in the United States.

Caetano Cedro Rebeiro of São Vicente, São Miguel, has an arresting garden planted in front of his small house with robust Agave, Opuntia *cactus,* Aloe, Escheveira *and other succulents.*

137

Herculano Vasconcelos and his daughter in Feteiras. The garden is hidden from view behind the house and low wall, a scene typical of this and other villages on the island of São Miguel.

Further investigation proved that the reason we were not discovering cottage gardens in front of houses is that often the family's main garden of vegetables, fruits and vines were located to the rear of the house and obscured by garden walls or joined houses. Even in villages, the streets are often shaped by the European tradition of houses built close to the streets and without a front yard. Where the pattern of connected row houses

The horta *and the* jardim *near São Vicente, São Miguel.*

A path bordered by bright flowers is characteristic of the cottage garden style.

138

prevails, often the only access to the garden is through the house itself. This back yard garden is called the *quintal* in Portugal, and it may include the *horta* and *jardim* if the kitchen and flower gardens are also in the back. The *quintal* is present in the backyard of almost every rural home in the Azores, and it is this landscape pattern that has strongly influenced the garden style in Portuguese communities in the eastern United States.

Hollyhocks, perhaps more than any other flowers, define the cottage garden style. Part of the jardim, they stand against the stone wall of this house near the village of Candelária.

Along the country road to São Vicente, São Miguel, quintais lie behind the houses. In the distance the fields are surrounded by tall hedges, abrigos, to block the wind.

From his balcony, Manuel da Cunha looks out to the village square where his wife Maria da Glória and a friend (below) were tending the flowers in the civic square.

Maria and her friend enjoy a laugh about her husband being photographed on their balcony.

A privy garden with a variety of exotic begonias.

The densely packed herb garden, including a few flowers, behind the home of Manuel and Maria da Glória da Cunha. Efficient utilization of space for plants is a characteristic of Portuguese gardens, especially in small house lots as the da Cunhas' as well as in urban yards in the eastern United States.

In the village of Feteiras do Sul, the village green was surrounded by houses closely built up to the road. There was little visible evidence of private gardening. Then we spotted two women gardening in the public green, engaged in conversation with an elderly gentleman overlooking their activity from the upper window of a house across the street. This house of Manuel and Maria da Glória da Cunha was physically joined to other houses on either side, and no *jardim, horta* or *quintal* was in evidence.

But they told us that they had a *quintal* behind the house, and we were cordially invited to see this tiny, well-used plot of land. On the left was a pot garden with perhaps 30 types of flowers and herbs; on the right the privy was planted with begonias. The wall itself was planted with herbs. An arbor of *maracujá*, or passion fruit, covered the steps, with ferns and flowers to one side and chickens on the other.

At another terrace level a beautifully planted privy had no fewer than five different kinds of begonias. Roses and lilies were planted in the upper terrace overlooking the very narrow and well cared for *quintal*. As with most others living in village centers on São Miguel, the da Cunhas had a small parcel of land outside of the village on which they grew potatoes, corn and other crops of the *quintal*.

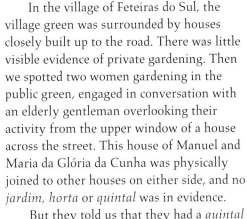

The urban cottage gardens in the northeast United States reflect more than a copy of the *quintais, hortas* or *jardims* of mainland or insular Portugal. In our view, these gardens are an expression of *saudade*. They recreate a memory of a much broader landscape and way of life on mainland Portugal or the Azores. The cottage gardens in the United States celebrate a composite memory, a microcosm of the whole Portuguese landscape of colorful civic parks, village squares with the church at the center, promenades, roadside shrines, favorite plants and the naturalized flowers of the countryside. Each garden in the United States provides a personal, memorable piece of the Azorean landscape for everyday life in New England.

Nasturtiums and morning glories paint the volcanic rock of the walls on São Miguel (far left, top and bottom).

The vegetation of these warm temperate islands is lush and vibrant with color. The common pink rose, roseira portuguesa, is almost a national flower and has naturalized, throughout Portugal. Below, wild flowers fill open spaces and vacant lots throughout the countryside.

Religious shrines similar to those in New Bedford gardens (right) are part of everyday life in the Azores found not as often in private gardens as along country roads. This residential shrine (left) was in a residential garden in Candelária, São Miguel, but was not typical of most private gardens we saw on the islands.

Churches, such as this one found on the road to Lagoa are the organizing centers of town.

142

The religious shrines seen in some New England Portuguese gardens might be interpreted as part of this symbolic recreation of life in Portugal. These religious symbols are typically erected in residential gardens in the United States, but not in Portugal where a shrine is more likely to occur at a crossroads or public square than in a private garden. The churches in Portugal are central features in many towns and villages, the organizing center of town, landscape and way of life. The individual religious shrines in Portuguese gardens in the United States invoke that centrality of religion in the homeland.

Abandoned man-made structures soon become covered with flowers and vines in the warm temperate climate of the Azores.

Delivering milk to the local cooperative, this man passes open fields once planted in a variety of fruits and vegetables and now planted in grains and hay for the growing dairy industry.

Hydrangia *in New Bedford's South End is similar to the hortensia growing along a waterway in Furnas (bottom), or that grows along the roads and forms hedge-rows between fields on the islands.*

Conteira (Canna indica) *is cultivated and naturalized along the rural roadsides of São Miguel and is the same as the vivid flowers in Gil Tavares' garden on Field Street in New Bedford. The urban cottage gardens of southeastern New England represent the whole Azorean countryside.*

Hydrangias along a waterway in Furnas, São Miguel.

The jardim, or flower garden, of the Carreira's home on Princeton Street, New Bedford (left) like the one in front of this home in São Miguel (right) is visible from the street and contributes to the neighborhood identity.

Arbors of grape vines, simply called "vines" are as popular in urban Portuguese communities in New Bedford as they are in mainland Portugal or the islands. They create a shaded room and provide grapes (uvas) for eating and winemaking.

An arbor on the south side of this house in mainland Portugal creates an outdoor room and shades the house.

145

The urban cottage garden, belonging to the Mellos on Gosnold Street (above) and the arched entranceway on Osborne Street (below) in New Bedford, define neighborhood identity more than any other material element in Portuguese neighborhoods in southeastern New England.

The dos Santos Garden and Vineyard

António and Mary Lou dos Santos came to New Bedford almost 35 years ago, from the mainland, where António was a machinist and engineer. The front of their home is planted in flowers typical of the *jardim*, and a tribute to St. Anthony is tucked into the patio garden behind the house. Beyond the house and patio lies the extensive garden of the *quintal*, and it is in the *quintal* that the gardening genius of the Santos' is revealed.

The Santos' relationship to the land developed while working on their property with their fathers here in New Bedford, and Mary Lou's father still comes from the mainland every year to make sure the weeds are kept down. Their garden has won several prizes for its productivity and variety.

Kale is heavily planted here as it is in most Portuguese gardens. Its many cultivars are a staple in certain Portuguese dishes, especially soups. The large heads of crinkled leaves of *couve lombarda* are impressive, and so are the Santos' corn, watermelons, and a variety of cucurbits (squash and pumpkins). *Feijão riscado*, striped bean, is only one of four types of pole beans grown in the garden. Peaches and pears are planted by themselves, or with under-plantings of more *couve Portuguesa Favas*, a broad bean, are accompanied by potatoes, tomatoes and many other vegetables.

The most striking crop in the Santos' landscape is in the *vinha*, or vineyard, with its 500 feet of *vines*. António's and Mary Lou's grapes are muscatel, originally brought from mainland Portugal near where they lived. The rows of productive vines are aligned in a north-south orientation to provide for maximum exposure to the sun. The land slopes downward to drain cold air away from the vines. These structural features of the *vinha*, together with exposing clusters of grapes to direct sun by pruning away some leaves late in summer, contribute to producing the extra sweetness of their muscatel grapes.

António described how he grafts his slips of muscatel vines brought from Portugal onto root stocks of the native New England Concord grape. Digging out a few potatoes intercropped near the base of the vines, he exposed the graft union of these two varieties.

To a Concord rootstock such as this, Antonio showed how he spliced the muscatel scion into the V-shaped cut in the stem of the rootstock, being sure to line up the growing regions of

The Santos display the fruit of their harvest.

Below, Mary Lou's father, José Cruz, helps with weeding when he visits from Portugal.

At bottom, vindima, *early October at the Santos', is when family and friends pick grapes and celebrate the harvest.*

Couve lombarda, *peaches, and sun ripened grapes from the prize winning garden of the Santos.*

the stems. From these grafts, and later, by ground layering new vines, Antonio propagates enough vines to harvest almost a thousand pounds of muscatel grapes, more than enough to make a year's supply of wine for the family and for gifts to friends.

The *vindima*, or grape harvest, takes place in fall at the Santos' *vinha*. This traditional gathering of family and friends on a sunny day in early October brings to mind memories of harvests in the old country. Gertúlio Magalhães notes how "Portuguese" the day feels, how many memories it brings to him of a life he had left behind years ago in Portugal. These memories recall not only the long hours, hot sun and sore backs but also the companionship, the joking, singing and meals together in the fields, and the sensuality of working hand-in-hand with nature.

António demonstrates how he grafted muscatel grapes from Portugal onto Concord grape root stock. Throughout the harvest, the grapes are brought in buckets to the cellar to make the wine. Green and purple muscatel grapes are crushed in a home-made hopper over the built-in, 400 gallon cement primary fermentation tank. After two or three days of open fermentation, the juice is pumped into oak casks for further fermentation. The barrel bung is left out until the bubbling from the fermenting juice stops. Traditional dishes are served to celebrate vindima (middle left).

A Garden of Surprises

Ligia and Basilio Sousa's front yard is similar to others in their suburban neighborhood near the George Farm in North Dartmouth, but once in the backyard you know you are in the garden of an accomplished gardener and horticulturist. Basilio's introduction to working the land began with his father on their small farm in the Azores on São Miguel. He attributes his close relationship to nature and much of what he now knows about gardening to having worked with his father on their family farm.

Extensive alleyways covered with vines and a centrally placed arbor divide his land into a variety of well-defined spaces. Small potted plants form a transparent curtain at the upper edge of the arbor; at its base, kale, young fig trees, a tomato and marigolds are densely tucked in and *agraõ*, or water cress, neatly wraps around the corner. Four types of kale provide food for the kitchen and greens for the rabbits in their warren at the back of the yard. Basilio recalls, "When I was a child my father let me have rabbits, lots of them. I have chickens too. All of these things, these traditions, I brought from the Azores. I like to have the things here that I had there. I like to remember all of that."

Basilio enjoys growing the plants needed to prepare favorite dishes from his childhood:

In the Azores we had lots of inhames *(a kind of yam, pronounced 'in-yams'), so I decided to have a few here. I get the tubers at*

Inhames *provide Basilio with decorative foliage as well as the edible underground tuber.*

A multiple grafted quince tree with several varieties of pears and apples on a single tree.

In a South Dartmouth cottage garden, utility and aesthetic are combined with clematis sharing an arbor with grapes.

the fish market in December, and plant them in old grape boxes with soil. After planting them out here, I sometimes cut off the lower leaves and plant strawberries below for next year. Because of the short growing season, they don't get very large in New England, but I like to eat inhames with fish fixed the Portuguese way, and I enjoy seeing the green leaves in the garden.

Basilio also enjoys exotic fruits such as kiwi and loquat, especially those he knew in the Azores. In addition to these tender fruits, he grows numerous potted and in-ground figs, persimmons and *araçais*, a small type of guava which turns yellow when ripe.

Altogether Basilio has well over 40 kinds of fruits, these growing on less than 20 trees in his modest-sized yard. He does this by grafting several varieties onto a single tree.

On our farm in the Azores we could plant each tree by itself. I want a variety of vegetables and fruits here, but there is not as much land here in Dartmouth, so I double up. Here I have an apple tree, and on its branch to the right is a pear, and in the middle an apple, and there on the left a quince. My father said that every fruit has a seed inside, and as long as the seeds are alike, their plants can be grafted together.

The pear and apple both have five seeds and are thus suitable for grafting on the same root stock, whereas a peach and nectarine have but one seed, the pit, and would require a different root stock bearing similar kinds of fruits and seed. Basilio grafts peaches, Euro-

Basilio reveals a fruit tree seedling tucked behind the broad leaves of kale. Later, he will use the seedling as root stock for grafting multiple varieties of fruits. At left, the fruit of one of Basilio's fig trees is a living reminder of his life on the islands.

Efficient utilization of limited space is evident with this arbor of intertwined vines of blackberry, kiwi and grape. The inhame *(at the end of the arbor), commonly grown as an ornamental and known as the "elephant ear plant," is the focal point of the arbor and will provide an edible tuber in late autumn.*

151

pean and Japanese plums, apricots and nectarines together. A purple-leafed variety of plum contrasts with a green-leafed one on the same tree. Quince trees have ten to fifteen different grafted varieties of pears and apples, as well as quince, all on the same tree. Red and green varieties of apples grow on the same tree. By

multiple grafting, more clearly visible when the tree is without leaf, Basilio is able to extend his harvest and provide compatible pollinating varieties on a single tree. Top-working these fruit trees provides a diversity of fruits grown on few trees in a small garden. Multiple grafting makes efficient use of space.

Multiple cropping is another intensive practice that produces several different kinds of crops in a space normally occupied by one. One type of multiple cropping is interculture where annuals are grown beneath a tree. In Basilio's quintal, *the shade of a young fruit tree provides a cool micro-climate in summer for growing seedlings of kale, and other fall crops which prefer cool weather.*

Similarly, in Feteiras, Herculano Vasconcelos grows kale seedlings in the shade of a boxwood hedge.

At right are ripening fruits with next year's seed

In the Azores, Herculano intercrops potatoes between rows of corn. Interplanting is a high-intensity horticultural technique advocated by modern organic gardeners. While often thought of as novel, to these gardeners it is part of the legacy of traditional Portuguese agriculture.

Harvest Patterns

There are several harvest patterns in Portuguese garden culture. Dried in the Azorean sun, onions are later braided together to form *restias* or *cambos*, a traditional aesthetic and functional pattern for drying, storing or transporting part of the harvest.

Cottage gardeners traditionally collect, save and exchange seed for planting the next year. In adapting to New England conditions, the Portuguese gardener is sometimes forced to use alternate varieties. The *abrigos* surrounding the fields and *quintais* in Portugal provide *incenso*, an evergreen hedge of

Bright filaments of the safleur plant (Cartamus tinctoria) are dried in the sun before sprinkling the orange powder on fish.

Onions braided into restias *for ease of handling.*

Nelson Carreiro grew a tomato from seed from Madeira given to him by a neighbor seven years earlier. The fruits were about five inches long and of a solid, sweet flesh.

The traditional hand garden tool in Portugal is the enxada.

The enxada, *carried over the shoulder from home to field every day. This versatile hoe-like tool serves as hoe, shovel, spade and rake. The* enxada *is still Basilio's chosen tool. Gil Tavares recalls using the* enxada *as a boy, and by the time he was 12, he worked with it in the field for 12-14 hours a day. He, too, prefers the* enxada *over the American shovel or hoe, and he dug these potatoes (middle left) without cutting a one. There are probably as many* enxadas, *or its smaller cousin, the* sash *and* sashu, *in New England as there are Portuguese gardeners.*

153

Pittosporum, which is used for decorating the streets and houses at festival time. *Incenso* is not hardy in New England, so arbor vitae, hemlock or other native evergreens are used instead.

Another interesting plant not commonly found in most New England gardens is *Carthamus tinctoria*, a member of the composite family known in Portuguese as *açafroa*. Its orange flower parts are a saffron substitute in Portuguese cooking with potatoes and fish; its seeds are the source of safflower oil. The stamens and pistils poke through the prickly, but otherwise undistinguished, flower head and are removed for drying and use.

Broad beans hang to dry on a garden wall in São Miguel.

Plants have come to New England with the Portuguese as well as traditional gardening patterns. In this 1984 photograph, Mr. Matos grew Sorgham bicolor, *a tall broom corn, partly for fun and memory's sake, but also out of the tradition of making a few brooms from the dried grain stalk.*

Fresh vegetables for sale at a weekly outdoor market near Ponta Delgada, São Miguel.

Children are busy shelling peas along the roadside on the island of São Miguel.

Mike Araujo stands proudly in front of his crop of tall sugar cane in South Dartmouth, a crop that is prevalent in Madeira. These plants are generally not found in American gardens outside of Portuguese communities but are commonly grown in Portugal.

155

Outdoor Rooms

A traditional Portuguese garden pattern which maintains cultural continuity is seen in outdoor rooms. In New Bedford, these outdoor rooms are a version of a more ancient pattern in Western culture brought to a peak of development by the Romans. Outdoor rooms are one of a dozen pre-industrial garden patterns noted by Christopher Alexander in his book, *A Pattern Language*.

The outdoor room is one of the most often seen features of the Portuguese gardens in New England. Vine covered arbors, partially open to the sky, are sometimes enclosed by foliage walls, trellis or shelves for plants. Sufficiently protected from the summer's sun, people use these outdoor living rooms for cooking, eating, drinking, working, enjoying grandchildren and playing—all in the context of sun, sky, breezes, protective trees, hanging fruits and scented flowers.

With these handsome, productive patterns of garden design, crop propagation and harvest, these medicinal, culinary and ritual traditions of crop use, all within the sociable context of home, family and community, we see again the integration of the Portuguese culture even in its transfer to another country. We have abstracted "the garden" out of the continuous fabric of this culture which was and still is capable of producing what it needs for its people, even as it enriches the earth and the quality of life of the community.

As members of an industrial culture with few ties to our agricultural past, we have much to learn from the integrated gardening traditions of the Portuguese culture. Indus-

156

trial work and settings seldom promote a positive relation to the earth. Unlike these veteran gardeners, many children and adults in industrial societies have little direct knowledge of how their food is produced, or where it comes from, or of the lifestyle which generates it.

By this gentle, inventive, unpretentious cultivation of the smallest pieces of urban land—a strip along the driveway, an arbor over the car, vegetables between the houses— a yard is transformed by cultivation into a place of delight that bonds the owner to nature and culture. The care and imagination for the land touch the heart; the finely-honed skills and remarkable productivity inspire admiration. One feels at home in these neighborhoods. These cottage gardens, microcosm of the organic world set about each home, are a gift from their makers to us all.

The roof of Cataeno Ribeiro's outdoor room is formed of maracujá. The unripened fruits of passion plant are still green in June and its vines are intertwined with grapes. White ducks occupy another room defined by a box hedge. The orderly rooms provide places for his daily life and domestic animals. Basilio Sousa, in his outdoor room, reflects: "As I come out of the door to the yard, I think of the Azores, and I live a happier life."

EARLY NEIGHBORHOOD

JOSEPH D. THOMAS

Today when I visit my old Rivet Street neighborhood, along the sidewalks that I walked up and down so many days, so many years, I remember the little shop where John the Cobbler (Medeiros) fitted shoes, chewed his cigar and spat on the floor; the air soaked in a fog of leather, shoe polish and cheap cigar. I smell the sharp aroma of fresh fish that fills the air on both sides of the street where Cabral and Franco faced each other. Along the sidewalk, I dodge the fruit stands outside of Britto's and Rebello's meat markets. I peek inside the poulterers' live chicken market to see feathers fly with the fall of his axe (his face was always well hidden).

Life stood still on Rivet Street for many years. And as l remember, we were one of only two or three non-Portuguese families in the entire neighborhood. For nine years, through grade school, we walked nine blocks back and forth to the French school everyday, twice a day (we went home for lunch). Along the way, on one side of the street were butchers and cobblers, bakers and druggists, fish markets and grocers, sundries and second hand stores. On the other side, some of the same, but mostly three deckers, a park, a church, a grainery and another school. Just your common New Bedford street.

Intersecting lower Rivet Street is County Street, where you could find fish & chips (on Thursday and Friday only), soda fountains, shoe stores, furniture stores and more. And a few more blocks east, toward the river, was South Water Street—a virtual downtown—with movie theaters, fancy men's and women's clothiers, jewelers, fine furniture, drug stores, bridal shops, grocers, bakers, and more.

The Beginnings: South Water Street

The Rivet Street neighborhood is an outgrowth of a much older Portuguese neighborhood—probably the oldest in the United States—that had its beginnings along the city's 200-year-old main thoroughfare, Water Street, which ran adjacent to the waterfront. At some point, Water Street begat South Water Street, the district south of the central city, where many banks, merchants and

Weekday afternoon, Mt. Carmel Church, 1979

Joseph D. Thomas photograph

money changers plied their trade, and where fine dwellings and commercial buildings were erected, then vacated for bigger buildings, and left for the denizens from foreign shores. South Water Street became the city's Plymouth Rock, where pilgrims from Europe, Asia, Africa and exotic isles brought their baggages of hope, family, and freedom to this gray corner of the New World.

This is where Joseph Pedro set up his dry goods shop in the late 1830s. Pedro, according to newspaper accounts from the turn of the last century, was the first Portuguese immigrant to establish business in New Bedford. Certainly, men and families of Portugal were all around the continent even before the American Revolution, and Portuguese seamen hung their hats in homes in Nantucket, the Vineyard and Provincetown. But Pedro's establishment in the upscale mecca of liberal thought and pious wealth—New Bedford—is significant because it marks the birth of a Portuguese community that would become the largest in North America.

In 1840, Water Street was still an avenue of quaint federal-style houses, mariner flop houses, boarding quarters, churches and commercial buildings. As the whaling industry grew and commerce increased, capitalists looked for land-based ways to invest their wealth. They needed to look no further than Fall River, Lowell and the Blackstone Valley to see the inspiring success of the cotton textile industry. By 1850, Wamsutta Mills was born and calling out for labor. The first to answer were the Irish, followed by farming families imported from Quebec, then immigrants from Italy, Poland, Portugal, Russia, Syria, Greece and elsewhere.

The success of Wamsutta spawned growth to the city's south end and expansion to the north. By the late 1800s, because of terrible working conditions, whaling captains found it impossible to fit-out with American-born sailors, and crews were gathered at the Cape Verde, Azorean and West Indian islands. Most of these men sailed to escape turmoil, poverty and imprisonment, and upon arrival turned to land-based work, usually the cotton mills. As they settled in, and sent home for wives and families to join them, the neighborhoods took shape.

As seafarers gave way to mill workers, growth along South Water Street emerged as rapidly as a Western gold-mining town. Just as wharves expanded to accommodate thousands of bales of cotton, so too did the rambling construction of brick and mortar and the installation of steel mechanics transform a Yankee seaport into a jungle of the Industrial Revolution.

And so they came to New Bedford, first to build her ships and industry, then to sail and render their ballast into liquid gold; and finally to work in her giant temples of sweat and noise and air so thick you could cough it up.

South Water Street was New Bedford's 42nd Street. It's where old women enshrouded in kerchiefs shopped tenaciously for the freshest produce at the fairest price; and mustachioed men bellowed coarsely for anyone to sample their wares. South Water Street soon belonged to the immigrant. It's where stores of every kind abutted stores; where multi-family dwellings sprung from sandy soil; where two- and three-story clapboard buildings were raised from their foundations to add more ground-level stores. It's where children ran half-naked along the sidewalks, where street urchins hung out on stairways and storefronts, and where they chose to play pool or sell papers instead of going to school. But most of all, it was the district that served and housed the working class and the foreign-born, most of whom, from youngster to parent, worked from dawn to dusk in the damp, close air of the cotton mill.

John "the Cobbler," taking a break to talk, 1980. John Medeiros set up his cobbler shop on Rivet Street in 1927. He worked until he passed away at age 82 in 1986. "Fixing shoes is the best thing I can do. I've been doing it since 1917. My uncle taught me how when I came over from Portugal in 1914. I used to get a dollar a week back then. Those were the best years for shoemakers. We had 110 in the city. We had seven in this area. People didn't want to buy shoes from the factory then, they wanted their shoes made for them. Nowadays, nobody wants to start a shoe repair place. I was born in Ponta Delgada. I went back after 55 years and found the same streets. I could name all of them. They're still there, been there 200 years the same."

Joseph D. Thomas photograph

Such was the setting of the Portuguese immigrant between 1880 and 1920. As the city's eastern shore expanded into the harbor, Water Street was no longer on the water. Expanded bulkheads were prepared for an expanding textile industry. Mills were built alongside each other in rapid succession until nearly 15 miles of waterfront along the river and the cove were occupied. With names like Potomska, Quisset, City, Acushnet, Hathaway, Pairpoint, Dartmouth, Butler, Holmes, Booth, Kilburn, Page, Howland, Fiske, Rotch, and Sharp, they dotted the south end waterfront until there was hardly a waterfront left. And behind these factories, in well-designed rows of corporate planning, blocks of three-decker houses stood squarely laid out.

While South Water Street marked the commercial district, parallel streets of resident housing to the west were occupied by a variety of groups: including Portuguese, French-Canadian, Polish, East European

Jewish, Irish and English. Soon, however, the Portuguese would dominate. Cultural organizations, churches and social clubs proliferated with the expediency expected from tight-knit ethnic communities. The first Portuguese Catholic parish in North America, St. John the Baptist, was established in 1871. In the church basement, in 1882, the Monte Pio Society was organized—the oldest Portuguese society in New England. By 1920, several newspapers were being published, including *Diário de Notícias*, the first Portuguese daily newspaper in the country.

The south-central district, from Allen Street to Clark's Cove, from the Acushnet River to Dartmouth Street, would become, by the mid-20th century, a distinctly Portuguese enclave.

Meanwhile, Rivet Street, which bisected this district, continued to grow westward. In 1902 on a parcel of land just three blocks west of County Street, the Portuguesee community

South Water Street in 1907, looking north between Howland (right) and Walnut Streets. This was the city's early immigrant district.

gathered to build a new church that would compare in size and glory to the numerous Catholic churches that were springing up throughout the city. Our Lady of Mt. Carmel Church, facing the small storefronts and multifamily dwellings on Rivet Street, is today (and has been for nearly 100 years) the largest Portuguese parish in the United States.

In the decades to follow, the district has grown and strengthened. The Casa da Saudade, the only Portuguese Public Library in the United States, anchors the community with programs, services and events; parochial schools nurture religious traditions; sports clubs abound, and a commercial district survives, even in hard economic times.

While most urban neighborhoods in most cities have changed completely in ethnic makeup, if not in physical appearance, the south-central neighborhood surrounding Rivet Street and Clark's Cove has maintained its cultural identity. Today, the stores have different names, but one thing is constant— they are nearly all owned and operated by

Luso Americans. Though most of the neighborhood factories have been either razed or refitted for small business, retail and warehousing, the residents still flourish in their traditions. With schools, a community center, hundreds of businesses and thousands of residents, the old neighborhood carries on. Culture spills onto the pavement with a flavor as rich as century-old Porto wine.

The south end district in this 1950's map roughly defines the perimeter of New Bedford's earliest and largest Portuguese neighborhood.

Bottom, people fill Rivet Street on the occasion of the consecration of Mt. Carmel Church, 1913.

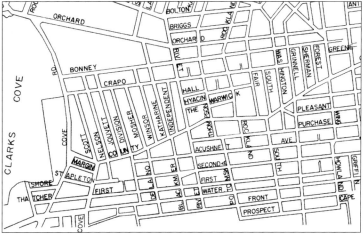

Spinner Collection

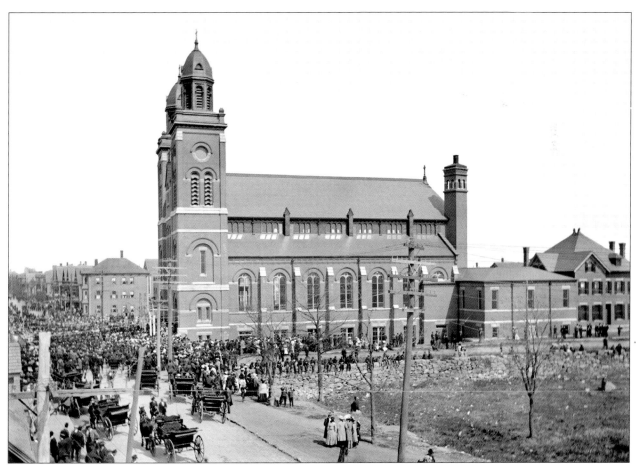

Spinner Collection

by Christina Connelly

Little Faial

"A part of New Bedford at the south end of Water Street is now known as Faial, from the large number of the Portuguese from that and other ports in the Portuguese dominions." So writes Daniel Ricketson in his 1858 *History of New Bedford.* The mention of a Faial in New Bedford at that early date clearly demonstrates the scope of the island's contribution to New Bedford's whale fishery. The principal Azorean port at the time, Horta, Faial, is where New Bedford's whaleships took supplies and enlisted crew.

The "Little Faial" designation was used at least into the 1920s. Even today, people with a connection to the old neighborhood

From New Bedford Illustrated, *1892*

remember it. Mary Silvia Vermette recalls driving in the area just a few years ago and hearing her mother tell her to take "Rua de Faial," the common nickname for South Front Street.

Immigrant Parish

As the Portuguese population swelled in the latter half of the 19th century, the community felt the need for its own church and built St. John the Baptist, the oldest Portuguese church in North America. St. John's foundation was laid in 1874 under the direction of Rev. António M. Freitas. As the new century approached, the promise of mill jobs swelled the numbers of Portuguese citizens. Bishop Matthew Harkins, in agreement with the pastor of the church, Rev. Antonio G.S. Neves, agreed to form a new parish for the Portuguese who lived south of Rockland and Potomska streets.

Ground was broken at the Rivet Street site in April of 1903, and the erection of Our Lady of Mount Carmel was begun. In July, the cornerstone was blessed by the Bishop of the Providence Diocese, of which New Bedford was then a part. In July of 1904, Bishop Stang, of the newly formed Fall River Diocese, blessed the basement of the church, and celebrated Mass for the first time.

Spinner Collection

Spinner Collection

Mount Carmel was literally built on nickels and dimes, and owes its beauty to individual parishioners who were determined that it rival in ornamentation and grandeur the other Catholic churches in the city. The upper church was completed and blessed in October of 1913. Within the next three years, all of Mount Carmel's 18 stained glass windows were installed. In 1918, the sanctuary was decorated; in 1923 the pastor, Monsignor Vieira burned the final mortgage in a grand ceremony.

Monsignor António Pacheco Vieira, a native of São Miguel, Azores was named pastor on December 7, 1907 and remained for 56 years, one of the longest pastorates in American Catholic history. At his death at 98 years, he would be acknowledged as the oldest active priest in the United States.

Throughout the years Mount Carmel has demonstrated a dedication to ethnic values, celebrating feasts and devotions unique to the Portuguese: the Feast of Our Lady of Fatima, the Feast of Our Lady of Miracles, and the Feasts of Santo Christo and Espirito Santo. In 1940, the parish made the decision to build a school dedicated to teaching the Portuguese language and preserving the culture and spiritual values of Portuguese on this side of the Atlantic. In September of 1941, the first classes were admitted, and in June of 1946 the first graduation took place. Our Lady of Mount Carmel Church and Our Lady of Mount Carmel School have been, and remain, vital components of the Portuguese experience in New Bedford.

The First Publisher

The first Portuguese language newspaper in the United States, the *Luso Americano* was founded by Manuel das Neves Xavier. Xavier came to America from Pico aboard a whaler, landed in Provincetown in 1872 and moved to Boston shortly after. In April of 1881, he and Miguel M. Sereque published the newspaper *A Civilisação*. The name of the paper was later changed to *Luso Americano*.

Xavier moved to New Bedford in 1884, and began to publish *O Novo Mundo* in partnership with Garcia Monteiro. Due to problems in the partnership, the paper was discontinued, and in 1895, Xavier started

another newspaper, the *Correio Portuguez*. He also published a magazine in New Bedford called the *Aurora Luzitana* as well as an almanac called the *Almanach Luso Americano*. A talented graphic artist, Xavier created all the artwork on the covers of both the magazine and the almanac.

Diário de Notícias and Guilherme Luiz

Guilherme Machado Gonaçalves Luiz was born in 1877 in Angra do Heroismo, Terceria, Azores. Arriving in Boston in 1891, Luiz followed many of his countrymen to New Bedford to seek his fortune in the city's burgeoning textile industry. In 1909, he established the firm of Guilherme M. Luiz and Co., a travel agency located at 101 Rivet Street. The agency was authorized to remit funds and possessions for Portugal and its possessions, serve as a foreign exchange, issue drafts, sell steamship passage, and serve as a commission merchant for importers and exporters.

In 1917, Luiz purchased *A Alvorada (The Awakening)*, a weekly in 1917 and renamed it *A Alvorada Diária*. In 1919, the paper became the *Diário de Notícias (Daily News)*, the largest and most professional Portuguese newspaper ever published in the United States. Its bustling Rivet Street office turned out the only daily Portuguese newspaper in the country. *Diário de Notícias* was sold to João Rocha in 1943.

Above, Manuel das Neves Xavier, founder of the first Portuguese language newspaper in the United States.

Cover of *Aurora Luzitana, 1900*, a magazine published by Xavier.

Courtesy of Xavier family

Courtesy of Xavier family

Manuel and Laura Machado Gonaçalves Luiz, Sr. and children. Left to right, José, Prazeres (Mrs. António Mello), Manuel, Jr. and Guilherme, 1891.

Courtesy of Luiz family

163

Luiz was also one of the most prominent figures in the Portuguese community during his time, entertaining and welcoming into his home many of his homeland's best and brightest. He was a devoted advocate for the interests of the Portuguese and his businesses were a center of Portuguese activity. Luiz assisted many of his countrymen in immigrating, finding work, and assimilating into their new lives. When he was honored by the Portuguese government for his many contributions to the community, Luiz was called one of the "most prestigious members of the Portuguese Colony of North America."

Monte Pio

Monte Pio, the oldest Portuguese organization in New England, was founded in 1882 "to promote benevolence and charity, to advance morality and social intercourse, to aid the sick and the indigent, and to assist at the

Courtesy of Xavier family

burial of its members." Its name, roughly translated as "holy mountain," is the common name for charitable organizations in Portugal. Typical of fraternal organizations of the day, members of the original Monte Pio Society had to be men of the white race who were of good character and in good health. They were also required to speak Portuguese.

Among its founding members and early officers were prominent Portuguese citizens, including whaling captains Narcizo D. Azevedo, George M. Chase and Joseph T. Edwards. Other names include ship chandler Antonio Leo Silvia, Manuel Enos, Charles A. Serpa, Frank Paul (the proprietor of a grocery store on Howland and Water Streets), Rev. A.G.S. Neves, Joseph B. Smith and John N. Morris.

After meeting for several years in the basement of St. John the Baptist church, the group dedicated its first building, the original Monte Pio Hall in 1890. The three-story structure, located on the corner of Acushnet Avenue and Howland Street housed the organization's offices on the second floor with a grocery and clothing store at ground level. Now located on Orchard Street, Monte Pio has been a center of religious, cultural, and political exchange in New Bedford's Portuguese community and continues to play an active role.

Courtesy of Luiz family

Courtesy of Luiz family

Casa da Saudade

Casa da Saudade, a branch of the New Bedford Free Public Library, is the only Portuguese language library in the United States. Situated on the corner of Crapo and Thompson Streets in the south end, "Casa" opened its doors on April 25, 1971 in a small storefront on Rivet Street to serve those who speak Portuguese as well as those who want to learn about the Portuguese-speaking world. Four years later, the demand for the library's services grew and Casa moved to its present location in the old Thompson Street School.

The library's mission is to provide materials and services to help community residents obtain information and knowledge about cultural, educational, and professional matters. To accomplish this, Casa's collection is geared toward Portuguese language materials and Portuguese-speaking groups. Starting out with close to 3,000 volumes, the collection has grown to 20,000, making it the most extensive Portuguese language collection outside of Portugal. The library subscribes to all the major Portuguese newspapers, affording people a way to ease their longing for their homeland while developing a new understanding of America.

Signage on south County Street.

John K. Robson photograph

About the Authors

Joseph D. Thomas is publisher of Spinner Publications, Inc. He also writes, edits, designs and photographs for Spinner. He attended Providence College and UMass Dartmouth before graduating from The Art Institute of Boston with a degree in photography.

Christina Connelly of New Bedford holds an M.A. in English from Boston College. She is also a writer, editor and sales representative for the South Coast Insider.

Librarian Dineia Sylvia assists school children who are learning about native wildlife. They are getting hands-on experience petting a wolf's skin, 1997.

Dineia Sylvia, active community member and faithful librarian for 20 years, serves patron Donna Huse in 1980. The Casa staff are themselves a vital resource, providing knowledge, advice and service on various levels to patrons.

Joseph D. Thomas photograph

DOWN ON COLUMBIA STREET

BY KEN CHAMPLIN

Birth of a Neighborhood

A brisk wind sweeps up Columbia Street from Mount Hope Bay. Loose sand and pulverized tile are blown across a depression in the street. Below, a telephone pole rises like Christ crucified; other poles and wires are arranged like the masts of ships in port.

Columbia Street runs a quarter mile up and down hill, a stretch of urban thoroughfare replete with bakeries, fish markets and groceries, restaurants, coffee shops, small shops selling women's and children's clothes, a furniture store, a credit union, a funeral home. The street is alive with people and cars.

It was not always so. Over a century and a half ago, a man on the hillcrest stood smoothing out a sheet of onion skin paper. The wind had folded over his survey plans. He'd just traced the lines of the new streets, Washington and Columbia, he had plotted out for Mr. Charlton Shearman Pearl. He shifted the board beneath his papers and wrote, "Simeon Borden, 1828."

In 1850, Andrew Robeson, who owned the hillside, smiled as he slammed shut the door to his vacant granite residence. Big doings. Surveyor Josiah Brown had divided the whole hill into house lots of about 24 square rods each. The lots formed a keyboard encircling his former home, on a block bounded by new streets—lower Columbia, Eagle, Hope and Fountain. A new tune would be played around here soon.

Streets crisscrossed the hill in haste. Union Street intersected Columbia before plunging northward to arrive at Mr. Robeson's Print Works on Pocasset Street. Ferry Street skirted the Fall River Iron Works property. Pearl, Washington and Canal dashed headlong into Anawan Street. One street over was Pocasset, lined with the Quequechan River mills, most of them erected between 1820 and 1850.

South from Columbia, uphill, newborn streets reached like fingers toward open land. Columbia Street straddled the state line until the border dispute with Rhode Island was resolved in 1862. After that, the expansion of Fall River, southward along the hills above Mount Hope Bay, was uninhibited.

In 1870s Fall River, tired ex-whalers from Newport and New Bedford mingled with Azorean families who recently arrived aboard commercial transports. Eventually they

Among Columbia Street's oldest buildings are these two survivors of turn of the century architecture across from Santo Christo Church.

became rooted in the 15-block area bounded by Broadway, Hunter, Columbia and Division Streets. Close by, linguistic cousins, French-speaking Canadians, had already settled in the area of Broadway, Division and Bay Streets.

The American Linen Company, at the foot of Ferry Street, recruited French-Canadians to perform unskilled labor—and to counteract the militant trade unionism of English and Irish textile workers.

Santo Christo dos Milagres

The First Baptist Church erected a community house in the midst of this non-English-speaking population, making a substantial number of converts among Portuguese Catholics. The Catholic Church reacted by sending a priest from the Portuguese community in New Bedford. Reverend António de Matos Freitas, the Azorean-born pastor of St. John the Baptist Church in New Bedford, initiated the first mission to Fall River on March 10, 1874.

Fall River's Portuguese immigrants attended Mass in Irish churches, St. Mary's, St. Louis and St. Joseph's, conducted by New Bedford priests. Masses were also held at Hibernian Hall. In 1889, the diocese acquired the Baptist Community House on the corner of Columbia and Canal Streets and converted it into the first Portuguese Catholic Church in Fall River, Santo Christo.

Around this time, there were about 300 Portuguese in Fall River; six years later over 1700. Some 10,000 Portuguese, mostly Azoreans, were living in the city by 1909. Pastor Cândido d'Ávila Martins called his church "Santo Cristo dos Milagres."

The Feast of Santo Christo

Today, the majestic Santo Christo Church is Columbia Street's centerpiece. Designed in 1924 by Providence architects Murphy and Hindle, its Greek Revival splendor is a focal point during the Feast of Santo Christo, a three-day celebration culminating in a solemn Mass on the last Sunday of June.

Ronald Caplain photograph

Young marching musician during the Feast of Santo Christo on Columbia Street, 1990.

Santo Christo Church, the first Portuguese parish in Fall River, started as a mission in the center of the city on March 10, 1874 by Rev. Antonio de Matos Freitas. He named the mission the "Portuguese Congregation of St. Anthony." The church that stands today was built in 1925.

Joseph D. Thomas photograph

167

For the 40,000 visitors, this is a feast of lights and color as well as food. As the church's yellow brick facade fades with approaching evening, an illuminated brocade emerges from the darkening walls. Hundreds of colored bulbs form patterns similar to those on the front of the cathedral at Ponta Delgada, São Miguel where the feast originated in the 1700s.

The statue of Christ (Ecce Homo) carried through the neighborhood is a replica of one kept at the Convent of Hope in Ponta Delgada. Feastgoers point and cameras click as they take note of the stained-glass windows and tracery, the tiled roof with copper coping and the cast stone pinnacles. The doors and stairs could serve as a setting for medieval pageantry. The smells of Portuguese and American food draw visitors to an adjoining parking lot.

Feast of the Holy Ghost

In previous decades, Holy Ghost feasts had been held locally in various locations. In 1986, the Portuguese community decided to bring all the area churches and Holy Ghost organizations from throughout New England to Fall River. The single feast of the Holy Ghost is now celebrated in the Columbia Street neighborhood during the last weekend in August.

Ronald Caplain photograph

Though it originated elsewhere in Europe, the feast gained popularity in Portugal under the reign of Queen Isabel. During one feast a poor man was crowned at a Mass attended by royalty and nobility. According to tradition, the man dined at the palace and was served by the king and queen. Portuguese navigators later brought the

Ronald Caplain photograph

festival to the Azores, and Azorean immigrants in Fall River have kept the tradition alive.

The *Bodo de Leite*, a small parade of floats (decorated ox carts or *carros de bois*), brass bands and other contingents move down South Main Street, down Columbia Street, along Broadway and up Middle Street to Saint Anne's Church and Kennedy Park. When the procession reaches the site of the feast at the park, the gathering crowds are served milk and Portuguese sweetbread.

From "Colony" to "Cultural District"

The route of the Holy Ghost procession encloses a "Portuguese Cultural District" created by the city in the mid-1980s, bounded by Washington, William and Broadway Streets and a few blocks north of Columbia Street. At the turn of the century, this area was referred to as the "Portuguese Colony," a colony that suffered greatly during the mill strike of 1904.

In July of that year, mill agents posted notices of a 12.5 percent reduction in wages, and union and nonunion workers responded by striking. As the dispute went into January, nonunion and largely unskilled Portuguese workers from the "colony" appealed in desperation to the unions for aid. Faced with dwindling resources, the unions suspended aid to the Portuguese, pending a review of their situation. Angered, residents met union officials with hostility and derision when they appeared on Columbia Street. Finally, Governor William Douglas met with both labor and management. Two days later the strike was "settled." The union accepted the wage reduction but won amnesty for strikers.

Today the neighborhood looks ahead as the former "colony" works to become a full-fledged cultural district. The city's $2.5 million plan for neighborhood revitalization includes the creation of three city squares—Columbia, Santo Christo and Medeiros.

Dedicated in 1987, Medeiros Square occupies the former site of a basketball court in front of the John J. Doran School. Near a set of concrete benches is a monument dedicated to William R. Medeiros, Business Agent for the Laborers Union (AFL). The inscription reads: "A man who devoted the best years of his life to the American Labor Movement. It can be rightly said that as a result of his untiring efforts the working man and his family have lived a happier and healthier life."

Ronald Caplain photograph

*Holy Ghost crowning,
Fall River, 1990.*

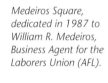

*Medeiros Square,
dedicated in 1987 to
William R. Medeiros,
Business Agent for the
Laborers Union (AFL).*

Joseph D. Thomas photograph

169

A Bustling Commercial District

During the late 19th century, Columbia Street emerged as a small-scale commercial district tangential to South Main Street. By 1895, the Globe Street Railway's new electric cars were running on Columbia Street, on Broadway, near the Ferry Street railroad station and along William Street. The presence of the streetcar line insured Columbia Street's viability as a commercial thoroughfare.

Substantial mansard-roofed tenements with stores beneath were erected along the street. Housing the Sagres Bar & Restaurant at number 179 is an elaborate Italianate structure with colonnaded porches. A 19th-century brick warehouse rises over Irene's Dress Shop. Near the foot of the street, a young woman emerges from a Greek Revival tenement to retrieve her mail.

Street numbers begin at the bottom and climb with the hill toward the center of the city. At number 49 is Chaves' Market, its walls a gleaming weave of gray and black ceramic brick.

Manuel Chaves, Sr. migrated to Fall River from São Miguel, Azores, in 1954 and three years later opened Chaves' Market and

Even Jesus partakes in Columbia Street action. From the corner of Hope Street, He emerges from the side of a local club to welcome the flock.

Well-kept buildings, like Oliveira's Funeral Home and the Sagres Restaurant in the distance (with the mansard roof), date to the early 20th century and are part of the renaissance that has made Columbia Street an important cultural district.

Joseph D. Thomas photographs

170

gift shop near the top of Columbia Street. His customers were the aging residents of the neighborhood who sought out the old-style foods, blood pudding, marinated pork, salted fish and sardines.

In 1966, when Manuel Chaves opened his new market on the site of the old Silver Dollar Cafe, it was a time of change. New immigration from the Azores brought younger people into the neighborhood. Highway construction and urban renewal had eliminated much of the old housing stock north of the upper half of the street. The southern border of the old Portuguese

Duke's Variety Store, 1998. John and Mary Caetano, who emigrated from Lisbon in 1962, bought the Columbia Street bakery and variety store in 1980. The new "Duke" begins his day baking at 2AM and finishes around 6PM. "Columbia Street is very good for business," he says. "People come in to talk—they talk about sports (group at left) and missing Portugal. Since I was five years old I wanted to come to America. Only to live here will I be satisfied in my life."

E. Manuel Chaves (cutting meat) is one of the owners of Chaves Market, a fixture on Columbia Street.

Costa's Fish Market, 1998. Antonio and Dora Costa bought Costa's Fish Market on Columbia Street in 1991 from Manuel Paiva. Even though she does not especially like the fish business, Dora (serving a customer) loves talking to people and making friends. Their day begins at 5AM when Dora prepares the food dishes and Antonio cleans the fish and the showcase. Dora and Antonio emigrated from São Miguel, Azores. Says Dora: "My family came to Fall River to have a better life, an American life."

Joseph D. Thomas photographs

"colony" shifted uphill toward Kennedy Park. The area became inhabited by people from different Azorean islands, now living within the same neighborhood and parish.

Manuel Chaves was the first to pattern his sidewalks with gray and white concrete pavers, an idea incorporated in the city's revitalization plan for Columbia Street. Mr. Chaves died in 1986, the same year the trees and shrubs were planted and new tile sidewalks showed under recently erected street lamps.

The trees along Columbia Street have grown up, upsetting some of the tiles, and automobiles have worn their own patterns over the street. Manuel, Jr. and his brother Octavio, now run the market. The bold Sagres has become less salty and more refined. The Cinderella Coffee Shop has found its glass slipper, having traded in old red vinyl and chrome for more elegant attire. And the wind still sweeps up the street from Mount Hope Bay.

Family portrait of the Trindade family taken in Lisbon, 1934, shows (left to right) Abilio, Joseph, Maria do Ceu (sitting), Maria, Irene, and Natalie (small child).

At right, the Santos monument at the foot of Columbia Street honors George F. Santos (1917-1944) who was killed in Italy during World War II. The monument reads "Erected by Friends and Members of the Portuguese American A.C., 293 Almond Street, Fall River, Mass."

Courtesy of Irene Braga

Joseph D. Thomas photograph

In 1966, Irene Braga purchased a small store at 253 Columbia Street and established "Irene's," the first clothing store in the downtown area that catered to the needs of Portuguese immigrants. Irene's daughter Carol (right) assumed management in 1984 and shares her mother's passion for the business: "I've worked in the store since I was 14."

Joseph D. Thomas photograph

172

Neighborhood Clubs

"I wish people would think of these clubs as more than places where men sit around talking, drinking and playing cards," observed Carlos Medeiros, president of the Associação Cultural Lusitânia. "Our club's purpose is to recreate life here as it was in the old country, through folklore, theater and dance."

Though culture, music and sports are the focus of many of today's clubs, most Portuguese clubs were originally formed to give men a place to socialize. Several clubs remain primarily social and are little more than a room with a bar and a few card tables. The social and sport clubs are still for men only; the band and cultural clubs welcome girls and women.

When a Fall River club closed its doors in June 1997 after a police raid, the press emphasized that the club shared virtually nothing with the city's present-day Portuguese community. The name and date on the weathered sign outside the closed building—Portuguese American Athletic Club, 1901—provides a link, however rusty, to the first wave of Azorean immigrants who settled in Fall River.

Trophies and awards encased at the Fall River Sports Club on Hope Street, 1998.

Joseph D. Thomas photograph

Fall River Sports Club

Further down Hope Street is the home of the Fall River Sports Club. A year after the club's founding in 1955, the club began sponsoring a soccer team. From 1972 to 1984, the club was associated with the Luso-American Soccer Association (LASA) but left after 12 years in a disagreement over alleged professionals playing in the amateur league. After several years without a team, Fall River Sports affiliated with an amateur, all-volunteer league, with a roster of 12 teams. Team

Courtesy of Santo Christo Club

The Santo Christo Club officers and members parade along Columbia Street during the Feast of Santo Christo, 1983. The Santo Christo Club, a social club near the corner of Hunter and Hope, is housed in a small powder-blue cinderblock building. To the left of the doorway, Christ is depicted on a tile panel. Chairs line the terrace and, on a pleasant day, the men drift outside to smoke and chat. Hope Street, which begins at Union and extends to Broadway, plays host to a number of Portuguese clubs.

The Associação Académica, or Académica Club, restored the three-story red brick building, formerly known as the Moose Hall, located on South Main Street. Built in 1890, the original occupants were the Young Men's Protestant and Benevolent Society.

Joseph D. Thomas photographs

The Académica Club team on tour in São Miguel in 1963.

Courtesy of Associação Académica

The Associação Académica team, known for their black uniforms, pose in a city lot, probably near their headquarters at Ferry Street, 1965. Académica has long been one of the top teams in the LASA league and has won several championships. An inscription on the photo indicates that the group features two Columbian professionals, William and Humberto, who played for the club during the off-season. It's not uncommon for LASA teams to enlist the services of professional soccer players.

manager John Pereira, a 34-year-old construction worker, has high praise for the team in good times and bad. He spins off the names of several teams in the league, teams that may or may not have a home club—Fall River United, Fall River Astros, Columbia Tavern, Madeirense. Several of the teams are from Washington Park, a neighborhood in East Providence.

The Fall River Sports Club began in a building at Fountain and Hope Streets. In 1972, it moved to its own home at 233 Hope Street.

Académica Club

When the Associação Académica was founded on Ferry Street in 1962, Fall River's textile industry was uttering its final death rattle. Ferry Street once divided the Fall River Iron Works, brick textile mills from the granite mills of the American Linen Company, two corporations that employed large numbers of immigrant Portuguese. Immigration from the Azores declined with the decline of the industry.

After the American immigration laws were liberalized in the 1960s, a new generation of immigrants arrived and the time was right for a new club. Four Azoreans, Paulo Carneiro, Manuel Nunes, Alfredo Correia and

Courtesy of Associação Académica

António Reis and a Brazilian, António Nunes, established the Acádemica Club within the environs of Santo Christo Church.

Today, the Acádemica Club, a social and sports club, has a membership of about 300. Nelson Paiva, the president, points with pride to its soccer team, whose home field is Britland Park. Many weekends the team travels all over Massachusetts and Rhode Island. As members of the LASA, the team has won its share of championships, including the New England championship in 1965-66.

Enter the club. To the left is a bar. Over the door on the right, a sign in Portuguese reads, "Social Club Members Only." In a back room, groups of older men surrounded by display cases filled with cups and trophies sit at tables playing board games. On the wall are team pictures of the Acádemicas going back at least one generation.

"I've done everything here," remarked Mr. Paiva as he wiped the top of the bar. "I've played soccer, coached, tended bar, mopped floors. This old building needs lots of work." The Acádemica Club purchased its three-story red brick building located at 627 South Main Street (formerly the Moose Hall) in 1966. Built in 1890 at a cost of $12,000, the initials of the original occupants are chiseled in the date stone above the roof-line—Young Men's Protestant and Benevolent Society.

Açoreana Band Club, formed in 1913

The Açoreana and three other Portuguese band clubs from Fall River and communities in Massachusetts, Connecticut and Rhode Island gathered in the auditorium of East Providence High School for the "VII Festival de Bandas de Música Luso-Americanas da Nova Inglaterra" in November 1993. The event was organized by Heitor Sousa.

Musical selections included *Saudação a Sobral do Monte Agraço,* a concert march by T.G. Figueiredo; *Festa por Sousa Morais,* a rhapsody by Sousa Morais; and a concert march entitled *Fall River, Massachusetts* by Manuel Canito.

Other band clubs active in Fall River that year were Banda de Santo António, founded in 1904; Banda Nossa Senhora da Luz (Our Lady of Light Band Club), 1969; and de Bandas Senhora da Conceição Mosteirense, 1984.

Our Lady of Light Band Club

Manuel Canito served as maestro of the Our Lady of Light Band Club since its first public performance in May 1969, when the original 28 members took part in an Espírito Santo parish procession. Several founding members, among them João Pinto Angelo, president; Manuel Costa, secretary; João Costa, treasurer, and António Costa came from a small Azorean village whose main church was called "Our Lady of Light."

Mr. Canito was born in Arrifes, São Miguel, and was a well-known conductor before coming to America. In 1978, under the maestro's direction, the Our Lady of Light band released an album, "The Best Portuguese Brass Band in the U.S.A. Plays the Bicentennial," which included several of Mr. Canito's compositions.

In 1979, the club moved from its first home at 220 County Street to an old building on a lot across from the Barnard Mill. A new facility was built in 1995. A picture of the old and new buildings together hangs on the wall of the recently completed club. The

Another vintage building, the "Broadway Mission" built around 1890 as a mission of the Baptist Society, was noted for its relief and outreach efforts among Fall River's immigrants. In 1916, the Portuguese Azorean Association occupied the building, and for more than 80 years it remained in the hands of Portuguese cultural organizations. The Açoreana Band Club, formed in 1913, acquired the property in 1940. Fifty years later the building again passed into private hands.

Below is the new building of Our Lady of Light Band Club.

Joseph D. Thomas photographs

175

new facility contains a kitchen and banquet hall seating about 450 people with a small, intimate bar. The small parquet floor serves as a stage or a dance floor. The exit to the club grounds is through a foyer furnished with over-stuffed easy chairs. On the grounds is a one-story concrete kitchen pavilion; near the exit to Quarry Street is a portable bandstand used for free concerts at Kennedy Park.

The 50 members of the band range in age from eight to 60 and is mostly boys and girls. "For the past 15 years we've been running a music school for the kids, to teach them to play in the band," said António Carvalho, former president for 19 years, now the treasurer. "Members come from all over, including Rhode Island and New Bedford. In one family the father, three daughters and a son all play in the band."

The band, sporting its blue-gray uniforms, has traveled to the Azores twice, in 1975 and 1985. It plays at all the Holy Ghost Feasts throughout New England as well as at feasts in Toronto and Montreal. In 1991, the band was invited to Washington, D.C., hosted by Representative Barney Frank.

The club hums with activity during the third weekend of July when band members play at the Holy Ghost Feast in the Flint. The crown and scepter of Queen Isabel are on display in the rehearsal room, and nearby a large statue of St. Peter gazes into the viewing room through a glass partition.

"St. Peter is the patron saint of the band. He goes in the procession with us, but his home is in Espírito Santo Church," Mr. Carvalho points out. On Saturday, the *Bodo de Leite* ends at the club grounds with the traditional distribution of milk and sweet bread. On Sunday, the band is featured in the Holy Ghost procession to Espírito Santo Church.

Our Lady of Light Band played for President Clinton during his visit to Fall River in September 1996. Mr. Carvalho proudly shows a framed memento containing a photo, a letter and a program: "To our Lady of Light Band, with thanks for making my wonderful visit to Fall River even better. Obrigado—Bill Clinton."

As the new wave of Portuguese immigrants who arrived during the 1960s and 1970s settled down and raised families, the need for a new type of club emerged, the "cultural association." Two such clubs are active in Fall River.

The Lusitânia Cultural Association, est. 1982

President Carlos Medeiros explains that the club is primarily cultural, devoted to recreating life here as it was in the old country through folklore (*folclore*) theater and dance. Enrollment is by family and membership is now 205. The majority are Azoreans but Brazilians and Luso-Americans also participate. "In America, we are all immigrants," said Mr. Medeiros, "new immigrants and old immigrants." Mr. Medeiros arrived in 1979 and became a citizen in 1988.

Club members inside Our Lady of Light Band Club's headquarters enjoy a round—not on the photographer.

Joseph D. Thomas photograph

The Lusitânia Cultural Association, like most clubs, is an all-volunteer group. "We pay rent so we must ask our members for an annual fee," Mr. Medeiros explains. The club, located at 80 Pearl Street in downtown Fall River, hosts seven parties a year in celebration of Azorean and American holidays, among them a Mardi Gras or carnival, Thanksgiving and Christmas.

The club is also involved in a program with Boston Children's Hospital, whereby disabled children are mainstreamed into the folklore, music and dance activities. "The emphasis is on youth. We try to keep our heritage and to keep our children safe," said Mr. Medeiros. Cultural activities keep youth off the streets and away from drugs and crime.

Some 40 Lusitânia Club members (eight from the Azores) are engaged in "dancing folklore." An ensemble of ten or twelve dancers revive the steps to late 18th, 19th- and early 20th-century Azorean dances. The dancers dress casually for rehearsals. Slacks and T-shirts save their colorful costumes for performances.

Azorean Cultural Society

The Sociedade Cultural Açoreana, 1438 Pleasant Street, is a social and cultural organization with a 300-family membership, or 600 people. While the club has a youth soccer team in the local league, the club puts particular emphasis on folklore activities.

On an evening in July 1997, the folklore group is rehearsing for a performance at the Senhor da Pedra feast, St. Ines Church, Toronto. Dancers, men and women, boys and girls, some as young as ten, are arranged by Norma Santos in double lines of six. In the background, a vocal group sings in Portuguese, accompanied by an acoustic band that includes two accordions. The Portuguese dances resemble English contra dances and many have agricultural themes such as the harvesting of grapes in preparation for feasting.

One dancer calls out the moves from the end of the line, and dance instructor Carlos Melo asks them to focus on the accuracy of the steps. A native of Fajã de Baixo, Mr. Melo learned traditional music and dance while in a *grupo folclórico* there. Checking a roster, Mrs. Santos asks them to take their places in each

Joseph D. Thomas photograph

The Lusitânia Cultural Association is primarily devoted to recreating life here as it was in the old country through folklore, theater and dance. Enrollment is by family membership. Like most clubs, it is an all-volunteer group. Their activities include involvement in a program with Boston Children's Hospital where disabled children are mainstreamed into cultural activities.

new dance—the *Pézinho da Vila*, the *Baile da Povoação*, and the dance, *Raminho de Salsa*.

Mrs. Santos and her brother-in-law Eduardo Santos were the original instructors of the group and started the dancers off with the *Bailo Furado*, one of the most popular traditional dances in the Azores. Mr. Melo performed with the *Grupo Folclórico Lusitâno* before taking on instructor duties here.

The cultural society has had several homes. The fledgling group first met at the Açoreana Band's headquarters on Broadway in 1986, where Mrs. Santos played trumpet. Other times they met in a first-floor apartment on Alden Street in the Flint and at the Portuguese Cultural Center on South Main Street before moving to Pleasant Street.

While Mr. Melo works with the dancers, Mrs. Santos instructs the chorus, a task with which she's familiar, having introduced children and adults to songs such as *Olhos Negros, Primavera, A Lira* and *Serenata ao Luar.*

During a break, Mr. Melo and Mrs. Santos provide details of the acoustic instruments left on the chairs by the departing musicians. One is the 12-string, teardrop-shaped Portuguese guitar or *guitarra*. Another is an older, mid 19th-century instrument called the *viola de terra*, which is made like a violin but played like a guitar.

Both the Associação Cultural Lusitânia and the Sociedade Cultural Açoreana offer more modern pastimes to their members— aerobics, movie nights, plays and pageants. Or, as Mr. Medeiros of the Lusitânia Cultural Association said, "We get together to have a good time, mixing both countries in one."

Change and Tradition in Fox Point

by Miguel Moniz

Even the sky shows the colors of the Azores on this sunny, spring morning in Fox Point, the acid aqua-blues of an Azorean summer. More colors of the Azores catch the eye in a parade winding down Wickenden Street. Children dressed in clean, cool white sparkle as the sun reflects off the silver crowns some carry in their small hands. Others holding brightly colored flags lead the marching beat of a brass band.

The wind plays with the banners—the yellow, white and blue of the Azores; the burgundy velvet and quilted white dove of the Holy Ghost. The colors, the flags, the band, the children and the crowns in this parade are part of a centuries-old Azores tradition, the Festa do Espírito Santo, the Holy Ghost Feast.

As the parade progresses through Fox Point, down the hill toward *Nossa Senhora do Rosário*, the Holy Rosary Church, one imagines the Portuguese community is waiting on this Sunday morning to embrace the

colors at the church's entrance. But there are not many Portuguese watching this parade. From the windows of a coffee shop, the non-Portuguese patrons—students, artists, professionals and assorted others—crane necks away from lattes and mochachinos to gawk in bewilderment at the procession.

The more inquisitive go outside to get a closer look. "How cute," says one girl with a nose ring and streaky blond hair. "I think it's Spanish or something," says a man in a sweatshirt. The coffee shop is located in what was once the heart of the Portuguese community on Fox Point.

The patrons are told that the parade is part of a ritual dating back to the 13th century in Portugal. They are told that the crowns held by the children represent Queen Isabel of Portugal who gave a feast for the poor of the Kingdom, in thanks to the Holy Ghost.

As the procession rounds the corner to the church, some of these spectators return to their drinks while

A view of the East Side and Fox Point looking southeast from the Hospital Trust Bank building in downtown Providence, circa 1924. In the foreground is the Providence River and the commercial district along South Water Street. The Fox Point neighborhood is at the center and right-center in the photograph and faces the Seekonk River in the distance. The cliffs in the far distance are on the East Providence riverfront.

others go home. They do not have far to walk. Most live in what were once the homes of Portuguese families in Fox Point.

This juxtaposition of tradition and change is typical in most urban communities. Neighborhoods never stay the same—shops come and go, characters that control the life of a neighborhood move away or pass away, community traditions important to one generation are rarely as important to the next. Over the past 40 years, Fox Point has been physically transformed by so-called "urban renewal" and by wealthier outsiders who have taken advantage of cheap rents in a "quaint" ethnic neighborhood.

Where exactly is Fox Point? Roughly, the boundaries are Route I-195 and the ocean beyond to the south, Gano Street and the Seekonk River to the east, with Brown University and the more affluent East Side of Providence wrapping around the west and to the north. But the specifics of these rough physical borders are constantly in dispute among longtime residents. Is it Benefit Street or Brook Street to the west; is it Power Street or Arnold to the north? Argue two Fox Pointers.

Residents talk about how big their neighborhood was before the arrival of students and urban professionals, before businesses catering to these newer residents displaced many older Portuguese storefronts. Today the neighborhood has shrunk to a small, five-square-block area around Ives Street, they say.

But Fox Pointers agree that the boundaries of their community have less to do with geography than with a sense of the spirit the Cape Verdeans and Azoreans brought with them when they arrived; the spirit that developed along with the community over the years. As cousins and relatives joined family, as neighbors became like family in the tenements off South Main, the spirit grew. That spirit remains in spite of the changes.

A Legacy of Community

Portuguese from the Azores and the Cape Verde Islands began coming to Fox Point in the mid-to-late 1800s. Most traveled overland from New Bedford to settle in Providence; others arrived on boats and found affordable housing in what was then a largely Irish community. Living and working with family and friends, they settled into a neighborhood that was (and still is) worlds apart from its surrounding environs.

Fox Point was an immigrant neighborhood bordered by the homes of Providence's original blue-blood settlers such as the Browns, the Tillinghasts and the Powers. On College Hill, as Brown University students celebrated commencement ceremonies, down the hill the Portuguese were celebrating feasts. Because of Fox Point's proximity to the India Point docks, many found work as fishermen, sailors and longshoreman. (In 1960, Interstate 195 was built, cutting Fox Point from the waterfront.)

With the packet trade, boats were constantly landing from the Azores and Cape Verde. Fox Pointers crowded the docks seeking news of the old country from the newcomers. Maria do Couto Tavares arrived in November 1928. Though snow covered the ground, the docks were filled with people craning to see relatives and hear news from the Azores. Among them was her husband

A young Cape Verdean girl and her family appear outside their South Main Street apartment on the day of her Holy Communion, circa 1940.

José who had made the trip from São Miguel a year earlier to find work and arrange for her arrival. They stayed with family in Fox Point before moving to their own home.

Fox Pointers have always looked out for one another, helping newcomers find homes and work and giving food and clothing to those facing hard times. When Azorean and Cape Verdean residents worked as migrant labor in the cranberry bogs and strawberry farms of Wareham and Falmouth on Cape Cod, they usually went together, worked together, lived together and then returned to Fox Point together.

A large Portuguese extended family

Roger Amaral, 27, grew up here and now works at the Fox Point Boys Club. His family emigrated to Fox Point from Vila Franca, São Miguel, before he was born, and most of his family still live here. "It was like a little Portugal, everybody stuck together. If a family was struggling, another family would help them out. If somebody got into trouble, people would go and help. Family, neighbors, it was just people sticking together," he says.

Echoing these comments is Lori Silvia, 41, director of the Fox Point Senior Center, where old-time residents come to eat, talk, play bingo and cards, dance and reminisce. Of Azorean descent, Ms. Silvia grew up in Fox Point in a house with her mother, grandmother and uncle. "We used to play a game where we would go down each street and name everyone who lived in every house. We could do it for streets and streets. Everyone grew up together, we shared our lives. It was a family."

An important member of the Fox Point "family" is Johnny Britto, a Cape Verdean man who runs the Fox Point Boys Club. Tall, with a crown of white hair, he can command a room with a simple look. Relaxed but vigilant in his chair at the Boys Club, he sees some children roughhousing; a boy shoves a girl off a chair. In mid-sentence, Johnny Britto looks up and stares. They stop. "It's just a game, Johnny," says one little girl. The boy, encouraged by her words, readies to push again. "Seems like a pretty rough game to me," he says. That ends it.

Then Johnny is laughing with an adolescent boy who wants to coach a soccer game between younger children later that afternoon. The boy is talking up his qualifications as Johnny listens and kids. He does not talk down to the children, and one can see the affection and respect they have for him.

Johnny Britto has made a life of helping Fox Point's less fortunate residents. "When we first came to Fox Point we struggled," says Roger Amaral. "My father and mother working, with five kids, that's a little tough.

Johnny Britto and Roger Amaral run the Fox Point Boys and Girls Club.

Some of the featured artwork adorning the walls of the Fox Point Boys and Girls Club.

Joseph D. Thomas photographs

My dad would drop us off at the Boys Club. Say we had a hole in our sock or sneaker, there goes Johnny to talk to somebody. 'Hey listen, I have this family over here and they are struggling.' Bang. At Christmas he would give us turkeys, food and presents. Johnny is like the Mayor of Fox Point.

"This past Christmas, I went with him," Roger continues, "and we dropped off 15 turkeys. It's just beautiful. A family has a fire in their house, everyone comes together to help them out. If you're doing bad, people here help you get back on your feet."

The plight of a little girl on a waiting list for a kidney brought out the best in Fox Point. She had lost her sight and was about to die. Although she was not from the neighborhood, her father was a regular at the Family Pub, a Fox Point tavern. The community put up posters entreating anyone who might donate a kidney to contact the hospital. One Cape Verdean man visiting Fox Point saw the posters and donated his kidney.

"The bond is not so much ethnic as it is Fox Point itself," says Lori Silvia, who nonetheless recognizes the importance of being Portuguese in gaining acceptance. "Professional people, other outsiders were not so easily accepted, especially when they first started coming in."

Although no place is completely free of racial or ethnic prejudice, Fox Point has been a place where racial distinctions have had minimal impact. Residents will use "Portuguese" to refer to all of the Portuguese-speaking populations in the neighborhood, while using terms like "Azorean," "Madeiran," "Continental" and "Cape Verdean" to make finer classifications referring to point of origin rather than racial identity. Naming the ethnic groups in the neighborhood, one Azorean man listed all of the above including "Cape Verdean" and then added "African-American."

Encroaching on the community

How did this once-sprawling community get squeezed into a fraction of the old neighborhood? Many Fox Point homes were demolished in the construction of I-195. Well-intentioned efforts at urban development by federal, state and municipal governments caused more changes. The homes in Fox Point, some over 200 years old, were researched, and those granted historical landmark status were then revalued for the purpose of assessing taxes. Many could not pay the higher taxes and were forced to sell homes that had been in their families for generations. One Cape Verdean woman commented, "If putting a plaque [demarcating historical landmark status] on my

The Science Library at Brown University, as if it were watching over the community, emerges from the crest of the Fox Point neighborhood. The view is from the East Providence side of the George Washington Bridge on Interstate 195.

Joseph D. Thomas photograph

181

house means I can't afford the taxes, then they can have their plaque back. A piece of wood with a date on it means nothing to me, but I've lived in this house all my life."

Those not forced to sell took advantage of the tremendous profit to be gained. Homes bought for $10,000 were now being sold for $250,000. Others capitalized on the new found attractiveness of the neighborhood and remodeled their homes to accommodate numerous students. A family paying $200 a month for a house could rent to ten students for $1000 a month. (A Providence law,

designed to help Fox Point, now prohibits the cohabitation of more than three unrelated persons in one apartment, but the law came late.) Many who rented to students in this initial period were shunned by their neighbors. Although most say the students are well behaved, others are bothered by loud, late-night parties, activity not usually seen in a working-class Portuguese neighborhood.

Brown University is now making efforts to discourage students from renting in the neighborhood on the grounds that the ethnic composition of the community should be respected. "This is like closing the barn door after the horse has been let out," says Lori Silvia. Here and there lines blur; some longtime residents *are* students. Carla Galvão, whose parents own a Portuguese market on Ives Street, entered Brown in the fall of 1996. Several graduate students, both from the Azores and of Azorean descent, live here. By urging students to stay out of Fox Point, Brown University unintentionally implies that Portuguese members of that community would not be students.

The university contributes to the community in helpful and positive ways: student volunteers serve as tutors in the community center. The school helped build a community garden in an abandoned lot. The Fox Point Day Care Center was given a free year's rent. The university is also the home of one of the world's largest and most important centers of research of Lusophone history, diaspora and literature. Many Portuguese cultural events attended by the wider community are hosted there every year.

A walk down Wickenden Street today

The Portuguese stores, the people, the gossip and the community that once thrived on Wickenden Street are gone now, replaced by Japanese sushi bars, an Indian restaurant, coffee shops and upscale restaurants. Antique shops and art galleries cover the south end of Ives Street, and a cycle shop, boutiques of new and vintage clothing, a video rental store and smoke shops dot the rest of Fox Point. The stores on Wickenden Street, once the heart of this Portuguese and Cape Verdean community, now cater to students and wealthier professionals.

Not so long ago, one could stop at the Portuguese meat market, buy some chouriço and spend the next ten minutes talking to friends and laughing over the latest community gossip. Stop at Lisbon Dry Goods and learn that someone's cousin needs a job, and did anyone know where he might find one? Stop at the Portuguese linen store and discover your son skipped school. He was, of course, caught by one of the many watchful eyes that looked out for others.

The center of the community is now Ives Street. At one end is the Fox Point Elementary School, the Community Center, the library, the Boys Club, the Senior Center, the Health Center. Traveling north one encounters stores such as the Eagle Market, a Portuguese grocery store that sells cheese from São Jorge and videos of *touradas* (bullfights) from Terceira; the Silver Star Bakery, a Portuguese *padaria* featuring *massa sovada* (sweet bread), *pap secos* (rolls), pastry and the best croissants in Providence; also Cardoso Travel, a Portuguese travel agency where one can find the cheapest flights to the Portuguese world. Although an occasional antique store may be found among the Portuguese stores, Ives Street is solidly at the core of contemporary Fox Point.

Other Portuguese stores in the area include a meat market, a general store, and two Portuguese-owned liquor stores, but the changes are evident here as well. At the Central Meat Market, signs announcing Portuguese sausage and food items are written in both Portuguese and Spanish. One of the workers is from the Dominican Republic. The meat market serves a broad clientele, including the large Providence Hispanic population. The ability to communicate in Spanish helps business.

Most residents who sold homes or left to pursue other opportunities moved to the large Portuguese community in East Providence; others moved to outlying cities including Pawtucket, Cranston and Warwick. But leaving the neighborhood does not mean leaving the community—once a Fox Pointer always a Fox Pointer. Fox Point's Portuguese church with its Portuguese Mass, *Nossa Senhora do Rosário*, recently added a large parking lot in order to accommodate the

majority of parishioners, former residents, who live outside Fox Point.

The Boys Club also sees a lot of traffic from outside Fox Point. Fathers who went to the club as children now bring their own children to spend time with Johnny Britto as they once did. The Senior Center also attracts former Fox Pointers who come back to socialize with old friends. Fox Pointers from all over Rhode Island attend social events, and proceeds help the community center and other charities. A highlight of summer is the annual reunion in which members of the Fox Point community, past and present, come back to eat, drink, laugh with old friends and reminisce about the old days.

"I was born here. I haven't always lived here, but my heart has always been in Fox Point," says Yvonne Smart, of Cape Verdean descent, who works as head librarian at the Fox Point branch of the Providence Public Library. Ms. Smart, too, regrets the losses of a changed neighborhood. "Up until this year,

Eduarda Ferreira (right) owns and operates the Silver Star Bakery with her husband Pedro. Suzette Vieira (left) works with them. The Ferreiras came here from São Miguel 25 years ago and now live in Seekonk. "Only about 20 percent of our customers are from the neighborhood, and 20 percent are students. We get along well with the students. Sometimes they send us cards after they've moved away. The rest of our customers are from the shipyard, East Providence, Warwick… Most of the families who lived in Fox Point have moved to East Providence over the years. Only the older generations live here now."

Joseph D. Thomas photographs

Fish monger Antonio Cabral (left) from Pawtucket is selling mackerel he caught this morning with Antonio Vieira. Both Antonios fished off a friend's small 22-foot boat out of Sandwich just outside the canal in Cape Cod Bay. "This is about the last day for mackerel," he said. "After this we'll fish for scup. We sell the fish here and in the shipyard (neighborhood)."

and always keeping a quiet presence. Unfortunately the two have passed away. You just
don't see that anymore."

For most members of the Fox Point
family, it is impossible not to think about the
way things were, but some are more accepting of the changes than others. "There are
many different people in this neighborhood
now—Indians, some Hispanics, even some
Russians, but everyone gets along. It's not
the same as it was. Things do change. There
is nothing you can do about that," says
Roger Amaral.

three elderly immigrant Cape Verdean men
would stand across the street from the school
every morning. They were very proper, they
would tip their hats to me and I loved it
because they would watch the kids in the
school to see that nothing bad happened to
them—watching the kids crossing the street

Echoes of the past are seen in the present
in the brown, wrinkled faces of two black-clad
widows walking arm in arm down Sheldon
Street; in the Christmas turkey Johnny Britto
and Roger Amaral bring to a struggling family;
in the voice of Yvonne Smart as she recom-

Joseph D. Thomas photographs

mends books to a young Azorean girl whose mother is impatiently honking the horn outside the library; in the fact that one can still function here in Portuguese only, whether buying bread, booking a trip or going to Mass. The echo is here in the trumpeting march of the Espírito Santo parade and in the humor of a Sunday afternoon crowd at the Cape Verdean club. Yes, things change, but as long as there are people who hear these echoes and live the spirit that is their community, there will always be a Fox Point.

Miguel Moniz is working on his Ph.D. in anthropology at Brown University. His thesis will examine the issue of repatriated Portuguese living in the Azores. He is widely published and has given presentations on Portuguese feasting and festivals, and on Azorean and Azorean-American identity. His current projects include a forthcoming chapter on wage-earning Portuguese-American women.

"I would like to thank the many people of Fox Point who opened their lives to me, especially Roger Amaral, Johnny Britto, Lori Silvia and Yvonne Smart." – Miguel Moniz

The chic, clean, collegiate look has spread to upper Wickenden Street.

An elderly Ives Street resident takes the time to clean the sidewalk and gutter in front of her house.

Joseph D. Thomas photographs

185

ADRIAN

SHORT STORY BY ONÉSIMO T. ALMEIDA

(TRANSLATION BY NAOMI PARKER)

Do you know Adrian? A pair of swift and penetrating eyes in a restless body, eleven years of pure dynamite, five of which still bear the mark of Terceira in the rare Portuguese he speaks.

I saw him for the first time picking up a huge stack of newspapers next to College Travel, on the corner of Waterman and Thayer. The *Providence Journal* truck had left that Himalaya there minutes before; arriving from school, he pulled pliers from his back pocket and cut the thick cord. The wind spun around the Sciences Library and the thermometer nearby read 28 degrees. He grabbed a sack he had brought, overturned the papers into it, and started off, his trunk bent and his right arm at a forty-five degree angle while the other arm tried titanically to balance the weight. He went along lightening his load, leaving copies in University buildings—Barus and Holley, Linguistics, Applied Math, the Computer Lab.

I followed that small bundle of energy and determination. Near Anthropology I started a conversation which he wasn't much interested in because he had to be on time; his clientele was waiting at home for the afternoon news. But yes, he would show up at the department the next day when school was out at noon.

He came to see me, as promised. He sat in the chair facing me as if we were longtime colleagues.

He always spoke English, but he knew I was Portuguese because he had already heard me speak it on the street. He spun himself out to me, talking about himself and his world.

He's a "businessman" and doesn't want to be anything else. Besides the papers, he has other dealings. He sells flower seeds, for instance. And postcards. He gets the orders in the mail. There's poetry in his speech, the prosaic businessman-like language of the big American world coming from a small Azorean body.

"I want to be a 'businessman.' That's all that interests me because I love money. I love money."

He had left Terceira six years ago and so was already more of an American than Portuguese. He wanted to forget, moreover, the little he did

remember of the islands. That he had smashed his head against a wall, that he had broken a leg…, a hill here, a plateau there, the ugly gray sea, cows…uh! Milking them into a washbowl, the cow stepping in the milk…

"But that stuff isn't worth remembering. I hate the Portuguese. I don't like being Portuguese. I'd like to have been born here. My blood is already totally American. The best deals I make are with stupid Portuguese. I'd rather not know Portuguese. I'm really trying to forget it. But all the 'businessmen' I talk to tell me it's good for business to know Portuguese. It's true, but what a drag! I'm Portuguese. What can I do? But I detest it. I don't like it when they call me Portuguese. And it's not even shame. It's hatred! On that subject no more

Boy tending his cow on São Miguel, 1985.

questions. No more answers. I don't even like to talk about this stupid stuff.

"Ah! Still good thing I'm from Terceira and not St. Michael. I hate the St. Michael people. At my school, almost everyone's from St. Michael. I never heard about St. Michael before I came to America. It's only here that I found out these bastards exist, and Asia, too, and California. But California's great! I'd even like to live there. A house in Beverly Hills, be a Hollywood producer! Well…dreams!

"The only thing I like about the people from St. Michael is hearing them fight. They talk funny. It sounds ugly, but it's kind of cute, and I love to laugh. The words are the same, but they do something with their mouths—I don't know what it is—and those weird sounds come out. I'm not the only one who doesn't like them. My father doesn't either. He doesn't like blacks or anybody from St. Michael.

"But I do business with them. Not just them, of course! Americans too. And with Brown students. A lot of them are my friends. They buy the paper and other things. I already told some of them that if I ever find out that they buy things from me because they feel sorry for me, I'll throw their money in their faces. I sell books. I make a dime a copy. I have two bank accounts. I opened one by myself without anybody knowing. How? It's a secret! The other one I opened with my father. I have 425 dollars and 80 cents in one of them, mine, the secret one, in the Old Stone Bank.

"I gamble for money. I do whatever I have to do to make a buck. I never take money out of the bank. I can take it out whenever I want, but when I do take it out it has to be for something big. One day I'm going to set up a big business. I'm going to sit in my office like a big shot and then you'll really see me doing business, only by telephone and computer. The money's going to roll in. A big house. Swimming pool. A summer house on the Cape and a winter house in Vermont. And blond chicks at my side. Vermont is beautiful, real nature. They have cows up there but they don't shit in the road like in the Azores. They have class.

"TV? I watch 'Charlie's Angels.' Because of Farrah Fawcett's breasts. Gorgeous! I like Elton John, the Beatles, Elvis. He was a drug addict when he died, you know that? He didn't learn the secret: just a little to feel good, but no more. If you do, there goes the business.

"On television, what else? I watch everything. Did you see that show last night where the father raped his daughter? What a son of a bitch. You need to be really hard up. I watch TV as much as I want. My parents don't understand it. They don't know what's going on. They ask me, and either I pretend I don't hear them, or I give them some bullshit answer. That stuff is too much for them. What do they know about the world? They only go to East Providence! My mother? She'd pass out. But they almost never watch TV. All my mother does is clean. She's always cleaning. When she finishes, she starts all over. All my father does is work. After he leaves the factory, he works from six to ten, cleaning, in two banks downtown. On weekends, he cleans in a factory in Warren. If he could live without sleeping, he'd get himself still another job. For the hours I work, I almost put more money in the bank than he does. It's business that pays off. He works like a slave. A Portugee's job. Sundays he doesn't work. He stays home. That's why I hate Sundays. He's already given me three beatings with a rope. I have marks on my back, want to see them? He was almost divorced a number of times. I know everything that goes on. They should hide certain things from me, but they don't. But I think that even if they did, it wouldn't make any difference. I have feelings about everything that happens to them. What do you want? It's

Milk delivery on São Miguel, 1990.

Ronald Caplain photograph

187

all the same blood. It's like they think I don't see, or don't understand. And anything I want to find out, it's only a matter of seconds. I'm a detective. But at home I don't like to know certain things. Sometimes I come home really late so I don't have to see what goes on. If I were of age, I'd take off. I wish I could. I don't think they like me.

"My sister got married early because of my father. He's strict. My mother pays the bills, but everything's in his name. At the bank, to open my account, he signed some papers so I wouldn't be able to do anything without his permission. But here, in this country, he's blind, you know? I've already gotten used to living without them, in my mind. It's only at night that they really bother me. And I'm not there, even when I am. In the summer they go to the beach and my mother doesn't even take her dress off. And they bring food from home. They really hang on to their money. Not me. I like money, but not like them. I like the good life."

I broke into that whirlwind, cascade, sluice, torrent, waterfall. I invited him to lunch.

"Why not? Too bad I can't call it a business lunch and take it off at the end of the year, but I don't pay taxes."

I pretend I hadn't heard him, and we went off to Spats. He was already familiar with the place-that place and all the other restaurants on Thayer Street and more. He had gone in to them to see what they were like. In some cases, he had been thrown out because he was underage. In that moment he had managed to see everything. To know what the place was like and, later, to be able to tell what it had been like. Once he even went to a really chic restaurant in Newport, one the rich go to by yacht and the poor people by car. He went by yacht with some gentlemen from the East Side.

"My parents have never been to a restaurant. Not even MacDonald's. To them the Biltmore Hotel must be like some beast out of Africa. And I've already eaten there. For free. Like a real big shot. Soon,

in addition to East Providence, my mother is going to see the road to Boston again. She's going back to the islands to keep her promise to the Holy Ghost. It seems like the Holy Ghost is on Terceira's side and Santo Cristo is on St. Michael's. When I was born I nearly died, and she said if I lived, she'd—I don't know how to put it in English, only Portuguese—pay off on a vow. There are things I only know how to say in English and others I only know in Portuguese. But the Portuguese things I don't know how to say in English…How can I say it?…Sound funny, foolish.

"I didn't die. Well and good. If I had had to stay there in the islands and get my feet plastered in cow shit, I wouldn't have cared if I had kicked the bucket; but since I'm here, she can go there in peace to fulfill her vow. Just in case. Anyway you look at it, it can't hurt I'm better protected."

"Ah! You know my son Adrian, Sir? That little devil, God forgive me. I don't know what to do with him. It was in an evil moment that I came to this country."

Young street urchin in Ponta Delgada, São Miguel, 1992.

Ronald Caplain photograph

I listened quietly to the father's picture of Adrian, the kid I had met a few short weeks before. He was in the middle of buying some Portuguese things in the Family Market, a tiny supermarket—simultaneously a mall—translated into a Beira-style store close to Wickenden Street.

"His mother's had it with him. He refused to speak Portuguese, and when he does speak, it's to say we don't understand anything. He's fed, clothed.

"We work like donkeys, night and day, and even weekends. For nothing. He doesn't give us any credit at all. He goes around mixed up in business, buying and selling things. He hangs out with students from the big university up there and he's on his way to the devil with them. They tell me he's already been in barrooms, and has a police record. I've been told he's friends with some boys who sell drugs here in Fox Point.

"I came to this country for a better life and ruined the boy's. He's lost. I don't know what can be done with him. He'll do business with the devil, if need be. Even if I left this country today, he wouldn't go. I give him a few good whacks once in a while, but it doesn't do any good. Maybe I didn't hit him enough. What can I do? My hands are tied

in this country. He's lost. He doesn't want anything to do with his parents, or the church, or our things, which is what we have, which is ours."

"So, you know Adrian too, huh?" Steve, a fourth-year med student, asked me some days ago in the Graduate Center Bar.

"Yes, of course, I did."

"What a wonderful kid! Quick, smart, lively. He understands everything. He picks it all up. What a way of looking at things-what a perspective on the world! He's a real entrepreneur. Everybody in the dorm knows him. He roams the halls and goes into everyone's room. He talks, asks questions. He answers without reservation. He has friends all over the university. He spent a weekend in Vermont with my classmate Dave and learned how to ski. Dave told me that he threw himself down the trail like a nut…But he's been well brought up. He lets people have it if they step on his toes even when they do it just to test him out, but he has an incredible sensibility. He has an extremely mature perspective on life and the world. He has incredibly deep feelings for someone his age. We took him to New York this weekend to see the basketball game—Brown against Columbia. We spent the

The milk must go through—hard at work on São Miguel, 1992.

afternoon in Manhattan. He wanted to go everywhere. If we'd let him, he'd have covered the whole place in no time at all. He says New York is what a good jungle is. Challenging. It's there if one really feels like digging right in. That's where one can grow, set up in business, tall as the skyscrapers.

"I first met him when I was working part-time in the Sciences Library. The security guard came over to tell us that some kid had come into the building and disappeared among the students in one of the elevators. We found him on the 14th floor admiring the view. When the guard told him he couldn't come in, he answered that he knew that very well and for that very reason he had sneaked in behind our backs. The restriction didn't matter to him anymore since now he knew what the view was actually like from up there. No longer would he be nagged with wondering about it when he walked by on the street.

"Once, to see the Harvard game, he squeezed into the back seat of the Brown football bus going to Cambridge. He isn't big enough to play football, but he doesn't like soccer either. He says it's a game for greenhorns and Portugees. He's at the stage of rejecting his culture, but he could come out of it all a great man. Why not? A great entrepreneur, his very dream. He's a phenom. The boy's

Working boys set out to gather vegetables, São Miguel, 1992.

Ronald Caplain photograph

brilliant. Very talented. A prodigy. The way he's going, he's a cinch. Great future. He's going to be very successful; he's already a bit of a big man."

"Do you know Adrian? That young boy from Terceira, from my parish, who hangs out over at the university and sells papers after school?"

"Of course. But why do you bring it up, my good Father?"

"You know, several people have talked to me about the boy to see if something can be done. Given what they tell me, I don't think there's any possibility. The boy must already be completely enmeshed in the webs of vice. So much bad company. They say he goes off with students to ski in the mountains, to New York, to jazz concerts in Newport and concerts at the Civic Center where they play that disgusting stuff they call punk. They say he smokes marijuana and makes the money to buy drugs by selling things around here. He won't have anything to do with the church. He showed up only once, in the rectory, to ask me for permission to sell Christmas cards at a dance in the church hall.

"They say he goes to bars (and the police don't do anything about it!) And that he says indecent things to girls walking by on the street. At the procession honoring Senhora da Saúde he stood on the sidewalk jeering the little children who were making their first communion, then crossed right through the procession to take a picture of a little boy dressed up as St. John the Baptist, so that he can now go around showing it to everybody and calling the child a sissy.

"The father doesn't care and the mother doesn't have any idea what's going on. The Brotherhood of the Holy Rosary offered to pay some of the cost if he were sent to reform school. He got really involved with a gang of American delinquents and now he's just like them—worse. Couldn't you talk to someone over there who could exercise some control over him and straighten him out? He influences a lot of boys, even those older than he, and already some stay away from Saturday Catechism because of him. And on top of it all, he has set them up as a ring of dealers under his command. So young and already his soul is the devil's."

"Do you know Adrian? He's Portuguese! What a kid!" The head of distribution for the *Providence Journal* said to me last week.

"If I were Portuguese, I must know him. He was nothing like the other Portuguese kids, passive and timid. He was adventurous. He had the aggressiveness required of businessmen. He's brave. He doesn't have problems. He has presence of mind. A sense of responsibility. He's a hard worker. He works hard like a good Portuguese, but he has the guts, the aggressive spirit the Portuguese lack. And he's a tough competitor. He wins all the prizes for best paperboy. He's already contacted several companies that advertised for salesmen. He gets their merchandise in the mail and delivers the goods. He's already gotten a prize for the best retailer in the area. He's got a P.O. box in his name and tells me that there's always merchandise arriving there. If Portugal has a few more like him, not so many people would find it necessary to emigrate here. What you people lack is that grit. In a few years, if he wants it, there will be doors open at this company for him. And not only at the newspaper. With his talent and some training, he'll go a long way. He'll end up heading a multinational yet."

"Do you know him? He's the devil incarnate." Those were the comments of Senhora Olinda Ferreira, pressing her hands together and lifting her eyes heavenward, while Senhor Machado wrapped some Azorean sweet bread for her. Adrian had come and gone in a flash, leaving a dripping stack of soaked newspapers. Senhora Olinda had witnessed the quickest of his exchanges in the scant seconds that Adrian paused in 'Machado's Portuguese Sweet Bread' shop.

"What that one's up to, God help us! And his parents know, but they don't care. He claims he even has his own bank account and that his father can only take out money with his permission. He's into drugs. He leaves the house and comes home late, if he comes home at all. He already goes around with women and won't have anything to do with religion. He says the Portuguese are dumb, that they are greenhorns, but he doesn't seem to notice that he too, is Portuguese. Flesh and blood, like the rest of us. Made and born there, entirely; the work of God. Or is it the devil's, God forbid! I wouldn't put it past him to have had dealings with him already. Oh, what they say he has done, Lord help us. It's a disgrace to us, the Portuguese people. We who've always been well-behaved and have respected the ways and customs of this country. What must the Americans say? That the Portuguese don't teach their children, that they let them do whatever they want. It looks terrible. It gives the Portuguese community a bad name."

"Oh! Do you know Adrian? I guess everybody knows him," commented a teacher between sips of coffee after a meeting, the purpose of which I've already forgotten.

"He's very intelligent. Or, to be more precise, perhaps smart, but not very studious. What he says and does is always amusing. Sometimes it is really incredible. The other day he was having fun with a girl who didn't know Portuguese. He called her 'my girl' and then he turned to his Portuguese friends and made fun of her, 'My girl, minha querida gal...inha (my dear chick...en).'

"He punned when he overheard one teacher talking to another about a gentleman who had never been introduced to her. 'I was never introduced!' He broke into the conversation and insinuated boldly: 'You've never been introduced to it, never done it?'

"They gave him a good dressing-down, but later in the teachers' lounge room they laughed till their sides split.

"It's a shame he's not a bit more studious. He's not a bad kid. It seems he has problems at home, but he never opens up about that. Only once do I remember his talking about his father. In the classroom of a teacher of Cape Verdean extraction, Adrian picked up a book by Manuel Ferreira-which also happens to be his own father's name-and started to show it around to his classmates as if it were a book his father had written. When he had everybody believing him, he burst out laughing and said only: my father's already dead.

"He doesn't like to do his homework at home. So he does it during free period. It seems that his parents make him work to help pay off the house. That happens with so many immigrants, incidentally. Only it'll be a shame if they make him leave school when he's sixteen."

What else? He's a kid like all the others. He watches "Soap" late at night and doesn't miss a trick. He knows one character is a homosexual, another a transvestite, and that Danny and Helen had a shotgun wedding. But what kid his age today doesn't know all about those things and more? He has great eyes. He doesn't offend people when he's "pushy," in spite of the fact that sometimes he really goes too far. But he's a sweet kid. Maybe it's that Portuguese sweetness the islands give to people. He's a little volcano born of that peace but one whose fire doesn't burn or, if it burns, doesn't hurt. I love him.

Ah! Do you know Adrian?...You do? He's a...

THE PORTUGUESE FEAST

TRADITION & TRANSFORMATION

BY STEPHEN L. CABRAL

At Catholic churches throughout Portugal, the Azores, Madeira and Portuguese immigrant communities in southeastern New England, parishioners observe public rituals devoted to images of patron saints, the Blessed Virgin Mary and Jesus Christ. These figures are viewed as intermediaries to God the Father. Devotees pray to their favorite patrons for divine intervention that will bestow good health, fortune or employment for relatives, safe passage for migrating kin or indulgences for the souls of departed family members. If these prayers are answered, the Portuguese pledge sacred vows called *promessas* to sponsor or to celebrate a specific feast. These patron saint feasts are a pan-Latin phenomenon combining Medieval Roman Catholic liturgy with more ancient pagan agricultural festivities.

Portuguese feasts are colorful and fascinating ritual dramas. These public events illuminate the dynamic interrelationships that link family, economics, politics, folklore and religion in a Portuguese community. They are clearly set off from ordinary space and time. Customarily a voluntary committee of adult men transforms mundane village life into sacred experience by coordinating ritual performances. Villagers often help decorate the church and the streets with arches of greens, colored lights, banners, flags, flowers, grapes and wheat. The altar and images of the saints are also adorned in their finest garments and surrounded by flowers, candles and incense.

Devout Portuguese travel considerable distances to attend a feast and pay homage to a decorated image. After visiting the church and praying to the saint, pilgrims often leave money donations. These alms, which help defray the expenses of the feast committee, are left in fulfillment of a promise to repay a divine favor. Any remaining cash is distributed to the poor. Portuguese Atlantic islanders from

Holy Ghost festival in the Azores in the 1890s. On the facade of a chapel, small lanterns with candles illuminate the ceremony. The imperiador *(emperor with crown) oversees the festivities. Elder men are armed with staffs for the long march, the young carry candles. While the band plays, people crowd around open windows to observe.*

Spinner Collection

the Azores and Madeira believe that the saints appreciate the effort, beauty and generosity shown in their honor.

Azoreans and Madeirans keep ritual time by firing aerial bombs, observing liturgical ceremonies and conducting secular festivities. Many feasts begin with a novena, a week of prayer and a recitation of the Rosary. The weekend of the feast usually opens with a Benediction of the Blessed Sacrament. A solemn High Mass and procession of the images of the saints and the Blessed Sacrament are held on the feast day. A carpet of flowers and leaves marks the procession route through the village streets.

At the conclusion of the religious ceremonies, villagers feast on the decorated church grounds. They share food and

Spinner Collection

In the 1920s, Portuguese immigrants in the U.S. celebrated in the same manner as they do today, and as they did in the Old Country—with banners of the Holy Ghost leading the way, regalia, children in white, spectators on their porches and people in the streets. This march, which originated at St. John the Baptist Church on County Street in New Bedford, is heading south on Bonney Street.

Milton Silvia photograph

In the Portuguese villages, a carpet of flowers marks the procession route, 1979.

Our Lady of the Sorrows at the Festa do Senhor da Pedra, 1980s.

Procession of the image of Santo Cristo through the streets of Ponta Delgada, São Miguel, 1967. The men are dressed in traditional medieval vestments and carrying lanterns. The statue of Christ was presented to Azorean nuns from the Pope in the 16th century.

At right, in Fall River, parents get children involved through direct participation, including elaborate costuming.

Young angels march at the Santo Cristo procession in Ponta Delgada around 1940.

At right, a man reviewing the procession from his balcony adorns his house with a colorful bedspread in tribute to Santo Cristo.

The Convent of Esperança in Ponta Delgada (lit up in the background) houses the statue of Santo Cristo.

indulge in drinking. Commerce, auctions, and brass band concerts are held in the shadow of the church. Villagers perform folk music, singing and dancing. Parishioners can be seen posturing, courting, gossiping, and storytelling. Finally, everyone passes judgment on the entire display by comparing it to previous festivals or those of rival villages. The Portuguese refer to these secular festivities as the *arraial*.

The Portuguese regard the religious and secular components of their feasts as parts of an integrated whole. Furthermore, they

expect each observance of a feast to be distinctive and memorable without radically departing from tradition. Each year the feast committees must compete with the memories of previous celebrations and rival feasts in neighboring villages. In this manner religious devotion is transformed into social prestige and regional group identity.

Feast of the Blessed Sacrament

Four Madeiran immigrants established the Feast of the Blessed Sacrament in New Bedford at the Church of Our Lady of the Immaculate Conception on the first Sunday of August 1915. The date corresponded to a similar observance in the village of Estreito da Calheta, the birthplace of the founders.

Madeirans have sustained a fervent devotion to the Blessed Sacrament, a symbol of power and control represented by the Eucharistic Host since the 15th century. Knights of the Holy Order of Christ, who discovered the uninhabited islands off the Moroccan coast in 1418, observed the initial festival to sanctify Prince Henry the Navigator's program of colonial expansion and settlement. Local parishes throughout the island continue to celebrate their version of the feast on a different Sunday between Easter and January 15.

The Feast of the Blessed Sacrament enabled Madeirans to retain part of their cultural heritage while adjusting to the American immigrant experience. Most Madeirans originated from small village farms in the countryside. In America they encountered a foreign language barrier and economic insecurity associated with living in a city and working in textile mills. They were estranged from each other and faced discrimination in New Bedford. The Feast of the Blessed Sacrament united Madeirans from different villages and enabled them to sustain their regional identity and pride while minimizing the threat of change in a foreign setting.

The initial observance of the Feast of the Blessed Sacrament required a cooperative effort by Madeiran immigrants who voluntarily sponsored it with the assistance of family and friends. They invested time, money and labor to transform their neighborhood of tenements and textile mills into a festive setting that resembled Madeiran village celebrations. The streets were lined with flagpoles, banners, colored lights, flowers and arches of bayberry leaves leading to the decorated church.

Several devotional services were conducted in the church throughout the weekend including Vespers on Friday, Benediction on Saturday and a High Mass and procession of the Blessed Sacrament on Sunday. These ceremonies invoked the divine intercession and protection of the Blessed Sacrament on behalf of the entire Madeiran immigrant community.

In the adjoining churchyard, Portuguese food, beverages and handicrafts were sold from wood-framed stalls called *barracas*. They were operated by *festeiros*, men who sponsored the feast, and their families. During the entire weekend, these Madeirans served the larger community. Profits generated from the *barracas* were donated to the church. Brass bands, roving musicians, dancers and fireworks enhanced the festivities.

These old-world feasting customs were maintained for 30 years because of the membership criteria for the feast committee. Only Madeiran-born adult males or their male descendants were eligible to serve. The sons of Madeiran daughters who married outside the group, including Continental or Azorean Portuguese, were excluded from official committee membership.

Group of Madeirans celebrate with music, food and laughter in the local countryside, 1930s.

Madeiran folkloric dancers march down Madeira Avenue in the parade of the Feast of the Blessed Sacrament in New Bedford, in the 1980s.

Courtesy of Joseph Sousa

Stephen Cabral photograph

A young dancer performs before thousands of people at Madeira Field, 1978.

Grupo Folclórico do Clube SS Sacramento perform the bailinho, *the national song and dance of Madeira, during the parade on Madeira Avenue, 1980.*

From 1915 through 1945 the committee was dominated by Madeiran immigrants who came to America at the turn of the century. These *festeiros* shared a common definition of a good Madeiran feast. Over the years the committee grew from four to ten members in response to the popularity of the feast. The original celebration attracted 2,000 parishio-

ners. By 1930 over 15,000 people attended, including many "outsiders." The pastor of the church and the bishop of the diocese advised the feast committee to keep the Blessed Sacrament inside the church where only Madeirans and other Portuguese parishioners would offer proper respect and worship. The street procession was discontinued and replaced by a parade in 1932.

The descendants of Madeiran immigrants further modified the feast after World War II. At this time, feast committees included many American-born sons of immigrants. They had been educated in American schools during the Depression, and many had served in the armed forces during the war. This second generation of *festeiros* used their feast to reaffirm their Madeiran heritage and pledge allegiance to their new homeland. Under this new leadership, the feast parade added color guards, veterans' groups, drum and bugle corps, floats, motorcades, beauty queens and politicians.

During the postwar years, the feast was held in the church lot and the Ottiwell school grounds across the street. As attendance

Stephen Cabral photograph

The Standard-Times Library

surpassed 25,000, further expansion of the feast grounds became necessary. In 1951 the feast committee purchased a piece of private property across from the school with a part of the feast profits. To secure the deed, the Madeirans incorporated the Clube Madeirense S. S. Sacramento, Inc., in 1953. The chief purpose of this group was to advise and to assist the committees in the promotion and celebration of the feast on Madeira Field.

Religious Feast to Public Extravaganza

The Clube Madeirense S.S. Sacramento, Inc., comprised exclusively of former *festeiros*, rapidly acquired the status of a parent organization. The feast committees were reduced to the working arm of this new association. Under the auspices of this new organizational structure, the Feast of the Blessed Sacrament was gradually transformed from a private, religious feast to a public extravaganza. The feast became a promotional display of selected Madeiran customs that were packaged, marketed and sold to the Greater New Bedford community.

Since the 1950s, feast committees and the Clube Madeirense S. S. Sacramento, Inc., have used feast profits to acquire more private property and improve Madeira Field, the feast ground. A clubhouse was constructed as well as a pavilion, modern kitchen and toilet facilities, stages, bandstands, permanent *barracas* of cinder blocks and a gas-fired barbecue pit. According to the local media, the Feast of the Blessed Sacrament attracted a crowd of 200,000 people in 1986. As the feast grew in popularity and size over the years, a diminishing percentage of the profits was donated to the church, local charities and a scholarship fund because of the high costs of developing and maintaining the feast grounds.

A memorial stone dedicated to the four founders stands on the southwest corner of Madeira Field. During the opening ceremonies of the feast, the presidents of the feast committee and of the Clube Madeirense S.S. Sacramento, Inc., lay a wreath of flowers at the stone and observe a moment of silence as taps are played on a bugle. The solemnity formerly reserved for the Blessed Sacrament has been replaced by a memorial ceremony focused on the founders.

The feast has endured, in part, because of its ability to change and meet contemporary needs. Most importantly, it endures because of the inclusion and socialization of children in adult activities throughout the preparation and celebration of the festivals. The transformations result from the degree that Portuguese descendants accept, reinterpret and act upon the values, understandings and meanings imparted to them by their parents and grandparents during feasts.

The membership of the Clube Madeirense S.S. Sacramento has dwindled during the past twenty years. Madeiran immigration did not keep pace with the inevitable loss of old timers and their sons. The organization addressed this crisis by revising their by laws to include the sons of Madeiran women. Feast committee membership, which was originally traced exclusively through the father's line, now acknowledges matrilineal descent. This modification immediately expanded and revitalized the pool of eligible festerios to perpetuate the feast.

The feast, as celebrated in New Bedford, therefore, is not simply a survival or extension of traditional Portuguese culture. It is a dynamic ritual drama that is constantly recreated by successive generations responding to their changing needs and circumstances. What counts most in the minds of the participants are the memories of the origin of the feast, the esthetic beauty of previous celebrations and how the Madeiran community has maintained the tradition for over 84 years.

The entrance to Madeira Field is marked with a tribute to the people who helped establish the feast.

Carne d'espeto and vinho da Madeira *are two of the greatest attractions for feastgoers at the Feast of the Blessed Sacrament in New Bedford, 1997.*

Joseph D. Thomas photographs

Finding Love at the Feast

Interview with Teresa Freitas

by Rhondalee Davis

I met my husband Tony, ha!, at the Portuguese feast. That was the only place my parents would allow me to go. I couldn't go to dances, or anywhere. I had an older brother who went to dances but he didn't want to take me 'cause he didn't want anyone to think I was his girlfriend. So I didn't go anywhere, just where my parents would go. And being from Madeira, we'd be involved with the Madeiran feast. That particular day, it was very surprising, my mother and father let me go to the feast with Mrs. Perreira and her daughter. Mrs. Perreira was also from Madeira and my parents liked her.

It's funny 'cause—I was 16, back in 1976—and I had this thing about Kris Kristofferson. He had a beard and I thought he was very handsome. Men with beards attracted me. So we were walking around and this guy bumped into me. I was all set to make a fuss. I think it was just for my ego 'cause I used to have all these guys following me around telling me how beautiful I looked. And I just loved it, not because I could talk to them—I wasn't allowed to, but just to have the attention. I think everybody likes to hear how nice they look. And when this guy bumped into me, I looked at him and said, "Hmmm… Not bad!"

He had a beard and was good-looking. My girlfriend and I walked around outside of the feast area and his car was parked out there. It was a little MG and he was just kind of leaning against it. He had on worn-out blue jeans, but clean, and a white sweater and new shoes. I said to my girlfriend—"I'm gonna get him." She said, "Oh, Teresa, no way! He's so stuck up." I said, "No, I'm gonna get him. I'm going to meet him."

She said, "Oh, God, just forget it. He's too snobby." And I said, "I noticed he was looking at me." I walked right by him. I didn't say anything.

Then I walked by him again and he said to me, "Where are you going?" In a very grumpy voice. And I don't know, I just turned around and said, "By the way, what time is it?" It was funny 'cause I hadn't really noticed his watch. I was just using a line. But he had one of those up-to-date watches, the black ones, you touch them and they light up. Very sharp. He clicked the watch and you could see the light on.

And my girlfriend was so silly—"Ah, I love your watch," she said. It was a conversation piece. We talked for a while and we walked. He followed us and then asked me my name because he had never seen me before. That's because I was not allowed to go out! So how could anybody see me? My parents had this attitude that if you live under this roof, you're going to follow the rules. I followed the rules and did what was expected of me. My brothers and sister gave my parents a lot of heartache for that, and my parents became hardened. But they are very accepting. They never said, "Oh, you have to marry Portuguese." It was just easier for me.

You don't date. He had to ask permission from my father before he could even talk to me. I said to my mother, "Get Dad ready for this. A guy is going to come over and talk to him." She said, "Don't worry. Don't worry. I'll get your father ready."

When he came to talk to my father, he had long hair and a beard and drove a sports car and had jeans on. So he is walking toward the driveway and my father looked at him. My mother hadn't told him anything about it. Tony said, "I want to talk to you about your daughter." My father said, "My daughter? Which one?" My sister was really young. He knew it wasn't about her. "About your daughter, Teresa."

My father looked right at him and said, "I don't have no daughter for you. Get out." Tony put his tail between his legs… and just left. Then he called me up and said, "Your father doesn't like me. He said he didn't have any daughters for me and to beat it." I was really upset and kind of depressed. My mother tried talking to my father but it didn't have any great effect.

Tony began coming around. He's got a lot of good qualities. He'd give you the shirt off his back. Very easy going. He bought my brothers skateboards and all these things and they loved him afterwards. If we did go out, I had to bring all of my brothers with me. I only really had to bring one brother but I used to bring all three. We would drive all the way down the Seven Hills and they loved it. We took them everywhere.

They've grown up now and some of them work for him. My father got to know Tony and he followed my father's rules. We couldn't go out alone, we couldn't do this, we couldn't do that. If he had been an American or some other nationality, he wouldn't have been able to put up with this. But being Portuguese, (his sisters were having the same problems), he kind of sympathized.

When I complained about the way I was being brought up, he said, "If you had had so much freedom, I probably wouldn't have wanted you." He has a lot of Portuguese in him because of his upbringing. Anyhow, when I met Tony at the feast, something inside told me—"This is the one."

WORKING THE FEAST

INTERVIEW WITH JOHN FERNANDES

BY BRIDGET CUSHING

John Fernandes, of Madeiran descent, grew up with the Portuguese traditions of his parents. In this hilarious account, he finds himself, innocent, in the ring with some old bulls, and he doesn't have a chance. The strength of the old-timers from Madeira, who haven't forgotten what work is, astonishes and humbles him.

· · · · · · · · · · · · · · · · · ·

You have to be of Madeiran descent to be on the feast committee, though anybody can work at the feast itself. In the mid-80s, I was nominated to be on the committee. After you serve your year on the committee, you are eligible to become a club member of the Clube Madeirense. Eventually I was elected to the board of directors. Being in the club is one of the best things that ever happened to me.

The real joy of it is working with these old-timers. Oh! Those guys are great! I mean, half of them don't speak English, which is fine by me. The other half, they are deeply religious people, very hard-working people. And they just love doing this. And they're bulls, sheer bulls. The Madeiran people are bulls.

End of November, beginning of December, one of the men on my committee had gotten a major gravel pit, Tilcon, to donate blue stone. We were eager to lay it in the side of the stakes. They asked for volunteers to go for the stone and I said, "Sure, I'll go.'"

They said, "Sure. You goin' to be there at six in the morning?"

"Yeah, yeah, I'll be there," I said.

So I get there Saturday morning at six o'clock. And we're all standing around having coffee. I'm listening to the old timers.

They say, "O.K., now, we are really going to see who's here to work."

I'm saying- "What's going on?"

So they all got these little brown bags under their armpits and there's a little bottle in there. They're all bringing their own homemade moonshine! And I'm looking at them and I'm saying, "These guys are lost!'" I mean, it's six o'clock in the morning.

And they say, "Only one. Only one." It's kind of like watching an old Italian movie. They make you try a little bit of everyone's or you're going to insult them. They are saying that this bottle really isn't the best they make, "It's just something I whipped up. I

could have done a little bit better. Here, try it." And it's really fun.

But they give you only one. I mean, you don't sit there and get sloshed. So now it's 6AM and I'm taking a shot of almost pure alcohol and I'm saying, "Up, I'm ready to work! Let's go get them!" So I'm figuring, OK, I've got all these old men with me, I'm the youngest guy here, the next youngest person here is about 50. Then from 50, you're up to 70. I mean they're in that age bracket.

So we get outside and we see these three huge dump trucks out there, like the ones the state uses. And I'm saying, "What the heck?" And I said, "OK, I'll just jump in the truck." And we go down this big huge pit. Boom! Boom! Boom! We get to the bottom of the gravel pit and it must have been a good quarter-mile deep. And I'm looking around for this nice little pile of stones, you know, tiny little stones. And I'm figuring, OK, where's the shovel? You know, let's get going, guys. And they're looking at me, laughing, because they know what I'm thinking. And they said, "No, no, no, Johnny."

I said, "What's the matter?"

And they said, "Over there!" I look and see we've got to climb the cliffs. Big boulders! Well, they're about 30- 60-pound boulders! And we had to fill these dump trucks up by hand. So, I'm a pretty big guy, you know, I'm not a little guy. It wasn't what I had in mind but OK, that's what we've got. So I'm carrying the block and this thing must weigh about, I don't know, 50 or 60 pounds. And lifting it is one thing, carrying it is another, and then trying to heave it so it goes over the top of the truck, that's the hardest part.

So I'm walking with this rock and I've got my arms laden. All of a sudden this little midget, about five foot one, comes by me and he smiles at me. He has a big, big rock in his hands. He smiles at me and he has a gold tooth. He says, "Not bad for 69, huh?" He throws the rock at his side like it was yesterday's lunch. Boom! Right inside. And he said, "Come on, little Johnny!" He started calling me little Johnny, like I was a little kid again. He said, "Come on, little Johnny, you've been away from work too long. It's time for you to get used to this again."

I got home and I was so sore! I couldn't believe it. All these guys were ready to go again tomorrow, these old guys. They're great.

OF WHALES AND FISH

On the island of São Miguel, Azores, whalers move on after the kill, while the processors tow the animal's carcass to the factory.

Courtesy of Miguel Côrte-Real

DOWN TO THE SEA FOR FISH

PORTUGUESE FISHING FAMILIES IN NEW BEDFORD

BY DANIEL GEORGIANNA

Good Times

The U. S. fishing industry needed skilled fishermen in the late 1970s and early 1980s. Georges Bank, one of the richest fishing grounds in the world, was now the exclusive property of New England ports. A new law, effective in 1976, excluded foreign boats from fishing in waters 200 miles from shore.

New Bedford had positioned itself well to take advantage of the industry's rebirth by rebuilding its docks and erecting state-of-the-art processing plants during the previous decade. The port responded to the call of riches from the sea, and fishing and its related industries boomed. From 1977 to 1983, the number of fishing boats, the number of fishermen, and the size of the catch all doubled. To increase profits, some boat owners alternated crews to keep the boats continually fishing. Because demand for fish by health-conscious customers grew even faster than the supply, the value of the catch almost tripled from $39 million to $109

million, thus making New Bedford the country's leading port. The docks on both the New Bedford and Fairhaven sides of the harbor suddenly awoke from their fitful drowsiness caused by loss of fish to the foreign fleets and pulsed with life not seen since the peak of whaling 100 years before. More welders, electricians, ships' carpenters and other related craftspeople were needed on the docks. Lumping, ship supply, boat repair and other marine services thrived. Processing plants called for more fish cutters, packers, floor men and others. Fishing was good, and the harbor beckoned to people who would work hard.

As always in New Bedford, the people who answered the call were mostly immigrants, or the children of immigrants, Newfoundlanders, Norwegians, and, to a lesser extent, Latvians and Poles who knew fishing and its kindred occupations. But most of the people who came to the docks were Portuguese whose families had fished and processed fish for generations.

Idle fishing vessels, mostly owned and captained by Portuguese immigrants from the continent, are tied up at Leonard's Wharf during the "Tie Up" of 1980.

Joseph D. Thomas photograph

Why They Left Portugal: *Os Bacalhoeiros*

Portugal faces the sea. For hundreds and probably thousands of years, people in villages on the coast lived from the sea. Life had been hard; only by working together in extended families could they survive. Men fished from small boats by day or, more recently, from large ships on long trips. Women farmed the land, gathered from the shoreline and processed the fish that boats brought ashore.

In 1934, after years of stagnation in the Portuguese fishing industry, António Salazar, the economics professor who ruled Portugal, decided he needed a new fleet to fish for cod on the Grand Banks. The Portuguese fishing fleet of wooden- and steel-hull sailing ships had been painted dazzling white during World War II so German submarines would not attack the fleet of a neutral nation. This fleet became the centerpiece of Salazar's Estado Novo, a state corporatist system called fascist by its enemies. Every spring, the *Bacalhoeiros*, referred to as the White Fleet by the others on the Grand Banks, set sail with much fanfare from Lisbon for six months or more on the Grand Banks, where fishermen fished from open dories and salted cod into the hold after setting and hauling back miles of baited hooks.

The official word from the Salazar regime was that cod fishing in the *Bacalhoeiros* was hard but that the state took good care of its fishermen and provided a good living for their families. Fishermen returning home with money in their pockets probably did relieve the grinding poverty in the small villages on the coast. But José da Silva Cruz, Second Fisher of Portugal when he fished on the Argus in the 1930s, remembered life on the boats differently from the national myth:

Life aboard the Bacalhoeiros *was a living hell. There, even the dogs were treated better than those of us who worked. It was quite common for the officers to say, "You shut up and if you don't I'll put you down in the Log Book, and when we get to Portugal you'll be taken as a prisoner, as a communist." Under the regime of dictator Salazar we were slaves from every point of view. We were not permitted to quit the ship for any reason whatsoever.*

In the early 1960s few fishermen wanted to fish from the *Bacalhoeiros*. Working and living conditions were bad and the pay low. Portuguese fishing companies began building large stern trawlers, 80 meters or longer, and powered by huge diesel engines, to catch and salt cod at sea. These boats were more efficient than the *Bacalhoeiros*, and required fewer fishermen, who earned higher pay.

The revolts in the 1960s in Angola, Guinea, Cape Verde, and Mozambique saved the *Bacalhoeiros* for a few years. To raise the army to fight in Africa, Salazar sharply increased the numbers of men drafted. Under a 1927 decree exempting fishermen on the Grand Banks from the draft, young men could work in the *Bacalhoeiros* rather than go into the army. Many preferred the low wages and harsh working conditions of fishing to fighting in Africa, where almost every family lost

The fisherman is always hopeful. In Sesimbra, Portugal, in the quiet afternoon sun, a fisherman mends his nets as he prepares for a dawn departure into the Atlantic and a profitable haul, 1961.

The Standard-Times Library

203

Their boats ashore, fishermen at Nazare repair handlines.

Bottom, the fishing village of Cascais, near Lisbon, 1974.

someone during the 13 years of war. The life of the *Bacalhoeiros* was prolonged until 1974, when the colonial wars ended.

In 1976 Canada extended its boundaries 200 miles offshore, shutting out Portugal and others from much of the cod on the Grand Banks. The Canadian government forced Portugal to buy cod from them in exchange for access to Canadian waters on the Grand Banks. Even when they complied, the Portuguese quota of codfish from the Grand Banks was kept low. Eventually these quotas were cut almost to zero.

Portuguese fishermen and their families looked for work away from Portugal. The fall of Salazar's successor in 1974 brought an end to the repressive regime, which considered emigration from Portugal a crime and only allowed passports to leave to those assured of returning. The new democratic government opened Portugal's borders, and fishing families, no longer able to find work in Portugal's reduced fisheries, left by the thousands.

Some left fishing and went to Germany, Switzerland, Brazil and the West Coast of the United States, which had land or jobs available and pockets of Portuguese immigrants already there. But many looked to New Bedford and the sea.

The Standard-Times Library

The Standard-Times Library

Fishing Families in America

New Bedford already had a large Portuguese fishing community, many of whom had come three or four generations earlier. During the 19th century, New Bedford whaling ships often stopped in the Azores and Cape Verde Islands to pick up crew. When they returned to port, the whalers jumped ship and sent for their families, who arrived in rickety packet ships plying the cross-Atlantic trade.

Portuguese seamen, also mostly from the Azores, fished in the American fleet of schooners on the Grand Banks. By 1885 most of the Provincetown fleet of 60 Grand Banks schooners had Portuguese captains. (A decade earlier, less than 20 percent had Portuguese captains). These Azorean seamen had risen quickly in the fishery, where they sailed 1,000 miles to the Grand Banks for weeks of catching and salting codfish. Around the turn of the century, they made the successful change to small trawlers supplying the Boston fresh-fish market. In 1915 about a third of the 3,000 fishermen in Massachusetts were Portuguese, most of them in Provincetown.

Manuel Avila brought his family from the Azores to Provincetown in 1899. In Faial he had hunted whales. In Provincetown he bought a schooner to fish the waters between Cape Cod and New Jersey, looking for swordfish and whatever else he could find. Around 1905 he brought his family to New Bedford to fish the inshore waters in and around Buzzards Bay.

His son John, born in Faial in 1872, had joined his father on the boats when he was a boy. In 1929 John built the *Clara S.*, a 40-foot wooden boat, in the Portuguese Navy Yard, a cluster of shanties at the southern edge of New Bedford's harbor, now occupied by fish processing plants. Here, Portuguese fishermen, mostly Azorean, kept their boats. John's son Manuel kept up the family tradition.

We fished for mackerel. We fished for lobster. We dragged for yellowtail. We handlined. We did everything. We'd fish off Nomans; we didn't have to go to Georges. There were plenty of fish around here.

We sold fish to a man named Childs, who had a little shack on Pier 3. There were still whaling ships there, when I was a boy.

In New Bedford, between textile mills, city slums and abandoned wharves, a quaint collection of shacks was maintained for several decades by local inshore fishermen. The shacks provided storage and shelter, and the surrounding marsh was used as a makeshift shipyard. The area, now embedded in local folklore, is affectionately referred to as "the Portugee Navy Yard." Located at the foot of Potomska Street, circa 1930.

We'd get a quarter of a cent, half a cent per pound. One cent was a big deal.

John and his wife Clara had ten children, nine of whom survived their mother. Clara died when the youngest was three. The six boys, Joseph, John, Frank, Manuel, Edmund and Gilbert, turned towards the sea, and each eventually captained his own boat. The three girls, Lena, Mildred and Tina, married into other Portuguese fishing families, and the next generation of Avilas found their way to jobs on family boats. The fifth generation of Manuel Avila's family in America now works the family trade. Four great-great grandsons, including Rodney Avila now captain fishing boats, owned by family members, in New Bedford.

I started fishing with my father when I was nine years old. I'd fish during summer and school vacations, and I made my first trip to Georges Bank when I was 13. What happened as you fished on these boats, you'd save up, and in 1967, I bought my first boat with my uncle. The whole crew came from Portugal. They were hard workers. They could handle the gear, they could mend the nets, they were fishermen. I came down to the dock one time with Manny Neves, who owned the Neves, and the guys on the crew told me they didn't want me to work. That

Painting by Rodney Avila

Courtesy of Frank Avila

was an insult to the crew, they said, if the captain has to work. "You go have coffee with the captains. You working makes us look bad; we don't want you here."

The Azoreans in New Bedford fished mostly inshore waters from small boats. This was a fishery they knew well; it was easy to enter and would support their families. Some bought the larger boats that could fish Georges Bank. Fishing families from Madeira mostly emigrated to Southern California to fish for tuna. But at least one, Manuel Pestana, owned a fishing boat in New Bedford.

Any business, industry or trade generates cooperation as well as competition, but fishing requires more cooperation than most trades. The sea can be cruel and dangerous, and the marketplace can be even harder and more dangerous. The Atlantic Fishermen's Union was formed in New Bedford in 1937, mostly by Newfoundlanders and Norwegians. The Newfoundlanders fished from the larger boats, dragging nets over Georges Bank for cod, haddock, yellowtail and other flounders. The Norwegians, also from large boats, dredged Georges Bank and waters south for scallops. Each group loosely stuck to its side of the informal agreement—cod, haddock, and flounders for the Newfoundlanders and scallops for the Norwegians. These groups supplied the industry with men, boats, ship supplies, gear, insurance and money. As Manuel Avila noted, there was little room left for the Portuguese.

One time I tried to get into the union, but the Portuguese couldn't get in. The only way you could go out on the big boats without being in the union was if they needed a man, they could take one off the dock. You had to be standing on the dock. You would have your clothes ready and jump aboard when they threw the ropes off. That's what made the Portuguese stick together. It's ironic that now almost all the boats in the union are Portuguese.

Rodney Avila attests to the persistence of this discrimination:

When I bought my first boat in 1967, it was very hard to get a loan. Then John Silvia, who owned a few boats, became a director of the Merchants Bank and that really opened up things for the Portuguese guys to buy

boats. He knew the Portuguese people; a lot of people didn't know the Portuguese. They wouldn't take a chance. But the Portuguese stood with the Portuguese.

The Cape Verdeans fared worse than the Portuguese and Azoreans either fishing in their

Spinner Collection

In 1939 more than 120 boats were listed in the "Georges Bank Fishing Fleet," hailing from New Bedford and the Cape and Islands. Of these, only eight of the owners had Portuguese names. The Clinton *was owned by Manuel C. DeMello of New Bedford.*

Courtesy of Manuel Avila

Four generations of Avilas outside their Dartmouth home in 1940: Manuel holding his son Rodney; next to him is his father John and his grandfather Manuel.

Photograph by Rodney Avila

Aboard Rodney Avila's boat, Trident, *70 miles south of Nomans Island and knee-deep in butterfish, is William Mello, 1980.*

own boats or finding sites on other New Bedford boats. On Cape Verde, where the sea is never very far away, men and boys fished from the shore or from small boats for sardines, and many learned to sail great distances on larger ships. In New Bedford, Cape Verdeans worked as longshoremen, fish processors and merchant seamen, but few found their way or were allowed access into the city's fishing industry.

The Fortes family were an exception. Three brothers came to New Bedford from Brava on a packet ship in the 1920s. They bought their first boat during the 1930s and owned a series of boats through the 1950s. Edward Fortes also fished on the *Alba V*, a boat owned by the Avila family. Ethel Lima noted,

My father, John Fortes, was working in a cotton mill, but he couldn't stand being indoors all the time. So he went fishing. First he fished on other people's boats and then he bought the John Henry Smith *with his older brothers Henry and Antone. When they sold their last boat, my father continued to fish until he retired, when he was 65.*

In the late 1970s and early 1980s, many Portuguese fishing families came to America, some to fish and others to work in construction and in the clothing trades. These latter ignored the call of the sea, but often not for long. Armando Estudante describes the process:

There is the guy who says that I can fish. I know how to mend nets. I know how to work on the fishing boats, and I'm going where there are fishing boats. And there is the guy who is sick and tired of fishing. He is done with fishing; he makes the sign of the cross,

The Portugal, *tied up at Leonard's Wharf while fitting-out for a trip, 1979.*

Bottom, fishing draggers at Homer's and Leonard's wharves, 1980.

and he says, "Good-bye, sea. I won't go work on you ever again." He comes to America. He goes to New Jersey, or he goes to Connecticut, and he gets a job in construction.

Then he gets that virus eating him, and he starts hearing stories about fishermen in New Bedford making $2,000 in a week. Two or three guys get together to come down to New Bedford. They see all the boats, and they hear all the stories, and they go to the cafes where they hear about the $2,000 or $3,000 in a trip. Of course when you make 100 dollars in a trip you don't brag about it.

So there he is, fishing again.

On the Picket Line

The Portuguese fishing families in New Bedford kept their heads down, worked hard and prospered from the bountiful landings and high prices. They saved their money to buy boats or to return home to Portugal. In the spring of 1980 the situation changed. Fuel and ice prices doubled, increasing costs by about $5,000 per trip. At the same time, prices set by fish dealers at the daily auction dropped. Between March and May auction prices were cut in half for cod, haddock and flounder to 10 and 15 cents per pound, while the retail price for fresh fish fillets, which average about a third of the whole fish weight, stayed around

two dollars per pound. The simmering age-old antagonism flared up between the fishermen who catch the fish and the dealers who buy it.

Fishing crews, captains and boat owners were united against the dealers because the three groups share in the value of the catch under a piecework system used around the world called "the lay." In New Bedford, after the costs of fuel, ice, and insurance are deducted from the money received for the fish, the crew receives about 50 percent of what's left. The captain gets about 15 percent and the boat owners get about 35 percent, which pays for the boat, gear and repairs. A typical crewman's share dropped from $1,000 to $300 for a 7-10 day trip, less than two dollars per hour for doing heavy, dangerous work at sea, day and night in all kinds of weather on a slippery, moving deck. Estudante explains the frustration that gave rise to the 1980 strike:

We went out fishing for one week or ten days, and we didn't see any money. We finished the trip even owing money to the suppliers. So I think, we do not have to be too smart to realize we have to do something. At the time there were a couple of cafes on the dock, and they were the meeting point of the fishermen, where we used to discuss these things. We decided to tie up the boats. It was about 11 o'clock, and there were a couple of

As tensions mount on the waterfront during the tie-up of 1980, families confront a police barricade with anger and disbelief.

Joseph D. Thomas photograph

209

boats going out: the Tina Maria *and the* Two
Friends. *They were leaving the dock, and we
told them we were talking about not going
fishing. They said that's what we need. That's
what we have to do, and let's do it. So they
tied the line back to the dock. And we went
around to the other boats, round the docks, to
tell the others.*

Led by the Portuguese fishermen and
boat owners, almost all the fishing boats in
New Bedford were tied up at the docks. Over
the next few days the Portuguese fishermen
and their families marched through the dock
areas, held rallies in front of City Hall and
picketed the processing plants to stop trucks
from carrying fish from other ports into the
plants. Their leaders met with the dealers to
discuss a fixed, minimum price that would
cover expenses for the trip.

The fish buyers had time and the law on
their side. They called the tie-up a constraint
of trade, a violation of the antitrust laws and
not a strike because they didn't employ the
fishermen; they bought fish from them. A
week into the tie-up, a few boats began going
out. Rather than lose their organization, the
Portuguese fishermen decided to go back
fishing but to limit catches and the length of
trips and to increase layover time between
trips. They had proven to the dealers that if
the prices went too low, they could shut down
the fishing fleet.

For the next few years New Bedford
fishermen did better. They brought in a little
more fish, and prices at the dock rose sharply.
But in 1986 costs, especially health insurance,
began to increase again, and a more troubling
problem could no longer be ignored: the long
term decline in the fish stocks. The bonanza for
New England fishermen from the 200-mile
limit had lasted for only a few years. By 1980
New England fish landings reached their peak
and began to fall. New Bedford was spared for
a few years mainly because of the large
flounder stocks, the port's major species. Also,
rising fish prices offset the decline in the cod
and haddock catch. But by 1984 fish landings
in New Bedford were clearly declining, and the
price increases weren't enough to offset the
decline in the catch. High retail prices were
driving consumers toward other products.

This time the fishermen turned on each
other. The Seafarers International Union
(which recently won an election over the
Teamsters) represented the fishermen. They
called a strike against the boat owners, who
were pushing for a larger share of the value of
the catch in contract talks. For many boats,
especially the Portuguese boats, the strike put
the owner (often the captain) on the opposite
side of relatives and close friends who formed
the crew.

Many boats left the port during the
strike, usually landing their catch at other
ports, and the strike essentially closed New
Bedford as a fishing port for two months. But
the strike split the Portuguese fishing community, and, in the end, the union could not
maintain its position. The crews were forced
to settle for a lower percentage, and many
boats left the union.

Joseph D. Thomas photographs

Hard Times

In the late 1980s landings of groundfish and scallops increased in New Bedford, but it was a false bloom. Between 1990 and 1994 landings fell by 40 percent. The value of landings (which usually rose, even when landings fell) plummeted. Fishermen were turning to less valued species including skate and dogfish, called "underutilized" by scientists and "trash fish" by fishermen, because flounder and scallops were increasingly hard to find. They suddenly looked more appealing to consumers, especially in Europe where fish prices were very high. They also began to look good to hurting fishermen and boat owners. Monkfish, an ugly but high-priced fish long popular in Europe, became a highliner in the port, ranking above flounders and second in value to scallops.

In 1995 the National Marine Fishery Service, charged by Congress to manage fish stocks, restricted days at sea to reduce pressure on depleted groundfish and scallop stocks. By 1997 draggers and scallopers were limited to 120 and 142 days fishing per year, respectively, about half the days they fished before restrictions. The fishery service also closed about 6,500 square miles of Georges Bank to fishermen.

These restrictions may cause recovery of the fish stocks, but they may not. Scientific predictions about fish stocks are far from precise. Other changes may have caused these stocks to decline more than overfishing. Global warming may be driving sea temperatures above the limits tolerated by groundfish and scallops, and pollution from large coastal populations may counter any recovery resulting from restricted fishing.

Whatever the future holds for the fish stocks, the current fishing industry is far from healthy. Many boat owners and fishermen are leaving the docks. The federal government buy-back program, initiated by the fishery service to take boats and fishermen out of the fishery, has also claimed many boats from New Bedford.

The Portuguese fishermen and their families who set out from New Bedford's docks for generations, however, are here to stay through good times and bad. Portuguese has become the language of the docks, at least on the New Bedford side of the harbor. Many immigrants return to their home countries eventually. But the Portuguese fisherman and his family are not about to go. They are a continuing presence here. Even in these difficult times Portuguese boat owners still send back to Portugal for crews. Portuguese fishing families have reached the critical mass necessary for the community to continue and flourish. As Rodney Avila states, they know about hard times and will survive.

The Portuguese will stick it out. They didn't go for the fancy boats with the microwaves and VCRs. They bought basic fishing boats. And now these boats are all paid for. There are no loans, no big mortgages.

But it all comes down to family values and family ties. For us, fishing is not just a job. It's a way of life, and we enjoy that way of life.

The sea still connects Portugal to her children, wherever they are. In December 1996 Nicole Avila, great-great-great granddaughter of Manuel Avila, threw a bottle with a note in it into Buzzards Bay as part of a class project for the Potter School in South Dartmouth. Six months later, a retired fisherman and his grandson were collecting seaweed on the shore of São Miguel in the Azores. They spotted the bottle washed up on the beach and mailed the note back to the Avilas in America.

The stern trawler West Wind *tows her trawl on the southeast part of Georges Bank, 1979.*

Joseph D. Thomas photograph

211

THE PROVINCETOWN FISHERMAN

INTERVIEW WITH CAPT. FRANK PARSONS

REPRINTED FROM *SPINNER*, VOLUME III

You know this place they call Georges Bank? God made this place, way back. The fish come from God knows where—from the eastern waters, from the deep waters of around the western bank, from Nova Scotia. That fish comes there every spring, just like clockwork.

When I was a young man out there, I would set five lines, 250 hooks and fill a dory with cod in no time. We used to put a little eye washer on the end of a trawl, set out the lines and then set the anchor. That dory would be flying around in the current. If I went right on the fish, I floated. In the spring, when we'd get the male fish, they'd be throwing out the milt and the female would be throwing out the spawn. When you bailed, you'd bail out the spawn and milt together. The bottom of the bank in that area is as fine as fine could be—fine, fine sand. When the fish is loaded with roe and loaded with milt, right on the bottom, you get there and you can see the gray of the bottom. With the weight of the roe and the milt, the fish are so heavy they can hardly swim. That is how you get so many fish that time of year.

I went in ships when they were called "wooden ships and iron men." Those days were tough days. We put in enormous hours. Everything was done with the power of arms. We had to bail water with a bucket. We had a big tub to wash the fish in. We had to hoist the sail by arms to get underway. There was no power until right after the First World War. We started to get a donkey engine into the stern to hoist the fish out. We used a gasoline-run winch to hoist the fish out and the sails up. Many a time my hands were so sore I couldn't close them. In fact, my fingers are flat on the end from using the heads on the trawl.

Handlining from the Gasela Primera, *the vessel that Frank Parsons' father and father-in-law fished from when their dory was lost at sea in 1903.*

Courtesy of Frank Parsons

My father, grandfather and great-grandfather were all fishermen. We came from the southern part of Portugal, Algarve. My father used to go to the Grand Banks and he got lost a couple of times. Once he was picked up by a French steamer and they took him back to London. He came back to Portugal and went the following year again, this time with my wife's father. They were on the vessel *Gazela Primera,* which is now in a museum in Philadelphia.

Another year he went out and got astray and a Canadian vessel took them up. They didn't fish with them but they helped the captain split fish on the deck and stuff like that until they went to St. Johns, Newfoundland. The American consul there was told by the captain that they were Americans off an American vessel. That's how my dad and my (future) father-in-law got to New England. It wasn't planned but he came here because there were already people from our part of the country here. He planned to stay until he could get money to go back home and return with his family.

My father's sisters didn't want my mother to leave Portugal until my father returned, but my mother said, "No, my husband's over there. My place is to be with him, not here." So she took all her belongings and sold them, peddled them out and turned them into money, and she bought her passage to come to America. They didn't stop foreigners then. Everything was open for immigrants.

We left when I was four, and I remember we went by way of Gibraltar. It took us two weeks from Gibraltar to Boston. When we got to Boston, we were guided to where my father was in Provincetown by this family from the same town my mother came from. I remember the time I went down to the dock, with my brother by the hand, to see my father. He couldn't believe we were all in this country. It was quite a surprise. It had been two years.

When I was a kid, I worked the freezer in a cannery in Provincetown. I used to can blue mackerel and herring, cut the heads off and fill a box. When a box was filled, it was put in a tank. Every time you went there, the foreman would give you a tag that was worth ten cents. That was piecework. The faster you worked, the more you

made. We also pickled herring with vinegar and sugar—kippered herring. They put them in jars now instead of barrels. We also split mackerel and put them in barrels. I was about 10 or 12 years old then; that was in the summertime.

I was brought up in Provincetown. I went to grammar school but I quit when I was 14 and went fishing with my dad. I used to go out with him on weekends. When he first came to this country, my father went to the Banks from September to April for $250. In the last two years he went, he would get so much in pay for every fish he caught. The generation growing up today don't realize what people before them went through, you know, when you figure you hadda work a whole week to make $15 to $20. I worked hard when I went fishing and didn't rest too much. I made up my mind I was gonna be successful.

My father decided to go down to Manset, Maine and we went trawling out of Southwest Harbor to Frenchman's Bay. I got up when my father called me at 1AM and we'd go out and set trawls, you know, long lines. We hooked tubs, 50 hooks on each line, 10 lines in a tub and four tubs, which means 2,000 hooks to bait. We'd have to bait it and let it go out and set it. For bait, we'd use either a squid or a mackerel or a herring. See, mainly we'd try to set the trawls at night, before daylight, because you get more hake. You have to

Portuguese dory fisherman out of Provincetown handlining in Cape Cod Bay, 1942.

John Collier photograph, Library of Congress

have a night set on them because the hake is a very funny fish. It will bite better at night than it will during the daytime. I fished there for three years with my dad. Just him and me, that's all. We'd get in in the afternoon, take the fish out and get 75 cents a hundred pounds for them. That's how they paid for hake, because they'd split and salt them down there.

In the early days, 1916-1917, when I was still in Provincetown, we shipped everything out from there. We didn't go by boat to New York. All my fish used to go to New York by truck. We used to come in at two o'clock, catch the express, and put it on the train which took it to market the next day. We had a dock there, and the train would back right down to the wharf.

When the boats came in, they'd pack the fish in 200-pound barrels, not even in boxes. They trucked the barrels into the freight cars and put tags on for the company they were going to. There weren't too many boats running to New York then. The boats from New Bedford started steaming there in the 1920s. They weren't landing much there till then. The Portland and Gloucester boats sold their product in Boston.

Parsons' boat Frances & Marion, *fitting-out for a trip, Provincetown, 1942.*

In the late '20s, I bought my first dragger, the *Arthur and Matthew*, a 60-foot dragger, and I had it until 1937. About that time, the scallop business came to southern New England from Maine, and the scallopers started landing on the Cape and in New Bedford. That was in the '20s and '30s. When we found a big run of scallops off of Provincetown, the fellas from Maine commenced to come here. They went down to Pollock Rip and went to the shoals. They kept finding new grounds. The boats from Maine, they were the great scallopers. They're the ones who opened the eyes of the guys around here.

In the thirties, a lot of Newfoundlanders were around Boston, East Boston, and south of Boston, and some of the guys could see that there was a better living (in southern New England) with less hardships than there was in longlining. They were on beam trawlers owned by the Atlantic Coast Fisheries, General Seafoods, and the Bay State Beam Trawlers. When they got too big, when they got above their heads, they all started falling out. They couldn't take out those boats, couldn't take care of the fish. No proper protection of quality. You get a bad product, send it out through the company, and you can't sell it right. I used to see fishermen in Boston… I don't know how they had the guts to put that fish on the market.

I went on one of those vessels one time. We got 65,000 pounds of haddock, but when the Boston company took out half the fish, we got a $1.50 for it, one-and-a-half cents a pound! We couldn't sell the rest of it, so we had to sail from Boston to Gloucester, to the smokehouse. We got seventy-five cents a hundred pounds for the rest. When we left Gloucester for Provincetown, the captain said, "We didn't make enough money for a settlement, but I'm going to give the crew $15 each for the trip. Next week we'll probably make it up." My hands were so damn sore from working!

In 1937, Danny Mullins got together with a man named Kurtz from New York, and they approached me. "We'd like you to become partners with us and start a business in New Bedford," they said. Well, at that time there was only Goulart here. There was line fishing and quahogging and some swordfishing, but most of the boats were running to New York from the grounds, unload and come back.

We put a platform out on the wharf and a catwalk and put a pillar at the other end of it so two boats could be unloaded at the same time. We started buying from the middle-sized boats, the 60- to 65-footers. They came into New Bedford every week on a Saturday or Sunday to unload. They'd go to Eldridge's, then come to me, and then to Goulart's until they'd get the final price. Sometimes it would take two or three hours before you'd come to a final price. We thought about establishing a place to buy, but no one looked into it until right around 1945 or 1946. That's when we started buying fish in an auction.

We used to sell to the A & P. They bought a lot of flounder and yellowtail, and they used to process them right in the yard. There was a big demand for flatfish, but there was no place that processed flatfish like we did. We had the people in New Bedford who started it and built it up, you know; for the A & P and the First National Food markets.

Back then it was a better life, a better living. What we have here today is just like Boston years ago. That's buying power. I remember going to Boston when I was a young man and millions and millions of pounds of fish were handled on the pier. Look at it today! You been there? Seen what it's like? That pier at one time had many stores handling thousands and thousands of pounds of different kinds of fish—mackerel, whiting, cod, haddock, sunfish. You name it, they handled it.

I think the whole secret of this whole, vital industry today is to get a bigger mesh, the cod ends, so the baby fish can escape the nets. Then we'll always have fish to catch. Years and years ago the old-timers told me, "Hooks never destroy the grounds, but with nets you will destroy the grounds." And they're right! They told me this fifty years ago when I was trawling.

If you use the mesh they use now, maybe two-inch mesh, nothing gets out of it. These fellas from down south, they're going for butterfish and catching it at five hundred-fifty count to a hundred pounds. They've got these small-mesh nets, almost like shrimp nets. Well, if they would use a three-and-a-half-inch or a four-inch mesh at the cod end, they'd just get the good ones and let the small ones go out. If you get a lot of scrod in the boat, that guy's got a sleeve in his net, in his cod end.

When the foreigners were here, the Russians and the Spanish and all, they cleaned up with the small mesh so there was nothing left. Not even a sculpin's left because everything was ground into fish meal. Sometimes our boats would go out off Georges Bank, back in the bay there to Stellwagen Bank, and not even get a bow of

haddock on the trip. With a small mesh they're hooked. They can't get out of there, even the bottom can't get out.

Three years ago the butterfish were two hundred to three hundred count. Now they get five hundred count. What's the asset? They get the fish too fast and they aren't letting the little ones go. Then it goes to those aquariums where they sell it for feed. Hey, we bring in half a million pounds of fish a day, and yes, it may increase, just as long as they're using the big cod ends. When I see a boat come in here and he's got small fish, I know the guy's using sleeving. I know. I'll tell him right to his face because I'm an ex-fisherman and know all about it. You hurt the grounds if you don't let the fish grow, if you don't have any young ones. We started closing that area, and after the fourth year of using big mesh, the spawning area returned on that end of the bank.

We have a lot of Portuguese fishermen here now. It's changed from Norwegians and Newfoundlanders to Portuguese. They have produced a lot of fish and they're doing very well. Some of these fellas have gone out with a small boat, then in a couple of years bought a little bigger one, and now they've got highly placed boats. You can see they're conscientious guys. They're hard working. They save what they can save and they invest it in something, and that's the fishing. Give them progress. That's the progress for this city.

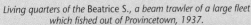

Living quarters of the Beatrice S., *a beam trawler of a large fleet which fished out of Provincetown, 1937.*

Edwin Rosskam photograph, Library of Congress

Azoreans in American Whaling

By Mary Silvia Vermette

The Bridge of Whaleships

Azorean whalemen made up the first phase of Portuguese immigration to the United States. From the 1750s to the 1920s, American whaleships left New Bedford to search for sperm whales in the Western Island Grounds, using the Azores as a first port of call. Here, whaling vessels could stop for fresh water and provisions as well as additional crew. Hard working Azorean men and boys took lowly jobs aboard the whalers for rock-bottom wages, but many regarded their time at sea as a passport to the United States. Jumping ship in New Bedford, many found shore work and eventually married local women. A section of New Bedford's south end was called Little Faial, and South Front Street was referred to as *Rua do Faial*.

The Portuguese government did not like its citizens leaving aboard foreign ships, especially those who had not yet served in the military. For the Azoreans, however, it was a flight from poverty, isolation and military conscription, and the government was unable to stop it.

Most of the Azorean whalemen were from Faial, followed by Flores and Pico, São Jorge and Graciosa.

The Azoreans engaged in low-tech whaling long before they joined the larger, high-tech American ships. Spotting whales from shore, they set out in small boats, seven men to a boat, and used only lances and harpoons. After the kill they dragged the whales in and melted them down in small shoreside factories. In contrast, New Bedford whalers were manned by 35 to 40 men, and the whales were processed on board.

New Bedford's population went from 3,313 in 1790 to 33,293 in 1885, in part reflecting the presence of these Portuguese newcomers. The whaling industry reached its highest point in 1857 with a fleet of 329 ships, whaling outfits worth more than $12 million and 10,000 seamen of many nationalities. Though the Azoreans began as lowly crewmen and "green hands" on these long journeys at sea, in the final era of whaling they became the dominant force as masters, officers and owners of whaleships.

From the early 19th century through the 1880s, the Faial-Boston packet trade carried passengers and cargo to and from Boston and New Bedford. Cargoes consisted of oranges, island wines, and at certain times of the year, thousands of barrels of whale oil.

Tracking Down the Azorean Whaleman

New Bedford's rich history of whaling is contained in documents in the New Bedford Whaling Museum, the New Bedford Free Public Library, in local directories and town records. Another good source is the book, *They Ploughed the Seas: Profiles of Azorean Master Mariners*, by Pat Amaral. The Whaling Museum houses a collection of over 1,000 whaling logbooks and all extant copies of crew lists belonging to the New Bedford Port Society from 1832 to 1925. The museum is also home to an enormous collection of *Whalemen's Shipping List*, and *Merchants' Transcript*, the whaling newspaper published since 1843. It is sometimes difficult to single out all the Azoreans because some adopted English surnames as part of the naturalization process.

The earliest documented presence of Azoreans on American whaleships is found in material at the New Bedford Free Public Library. The crew lists of whaleships record over 800 ships and 4,000 departures from the New Bedford Custom House District from 1807 to 1925. They include Emanuel Joseph, mariner, sailing from Pico, arriving in New Bedford, height 5 feet 6 inches, dark complexion, age 17, aboard the ship *Sally* of New Bedford, with Capt. Obed Clark, date of whaling voyage July 29, 1808. Another (from the National Archives microfilm collection at the library) is Joseph Rose, seamen, Flores, Nantucket, 5 feet 11 inches, dark, age 17 .

The marriage records of New Bedford also provide insight and information. On Oct. 7, 1834. Joseph (Silvia), New Bedford, and Miss Sarah Cheedle {int. Chedell} of Providence, RI. On November 30, 1843 Joseph (Silvia), New Bedford {int. Fairhaven}, and Mary Ann Hammond of New Bedford.

Distinguished Captains and Merchants

Frederic Joseph (1817-85) of Faial, master of the bark *Peri*, appears to have been the earliest captain born in the Azores.

Joseph Vera (1816-76) became one of the most prominent Azoreans to establish himself in New Bedford. Originally from Pico, he came to the United States as a youth, probably on a whaleship, and operated a ship's chandlery at 113 South Water Street. His first wife, Ann Rose Donahue, was Irish, and they

may have met at St. Mary's Church, the only Catholic church in New Bedford before the Civil War.

Manuel Costa (1849-1914), a native of Faial, left home at 13 to begin a 47-year career in American whaling. At 31, he commanded his first vessel, the *Eleanor B. Conwell*, and sailed on the first of four voyages as master. He was captain on seven more voyages on other vessels. His wife, Philomena Nunes Costa, sometimes accompanied her husband and wrote 44 stanzas of verse on her experiences including this one: Lá estão os pobres pais/Os pobres pais a esperar/Para que eles a vão ver/Só para os consolar. (There are their poor parents/Their poor parents waiting/for them to visit/and console them.)

Henry Clay (1836-1901), who was born in Flores as Acquilla Rodrigues, shipped out at the age of 14. Taking on the name Henry Clay, he worked his way up to the position of master, first of the brig *Star Castle*, then of the barks *Cicero* and *Seine*, and finally of the schooner *Golden City*. At St. Eustacia in the Dutch West Indies, Clay met Alice Avery, his future wife. After they married her brother James later joined the couple in New Bedford and become associated with Clay in the whaling firm of Henry Clay & Company. Henry Clay (Antone Silvia) became one of the largest owners and investors in whaleships during the final decades of New Bedford whaling.

With the Charles W. Morgan *on the ways in Fairhaven in early summer, 1918, Antonio C. Corvello, James A. Cook and James A. Tilton (left to right) may be discussing the price of oil as they walk along the wharf. Corvello had recently arrived as captain of the bark* Greyhound. *James A. Cook, a retired sea captain, was the agent for the* Morgan *and owner of the* Greyhound. *Captain Tilton was semiretired.*

Arthur Packard photograph, courtesy of T.M. Holcombe

Antone L. Silvia (or Sylvia) (1840-1920) arrived in the United States at 15 and found work in the outfitting shop of Joseph Frazier, one of New Bedford's first Azorean whaling merchants. After Frazier's death Silvia married his widow and became stepfather to the Frazier children, including Edward, who was to become a whaling master. As a merchant Silvia operated a large outfitting store and invested in numerous vessels including the *Veronica*, built for packet trade with the Azores. The *Veronica* carried supplies and mail to the whaling fleet and general merchandise to the islanders. On her return she brought immigrants, whale oil and island products. When the *Veronica* was wrecked in a gale, Silvia and others acquired the larger *Moses B. Tower* to maintain the link between New Bedford and the Azores. Silvia also served as a director of the Union Street Railway, the Pairpoint Company, and Monte Pio, the Portuguese Benevolent Society. His success demonstrated the opportunities available to young immigrants with abilities and determination.

Captain Antonio C. Corvello with his wife, child and crewman on the deck of the Wanderer, circa 1918.

Mr. Silvia and his wife are memorialized by two huge stained glass windows in St. John's Church in New Bedford. The bark *Veronica's* eagle figurehead is on permanent display at the New Bedford Whaling Museum. The men who climbed the ranks to become captains, outfitters and owners also donated stained glass windows to Our Lady of Mt. Carmel Church.

Nicolas R. Vieira (1856-1913) was born in Flores and came to the U.S. in his 20s. At 45, Captain Vieira took his own command and made three highly successful voyages. On his next voyage, as master of the bark *Bertha*, Capt. Vieira became ill and left the vessel in Faial with his son Joseph, the fourth mate, in charge. He recovered from his illness but never returned to sea. An impressive monument, embellished by a sculptured anchor, marks his grave in St. John's Cemetery, where many Azorean captains are buried.

The "bridge" between the Azores and America was reinforced over the years, especially when the art of photography came

Arthur Packard photograph, courtesy of T.M. Holcombe

218

into vogue. The brothers, Manuel and José Goulart, from Faial, were talented photographers who captured "people and place" on both sides of the ocean. Manuel left the Azores for New Bedford in 1889 and eventually set up his own studio on South Sixth Street. José set up shop in Horta, Faial. The brothers, who had similar styles, specialized in portrait photography. For 40 years Manuel produced portraits of countless Azoreans and other New Bedford residents. José photographed island life and American whaleships in port, including the well-known "Horta Harbor," where 11 American whaleships are pictured at anchor.

António C. Corvello (1879-1920) of Flores is one of the most well-known captains photographed by José Goulart. At 15 he set sail for New Bedford and rose through the ranks. He captained the bark *Greyhound* on three voyages, the latter especially perilous because the U.S. was involved in World War I and German submarines were cruising the Atlantic.

Capt. Corvello was also photographed with his good friend Capt. Manuel F. Santos (1869-1919) and their wives. Capt. Santos, born on Corvo, embarked for New Bedford as a 14-year-old cabin boy and rose through the ranks to serve as captain on seven voyages. Perhaps finding it hard to retire from the sea, Capt. Santos decided to accompany Captain George L. Dunham as an aide on the schooner *Ellen A. Swift*. The vessel departed New Bedford on January 14, 1919, and was never heard from again.

Notable Families

On land and sea, Portuguese fathers, sons, uncles, nephews and cousins all participated in the whaling industry. Nearly every captain had a relative who was part of the crew. Two Azorean families became locally famous: the Edwards and the Mandlys.

Joseph T. Edwards (1856-1913) left his native Flores at 16 on the bark *A.R. Tucker* of New Bedford, thus beginning a long, successful career as a mariner, first on merchant vessels, then on whalers. He enjoyed teaching navigation to the young men who sailed with him. Some of his friends referred to the *Greyhound*, which he captained, as the school ship.

Three nephews of Joseph T. Edwards, Antone, John, and Joseph, also became well-known whaling masters. The four Edwards completed 25 voyages as masters of New Bedford whaleships from 1887 to 1927.

Capt. Joseph T. Edwards had a dramatic near-death encounter on St. Kitts when he had a cataleptic seizure following rheumatic fever. For 30 hours he was laid out for dead. Everyone but his wife, who had accompanied him, thought he was dead. She fought the regulations, which prohibited the keeping of a dead body overnight in the tropics, and persuaded authorities to relent for one day. Captain Edwards, not able to move a muscle, was perfectly aware of what was going on and later described his ordeal as an extremely fearful one. The next day, when even his wife had nearly lost hope, a priest, called aboard to administer the last rites, noticed beads of perspiration on the captain's forehead. The physician, who previously pronounced him dead, soon had him on the road to recovery.

His nephew Antone (1882-1936) became the youngest master in the whaling fleet at that time and first took command when his uncle became ill. He left the *Greyhound* in 1905 and eventually became master of the bark *Wanderer*. Between 1913 and 1922, Capt. Edwards made six voyages in the *Wanderer*, taking in 12,800 barrels of sperm oil worth $168,674. This was the return for ten years of work when the average annual earnings for nonfarm laborers in America averaged $1,500.

Group of whaling masters shmooze it up at a clamboil on the deck of the Wanderer. *Among the group are the Edwards brothers, Captains Antone T. (right of center with light gray suit and hat in hand), Joseph F. (far left, first row with hat off), and John T. (behind Joseph).*

Courtesy of Edwards family

Captain Joseph F. Edwards (right) took his first command on the famous bark Charles W. Morgan.

Captain Antone T. Edwards was a prominent, well-respected man and master of the *Wanderer* on the day it was wrecked on Sow and Pigs Reef off Cuttyhunk in 1924. It is said he wept when he saw his ship crushed on the rocks by the storm as it rode at anchor. This day marked the end of the long history of square-rigged whaleships sailing from American ports.

Captain Antone's two brothers also had significant careers as whaling masters. Capt. John T. Edwards (1884-1957) was captain of the *Cameo* (1912) and *A.V.S. Woodruff*. He later became a merchant marine graduate and first officer on the *SS Coldbrook*. During World War II, he was a lieutenant in the Navy assigned to the *USS Curtis*, which was anchored in Honolulu during the attack on Pearl Harbor.

The youngest of the brothers, Joseph F. Edwards (1886-1933), traveled west as a young man to try his hand at ranching, then returned east to work at Morse Twist Drill and Machine Company in New Bedford. Eventually he became a master at sea and took his first command on the famous bark *Charles W. Morgan*. After he retired, he worked as a custodian of the half-scale model of whaler *Lagoda* at the New Bedford Whaling Museum.

Three members of the Mandly family commanded more whaling voyages than any other family group in the history of American whaling. From 1876 to 1925 the Mandlys (originally Mendonça) made 52 voyages as captains.

Courtesy of Edwards family

Henry Mandly, Sr. was born on Graciosa, Azores, and shipped out at 15 as a cabin boy on the bark *Bartholomew Gosnold*, bound for the Arctic. Two years later, at San Francisco, he left ship for the gold fields but had no success. He returned to New Bedford and eventually served as captain of the *Mary E. Simmons* through 12 voyages. A respected whaling masters of his time, he was known along the waterfront for hiring a crew of Filipinos. They were a model crew, and, it is said, they eventually became officers aboard whaling vessels. After his retirement he became a director and stockholder of the Luso Corporation of America. White-bearded and mustachioed, the captain was said to have made an impressive sight along the streets of New Bedford, "walking as if he still felt the deck of a ship rolling under his feet and carrying an ivory-fisted cane carved from the tooth of a sperm whale." He lived well into his nineties and is buried in St. John's Cemetery.

The schooner *John R. Manta* was a significant ship in respect to Azorean captains. The ship made 19 whaling voyages, 18 of which were commanded by masters of Azorean birth—Joseph T. Edwards (Flores); António J. Mandly (Faial); Frank J. Garcia (Faial); Henry Mandly, Sr. (Graciosa); Joseph Luis (Faial) and Manuel F. Santos (Corvo).

Charles W. Morgan, full sail on the high seas. On the historic whaling ship's last voyage (October 1919 to July 1920), she was commanded by Captain Joseph F. Edwards. This photograph was taken from one of the whaleboats by William Tripp, head of the New Bedford Whaling Museum, who sailed on that voyage.

Courtesy of Edwards family

Antonio J. Mandly made ten voyages on the *John R. Manta* to the Atlantic whaling grounds between 1915 and 1925. Born in Faial, Mandly shipped out when he was only 11. His first command on the *Franklin* out of New Bedford was filled with mishaps until he came upon a large amount of ambergris worth $14,000. He made 28 voyages in a distinguished career at sea. His final trip on the *Manta* in 1925 was the last successful voyage made by a whaling captain out of New Bedford.

Capt. Henry Mandly Jr. was born in 1879 in Provincetown. As a youngster he accompanied his father on whaling cruises and learned the trade. During a voyage on the *Margarett*, Capt. Mandly had to perform surgical duties, cutting a harpoon out of the foot of his boatsteerer where the whale's flukes had driven it. Mandly himself was suffering from a tropical fever but managed to complete the operation, and both fully recovered. Whaling masters had to perform many unusual duties. On this same voyage Capt. Mandly had a pet pig, Betty, which performed tricks for the shore crowd that greeted the ship upon arrival.

Capt. Mandly became a hero at sea when he and the crew of the *Valkyria* responded to a distress call and rescued a 12-man crew from the burning freighter *Roy H. Beattie*. This was his last voyage as captain of a whaleship.

When Capt. Mandly retired from the sea, he operated the area's first car rental shop, which flourished until the mid-1930s. However, his absence from the sea was short-lived. The Woods Hole Oceanographic Institute of Cape Cod was looking for mariners to man its research vessel *Atlantis*, the largest ketch in the world. Henry Mandly signed on as second mate, a position he held from 1934 to 1945. When World War II broke out the *Atlantis* was in the Caribbean. Fearful for her safety, the Institute ordered her to Lake Charles, Louisiana, where she spent her war years. Second Officer Mandly stayed with the ship until she returned to home port.

Borges de Freitas Henriques, an Azorean whaler and native of Flores, eventually became Consul of Portugal in Boston, a post he held from 1867 until his death in 1873. In order to make Boston more familiar with the Azores and the large number of Azoreans living there, he authored several articles in the *North End*

The three Captain Mandlys (left to right), Henry Jr., Henry Sr. and Antonio J., commanded more whaling voyages than any other family group in the history of American whaling. From 1876 to 1925 the Mandlys (originally Mendonça) made 52 voyages as captains.

Mission Magazine as well as a book entitled *A Trip to the Azores, or Western Islands.*

The Azorean captains whose stories are told here form only a partial list of the many men who became masters and owners of whaling vessels. Scores of others were mates and boatsteerers, and hundreds served as crewmen. The exact number may never be known because of the loss of the crew lists. In the last two decades of the whaling era, the Azorean owners, masters, mates and crewmen were a commanding force on the whaleships.

Very little was written by the whaleman themselves. In addition to Philomena Nunes Costa's unpublished verses of a whaling voyage, Manuel T. Lopes wrote a long poem entitled, *A Vida Dos Marinheiros (The Life of the Whaleman)*. The poem recounts the adventures of three men from Flores who fled on a New Bedford whaler to avoid the army. Joining them was a fourth man from Corvo, Manuel Francisco Santos, who later became a master of New Bedford whaleships. The second verse of the poems emphasizes one of the main reasons why Azoreans left on whaleships at an early age:

Tinha 16 anos de idade / Um moco bem educado
Fugi a minha mae / Para nao ir para soldado.
I was 16 years old / And a well-mannered lad
I left my mother, so as / Not to become a soldier.

Mary T. Silvia Vermette received her Ph.D. from Harvard University in Romance Languages and Literatures. At UMass Dartmouth, she directed the master's degree bilingual program and, for 17 years, was staff associate for the Center for the Portuguese Speaking World (now the Center for Portuguese Studies and Culture). She has been visiting curator for three exhibits at the Whaling Museum, including the Azorean whaling exhibit.

Luzo Whalemen

Interviews with Alberto Cordeiro, José C. Pinheiro and José P. Ávila

by Eva Cordeiro

Alberto Cordeiro was born in 1928 in the village of Capelas, São Miguel. His father was a fisherman and a whaleman. Following in his father's steps, Alberto, at 16, was already catching whales in the Azorean waters. He was a harpooner and is still disturbed by it.

. . . .

My father prepared me to be a fisherman and a whaleman. I remember him saying, "Son, you are a very courageous young man. In life, you are going to face many challenges, and nothing better prepares you than being a whaleman. In this job you prove you are a real man." To be a man was real important for my father. He wanted his sons to act like men, no matter what it took.

Whaling was a fight, heroic and difficult, a fight between a man and a whale. It was a pilgrimage without a definite return, the hardest job I ever had in my life. We never had a fixed schedule. Nights and days we had to go out to catch the whale. I knew I could face that enormous creature. To make the throw, I concentrated on the target and threw the lance with no pity. Using this concentration trick, I triumphed over the animal. The use of hand-thrown harpoons and lances made our lives primitive and deadly-dangerous.

We hunted whales in small open boats without power, only oars and paddles, no advanced technology. We had to count on our strength and willingness to kill, and speed and ease was vital. When I heard the alarm, *"Baleia, Baleia à vista,"* my heart pumped hard. It was one more day not knowing if I was going to return home, a poignant time for all of us. In Capelas, we had a house called *A Casa dos Baleeiros* with a phone. We would receive a call saying they had seen whales and we should get ready.

Whaling is extremely cruel. Some of the whales take up to a half-hour to die. The biggest one we caught was 22 meters. We were only allowed to kill whales of 8.8 meters and above. With only seven in the boat, the strength and courage of everyone in the crew is extremely important. Our bravery and humanity distinguished us but, during this time, we were also broke financially and spiritually.

I still remember the scene: An enraged sperm whale shatters our whaleboat with its flukes, and the mate of another boat prepares to drive his lance into the whale's lungs. We hope he is able to kill that whale. If not, she will attack us and there is no refuge. Oh, thank God, he did it. The struggle to survive… triumph. One day, a whale flipped our

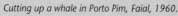

Cutting up a whale in Porto Pim, Faial, 1960.

Spinner Collection

boat and two of my friends lost their lives. One disappeared in the ocean; the other got tangled in the rope. Everyone yelled for a knife to cut the line. We pulled it in and were devastated to see our friend already dead.

On other occasions we saved each other's lives. Once I saved the life of my best friend when his boat flipped; I rapidly got to him before the whale came. These fatal accidents are the biggest drawbacks of whaling. Many of my friends lost their lives on the ocean, without having a chance to say goodbye to their families. This was unforgivable and unforgettable. One time the whale bit the bottom of my boat and lifted it three times in the air with the crew inside. That day, I said to myself, "This is it. I am going to die today." Some jumped in the water on the first lift. I just stood with another man. The third time I screamed, "Jump. She is going to kill us." When the whale saw no more men in the boat, she went away. As incredible as it may sound, I felt pity for that animal. I realized the whale was only defending herself, showing us she was more powerful than we were, and we should be careful with her.

But the whales were not the only resistance we had to fight against. We also had to confront the weather, when tornadoes and strong winds attacked. We had to use our strength to get back to land as soon as possible. Sometimes we were far from our villages and had to stay days out, without having an opportunity to tell our wives. I imagine how the wives were feeling, seeing the bad weather and knowing their husbands were on the ocean. Whaling was not only difficult for men but also for women. Many times they had to replace the father figure at home, and that was not easy.

After the arduous catch, the men still had to work in the factory melting the whale, which is drawn slowly up the stones and lubricated with the fat and blood. I lost half my finger pushing the whale to land when the metal instrument went through it. Oh! It was painful. It got infected and had to be cut off. I always tell my family my finger is a physical way of remembering my whaling days.

Azoreans are devoted to their large extended families. Even though my father was whaling, I was never in the same boat as him. I think it was a way of preventing pain in case something fatal happened. I was never afraid. No, I had to lose all the fear. If I didn't, I wouldn't be able to kill the animal, and I could cause my death. The ocean was my only job. It was the only thing I could do best. I

heard people talking about coming to the United States for whaling but I did not want to leave my family behind and it was a strange and different country. Who was going to take care of my offspring?

Alberto Cordeiro with granddaughter.

I was happy when I was transferred to Vila Franca do Campo because I did not have to go to the U.S. From Capelas, I lived in Vila Franca for three years. You can imagine how it is to move to a different town with a wife and two children. We lived in a house with other whalemen. After three years I moved back to Capelas and in 1959, I moved to Faial da Terra for three more years. By this time I was a father of three children. When I was out in the ocean, I didn't know what was happening to them. I only asked God to protect them. After so many years I moved to the United States. My coming here was not due to necessity. I came to provide the best education for my youngest daughter. I was certain that was the best gift I ever could give to her.

Were we searching for challenge and status in whaling? Absolutely not. My salary was very low. I still remember the amount—nine escudos and eighty. At the end of the year, we usually got a commission on the quantity of the oil sold. For each bucket, we used to get one escudo.

What do I recall the most about whaling? Death. I saw death so many times I am not scared of it anymore. I never saw whaling as a revenge. I killed whales in order to protect me and earn my living, not to revenge against her. The infinity of the ocean astonishes me. The ocean does not have a beginning, neither an ending. At the ocean, as incredible as it may sound, I relax, I enjoy, and the ocean is like a dairy for me. There I laugh, I cry, I talk to myself, there I put out all my agonies, and frustrations.

Alberto Cordeiro supported ten children as a fisherman and whaler. This interview was conducted by his daughter, Eva Cordeiro, a graduate of UMass Dartmouth.

José Cardoso Pinheiro, highliner

José Cardoso Pinheiro, 81, was born in Faial, Azores, and emigrated to the United States in 1959. Considered one of the best harpooners of the 20th century, Mr. Pinheiro is well-known to Azoreans throughout the world. He still dreams of his whaling days.

. . . .

My father was a farmer, but he had a passion for whaling. As soon he saw smoke in the air, he knew whales had been spotted and would find someone to take care of the farm while he went on his pilgrimage. I think I got the whaling passion from him. When I was 18, I started whaling and still recall the first time I went offshore. I went to the pier to help the whalers and suddenly heard a voice tell me to jump in the boat. I was astonished and I replied. "I cannot go."

The man then looked at me very seriously and said, "Why not?" I was only an inexperienced young boy. I had no idea how to go whaling. I did not have the license to go whaling. How was I going to tell him? Suddenly I said, "I don't have the license and I don't have the money to get one." My father had died recently and I was responsible for my mother and my brothers. I had to work to feed five people. There was no way I could take the money necessary for the license. Life in the Azores was not easy at all. The man, who was the captain of the boat, looked at me and said, "Here is 100 escudos for you to get your license." And soon I went to get what I always had dreamed about, my whaling license.

At 20, I was a harpooner. We'd go about 10 miles offshore in small *conoas* with seven men to a boat. After killing the whale, we towed them to factories along the pier by motorboat. Sometimes we'd bring up to 12 whales to the factories. In the early days, before we had factories, we used to drain all the fat by hand and put them in big pots.

José Cardoso Pinheiro

This was a hard job. We were already extremely fatigued from being on the ocean, and we had to work on the melting process.

Whaling is an extremely dangerous job and we never know if we are going to return home. The biggest whale we ever caught was one of 61 feet. Another time, I killed three whales on the same day. I rarely missed a shot and people started calling me the whale killer (*mata baleias*). I never felt pleasure for killing whales. I did it in order to feed my family. I was forced to kill those innocent animals. I will never be able to erase the death of a whale out of my mind. I remember like it was yesterday. I would kill a female whale and in seconds her babies would be surrounding her, saying goodbye for the last time. That shocked me. I felt pity and shame for being able to do something like that. The whale harms nobody and has the same reproduction cycle as humans, nine months, and only one baby at a time. When this strongest of animals dies, she lays there on the waters helplessly. When she turns belly-up, we definitely know she is dead.

We used special techniques to catch a whale. First, the whale sees by the side of his head so we cannot throw the harpoon to his side—only as the last resort. We must kill the whale by the head or the tail. The tail is safest. If we kill by the head, she could touch the boat with her tail, and it will automatically flip. I remember seeing a whaler die because he killed the whale by the head. She came against him and killed him in a few seconds.

Whaling was very competitive. One time we were catching whales and there were boats from

An American whaleboat from the Charles W. Morgan on the hunt. Azorean whaleboats, designed and built on Pico, had slight variations in style: they were narrower, faster and used seven crewmen instead of six.

another company. A harpooner threw the harpoon and the line broke. I got his line and tied it to my harpoon. The other man screamed, saying the whale was his, but the harpoon was mine so I got the credit for killing that enormous animal. The Azoreans are a religious people. Some whalers had images of all the saints on their boats in order to give them luck. The saints would return them home safe. Nothing disastrous will happen if God is with us.

The salary was very poor and we got paid once a year. I had to buy all my food at the market on credit, then pay when I received my salary. The first year, I earned 1500 escudos, not enough to support my family. I had to raise chickens and go fishing too. Even though the salary was very low, my son went to high school. At that time, high school was only for rich people, but I knew it was my son's dream. I rented some of the rooms in my house to people from other islands visiting in Faial. With this extra money, I paid for my son's schooling. I did not want my son to be a whaler. Whaling was good for those who had no other choice. I wanted my son to have many choices in life, not to be forced to do something like I was.

I stopped whaling when the volcano, Capelinhos, erupted in Faial, very close to the pier where we kept our whaling equipment. We lost everything. An Azorean wrote a book called, *The Whale that was a Volcano*. The whale spotters saw something coming out of the water and thought it was a whale. I remember that day. There was smoke coming out of the water. I could not see my house; it was full of black ashes. My family and I did not sleep at home for three days. What scared me most was the shaking of the island. There was nothing I could do to stop it. Boats were bringing people to the other islands. When the American Congress passed a law authorizing 2,000 Azoreans from Faial to come to the United States, I came with my family to this new land. In the beginning, I missed my home, my way of living. But I started working and getting used to the new life-style.

I would not return to the Azores today but the islands will always be in my heart. Life has changed there. My old friends have died, my children and grandchildren are in the United States. I have lived here now for 39 years.

What I miss most is whaling. I dream of all the happenings, the frustrations, sadness and happiness. Even though it was a very difficult and dangerous life, it was the best time of my life. I will die thinking of whaling; this is what I call a true whaler.

José P. Ávila, Whaling Factory Worker

José P. Ávila, 75, worked in a whaling factory in Pico from 1950-1960. He describes the brutal process of cutting up and melting down the whales, but his most heartfelt memory is the sad, devastated expression on the faces of the whalers when they had just lost a friend on the ocean. Today Mr. Ávila lives in New Bedford and, in his spare time, makes models of whaling crafts.

Pico whaleboat model by José P. Ávila

. . . .

The spotters, the harpooners and other crew are not the only members of the whaling industry. The factory workers like myself are part of this fabulous industry. We were the workers who anxiously waited for the whales to land. The process of melting required skill and adeptness, just as catching the whale did.

Sperm whales (now protected under the Endangered Species Conservation Act of 1969) took the lives of many Azorean whalers. I recall one particular incident in the Azores. Pico is very mountainous, and especially in winter, we have lots of heavy winds. Because of this terrible weather, a boat coming from Calheta do Pico was brought to Terceira by the winds and only one member survived. His name was Eduardo Azevedo, a friend.

The sperm whale is one of the most spectacular and amazing creatures on Earth. We Azoreans call the sperm whale "cachalote." These animals are enormous. The males average 15 to 19 meters, females are 11 to 12 meters. Males tend to weigh 45 to 70 tons; females 15 to 20 tons. It was extremely important for us to know all the parts and characteristics of the whale, because in the process of cutting and melting, we had to identify every part and melt all of the whaling components.

Most of the sperm whales were dark gray or brownish-gray in color and have white at the front of the head, the mouth and on the belly. They have 20 to 25 large teeth in the lower jaw and up to 10 curved teeth in the upper jaw. When we were processing the whale, we buried the jaw and, after a month, because of decay we could remove the teeth. The teeth did not belong to the whaling companies. They belonged to the whalers and were distributed among them. They could sell them at a very high price. The teeth were like gold. Their value was very high.

I still remember those days when the factories were closed, waiting for the sign from the whale spotters. I recall the image of the whalers sitting down at the cafes, near the ocean, socializing and waiting for that critical sign. As soon as they saw the gesture of the spotters, a flare shot in the sky, the whole town became agitated, with whalers running to their boats and their family members waving goodbye with tears coming down their sad and hopeless eyes.

This was a journey with no certain return. Many hearts were broken and many others were kept alive by a string. The uncertainty was probably the reason I chose to work at the factories instead of going offshore whaling. I went twice on whaling trips but did not like the life of a whaler. In the factories, I did not have to confront this enormous animal and risk my life.

The first boats were made in New Bedford and brought to the Azores. Later, an Azorean who resided in Massachusetts returned home and made a similar but better boat. It was bigger and wider. The American boat took six whalers, the Pico boat took seven. While the whalers were offshore, the workers at the factories were getting everything prepared for the arrival of the whales. All we asked God was to bring our whalers back home alive. There was nothing that would pay for the loss of a dear friend.

Pico, the most active island in the Azores in the processing of whales, had three whaling factories, and they could process up to seven whales at once, whereas Faial had to bring them up one by one. These whaling factories were private and the government would oversee the operations. An official was there 24 hours a day to measure the oil we had to pay taxes on.

Pico and Faial were partners in the whaling industry. The oil was divided in half between these two islands, but each island could sell its oil for the price they wished, and the money was theirs. The striking fact is

Cutting and processing on Faial, 1960s.

that the factory workers got paid once a month whereas the whalers, who were risking their lives, were paid once a year. The whalers had to wait for the selling of the oil; that's where their money came from, like a commission. For each liter of oil sold, the whalers got a percentage. The meat and the bones were the property of the whaling factory. By selling these products, the factory paid us.

According to B. Venables in *Baleia! Baleia!*:

When the men were out, the village was in complete silence. Women were lighting candles, imploring their saints to protect the whalers from that enormous animal. But upon the arrival of the whalers, the village was again in feast, with agitation and a lot of work for everyone to do. At the harbor, there were the workers anxious to work and the family members praying to see their loved ones alive. Then the whales, one by one, were drawn slowly up the stones, lubricated with their fat and blood.

Cutting a whale on Faial, 1960s. According to José Ávila, Faial did not have the capabilities of Pico, where there were four factories and several whales could be processed at once.

Everything except the melting process was done outdoors, by hand, at the platform near the ocean. The first thing we did was cut off was the head. Sperm whales' heads seem to be square and take up at least one-third of the body. A cutting-spade would sunder the head from the trunk. Even today I shake just remembering that spade cutting the mouth of the whale. After the head was cut off, we put it aside to a corner of the platform so that one man with a cutting spade could chop through the blubber and another with a blubber hook would drag it away.

Next we cut the tail off and divided it in two and put it aside. Then it was time for us to cut the trunk. This cut was perfectly done, almost surgically neat. We cut the side of the trunk from the beginning to the end with no pity or regret. At this time, we were already able to see everything inside of the whale. There was lots of blood running down the platform. We used ponderous winches with massive chains and hooks to peel the skin off.

The blood was still flooding from the vast carcass to the drainage gutters as this grotesque butchery continued. I felt I was walking on blood, my feet were all bloody. As we continued chopping in or slowly cutting the trunk in slices, other factory workers were already carrying whale pieces in barrels to their final destination. We were standing between the head and the trunk, chopping, chopping, and all I felt was the heavy blood swirled around my legs. That scenery is like a horror nightmare, when we only see blood, and blood. I felt that we, the workers, were cold killers chopping that hopeless victim with no pity. But later I realized we had feelings. We only had to do our job to feed our family.

With incredible facility, the whole whale was stripped and ready to be brought to the factories. The barrels used for melting were enormous. One whale would fill four barrels, and we took approximately an hour to fill one barrel. For every barrel of oil, we had to mix one barrel of water to make the oil from the blubber. Pico does not have water. Rain water was used to melt the blubber. They'd tap into a stream coming from the mountains to the barrels. When it rained, we opened the door of the barrels so the water could go inside.

The Azores sold the whaling products to other countries, mostly to cold countries like Netherlands, Germany, and Sweden. The liver of the sperm whale was used for making vitamins, one more way we could earn money. A German scientist came to teach us how to make vitamins out of liver. The heaviest liver I ever worked on weighed about a thousand pounds. There was a technique to making these vitamins. First we had to weigh the liver, then add two percent calcium and 100 percent water before boiling it. The bones of the whale were also melted. The jaw bones had a lot of fat and gave five to six gallons of oil. These also had to be boiled at high temperatures.

The whales smelled, but it was the smell from the whale-factory that caused a bad smell on the island. I didn't complain about the smell. It was already part of my life. Without the smell, whaling would not exist. Though I loved whaling, I still didn't earn enough to support my family. I decided to come to the United States to look for a better financial life for me and for my offspring.

Today I recall my whaling days by making what I love most. I am a craftsman. I make model whaling boats. I also make the instruments used by whalers to catch the whales. This is the way I keep whaling alive in my life. The whaling era cannot be forgotten by those who worked on it. Even though it was a most difficult and devastating period, all the whaling crew including me will always recall the adventures, no matter if they were sad or happy.

Author Eva Cordeiro received her M.A. in professional writing and her B.A. in English both from UMass Dartmouth.

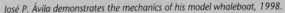

José P. Ávila demonstrates the mechanics of his model whaleboat, 1998.

Joseph D. Thomas photograph

Lewis Hine worked for the National Child Labor Commission and extensively photographed working and living conditions of children and immigrants across the United States. As a propagandist for the NCLC, he deliberately emphasized squalor, suffering and poor working conditions. His intent was to help eradicate child labor, and to demonstrate the shortsightedness of putting children to work. For this photograph he wrote: "Young doffer and spinner boys in the Sakonnet Mill, Fall River, 1912. The youngest are Manuel Perry, 111 Pitman St. John E. Mello, 299 Alden St. and Manuel Louis. None of these could write their own names. The last couldn't spell the street he lives on. They spoke almost no English."

WORKING TRADITION

Lewis W. Hine photograph, Library of Congress

THE PORTUGUESE WORKER

BY PENN REEVE

The story of the Portuguese worker and the region's booming textile industry can be read in the numbers. Few Portuguese immigrated to southern New England prior to 1870; the official census that year reported only 8,971 Portuguese-born individuals in the United States. Portuguese immigration soared with the expansion of the textile industry. By 1900, 17,885 Portuguese were living in Massachusetts alone. By 1920 the numbers increased to 50,294. Only a decade later, Massachusetts was home to more than 62,000 second-generation Portuguese.

Most settled in Fall River and New Bedford and took jobs in the textile mills. In New Bedford, merchant families had transferred their investments from whaling to the production of fine cotton textiles. By the beginning of the First World War, 32 New Bedford cotton manufacturing companies employed 30,000 people. New Bedford mills were built along the railroad tracks and river in the north and south ends of the city. To this day, these areas are largely Portuguese communities.

Fall River, the "Spindle City," was a leading cotton textile manufacturing city in the 1800s, but very few Portuguese lived there during that time. Of the total Fall River population, 132 individuals were from southern and eastern Europe and only 104 were Portuguese immigrants. Although the new immigrant population in Fall River jumped to 1,017 in 1890, this number was barely perceptible in a population of 74,398.

Over 80 percent of Portuguese mill workers in Fall River arrived after 1901. As late as 1880, all but 40 of Fall River's textile employees were either native-born or born in northern or western Europe. The Portuguese and Polish immigrants generally stepped into mill jobs held by departing English and Irish. By 1900, 6,000 originated from southern and eastern Europe; that number reached 10,000 five years later. Azoreans comprised half this total. According to Phil Silvia, "Fall River's entire Portuguese and Polish population were working in the mills by 1910."

"Phinney Bog, Falmouth, MA, 1911. The Texeira family of 50 Lombard Street, New Bedford. Mother and two children pick 40 measures a day at 7 cents a measure. There were two out of 18 workers apparently under 12 and they expected to work several weeks more—losing some weeks of schooling." – Lewis W. Hine

Lewis W. Hine photograph, Library of Congress

Transition to Factory Work

At the turn of the century, most of the Portuguese arrivals to southern New England were farmers from the Azores and Madeira with no industrial work experience. The transition from rural agriculture to urban industrial life was a shock for these immigrants. Some opted for life on small farms, but such opportunities were scarce. The jobs were in the mills.

Most of the island Portuguese lacked the skills to do factory work but could quickly learn the less skilled jobs. They worked as bobbin boys, doffers, carders, combers, sweepers and spoolers and at jobs that demanded only brief training. One had only to be willing to endure 10 to 12-hour shifts, six days a week at monotonous, tedious tasks.

Textile work had always been difficult. As historian John Cumbler points out, "Nineteenth century textile workers in Fall River rose daily in the early dawn to face exhausting, intensive labor, long hours, and low pay." Constant, close supervision, speedups, "stretch-outs" and dusty, poorly ventilated mills plagued the textile workers. In the early 20th century, conditions were only somewhat better, and periodic speedups and wage cuts led to great hardships.

In the face of such difficulties the Portuguese demonstrated their resilience. To cope with economic hardships they relied on family, religion, and community. While seeking employment they often lived with extended family members and friends in the local Portuguese community, a "family" that sometimes arranged work for them. Today's Portuguese immigrants continue to rely on these social networks for economic and emotional support.

To adjust, they relied on their traditional culture, planting gardens and raising animals. They sought help from Portuguese mutual aid societies, attended parish churches and feasts and joined Portuguese social clubs. These activities reinforced their ethnic identity and helped them cope with *saudade* for the old life. As John Cumbler notes, participation in the community "helped integrate the textile workers into the urban industrial world or served as a buffer against those forces which newcomers felt bearing down on them."

Many of these activities also helped the immigrant family economically. For example, gardens gave some relief from the costs of

Spinner Collection

In a mill lot that was once vacant, the Ferreira family tend their community garden, New Bedford, 1951.

Lewis W. Hine photograph, Library of Congress

One of Hine's most frequently published photographs of southeastern New England is this family portrait in New Bedford, 1912. Hine wrote: "Manuel Sousa and family, 306 Second St. On right end is brother-in-law; next to him is his father who works on the river; next is Manuel, appears 12, arms folded. He has been a cleaner in the Holmes Cotton Mill for two years. Next is brother John who works in City Mill. Next is his sister. At left end is cousin. All are very illiterate. John and Manuel are the only ones who can speak English and they only a little."

buying food. Families pooled resources, and when conditions deteriorated financially they obtained loans and credit from local Portuguese merchants, family, friends and aid societies. These cooperative efforts were evident during strikes when Portuguese workers and their families joined union efforts to raise money and food for striking workers. The oral histories of Eula Mendes, Manny Fernandes and Tina Ponte reflect this solidarity.

Ethnic Prejudices

Serious divisions arose between the "old immigrants," who arrived earlier in the 19th century, and the "new immigrants," such as the Portuguese and Polish whose numbers increased significantly at the end of the century. The "old immigrants" from northern and western Europe held most of the highly skilled jobs, and many resented the new arrivals. Some felt the Portuguese immigrants would work for lower wages and thereby threaten their jobs. Also, many "old" immigrants and American-born believed those from southern and eastern Europe were racially inferior.

However, even the Dillingham Commission Report in 1911, a document full of racial biases against the "new" immigrants, acknowledged that the main reason new immigrants hadn't advanced was they hadn't been here long enough. The report also pointed out that management still preferred to hire "old immigrants." English, Welsh and Irish workers supported the hiring and promotion of experienced workers from their own groups. Ethnic animosity at times led English, Irish and French-Canadians "to quit if they had to work under new immigrants, especially the Portuguese."

Mill owners and managers generally hired Portuguese immigrants for lower-skilled jobs, but evidence shows some bosses respected Portuguese workers and they advanced. Figures compiled about textile operatives in four New England states reveal that Portuguese males and females over 16 were "competitive in proficiency and wages with French-Canadians and American born doffers, ring spinners, speeder tenders, and spoolers."

Surveys from a 1912 report on infant mortality in New Bedford rated the disposition of immigrants in this order: *General efficiency and progress:* American, English and Irish, French-Canadian, North Italian, Portuguese, Polish, South Italian, and Syrian.

Stoking the furnace in the boiler room of the Gosnold Mill, 1912. For many immigrants, working your way up in the mills usually meant starting at the most hazardous jobs, like boiler room or card room laborer.

Courtesy of Thomas Whittaker

Industriousness: Portuguese, French-Canadian, North Italian, American, English, Irish, Polish, South Italian, Syrian."

Though the numerical impact of new immigrants on the textile industry was pronounced by 1910, they did not "take over" as many "old immigrants" feared. Many Irish and English were promoted or left the mills for other jobs; competition with "new immigrants" did not force them out of their jobs. Usually new immigrants could not compete for the more skilled, higher-paying jobs reserved for "old immigrants." Typically the "new immigrants" were qualified for only the lowest-wage jobs. But even if skilled, they were forced to take low-end jobs because of ethnic biases.

Work and Labor

Labor unrest was frequent throughout the 19th and into the 20th century. The goals of these "walkouts" and strikes were to pressure employers to improve the poor working conditions and low pay and secure the workers' right to collective bargaining. Unions became one basis of power and support for the immigrant.

The assumption that new immigrants acted as strikebreakers is largely erroneous. In fact, some Portuguese from the mainland had been involved in labor activities in the textile industry in Portugal. Even immigrants who lacked awareness of trade unions generally supported the push for the right to unionize and the fight for higher wages. Many joined walkouts and strikes. During the 1904 strike, John Golden commented, "I cannot help but compliment the French, Portuguese, Italian and Polish people for the splendid way in which they stood by their English-speaking brothers and sisters."

Portuguese immigrants played an active role in the 1928 New Bedford textile strike. They helped organize rallies, distribute food to striking workers, translate pamphlets and populate rallies.

However, friction continued between older, more skilled, northern European immigrants and the newer, less skilled, southern and eastern European immigrants. In 1920 the AFTO (American Federation Textile Operatives) consisted mainly of old immigrants who were skilled operatives. Though the union did not exclude Portuguese and Polish, it did not encourage them to join.

Both the New Bedford textile strike of 1928 and the national textile strike of 1934 underscored this rift among workers based on ethnicity and job skills. In 1928 and again in 1934 textile manufacturers cut wages and refused to improve working conditions. The federal government sided with the manufacturers. In 1934 the United Textile Workers (UTW), made up of less skilled workers and

Men and women, young and old, all nationalities, from New Bedford and Fall River, came together during the 1928 textile strike. Here, they prepare to march from one end of New Bedford to the other during the July 4th parade held by the Textile Mill Committee.

Spinner Collection

233

many "new immigrants," urged the AFTO to join them in the strike. AFTO refused, and on the first day of the strike its members crossed the UTW picket line. Despite this lack of support, the UTW got half of the work force to walk out including doffers and carders, who were mostly Portuguese immigrants. The police arrested and teargassed many workers on the picket lines, including the Portuguese.

Despite all the difficulties and hardships, from the 1930s on, many Portuguese immigrants joined the Fall River and New Bedford labor movement and its leadership. In Fall River, Mariano Bishop, Manuel Melo, and Mike Botelho led CIO organizing drives from the 1930s to the 1940s. Mariano Bishop was typical of these new labor leaders, taken from the ranks of the recent immigrants. He emigrated from the Azores and entered Fall River mills as a doffer at age 10. He lived in the Portuguese south end and socialized at the Liberal Athletic Club. In the 1920s Mariano became president of the dyers unit of the UTW. He and an Irish immigrant, Mike Doolan, organized hundreds of immigrant workers and successfully united workers from different ethnic backgrounds. In the national textile strike of 1934, Bishop and Doolan led the local efforts in Fall River and the surrounding region.

Decline of the Textile Industry

The movement of the textile industry south in the 1920s and the Depression of the 1930s created further hardships for immigrants. The Portuguese took a variety of jobs in the tight labor market. The garment shops hired only a fraction of the work force that had been employed in the textile mills. Some individuals left for other parts of the country, such as California and New Jersey, and others took whatever jobs were available locally.

Many more Portuguese immigrants in recent decades have higher levels of education and skills than in the past. The post-1965 immigration, with increasing numbers from the continent, represents a more skilled, educated population. Today, as the economy shifts from manufacturing to services, Luso Americans have increasingly entered the professions and service industries, including financial services, education, law, and engineering. Many have succeeded in businesses throughout the region. However, like much of the region's population, Portuguese without higher education often end up in lower-paid service and retail jobs.

Even after the decline in textiles led to a decline in textile union membership and power, the Portuguese continued to play an active role in the labor movement of south-

Fall River apparel workers, circa 1940. During the Great Depression, the city of Fall River went bankrupt and its administration was taken over by the Federal Government. As large textile manufacturers, employing tens of thousands, closed or moved south, Fall River's spectacular mill structures were left with millions of square feet of vacant industrial space. Many of these buildings could be purchased for as little as $1.00. With this opportunity, the garment industry, primarily from New York and Pennsylvania, came to town.

eastern Massachusetts. They built their local successes on tactics of earlier strikes—unity of the community, massive rallies, demonstrations, parades and efforts to unify the various skill groups and ethnic groups.

In the 1980s, author Ann Bookman challenged the common stereotypes that women, particularly immigrant women, resist joining unions. In the Boston electronics factory where she worked and conducted her research, she discovered that women, particularly Portuguese immigrant women, were instrumental in organizing and supporting the successful union drive.

Organizers faced many barriers. The factory was divided by ethnicity and race and between men and women. Even among the Portuguese, there were divisions—between Azoreans and "Continentals," between Azoreans from different islands, between urban and rural Portuguese, between more traditional and more Americanized immigrants. But these differences were less important than their dedications to improve their working conditions.

According to Bookman, "They tended to be neighbors, to have friendship and kinship ties which operated inside and outside of work, and to see each other in stores, social clubs and churches on weekends."

In the end, women joined the union drive in equal numbers to men, shattering the

Joseph D. Thomas photograph

stereotype that women were more hesitant to join unions. Also, Bookman discovered that first-generation Portuguese immigrants joined the union in even greater proportions than non-Portuguese (73.5 percent of Portuguese, 61.4 percent non-Portuguese).

In recent years the labor movement nationally and locally is showing signs of a modest rebirth. This is especially true in the unions representing the less organized sectors of the economy—government and service. The large number of current labor leaders of Portuguese descent reminds us that the legacy of the Portuguese contribution to the regional labor movement remains strong. As Peter Knowlton, United Electrical Workers Union organizer in New Bedford, commented, "I can't think of a single union local in this area which doesn't have at least one person of Portuguese descent in its leadership."

Women stitchers hard at work at Calvin Clothing in New Bedford, 1982. At the peak of the apparel industry's presence in Bristol County, around 1980, more than 20,000 people were employed in the manufacture of sewn goods. According to the U.S. Bureau of Labor Statistics, as of 1996, that number was down to 7,600. Union officials estimate that about 85% of their nearly 2,000 members are of Portuguese descent.

In 1980, Portuguese fishermen, with their families by their side, initiated and led the tie-up that crippled the port of New Bedford and brought redress to the economic problems facing the industry.

Joseph D. Thomas photograph

THREE LIVES FOR LABOR

EULA MENDES, MANNY FERNANDES AND TINA PONTE

BY PENN REEVE

The history of southeastern Massachusetts is a history of struggle—immigrants struggling to achieve the American Dream, a decent standard of living and opportunities for their children. Success required long hours of toil under less than ideal working conditions. Success also required the fight to improve wages and working conditions in the factories and offices throughout the region. This struggle therefore is also the history of unions and the labor movement.

The Portuguese played a vital role in the region's labor movement. Contrary to views that the Portuguese were generally antiunion, Portuguese immigrants have a long and distinguished history of labor activism. This essay explores the lives of several of the many local Portuguese workers who participated in the labor movement over the years— Eula Mendes Papandreu, Manny Fernandes, and Tina Ponte. We look at the circumstances that led them into the movement, their role in the labor movement, as well as their goals and accomplishments.

Young Portuguese spinner at the American Linen Company, Fall River, 1916.

Lewis W. Hine photograph, Library of Congress

Eula Mendes and the 1928 Strike

Eulalia Mendes was born in Gouveia, Portugal, in 1910, the year Portugal's monarchy was overthrown. Eula's father Edward saw the timing of her birth as a sign that she would become a revolutionary, a prophecy that was realized partly because of his own influence on her.

Blacklisted from mill work in Portugal for his radical politics, Edward, and others like him, fled to the United States. Many anarchists, syndicalists and communists from North Portugal came indentured to United States companies, as Eula recalls, "to the land of gold and honey." Edward obtained contract work in 1912 in a cordage factory in Plymouth, working alongside Bartolomeo Vanzetti (of Sacco and Vanzetti). He then got a job in a Brockton shoe factory. Eula, her mother and brother arrived from Portugal to join Edward in 1915.

After the family moved to New Bedford, Eula went to work at age 13 in the City Mill in 1923. The work was "tough." A relative worked next to her and helped her. Eula remembers that the mostly Portuguese immigrant women helped each other as much as they could. But she was too small to work the loom so she became a doffer in the card room. She worked nine hours a day, with four hours off one day a week to attend vocational school.

In 1928 the New Bedford textile manufacturers demanded a ten-cent-per-hour pay cut, a dramatic reduction in wages at the time. The mill owners were making a profit, but with a dip in demand. They decided to operate at the same rate of profit even though they were not operating at the same rate of production.

The only textile organization, the conservative Textile Council (TC), was made up primarily of English- and Scottish-dominated craft unions of weavers and spinners. They voted to go on strike. But this union didn't represent the majority of mill workers, including the less skilled, mostly Portuguese, Polish and French-Canadian workers, who also walked off their jobs.

A rival organization, the Textile Mill Committee (TMC), was formed to represent them. The TMC was made up of local workers and outside organizers, including communists with experience in other textile strikes. They began to organize on a more inclusive, industry-wide basis. The immediate goals of the TMC were to stop the wage cut and gain legal union representation for unrepresented workers.

At age 18, Eula immediately became involved in the strike and joined the TMC.

I remember the time of strike. I didn't know what to do. I was young at the time. My father said, "There is a strike. You must go on strike. You must be with the workers." I spent my 18th birthday on the picket line.

Eula was asked to join the TMC strike committee to translate leaflets and speeches from Portuguese to English and vice versa. She became secretary of the TMC and an active speaker, helping to organize Portuguese workers and maintain their morale.

When the strike began, the Portuguese people from the continent got involved immediately; so did those from the Azores, Madeira and Cape Verde. The people from the islands were a little more conservative. They had no background working in factories but they became more active.

The six-month strike ended when the Textile Council and mill owners worked out an agreement for a five-cent-an-hour wage cut instead of ten cents. The TMC was excluded from negotiations and the vote. The authorities attacked the TMC and arrested many leaders and members so they couldn't participate in the final settlement. (The charges were dropped after the strike.) They accused TMC organizers of being dangerous outside agitators and un-American. Eula was arrested several times during the strike. Immediately after the strike Eula, like many strikers, could not get work in the mills, though eventually she did. Then the TMC asked her to work for them as an organizer and office worker.

At the national level many workers and labor leaders were disappointed in the AF of L for its narrow craft-based organizing and lack of inclusiveness, as well as a failed 1934 national textile strike. At the 1935 AFL convention, the United Textile Workers walked out and joined the new CIO. They formed the Textile Workers Organizing Committee (TWOC) with financial support at the national level from the Amalgamated Clothing Workers (ACW) and the International Ladies Garment Workers Unions (ILGWU).

Eula worked for this new organization, competing directly with local AFL affiliates for members. Having signed up thousands of new members nationwide, in 1939 the TWOC

became the Textile Workers Union of America–CIO. From the 1930s through the 40s, Eula's life was filled with union organizing work and Communist Party political and social activities.

By the late 1940s leadership in many unions came to reflect the more conservative mood of the post World War II society. As a sign of the times, in 1947, the Taft-Hartley law passed, over President Truman's veto. (The Taft-Hartley Law have been judged by some as the most repressive labor law in the industrial world.)

The restrictions on labor unions included the notorious "loyalty oaths" which precluded many leftists from holding union office and led to the purge of many of the more militant and successful union leaders. The local textile union did not fight the Taft-Hartley loyalty oaths, and Eula was expelled from the union because of her communist affiliation. The union president told Eula, "Sorry, Eula, you'll have to go—you're a communist. Nothing personal."

"I Heard the Iron Clang Behind Me"

The conservative Cold War era gave birth to the McCarthy period of political repression, during which labor leaders critical of the United States economic and political system were persecuted. The Smith Act of 1940 and the Subversive Control Act (McCarran-Walter Act) of 1950 became tools for suppressing militant labor leaders. Under the 1950 Act, at age 42, Eula was arrested at her home in New Bedford as a "subversive alien." She was not a citizen, having been denied that opportunity because of her arrests during the 1928 strike.

They were afraid I was going to overthrow the government by force and violence, all by myself.

She went to New York as the only woman in New England arrested for deportation and got temporary work in a dress factory while awaiting deportation decisions. Despite support from various groups, Eula was deported in May 1953. She vividly remembers, "I heard the iron clang behind me." Portugal was a fascist state, and one activist, Augusto Pinto, who had been deported there, allegedly was killed in a prison

Eula Mendes, known to her fellow workers as "Guandacio," at work during the 1928 strike. The Times, *in New Bedford wrote: "Miss Mendes appeared almost daily on the speaking platform, while her ready smile and sparkling brown eyes coupled with a conservativeness of expression have made her a favorite at the Potomska and Diman Street halls."*

Eula Mendes at the time of her deportation in 1953. When she applied for citizenship, Eula noted: "They said, 'You're a criminal, you were arrested a number of times.' I said, 'Sure, during the strike.' They said, 'That's against you as a criminal...' When the plane took off from New York, I felt the Iron Curtain closing behind me."

camp in Cape Verde. Eula feared a similar fate. She sought and was granted asylum in Poland where she has been living since.

Most of these people who were deported had to go to countries they had not seen, had not lived in and most of them had been brought to the United States when they were children. And it meant quite a break for them to leave a country where they grew up. For some people it was also breaking up a home, where the husband was deported and the wife and children stayed.

Eula reflected on the chilling effect arrest and deportation threats had on the foreign-born workers at the time:

Picking on foreign-born people was used during the McCarthy days as a pressure against people generally. My arrest had the effect of creating a lot of fear amongst Portuguese people who were not citizens. Arresting so many at that time all over the country broke the progress of the trade union movement.

Forty years later, as part of an attempt to secure a visa for Eula so she could return to the United States for a visit, U.S. Representative Barney Frank stated:

We should keep people out because of criminal violence, but not keep them out because of their ideas. That's what Eulalia Mendes got caught up in.

Manny Fernandes: The Rise to Leadership

Manny Fernandes was born in New Bedford in 1913. His parents were from farming communities in Madeira. Though they grew up in villages near each other, they met for the first time in New Bedford. Both worked in cotton textile mills.

Manny doesn't remember much about the 1928 strike except that his father walked the picket line, and they got by in part by selling homemade "moonshine." They also raised goats, cows, pigs, chickens and vegetables on their two acres of land located near the Acushnet River. "My father used to get soup or bread from the union."

He also remembers that the leaders of the strike asked his father if Manny and the children could patrol the waterfront in their small rowboat with an attached sail "to see if anything was going on," such as scabs sneaking into the mill to work.

After Manny graduated from eighth grade, his father encouraged him to get a job in the mills as a weaver. It was considered a "clean job."

I didn't like weaving, period! It was noisy, repetitive. I didn't like the job and I wasn't learning because I was actually thinking, how soon can I get out of this. It wasn't my kind of cake.

Machinists at New Bedford Rayon Company, 1931. Manny Fernandes began working at the New Bedford Rayon Company around 1936, first as a helper, then as a churn room operator.

Because of family responsibilities he stuck it out, moving to a weaving job in another mill and finally to a synthetic yarn plant in Hartford, where his aunt and some friends lived.

Meanwhile he had a girlfriend in New Bedford and began looking for a way to return there. He landed a job at New Bedford Rayon around 1936 as a helper and four years later advanced to churn room operator. Here he mixed the materials for the yarn. Finally, he became viscose cellar operator, the best job in the plant with higher pay and less exposure to toxic chemicals.

The only thing that keeps you going is the money and a little security. We had one layoff in 1938. The plant continued to run steady and paid fairly good money in comparison to the (cotton textile) plants in the city.

"We are the CIO! You Know!"

During the Depression of the 1930s, the CIO was competing with the AFL, organizing unions across the country as well as locally. (In Fall River, Portuguese labor leaders Mariano Bishop and Ed Doolan became well-known CIO labor organizers.)

Manny's local became part of National Textile Workers Union of America–CIO. Tony England was director of the local Joint Board of this union. Under Tony England and John Chupka's efforts, New Bedford became a stronghold of CIO organizing. Twenty-four shops made up the Joint Board of New Bedford and included over 15,000 union members. At the time, Eula Mendes was working for Tony England on their organizing drive. However, Manny and Eula did not know each other.

We used to compete with the AF of L for different plants. "We are the CIO!" went over better than AF of L. The AF of L went after loomfixers, slasher tenders, mechanical loomfixers. They were the Crafts Union. The slasher tenders were an elite group and you had to know what you were doing, how to read and write and stuff, so you could set up the job. A lot of these people didn't speak English too well. The loomfixers were the elites of the union, so the others felt left out. And when we (the CIO) came in, we said you should all be represented. So in the election we beat the AF of L and came to represent 24 or 25 plants in New Bedford.

Union leadership

Manny became more involved in union activities in the late 1930s and '40s, eventually moving up the local board hierarchy to business agent of the Joint Board. He was highly motivated by the interesting nature of the work and liked making new friends and developing new ideas to improve the condition of workers. While serving as business agent he translated materials, including contracts, for Portuguese-speaking workers, the same important role that Eula played. Manny helped them resolve problems and gave financial advice.

He became steward and then head steward by 1940, when he was elected to the executive board. In 1944, after he intervened to help resolve a conflict between workers and the company, he was elected business agent. The incident recounted here is typical of his style of conflict resolution, and, like many conflicts between management and workers at the time, it was resolved on the shop floor.

In 1944, the union had requested a small wage increase, a few cents an hour. The company had referred the request, as was routine, to the Wage Stabilization Board. The Board was established during the war to make sure wage increases were not so high as to interfere with the war effort. But the Board was extremely slow responding, of course, since they tended to slow down wage increases in general. The union asked for a response and got none. We went to union president Tony England and he told us we couldn't rush them. We were making parachute shrouds. The shop steward said if

Manny Fernandes, 1949.

Workers leaving the Goodyear plant on Orchard Street in New Bedford, protected by police while strikers on the sidelines "boo" them, 1934.

239

Joseph D. Thomas photograph

Slasher tender Manuel Gonsalves straightens out a lap on the warp beam, Berkshire Hathaway Mill, 1985. Ernest Bourque, a slasher of Franco-American descent who worked with Gonsalves told Spinner, "The old slasher tenders were all English. They finally let the Irish and the French in before letting in the Portuguese around 1940. When the Portuguese came, they said, 'That's the end of this mill.' But this was the only mill that lasted through the '80s and it's 98% Portuguese." – Spinner, Volume IV.

they don't want to listen, maybe we should cut down production. When we agreed to walk out, the steward got stomach cramps and went home, leaving me in charge.

The manager came around and said a walkout would stop production for quite a while because the viscose in the pipes will harden and it will ruin the plant.

So I said, "Look, fellas, those guys (from another shift) are threatening to walk out after four hours but I'm going to leave it up to you. We've got to use our heads. We're not getting support so let's take a secret ballot." We did, and eleven voted to go back and two voted to stay out. We notified the company we'd go back to work but said we'll do this again unless some action is taken. They pointed out that our union head Tony England didn't agree with this action. I said, "Look, he didn't agree, but majority rules."

After that, the union local president came to me and suggested I run for business agent.

Taft-Hartley and the "Loyalty Oaths"

Manny Fernandes and others felt the chill in the labor movement from Taft-Hartley:

Anyone running for a union office must sign an anticommunist affidavit stating that he doesn't believe in the overthrow of the U.S. government by force and that he is not a member of any subversive organization or Communist Party. See, this was leading up to 1952—the McCarthy years.

The Taft-Hartley Law of 1947 had important negative consequences for labor. The amendments allowed states to pass laws forbidding the "closed shop," made unions and union leaders financially liable for losses incurred by businesses that were struck, made unions more vulnerable to court injunctions, outlawed secondary boycotts, wildcat strikes and federal strikes and gave the president the power to order workers back to work. Employers could sue workers for breach of contract. The "loyalty oaths" that led to Eula Mendes' expulsion from the local textile union mandated that all union officers sign an affidavit swearing they were not members of the Communist Party and that they did not advocate the overthrow of the government by force or by any unconstitutional means. Manny Fernandes continues:

In 1947, when I was president of the local, the Taft-Hartley law was new. So there's a big discussion about signing the affidavit. About 40 percent are against signing and 60 percent are for, more or less. "Look, you're not commies, why don't you sign it?" I asked. "The hell with it." And then the discussion flows into, "Why us?" They're implying we are communists, and if we don't sign it, we positively are. If you didn't (sign) you were automatically convicted. "By golly they have a point," I said. It didn't happen too much in labor, but if things got vicious, you could say, "Those Commies! They don't wanna sign!"

Finally, one of our attorneys from New York handed down the interpretation…We had to sign or we couldn't run for office. The records show I made the motion to sign the affidavit—being that the law required it. I honestly felt that, I was born in this country, I didn't know any communists so why shouldn't I just sign the piece of lousy paper that I wasn't a communist. That was my true belief.

According to Manny, Portuguese labor leaders were actively involved and represented on both sides of the "loyalty oath" debate:

The so-called active Portuguese were against the signing of the affidavit. The more conservative ones would say, "Well, it's the law, I'm gonna sign it." The liberal ones said, "I don't care if it's the law, I don't have to sign it and I'm not a commie." There were more Portuguese than any other nationality against signing the affidavit. We had a majority of Portuguese on the board but it was primarily (conservative) ones.

By the way, one member of the Board was a known communist and she worked in one of our plants. Even the Portuguese that were against signing the affidavit were afraid of, or careful about, being tied in with her.

Impact of the Loyalty Oaths

Manny Fernandes felt the impact of Taft-Hartley and agonized over its implications:

From now on, you didn't take the so-called procedures of settling a grievance in the old way because under the new law, if you caused the company some hardship or loss of production, the union would be liable for damages. That made the union leadership cautious in how they settled a grievance and sort of weakened our grievance procedure.

What we should have done is refused to sign it and still run for office. I did not realize the importance of legislation like this which intimated that if there are communists, that's where we've got to watch them—in the labor movement. I was not yet aware of all these implications.

McCarthyism

Taft-Hartley contributed to McCarthyism and the "witch hunts" of the early 1950s. According to Manny, the FBI was monitoring local union activities:

We had some fellow, Vena or Pena, who was supposed to be an undercover agent working in the New Bedford labor movement. He came out with a report I thought was ridiculous. For example, if you bought the Daily Worker *(Communist Party newspaper), that was supposed to make you a communist. He'd say, why didn't I go in there and take care of the company officials. "Shoot them," and I would say to him, "Well, I haven't got any guns." He was nuts, period. In the newspaper this guy became one of the noted communists in New Bedford.*

Manny discusses the first time he read the *Daily Worker* and the implications of reading such a paper during this period:

I said "What the hell's the Daily Worker?*" He said, "I'll bring it to you," so I read the damned thing. Then I find out these communists are all reading these newspapers, you know. The paper made comparisons, and most of what they said was true, exaggerated truth to some extent, but even at that time Russian workers were having vacations. Now remember, these guys (local union members) have fought for their vacations and it's difficult. Hell, the so-called powers that be in this country don't want us to get ideas that we should go for a vacation down in Florida, and the companies are gonna pay for it?*

They (communists) felt we should have substantial wage increases and every family deserves a good home, be able to take care of their children and send them to school, which at that time was considered communist propaganda, you see, because that's the way life was.

The 1955 Textile Strike

Manny Fernandes saw the 1955 textile strike as his most trying period in the labor movement:

You notice the reaction of people (workers) that feel helpless in that situation. They look at you to do something.

On April 7, 1955, the New England textile manufacturers demanded cuts in worker benefits—elimination of the cost-of-living increase-clause, reduction in holiday pay, fewer paid holidays and a decrease in insurance benefits. Textile manufacturers claimed that to be competitive with southern and foreign manufacturers, New England's textile industry must lower costs—including labor costs. A federal arbitrator had already mandated a 6.5 percent pay decrease in 1952.

After mediation efforts failed, the TWUA declared a strike of over 29,000 workers in 27 plants throughout New England. In the New Bedford/Fall River group, 13,000 workers in the 16 member-mills were on strike, including 3,100 at Wamsutta Mill and Berkshire Hathaway in New Bedford. The *Standard-Times* reported the event April 16, 1955:

A 100-man picket line set up at Berkshire Hathaway at midnight and a 56-man line at 5 this morning was led by Manuel Fernandes,

Manny Fernandes, 1979.

Nightworking strikebreakers get police protection outside the Wamsutta Mill during the 1955 strike.

business agent, and Manuel Caetano, chairman of the Berkshire Hathaway local.

At 12:15 AM, a lone striker walked through the Gifford Street gate, announcing, "I'm the last." A cheer went up and Mr. Fernandes shouted, "It's a 100 percent walkout. Let's go with the picket lines!" Dozens of marchers followed him. Pickets reported that no one attempted to pass the gates into the mills last night or today.

Manny recalled his approach to the workers:

Things had been going pretty good after the war. Now the company talks to union officials and you have to report to your workers. What did they used to say about the messenger of bad news—shoot them? You are their representative now telling them, "We don't go to work tomorrow because the company wants to cut your pay. You are still going to vote. I don't vote, you do."

A leader goes in there and he knows the wind is blowing from the south, he's not going to tell the members the wind is blowing from the north. The union heads thought the company was unjust and we pushed it. Hell, strike. Even the ones that are a little afraid. For instance, you might have a man and wife working in the same plant. Hell, that does affect them. They weren't enthused about fighting for what they believed to be theirs.

The first four weeks is a sort of enthusiasm. They talk, they sing. After that, there's a few who start to kick the pebbles on the sidewalk as they are picketing. Shuffling, I call it. After about eight weeks, they say, "Anything yet?" And I say "No." Then, "What are you doing? You are getting paid." They are starting to turn on you. You notice these things. That's why it's a difficult job.

Worker morale begins to deteriorate. You must hold their attention and build them up. That's why sometimes there is a little violence. To make matters worse, the police are escorting trucks to pick up the cloth. Then we know the cloth had to be processed in dying and finishing plants. We asked the workers in other plants not to work on Berkshire Hathaway cloth and they didn't. The company took the cloth elsewhere to have it processed. You didn't go tell the workers because you want to keep their morale up.

That was one of my most trying periods in the labor movement because you notice the reaction of workers that feel helpless. They look at you to do something. The average worker finds it difficult to understand the process we must go through in order to accomplish something.

During the fifth week of the strike, on May 19, 1955, the *Standard-Times* ran a front-page editorial condemning it. It blamed

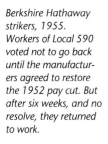

Berkshire Hathaway strikers, 1955. Workers of Local 590 voted not to go back until the manufacturers agreed to restore the 1952 pay cut. But after six weeks, and no resolve, they returned to work.

The Standard-Times Library

union leaders for the "grave injustice" in diverting textile business to the South and claimed their actions were creating the "same dire circumstances as caused by the 1928 and 1934 textile strikes."

There is but one issue involved in the Wamsutta and Hathaway strikes. It is very simple—shall the workers and their union leaders consent to conditions which enable these two well-equipped and efficient and well-managed concerns to sell their wares in the market in competition with other mills, particularly in the South? Or shall these mills be compelled to move to the South, as dozens of New Bedford's mills have done, or close up because they cannot compete?

An open letter with a similar message appeared in the May 17 *Diário de Notícias*, the local Portuguese newspaper. Written by the Berkshire Hathaway management and obviously aimed at Portuguese workers, the full-page letter blamed the union leaders for risking workers' jobs and suggested their jobs would be lost to southern workers.

On May 26, 1955, the strike ended, except at Berkshire Hathaway where workers of Local 590 voted not to go back until the manufacturers agreed to restore the 1952 pay cut. After six more weeks they, too, returned to work. The settlement was a partial victory because it reinstated most of the benefits of the prior contract, but the cost-of-living clause and the three holidays were eliminated.

The Standard-Times Library

Unfortunately, the issues raised in this strike reflected the symptoms of an industry that continued to decline in the region. At a national level, despite economic expansion and an apparent increase in labor power with the merger of the AFL and CIO, 1955 marked the peak of labor union membership. Since then and until recently, labor union membership has declined. This was most noticeable in the manufacturing sector, as manufacturing jobs were lost to foreign competitors and the U.S. economy shifted dramatically toward service and information.

Tina Ponte, 1985.

The Standard-Times Library

Tina Ponte and the UAW

Tina Ponte grew up in New Bedford. She worked for 44 years at John F. Pauldings Co., a wiring device company. Along with Henry Dunham and others, she helped organize a United Auto Workers local at Pauldings. Both Tina and Henry became recognized for their contributions to the local labor movement. When Dunham died in 1978, the SMU Labor Education Center created the Henry Dunham Award, presented annually to a rank-and-file union member for "promoting the cause of economic and social justice for working people" in southeastern Massachusetts. The following year Tina Ponte was the first recipient of this award.

Tina's parents grew up in Portugal, 50 miles from each other, but they first met in the New Bedford textile mills. Her mother worked as a spinner in the Wamsutta and Beacon mills. Her father started out at the Beacon Mill doing assorted jobs but later shifted to construction work.

As a young girl, I remember taking their lunches to the Beacon Mill because we lived so close. My mother used to tap bobbins. She would have her lunch and I would tap the bobbins for her so she could make her amount. We were taught at a very young age to be independent.

Three of Tina's four siblings died from influenza. When Tina was 15 her mother became ill and her father had an accident, so she was taken out of school to work part-time at a laundry and to care for her parents.

In those days Portuguese girls didn't have much of an opportunity to go to school.

Silbert T. Perry (center), Vice President of Local 590, is flanked by Arthur Hebert (left) and William Lewis as they walk the line outside Berkshire Hathaway.

That was left to the men in the family. The women had to work and take care of the household. There were very few Portuguese girls that went to college—very, very few. But there's so many now it's great.

In 1940 at age 17, Tina began working for Pauldings. She earned 40 cents an hour as a mold press operator, pressing plastic wall plates for receptacles. She did that job for 32 years.

The reason there were women pressers was because of the war. They couldn't get the men so they hired the women. We thought it was the same pay but it was a few cents less. We never knew of pay scales until the union came.

Because of seniority rules through the union, she was able to become stock clerk and tool crib attendant, handing out tools to machine shop clerks.

It was a little difficult but I learned it. It had been a man's job and they didn't want a woman. They made it very difficult. But we were unionized and now I had the right to bid on jobs.

In 1948 Tina left to give birth to her daughter. When she returned to Pauldings they hired her at the same pay rate she had received in 1940.

Even though I was one of the seniors, I had to wait five years to get a nickel raise. When the union came in, it was equal pay for equal work. Before the union, if you were a

friend of the boss, you would get a nickel raise. If you weren't, you wouldn't. If you were a man and did work for him at his home, then you received a raise much quicker. That happened a lot. All overtime was given to men—in my lifetime and in my mother's. I remember my mother carrying bags of potatoes to keep her job.

Union organizing

In 1958 Tina helped organize Pauldings. About 150 of the 250 workers signed cards to be presented to the National Labor Relations Board for union certification elections. But it wasn't easy. The workers went on strike for six and a half months to get the company to recognize the union. Hired strikebreakers (scabs) prolonged the strike.

The strike lasted from July through January. We knew all kinds of weather, all but the springtime, the best time. When we got extremely cold, we would stamp our feet or go sit in someone's car for a little while and then go back out and picket. It's not too bad when you're in a gang, and of course this was 28 years ago. We were younger and we could stand the cold. I doubt if I could do that today.

We had fun too. We became united and very together. Some of the people suffered, but the longing for that kind of union kept them going. The UAW took care of our insurance problems and hospital bills. We had union representation in the United Way. They helped some of our people with mortgage payments and getting food baskets.

During the strike, Tina became active in organizing Portuguese workers.

My job was to explain to the Portuguese people what the company's offer was and what we wanted. I would get up and say, "The company is trying to take away our vacation rights. They want us to become co-payers for our insurance plan, and they only want to give us a few pennies. Please support the union committee." I would take questions from them if they didn't understand certain language in the agreements.

But this role as interpreter and organizer was difficult.

We had people who were dissatisfied but others would come over and say, "Thanks a lot; you did a good job." The Portuguese

Tina Ponte walks the picket line outside Pauldings in the 1970s.

Courtesy of Tina Ponte

244

people were very appreciative. After the strike the workers recognized that without the union they wouldn't have anything. They became members. Part of the agreement with the company was the establishment of a closed shop. Quite a few received retirement pay, thanks to the union. It's true, no company gives anything without struggle. We struggled!

As union steward, Tina handled many grievances. The following involved Harry Dunham, a local labor leader, who was suspended for calling the personnel director a liar.

I was called to the personnel office and when I got there, a shouting match was going on between Harry and Arthur Tabor.

Arthur said, "What did you say, Harry?"
Harry said, "I said you were a liar."
"Say it again, Harry."
"You're a liar."
"What did you say?"
"You're a God damn liar!"
"You're fired!"
I said, "You can't fire him."
Arthur said, "I just did; get out of here!"

Arthur then told me I couldn't go downstairs with Harry. They escorted me out one way, Harry another. But, as he was driving out of the driveway, I handed him the grievance pad through the window. He signed it, gave it back and I filled it out. He was reinstated in three days. They didn't like Harry but they respected him because he was honest and sincere.

Tina relates another situation, involving her and Harry Dunham; this time the issue was the treatment of Portuguese workers.

At Pauldings we had what was called a kiln or oven. All these porcelain pieces had to be put in the oven to be cured. I remember one foreman sending Portuguese people into the kiln before it was cool enough. He would say to me, "What in the hell are you fighting for them for? They're only greenhorns," which would irritate Harry and me to no end. That foreman was Portuguese, too. Harry would say, "What in the hell do you think your parents were? They are human beings, not greenhorns." We straightened him out. The Portuguese people did all the bull work, the work nobody else wanted to do. Later on I would say to that foreman, "Hey, I've got regards from Harry Dunham." He'd say, "Why, that SOB!"

The plant closed in 1985, two years after the union obtained a decent wage settlement.

We had negotiated good pays, $6 or $7 an hour, not bad in New Bedford at the time. These same people were now forced to work out of town for $4 an hour. To think we had fought so hard and then have it go down the tubes because of two greedy men. They stuffed their pockets with the money instead of putting it into the company. I think the Portuguese people hurt more than anyone.

About the Author

Penn Reeve is Professor of Sociology and Anthropology at UMass Dartmouth. He received his Ph.D. in anthropology at Washington University in St. Louis and came to UMD in 1974. Dr. Reeve specializes in social inequality, ethnicity and labor issues. He has done research in Brazil, the Azores, and in the Alentejo, Portugal. He is a member of the Steering Committee of the Center for Portuguese Study and Culture, and the Arnold Dubin Labor Education Center at the UMass Dartmouth.

At J.F. Pauldings, employees assemble mechanisms used in lamp holders, 1969. "They are so expert at the job, there are no lost motions." –The Standard-Times

The Standard-Times Library

A Man of Steel

Interview with Emidio Raposo

by Gavin Hymes

Emidio Raposo, who emigrated from Portugal at 26, had a distinguished career at Morse Cutting Tool, Inc. and was an active member of the United Electrical Union. As a young boy he attended military school in Portugal and became an expert machinist; he took his knowledge and skills with him to Morse.

· · · · · · · · · · · · · · · ·

When my father died, my mother put me in a military school in Lisbon for the sons of army men. I was eight years old. My father fought in Belgium in the First World War and absorbed poison gas into his lungs. Little by little, the gas burned his trachea and he died slowly. He was about 32.

After my father died, my mother worked as a dressmaker. When the woman she worked for retired, she sold my mother the business. My mother didn't have a shop. She worked right in our house. Working with four or five girls, they measured, cut and sewed in a big room in our house. She had several sewing machines, the kind you have to pedal, and a big table for cutting. She would make her own designs and patterns on newspaper, then cut out the dresses. She made each dress to fit a certain customer, using chalk to mark the fabric and cutting carefully to conserve material.

In my time, people didn't have telephones at home but there were telephones in the stores. Next door to us was a bakery and if a customer or anyone else needed to contact us, they called the people in the bakery, who were kind enough to communicate with us.

My mother was a soft-spoken woman but she had her own ideas. She was somewhat strict with us because our father had died but she had a sensibility about the right way to guide us. She didn't need to say, "Do this and do that." She was the kind of woman who would say, "Nobody is any better than you, but you're not any better than anybody else either."

I came home from military school on weekends in uniform. We had classes on Saturday morning and were free to go home after the noon meal. We had to be back on Sunday night when they blew the horn at 9PM. My grandmother, who lived with us, would look at me and say, "Here comes my little general!" She was very proud that I had that uniform and she always asked that I wear it with dignity. If you were being punished at school, you could not go home on the weekend.

The teaching methods made it very hard for a child to learn. We had to repeat everything constantly. There was lots of memorization. One teacher I liked very much because he believed when you don't know something, you should use books and libraries to look for the answer. He'd say, "The book is your best friend. You don't have to know a book by heart, but I want you to know how to look at a book."

We had to go by military rules. We slept in a barracks with 30 to 35 beds. They played the bugle and woke us up at 5:30AM. At 6AM we had to make our beds, take showers and be ready to go downstairs for breakfast. If it was not raining, we would meet outside in formation and be divided into platoons. Then the ten- and eleven-year-old boys marched to their tables and sat with their platoon. We had a half-hour to get ready for school at 8AM and we marched to our classrooms.

When I was 11 or 12, I entered the vocational section of the military school. At that time, we could choose either industrial, commercial, shop or accounting. I took shop, which was a five-year

Emidio, a member of the Lisbon College Group, demonstrates his gymnastic skills at the school's anniversary celebration, 1940.

Courtesy of Raposo family

246

program. You went through different steps in shop, the first step was carpentry, then simple construction, or molding, or the foundry. My favorite was the machine shop. We used grinding machines, the lathe and the milling machine, but we filed by hand using rough files. They'd put a hunk of iron in your hands and you had to make a cube out of it. You had to meet certain measurements and learn how to use a micrometer and the rulers and all the tools necessary for a machinist. In Portugal, we were called mechanics. We were not automobile mechanics but machinists.

We put in ten hours a week in the shops but I had a lot of theoretical experience with different qualities of steel. You have carbon and cobalt and T-42 and T-15. The school bought the steel according to what you were doing. If you were making a screwdriver, for example, you'd have to have a little bit of temper, which is the hardness of the steel. You would apply the heat to that screwdriver after you mold it and file it into the right condition. We did it by hand.

The school taught us to stick together. One day at school a teacher was sick and there were 28 of us with nothing to do from 10AM to 12PM. We took off to the playing field and played soccer. We saw the officer on duty that day come walking over the hill between the school and the playing field. We ran away and he didn't catch anybody. Later, he put us in formation and wanted to know who was playing soccer. We didn't say anything. Then he took us to the director of the school, and still nobody said anything. The director said, "If none of you will tell me, then all of you must have been playing so I'm not going to give any of you permission to go home for the weekend."

Well, there was one boy whose parents came to visit him every day and I guess he didn't want to stay all weekend so he said, "I don't know who was playing soccer, but it wasn't me." You know what the director did? He told us, "You've got to stick together. That's the way it should be. Everyone is going to have liberty except for you (the boy). You have no respect for your friends. You told on them, so you're going to stay." I thought that was proper. I really respected that man. We stuck together like that.

When I reached the age of 18, I didn't go to college because I had to serve in the army. Portugal was not in the war in 1939, but they sent us to different colonies. Portugal had been one of the biggest, most powerful colonial countries in Europe. I was sent to the island of Terceira in the Azores in January 1943.

There was never any combat but sometimes it was close and we would man the machine guns, especially at night. Sometimes the German subs or the Americans or the British Navy was around there. I was the sergeant of a platoon and we had two posts. My platoon were machine gunners. One of my posts was aimed at the sky and the other was aimed at the bay.

I met my future wife Mariana while I was in the Azores. Her mother's house was across the street from my headquarters and I used to see her at the window. When the troops would be in formation or on maneuvers, all the townspeople would come outside to watch us march. I would see that girl there and think I liked her. And we started to talk and that's how we got married. In the Azores and in Portugal, we can only talk to a girl at her window. They don't come out to talk with us. You couldn't take a girl out to the show all alone.

I was discharged from the army in December 1945 and went to Lisbon and got a job. The work was not what I had studied but it was hard to get a job and you'd take the first thing you could get your hands on to make a decent living. I would like to have studied engineering but I needed to help my mother. She had married a second time, had another child, and my stepfather died too.

Emidio stands outside of the car next to Mariana in front of her house in Terceira, 1944. The first window on the right is where Emidio courted her.

Courtesy of Raposo family

Emidio on leave from army duty, with Mariana, Terceira, 1945.

I asked for a month of vacation from my job so I could go to the Azores to see my (future) wife for Christmas. I went and we decided to get married in June or July. When I was getting things ready for the marriage, I asked my boss for permission to go but he told me, "No, you already had your vacation at Christmas." In a way, he was right. So I got married by proxy in 1946. I asked a friend, a businessman, in Terceira to represent me. The priest in Terceira, another good friend, was the witness of my wedding. Of course, later, my wife came to Lisbon and we went to my church and got married.

I was not doing the kind of work I liked and was always looking for something better so my wife said to me, "Look. Why don't you go to the United States? At least you'll have more opportunity." I was able to come because my wife and her parents were American citizens. Coming here was a little scary but I feel I came at the right place at the right time. It's a new experience and you don't know what you're gonna face, right? I didn't know any English and went to school a little bit to learn. I don't talk that good but at least I've made myself understood and I try my best.

Portuguese people are different from Americans in many ways. We respect older people more. The poor people in my country always bowed to the rich because the rich were the ones who gave them jobs and food. Americans also don't know their neighbors very well. In Portugal, even if you live in a building with 12 or 16 floors, you always know everybody. Over here I found that people sometimes lived in the same house and the ones who lived on the first floor didn't know the ones who lived on the second floor. I don't think there was a lack of friendship. It was a lack of communication. In Portugal, whenever new people came into our neighborhood, my mother would bake a cake or something to welcome them. And you would go to a neighbor's house to borrow a cup of sugar or macaroni. You don't see that much in this country. I love this country very much even though we are different.

I wanted a job where I could work with metals—metallurgy, you call it in English? That's why I went to Morse. When they called me for an interview, I didn't know how to speak English at all. The personnel manager knew French because he came from Canada and I knew a little French because I had studied it in Portugal. So we spoke in French. Then he filled out my application in English.

When I went to work at Morse, the foreman was Portuguese and many Portuguese people worked there. Many didn't speak English, some who had been here 20 years or more. I was surprised. I didn't expect them to be experts in English—I'm not—but I expected they could help me with my English and they couldn't.

I had no trouble learning the job because I knew how to read a blueprint and use a micrometer and a ruler and so forth. The skills and education I got in military school were a big help at Morse and I became distinguished in my work. I did skilled work, the kind of work you do with your fingers. You had to work on these real small drills. Sometimes these drills are very thin, you know? From number 80, which is real small, like a dentist's drill, to all sizes. I worked on a four-inch drill.

I stayed on the job for 36 years. I was what they called the wheeling-out man. When the work

Gauging tool diameter, Morse Tool Company, 1986.

Joseph D. Thomas photograph

comes out of the grinding machines, it goes into the hardening room and gets all black from the fire. Those drills have to go through a process called sandblasting to get the black out. The groove of the drill has to be polished without spoiling the cutting edge. That was my job.

We had different kinds of grinding wheels and my job was to grind out the grooves with grinding wheels ranging in diameter from one inch to one thirty-second of an inch. The wheel I used depended on the width of the groove. You have to put that wheel in the middle of the groove of the drill and grind to take off what's necessary. Sometimes we had to take off only one-thousandth of an inch off each side. Do you know what a thousandth is? Do you have any idea how small that is? If you take one of your hairs, it's about three- or four-thousandths, depending how thick your hair is. The thinnest hair is no less than two-thousandths.

We also did a cut called the thin web cut and we polished the grooves so the drill would cut more smoothly. I not only worked on drills but on all kinds of cutting tools—reamers, mills, taps. In addition to the thin web cuts and the polishing, I did grinding to make the cutting edges as sharp as possible. We could also make drills of two diameters. For example, a quarter-inch drill might have a point an eighth of an inch. In other words, the specifications might say that the last half of an inch of the drill should have a step down to a smaller diameter. Sometimes there would be three or more of these steps. These machines couldn't do this themselves so I had to fix it by hand. The excess material of the drill had to be removed by hand on the grinding wheel.

The wheel goes around with the rotation of the machine and you just touch the wheel with the tool and the wheel grinds until it reaches the specifications they want. Sometimes you only

Making a precise measurement, Morse Tool Company, 1986.

have a tolerance of one hundred-thousandth, so you must have good vision and skill with your hands. Like I said, it didn't take me long to learn at Morse because I brought that knowledge of steel with me. So I knew the difference between working with carbon and working with high speed or cobalt.

Sometimes I can say that Morse was more like a country club than a place to work. A lot of people would abuse the system. The bosses never forced the workers to be on their machines for the full eight hours and they would take coffee breaks whenever they felt like it. I tried to do my work as best I could and put in my hours. I believe if I want the job, I have to produce enough for that mill to make money to keep me working.

I always believed in the union because in Portugal, we had no unions and never talked about them. The union needed me because I spoke

Morse Tool Company workers grinding drill bits, 1986.

Joseph D. Thomas photographs

English and Portuguese and could explain union matters to the workers. Sometimes I did interviews as far away as Springfield. The union paid me for this. I also helped Portuguese workers with any problems they had with the union.

The union's president, the vice president, the secretary and steward were right in the shop. We elected them. I disagreed with the bosses many times on the best way to do things, but I knew the union was behind me to protect me. I don't think I would have had a voice to express myself without the union.

One time a milling machine had malfunctioned and spoiled thousands of dollars worth of work. The machine had left a bump on each piece of work. Rather than scrap the work, I was asked to fix it. The supervisor told me I had to do it at the rate of about $6.35 an hour. At that time, I was making about $10 an hour so my piecework rate was about $8.80 an hour. I told him, "No, I'm sorry. I don't have to do it. If you want it done, you do it." He said, "I don't know how and the company needs you to do it." Well, I walked out the door. Why did I do that? I knew I was right. I knew the union would back me up.

But the union didn't protect me as much as I thought it would. The shop steward came and talked with the boss for about half an hour. Then they called me into the office. I was the only one who could repair the work to the specifications. The shop steward told me that if I wanted to, I could come to an agreement with the boss and accept the job. I said, "No, that's not right. I want you to tell him to pay me what's in the contract." Finally, the boss agreed to pay me the unrated wage and I worked on that job for two or three weeks.

Sometimes the boss wanted me to work five hours on Saturday but I also wanted to see my son play football on Saturday morning. I would go to work at 4AM and work until 9AM so I could do both. I've always believed that parents should take an interest in what their children do.

I am a Catholic. I try to obey the commandments. I believe in confession. We have to believe that God is not an instrument of punishment. He is an instrument of forgiveness. When you realize you've done wrong, you ask God to forgive you. That's your obligation. Sometimes you can't fulfill your obligations as you should. That's why you go back to church and confess.

My youngest son is a physical education teacher in the Dartmouth schools. He wanted to go into the army but I asked him to try college and see if he could make it. He went to Bristol Community College, then Bridgewater. All my children are college-educated. My other son is a priest. One of my daughters is a nun and has a master's degree in administration. My oldest daughter is married and has a master's degree in counseling. I have five granddaughters.

I am proud of my children because they've achieved what I couldn't. I didn't finish college because my responsibility was to support my family in Portugal. I made the sacrifices to get schooling for my children and America gave them the opportunity.

Reverend Luis Mendonça, who would later become Monsignor and pastor at Mt. Carmel Church in New Bedford, celebrates with the Andrade family (Mariana's family) at a picnic at Mount Brazil, Terceira, circa 1933.

Courtesy of Raposo family

The Union Representative

Interview with Noe Gouveia

by Lynne Wilde

Noe Gouveia left Madeira for America when he was ten, terrified of all that lay ahead. He and his family settled on a farm in Norton, Massachusetts. As a teenager, he worked long hours in a supermarket and learned every job in the store. After graduation from high school, he worked full-time for Fernandes Supermarket as a meat cutter and meat manager. Noe, who saw his father lose his longtime job in a woolen mill and walk away with nothing, fought hard for worker pensions and decided to work full-time for the union. "I can help people better in the union," he said. It was also his ticket to a larger life.

· · · · · · · · · · · · · · · · · · ·

In 1946 I was a frightened ten-year-old boy, waiting in Grand Central Station for a train to take me and my family to Providence. I could not speak English and everyone and everything seemed so strange. The last time I had seen my father I was very young and could not remember him. He and my brother Joe, who had come over years before us, met us in Providence at an emotional meeting. I was so hesitant about my reconciliation with my father. My mother actually introduced us and he was very glad to see me! I felt relieved after we had our meeting.

My father had come to America seven years before, in 1939. My father got a job in a woolen mill and eventually bought a house and 18 acres of land in Norton. He had to save to send for the family. In 1944 my brother Joe was the first to leave and I knew our time would be coming soon. I was very skeptical. Two years later we got word and I will never forget it. We went from Madeira to Lisbon and stayed in a hotel room where we waited for the air fare. My mother had to control five kids for two months in one hotel room. Finally air fare was provided and we flew to New York.

We went to the new house and everyone was excited except me. I just stood outside hesitating to go in. I didn't understand what was wrong with me. I was nervous and unsure of the new place. My brother Joe took me by the hand and slowly brought me up the stairs. Food was set up on the table and the bedrooms were ready for us.

The small community in Norton was mixed with many nationalities. They were very old-fashioned and strict. My father worked on the farm, where he planted half the land, and at the woolen mill. We kids didn't have too much time to play. I started work at 13 in a supermarket and worked on the farm too. We also had a couple of milking cows, a couple of pigs and chickens. Until we got our licenses at 16, we didn't have much of a social life.

I was fascinated with sports in this country and regret being unable to participate because I worked 35 to 38 hours a week all through high school. I looked forward to recess because I could go out and play baseball. As I got older, I started to stand up to my father a little more and let him know that times had changed and you need to get into the flow of life around here. After a while, my parents began to accept the change, but it was hard for them.

I remember my first date. We had neighbors called the Armstrongs, and their relatives from New York came to visit every summer. Mrs. Armstrong's sister had two daughters, Joan and Carol, who came over at night and we played games like hide and seek. I didn't know she liked me, but one thing led to another and one day we went on a bike ride through Norton Center and Norton Grove—my first date on a bicycle ride with a girl from New York named Joan!

By the time I started high school, the girls didn't think of me as different from the next guy just because I was Portuguese. That barrier was gone and I went to my junior prom and other functions. When I graduated in 1956, I was still working at the supermarket. In the '50s, the supermarket industry was growing by leaps and bounds. You graduate one week, start working full-time the next. I started as a service clerk, bottling groceries and loading potatoes and onions. Everything was in bins and we had to put the potatoes in peck bags—that's 15-pound bags. From there, I went to groceries. I also worked as a cashier—I worked in all phases of the industry. Even when I was 14, I was buying all the candy for Fernandes! Eventually I made my way to the meat department and that is where it all began.

I worked my way up to an apprentice meat cutter and became a meat manager in two years, which was fast. There was some resentment from some of the older meat cutters but I was accepted. I managed six different meat rooms, and also opened the stores in Somerset and Foxboro. I worked in Somerset, Foxboro, Quincy, Brockton, then back to Oak Village in Brockton. In the small towns, you got to know the people better than in larger cities like Quincy and Brockton. The clientele from town to town are very different.

I stayed a meat manager for about 13 years. They tried several times to organize the company and came up with an in-store union, an association made up of employees who actually work for the union and the company both. I didn't see how you could serve two masters. In about 1972 a group tried to get the international union to come in and merge with the association but that failed. It took about two or three years before I became active with the union movement.

I had an advantage because I'd worked for the company since I was a teenager and knew most of the people. I went to all the stores and tried to convince the workers to sign authorization cards. When you are young, you don't think of it as taking a chance. You just do it. Two or three times we failed. People get scared. The intimidation factor by the company is one of the biggest problems. You lose a certain percentage of votes from people who have signed cards when they get in the booth and feel intimidated. We finally succeeded in getting a union in 1974.

I was still a meat manager at this time and we became part of the Amalgamated Meat Cutters Association, or the old Butchers' Union. We formed our own local at Fernandes and signed our first contract in 1974. After that I was a shop steward and on the executive board. Suddenly, I became very active and took part in the negotiations in the first contract as a committee member. I was interested in seniority and wanted a pension program for employees. I had seen my father work in the woolen mills

The staff of the original Fernandes store in Norton, MA, includes Augustine Gouveia (Noe's brother, standing far left), José Fernandes (owner, with hat), Joe Fernandes (son, next to José), Evangelina (daughter, next to Joe), Noe Gouveia at far right. At its height, Fernandes had 32 supermarkets.

Courtesy of Noe Gouveia

for 20 to 25 years and lose his job when the company went south, ending up without a pension or anything. We were successful in the first contract. At 4AM I got a call and knew the company wouldn't budge and it was the final proposal. I remember saying I will not recommend this contract to the workers because we have no pension program. I talked to Mr. Fernandes and told him how important it was to the people. They went back and about one hour later we got it in the contract.

Fernandes meat cutter, 1979.

On March 24, 1975, I went full-time with the union as the coordinator, then got more training through the international. In September I was elected president. I had mixed feelings about it because it was like going into the unknown. As a meat manager for 17 years, I could have gone into management. But I never regretted my decision. The union was never dull. It was helping people out. I felt I could do more for the people with the union.

At this time, we had about 2300 people, which was not a large local, about 25 stores. It was a lot of responsibility. Then there were 32 stores and the company ran into some business problems and they started closing stores. In 1978, they went into Chapter 11 bankruptcy, but had the right to operate the business. However, the judge can decide everything and can even renegotiate the contract. In most cases companies didn't make it, but we did. Vacations were canceled and we had to file 1200 claims on behalf of the members, which amounted to $475,000. At that time, Springfield Sugar Company bought the store but kept the Fernandes name. Springfield Sugar was the same as Sweet Life, the biggest wholesalers on the East Coast. During its troubles, only Springfield Sugar would extend credit to Fernandes. Then all of a sudden, they pulled the rug from under the store and said we want our money—$600,000. They became one of the major creditors in bankruptcy court.

Noe's last day of work, 1997.

We were down to about 1200 members when we merged with Local 1325 in Fall River. That year, 1979, was a historical time for the union movement when the retail clerks joined with the meat cutters to form the United Food and Commercial Workers (UFCW), the largest international union in the AFL-CIO with 1.2 million people. Locally, we had about 4,200 workers. I became secretary-treasurer after the merger and that became a very educational job. Eventually we merged with the former meat cutters in Providence and became 12,000 members in 1995.

Sometimes I think about that little boy from Madeira in Grand Central Station, terrified to meet his father, frightened of the new country and all that lay ahead. But things worked out. Working in a supermarket took me farther than I'd ever dreamed. Through the union, I learned about workers and managers, met wealthy and poor people, stayed home and traveled, served on committees, negotiated contracts, endured scary times. The union has been better than a college education. It has enabled me to help people and that's what life is all about.

Noe Gouveia addressing the union membership, 1976.

Courtesy of Noe Gouveia

253

Man and his best friend admire their patch of kale in a "community garden" on the grounds of the old Cawley Field in New Bedford, September 1951. Community Gardens, prevalent throughout southeastern New England during the Depression era, provided opportunity for Luso Americans to practice the traditional pastime of planting and cultivating crops, while putting food on the table. In the background are the former Fairhaven Mills on Coggeshall Street. Today, Interstate 195 occupies this lot.

WORKING THE LAND

Strawberries and Cement

A Story of the Portuguese of Falmouth

by Miguel Moniz

A ruddy young man named Gene Moniz went back to his town of Lomba da Maia in São Miguel, in the 1920s, accompanied by his father José. Gene was a bit of a man about town in Falmouth, on Cape Cod, where the family had settled. His father didn't trust him to be alone so he took him on the trip. Gene got his hands on a white horse and, fancying himself a *cavalheiro*, he pranced about the village and often trotted over to the neighboring village of Lombinha da Maia. With a cock to his head and cap pulled low over his brow, he attempted to woo whichever young woman caught his winking eye. In the Lombinha, no one called a Moniz a Moniz, so Gene was known as "Catunto." On one amorous excursion, young Catunto was awestruck by a young belle in the village, Maria José do Couto. As their families were close friends, he determined to marry her and made arrangements through his father with her family. Maria José, however, was having none of it. "I don't know what he thought he was doing on that white horse," she would later recall. "He thought he was some kind of *cavalheiro*. I had no interest in that Catunto or his white horse."

Gene left his horse in the Lomba, returning to Falmouth where he used his tilted cap to impress a different young woman, Elvira, from Burguete (another town bordering the Lomba), and the two married. A few years later, Maria José would fall in love and marry a man from a respectable Lombinha family named José Tavares. José brought her to America and they also settled in the Micaelense and Cape Verdean enclave of Falmouth, where Gene and Elvira lived. The two couples raised their families in Falmouth: Gene and Elvira raised two sons, Gene (known as Mickey) and Tommy. José and Maria José raised five children, Helena, Cecília, Maurice, Gilberto, and Martha. Throughout the decades that followed, the two families were at the heart of the Portuguese-American experience in Falmouth, and the destinies of the Catunto on the white horse and the young belle from the Lombinha would yet intertwine again…

Young "Catunto," Gene Moniz.

Courtesy of Tavares family

Falmouth, one of the most beautiful and vibrant of the seaside towns on Cape Cod, has been the destination and home for large numbers of Portuguese since the late 1900s. From the Falmouth villages of Teaticket, Hatchville and East Falmouth, Portuguese—*Micaelenses*, Cape Verdeans and a newer generation of migrants from Terceira—have been the backbone of the town's labor force and the movers behind many commercial ventures; they have dominated the ranks of public office to serve as selectman, police chief, fire chief. The Portuguese have given the blue blood of this old Yankee town, settled by Mayflower descendants and Revolutionary War heroes, a distinctive Latin hue of red and green.

Planting Strawberries and Harvesting Dreams

Agriculture brought the Portuguese to Falmouth. Opting to escape from the dreary life of factory work in New Bedford and Fall River, many came to Falmouth to pick cranberries. Agricultural work was more *simpático* with the kind of work they had done in the Azores and Cape Verde. For the industrious immigrants, picking cranberries was soon abandoned in favor of the more lucrative enterprise of cultivating their own strawberries. Although the industry was first commercially developed in the town by a non-Portuguese, George Davis of East Falmouth in the 1880s, the Portuguese soon came to command the strawberry industry. In the period prior to World War II, the Portuguese were cultivating the berry on roughly 500 acres of land, providing Massachusetts with 50 percent of the state's strawberry production.

Helena Tavares and mother Maria José harvest the family fields, 1940s.

Courtesy of Tavares family

Strawberry cultivation was a family business and the biggest growers in this period were the Augustas, the Benevides, the Emeralds, the Furtados, the Medeiros, the Pachecos, the Rabesas, the Santos and the Vidals. Two of the biggest cultivators were the Tavares and the Moniz families. In the earlier part of the century, the two Tavares brothers, Leonardo and Francisco, cultivated strawberries on five acres of land, in the villages of Hatchville and East Falmouth. When Moniz, the elder Catunto, came to the United States, he and his family stayed with Francisco and his wife, Maria until they had saved enough to build their own home. Though the elder Catunto primarily worked for the state building roads, he was introduced to strawberries on the Tavares farm.

Eventually he purchased a 15-acre tract of land in the Teaticket village of Falmouth where he and his family cultivated strawberries. José had been increasingly frustrated by the non-Portuguese merchants who controlled the prices and inefficiently marketed the crop during the industry's rapid expansion. In 1915, he founded a labor association of Portuguese strawberry-growers. He also introduced a new plant, the Howard-17, which could be harvested earlier and yielded a larger and healthier berry. On three acres of land, Moniz could produce more than others cultivating on five acres.

Other families soon adopted the new plant as their own. Later, in 1935, José's son, Gene Moniz introduced the first tractor to Falmouth, fixing up an old 1928 Fordson tractor he acquired from a relative in Westport. He rented out his tractor at $5 an hour for untilled land and $4 an hour for tilled land, but many Portuguese did not see the new mechanized tiller as an improvement over the horse. Not until they saw his father's plentiful fields did the tractor become a sought-after commodity in the town.

Yankee Town to a Portuguese Community

The strawberry industry did much to alter the cultural and demographic makeup of the town. In addition to those who came to start their own farms, vast numbers of Azoreans and Cape Verdeans arrived for the picking season in the summer months. Many of these pickers favored long hours on rural farms over long hours in urban factories and stayed. The sparsely settled rural areas outside of the town's commercial and maritime centers soon became dense with Portuguese and Cape Verdean families.

Civic, political and religious organizations developed within the community to serve the new populations. The Portuguese-American Civic League, founded in the 1930s, aided Portuguese in the migration process. In need of a church, the community built St. Anthony's in East Falmouth, and the first Mass was said in Portuguese in 1923. Known as "the church that strawberries built," it was a Portuguese national Church until about 1980 and is the home of the renowned Henrique Medina painting of the *Vision of Fatima*. A stained-glass window offers a tribute to Portuguese strawberry cultivation. Within this church, the Portuguese worshiped, were baptized, married and interred.

Maria José and José Tavares (below) bring in the harvest, 1940s.

Photographs courtesy of Tavares family

257

Henrique Medina's renowned painting, The Vision of Fatima, *hangs above the altar at St. Anthony's Church in East Falmouth.*

The Standard-Times Library

From Harvesting Dreams to Building Them

After the World War II, strawberry cultivation began to wane and Cape Cod saw a boom in the housing industry. Two bridges constructed by the WPA in the 1930s made the virtual island of the Cape accessible, and the thriving economy gave everyone with a "car in every garage" the chance to drive it. Improvements in interstate transportation made strawberries coming from warmer climates, like California, more competitive. Many of Falmouth's strawberry families left the fields to start construction companies.

Of the big strawberry growers, the Augusta family became the town's primary providers of lumber; three Medeiros sons (Frankie T., Joe T., and Manny T.), the Rabesa family, the Santos family and the Vidal family became home builders. Francisco Tavares' son José became a carpenter, and the sons of the elder Catunto, José Moniz, went into the cement business. The children of the strawberry families, whose parents relied on one another during the harvesting season, came to work together in the construction trades.

But the transition was not always easy. Bank loans were necessary to raise the capital for start-up costs and expensive heavy machinery. George Sousa recalls his father's attempt to secure a loan from the Falmouth National Bank. When asked for collateral, he replied, "I have my children, and my jewelry is the callouses on my hands." Eventually, the money was secured. The story goes that when John Augusta, Sr. was turned down for a loan to start a lumber yard (the bank's board included a businessman who owned a lumber yard), he applied for a loan to go into the "molding business" and it was approved. Though he used the money for its stated purpose, he also sold the lumber used to make the moldings. The business grew into one of the area's largest lumber yards.

As the Moniz family played a primary role in strawberries, they also came to play a primary role in construction. Gene's brothers Adelino and Gile made concrete blocks for foundations, as well as ready-mix concrete for footings and floors. Soon they began making their own cement and developed a gravel crushing plant. In the meantime, the white horse-riding Gene, went into the masonry business. After leaving the Navy at the end of the war (all five living Moniz brothers served in the U.S. military), Gene went to work making foundations and learned the trade, leaving after a year to start his own business.

As the strawberry farms employed predominantly Portuguese pickers, the construction businesses hired mostly Portuguese laborers. And as the farms were passed down from one generation to the next, the construction firms went from father to son.

The Portuguese entry into the construction trade may be related to several factors: Many learned the trade when a nearby army outpost transformed into Otis Air Force base after the war. Many Portuguese (including José Tavares and his brother João) worked on the construction. Gile and Adelino Moniz sold over a million concrete blocks to the base during that period. The Portuguese also gained experience by laboring on the public works projects of FDR's New Deal; and many returned from the war with building skills. Further, anyone who has ever lived on a farm becomes handy with tools. For their children, the construction business became a way of life, much as strawberries had been to them. There was no going back to the fields.

In 1963 Gene Moniz' sons Mickey and Tommy attended a relative's wedding. At this Portuguese wedding, the only thing flowing more freely than laughter was wine. Tommy, 19, who inherited his father's penchant for gregariousness with the opposite sex, started to give his brother, 23, a hard time about not being married. Tommy had been married since he was 17 and already had one daughter and he decided his brother had been single long enough. "Mick, I think it's about time you get married." Mickey shook his head, "Marriage? I don't even have a girlfriend, never mind a wife." So Tommy, head full of red wine, set out to fix that problem. He staggered up to the stage and wrestled the microphone out of the band leader's hand. As Tommy tapped the microphone he scanned the crowd and spotted the most beautiful woman at the reception.

Clinking a glass, he said, "Ladies and gentlemen. I am very happy to announce the engagement of my brother Mickey to... Martha Tavares." Mickey turned crimson red and tried as hard as he could to disappear. Martha turned her head around from where she was sitting and said to no one in particular, "Who is that idiot?"

Embarrassed by his brother's behavior, Mickey walked over to Martha's table. She was sitting with her parents, José and the belle of the Lombinha, Maria José Tavares. He apologized to her and asked, maybe, to make up for the situation, if she would like to go out for dinner after the wedding. She agreed and a meal led to a few dates. One evening, Martha was getting ready for their date and she overheard her *avó* talking to Mickey. Her grandmother said, *"O Catunto, quando vai casar a minha neta?"* (When are you going to marry my granddaughter?) Martha dropped the mirror she was holding. Neither of them knew it at the time, but as it turned out, he could have said, "In two years, Sra. Tavares." And so, the wedding that never happened a generation earlier between the *cavalheiro*, Mickey's father Gene, and the belle, Martha's mother Maria José, finally came to pass by the marriage of their children.

The older generation began to hand over their construction businesses to their children in the 1970s, thus marking another transfor-

mation in the Portuguese community. These children, having grown up in the United States, but with ties to the Azorean community would play an integral part in the migration network that brought the next wave of Portuguese to Falmouth from Terceira, Azores. John Augusta Jr. took over one of the town's largest and most successful businesses from his father, and Mickey and his brother Tommy took over Moniz Mason Contractors in 1972.

Although these companies were taken over by a new generation, their hiring practices were similar to their elders; the firms were filled with Portuguese labor. In large part, because of these construction firms, the next group of Azorean migrants from Terceira began to settle in Falmouth. João Estrella was a *Micaelense* who came to Falmouth in the 1960s, as he had relatives in the town. But unlike most *Micaelenses*, his wife was from Terceira. Fewer people from that island find themselves in places like Massachusetts, due to a long history of migration networks to California. But João Estrela, through his connection to Moniz Mason Contractors, would soon change this pattern in Falmouth.

Estrella first started working for Gene Moniz in the 60s and is widely regarded as the area's hardest-working and finest artisan—Portuguese or otherwise—to work with stone. Estrela could pick up a large stone and with a quick tap of his hammer form the perfect fit for whatever he was building. He and his wife, from São Mateus, Terceira settled in the town, and were joined by some of her relatives from Terceira.

Crew of J&J Concrete (formerly Moniz Mason Contractors), 1997. Two of the three generations of Azoreans working for the company are represented in this photograph. Left to right, José Silva, Tommy Moniz, David Fernandes, João Silveira, Cory Silva, João Silva and Miguel Braga.

Miguel Moniz photograph

New Migration, the *Terceirenses*

As with Estrella's in-laws, other *Terceirenses* usually had jobs lined up before they even left the islands, and the companies always seemed to find room on the crew for an employee's out of work cousin. Although many of the *Terceirenses* initially found work in non-Portuguese companies—including factory work—many would leave these jobs to work with family and friends who knew their language and knew their way of life.

Two of the *Terceirenses* working for Tommy and Mickey eventually started their own construction companies. One of these men, José Silva, entered into a partnership with his former boss, Tommy Moniz and renamed Moniz Mason Contractors to J&J Concrete (after José and his son, Joe Jr.). At last tally J&J had a six man crew, all Terceirense migrants and Terceirense-Americans, and all related to the owner in some fashion.

The *Terceirenses* have been a large part of the revitalization of the town's Portuguese cultural community. They founded an *Irmandade* for the celebration of the Holy Ghost Feast, which now annually hosts about 1000 participants in the summer *festa*. They have also played a large role in the founding of a new civic club, the Portuguese-American Association which holds dances, dinners and has a club house for other community events.

In the early 1970s, Mickey and Martha built their house on Turner Road in East Falmouth. It was built on José and Maria

Taking a break from picking are: a cousin and Tavares children Martha, Gilbert and Maurice.

Courtesy of Tavares family

José's land, right next door to Martha's three other married siblings on what used to be family farmland. As each of the Tavares children married, they would receive a plot so the entire family all lived in a row in the same neighborhood. Later, José and Maria José would sell their old house and move down the street with their daughter Helena to a house next door to Martha and Mickey. Everyone helped out with yard work and family projects; all of the children played together and were one another's best friends; and every night, the whole family would gather at the house. Coffee and *cachaça* were poured, dessert was served, an accordion and guitars were brought out and cards were played over laughter and stories.

The youngest Catunto, Mickey and Martha's son, born in 1969, was always the happiest to be there. His parents named him for the family's island of São Miguel, and his work would eventually take him there. He still laughs when he thinks about his grandfather, Gene, the *cavalheiro* with the hat, and his grandmother, the young belle Maria José, who so many years ago, never married in Lombinha da Maia, and he wonders what would have happened if they had.

This young Catunto may have been born a generation earlier, and may have grown up in the strawberry fields and it would have been he who took over his father's construction company. Instead, the young Catunto was born a generation later, the product of the Portuguese migration story. Yes, it would have been funny had Gene and Maria José married. But then I would probably be in bed sleeping right now, getting ready to wake up early and plant strawberry runners or pour concrete (though I did do my fair share of that when I was younger) rather than writing this story about my family and about the Portuguese of my hometown of Falmouth.

I would like to thank the members of my family for their contributions to this story. Every fact that is missing makes me think of o meu avô, José Leite Tavares, who would have known them all were he still here to tell me. – Miguel Moniz

Miguel Moniz is working on his doctorate in anthropology at Brown University. He is the author of "Fox Point," in this volume.

DOWN ON THE FARM

THE GEORGE FARM IN DARTMOUTH

BY STEPHEN FARRELL

The George Farm, located on the corner of Slocum Road and Allen Street, is a landmark in Dartmouth. Every year townspeople and visitors look forward to the first day of a new season. Here they buy fresh fruits and vegetables in spring and summer, pumpkins and Indian corn in fall, Christmas trees and Poinsetta plants during the holiday season. Pink and purple flowers cascade from the greenhouses and brighten the driveways in spring and invite customers in.

When a visitor is given the chance to wander about the George Farm, he can see New England written all over the landscape—ancient stone walls, sweeping vistas, shades of green and brown as far as the eye can see. During planting season the view is breathtaking. On an early spring morning, one can stand at the corner of Slocum and Allen and gaze westward into the hollow of planted acreage. As the sun ascends behind you, mist rises from the fields while swallows dart through still air looking for insects. This is perhaps one of the most spectacular views in coastal Massachusetts. Here is a beauty that stays in the memory and, in our travels, compels us to return here and call it home.

The George Farm is one of the few working farms remaining in Dartmouth. Determined to continue the venture begun by Antone George in 1906, the George family braves storms, drought, insects and a host of other conditions bent on destroying their harvest. Though the farm has grown smaller in the past decade and houses now occupy some of the old farmland, this hardworking family prevails against the pressures on today's farmer.

As a young man in his teens, Antone George settled in the Dartmouth area after immigrating from Porto, Portugal. He left behind a life of tenant farming, working under desperate conditions with no hope of prosperity. He began his new life in America working for wages as a farmhand, striving to save enough money to buy his own land. Through frugality and grit, Antone eventually saved enough to rent land on Old Westport Road and begin his own spread. Over the next 20 years, he rented additional acreage. In the 1930s, when the Great Depression created financial ruin throughout the region, Antone was able to capitalize on an opportunity to purchase the old Dias Farm on Slocum Road, the site of the George Farm today. He became a landowner in 1932.

John George Jr., present owner and operator of the farm, takes time out to talk about the history of the farm and the plight of today's farmer.

My grandfather started farming in pretty much the same way we operate today. He was a truck farmer, one who grows his produce and trucks it to market himself. His main crops were corn, beans, carrots, tomatoes, strawberries, turnips and other staples. He worked long, hard hours by hand, picking and packing his own produce. Over the years, he hired more men during busy times, but the business remained largely a family-run farm.

View of the George Farm from the northwest corner during October harvesting, 1997.

Joseph D. Thomas photograph

Our regular market was downtown New Bedford, along Union and Water Street, near where the YMCA now stands. As a kid, I remember working with my father, getting up at midnight or 1 A.M., loading and setting up down there.

Private vendors like the Georges sold to a bustling Farmers Market in downtown New Bedford near the waterfront. Produce wholesalers including Jack and Saul Mickelson, Hime Faulk and the State Fruit Company were regulars at the market. Buyers from supermarkets, restaurants, fishing boats and the general public kept this outdoor institution going from the 1920s through the 1960s.

John George has witnessed dramatic changes in farming over the last 30 years.

Today's farming doesn't allow that kind of business. Profits are earned on a much tighter margin. Farmers cannot afford to transport their crops to market, maintain their equipment and pay their bills. Something has to give.

The farm stand on Slocum Road is a bustling marketplace for the freshest produce.

Following the October harvest, surplus pumpkins are left on the land for compost.

Joseph D. Thomas photograph

John K. Robson photograph

My father worked our farm his entire life, and probably always will. Both my parents still work on the farm and they're supposed to be retired. I have no idea how they still do it since both are in their '70s. My father goes out into the fields and works seven days a week, all year long. My mother puts in long days too, as well as doing the housework and cooking. That's the life of today's farmer if they want any chance to make a crop. That is the legacy of the George family. We work long and hard.

George family lore claims they follow a simple recipe for farming: When it comes to soil, you have to be able to feel it, touch it and taste it. The Georges employ tractors, plows, cultivators and other farm machinery, but the bulk of the work is still done by hand using traditional Portuguese methods introduced by Antone George.

We plant, hoe, weed and eventually harvest most of our produce by hand. During the season we hire help, kids putting themselves through school mainly, to work with my parents in the fields. Everyone in the family at some time has to help, even those who are working outside. We do a lot of hand work, especially picking because it produces a better crop with a long shelf life.

John George himself alternates between work pants and natty suits. When he's not farming, he's a New Bedford businessman. Formerly a State Representative and member of the State Board of Agriculture, Mr. George brought the plight of Massachusetts farmers directly into the State House. He continues today to be a respected advocate of New England farmers.

Seventy-five percent of Massachusetts farmers have some form of outside income. They have to work elsewhere in order to survive. Seventy-five percent! That is typical of southeastern Massachusetts. The public hasn't any idea of the costs involved in producing a crop on even one acre of land. If the government wasn't involved with subsidies, today's farmer could not survive.

Westport once produced the largest quantity of milk in Massachusetts, the majority of those farms owned and operated by Luso American farmers. Dairy thrived in our area. Today with land fetching $35,000 to

$80,000 an acre, few remain. Farms are actually becoming an oddity on the landscape. The most valuable commodity a Massachusetts farmer has is his land. Today developers are offering huge sums of money to farmers who just can't pass it up. In some cases, a farmer can realize a substantial profit after working a lifetime in a business where they go year to year without so much as breaking even. Farmers sell out because they have nowhere to go.

The George Farm sits on prime real estate, near the geographical center of Dartmouth. When Antone George retired in 1956, he divided his farm by giving his two sons, Joseph and John Sr., shares. In 1986, Joseph retired from farming and sold his share of land to developers. This very public sale reverberated throughout the community. "Our family respects my uncle's decision, but my father and I remain committed to continue farming," says John George.

We tend to take for granted the landscape of our own community, and we suppose it will always be there. The farmlands of Dartmouth are precisely what give Dartmouth its identity and beauty. The Portuguese contribution to farms and farming has been immense. In losing its farms, the town loses its charm. The George Farm not only gives Dartmouth fresh fruits and vegetables; it gives the town one of its most enchanting landscapes.

John George, Sr., 1954.

John Silvia and Antone George, Sr. 1934.

Workers give last-minute care to flourishing cabbage crop on the George Farm in Dartmouth, 1967.

John Silvia and Manny Mathews (on the digger), harvest potatoes the old-fashioned way.

Photographs courtesy of the George family

263

THE STORY OF MARTIN'S CHEESE

BY STEPHEN FARRELL

The Martin family arrived from the Azores in 1905 and began working long, hard hours in the Fall River mills. Their two sons looked for an escape from this bleak life and decided to try their hand at farming. In 1919 Manuel and Antone bought a farm in Westport and went into dairy farming. Eventually, Manuel and his family began turning a portion of the farm's milk into cheese, based on an old family recipe, and it soon became their principal product. Today Martin's Cheese is the oldest Portuguese-run cheese business in the country.

Paying off the Farm

On a summer day in 1928, Mrs. Maria Emilia Martin cooked a dinner of roasted chicken with potatoes and vegetables for her husband, children and their guests, Mr. and Mrs. Basile Michaud. For dessert, she baked a special cake. Hollowing out its center, she placed there a small Edgeworth tobacco can which contained the family's final mortgage payment on their Westport farm. Mr. Michaud, the former owner of the farm, was given the honor of cutting the cake. He quickly uncovered the tin and the final payment. The dinner was the celebration of a dream and culmination of a long journey.

The journey began in 1905, when Manuel Inacio Martin, a teenager, came to the United States with his family from São Miguel. They were millers of moderate means. The Martins were seeking greater prosperity and the means to pay heavy inheritance taxes back home. When they settled in the Flint section of Fall River, they soon realized that prosperity came at a heavy cost. Most of the family went to work in the textile mills, putting in 12-hour days and making barely enough to pay the rent.

This bleak life prompted Manuel's parents and most of his family to leave the United States and return to their former home in the Azores. Two sons, Manuel and Antone, stayed behind. When he first arrived, Manuel worked as a sexton at Mount Carmel Church in New Bedford. Seeking more income, he eventually left New Bedford to take a job as a third hand in the Davis textile mill in Fall River, where he worked primarily as a loom fixer. Here he met Maria Emilia Ferry. They married a year later and continued to work in the mills. Over the years Manuel and Maria had six sons and five daughters.

Their daughter, Mrs. Alexandrina (Lillie) Martin Smith, the oldest member of the Martin family today, recalls her parents' hard days in the mills.

The modern cheese room, 1998.

John K. Robson photograph

It was dangerous with the looms and spinning machines always running. People were always getting hurt and hurt horribly. If a machine broke, my father was one of the men who fixed them. He would replace the leather belts that connected the machines to the spinning shafts overhead. Many people lost eyes or worse when those belts would break.

The mill owners did not care about the Portuguese people. They worked like dogs and for what? They gave us the least money of all the workers, you know. But we needed the money and were willing to do any kind of work. The bosses knew it. My father always swore he would never see his children work in the mills.

As time went on, Manuel and Antone looked for a way to escape the harsh life of the mills. Though they had no experience in farming, they decided to plunge in. Helped by the advice of Mr. Antone Vieira, a highly respected Portuguese farmer in Westport, the two brothers decided to buy Mr. Michaud's 100-acre farm on Sodom Road in Westport. On June 29, 1919, the day after peace was declared in Europe, they bought the farm directly from the owner, without the assistance of a bank.

At the turn of the century, Westport was an old Yankee community of mostly farmers and fishermen. Between 1910 and 1920, a shift in population occurred when immigrants and first-generation Portuguese started buying farm land. David Martin, Manuel's son and present owner of Martin's Cheese, comments, "My father and uncle Tony were green and really had no idea how much land was worth. Some of the farms like my father's, about a hundred acres or so, went for $1,000 to $2,000. Others went for $9,000 to $10,000, like my father's. Do you think they would sell to the Portuguese at a fair price in those days? There was just as much resentment in Westport toward the Portuguese as there was in the cities. My father was lucky he had the ability to work like he did and keep the farm."

The early Martin farm was worked with horse-drawn equipment and human power, traditional farming methods found throughout the Azores. As the Martins discovered, the life of a farmer was difficult; farmers worked 10- to 16-hour days, seven days a week. The larger Luso American farms in Westport produced dairy and vegetables, which were transported to market in New Bedford and Fall River. Though some of these early farmers survived by producing only enough to feed their families, others began to supplement farm income with other products. Many created and sold traditional Portuguese foods at market along with their milk and produce.

Manuel started his farm with nine cows and cultivated about 25 acres, mainly corn and hay for the dairy. He also cut firewood which he carted to Fall River and sold. The early farm had a forge and blacksmith shop where Manuel repaired farm equipment for cash and, often, trade. The early Martin dairy farm had no electricity. After milking the cows, which was done by hand, the milk was strained, canned and picked up by the dairy driver. The farmers were at the mercy of the dairies, and the dairies were merciless. David Martin recalls:

My father decided to start making cheese because he was having too much trouble with the dairies. He and some men built a well in a structure next to the barn, which was lined with rocks and fed by a stream. We called it the water house. We could fit about eight or so of the old-fashioned 30-gallon milk cans in the well to keep the milk cool. The horse-drawn dairy cart would drive up, take the milk and leave the cans. One day my father noticed a can full of milk left in the well. The next day there was another. The following day, my father asked the driver why he had left the milk. The driver said he did not need all the milk and was going to leave another can today. "What am I supposed to do with the milk?" my father asked. The driver replied, "Wash your ass with it."

The dairy could also cheat you with classification. Milk was classified either to drink or to be processed into some form of milk product. It's the same today only the government makes sure everyone follows the rules. You see, if milk is for drinking, it is labeled class one and both the farmer and dairy receive the highest price for it. If the milk is class two or three and processed, then the farmers and dairy receive less money for it, say half as much or less. The dairies in those days, besides not buying milk, would pay you for class two or three when you had a contract for class one.

Manuel Martin, Sr. and Basile Michaud, circa, 1925.

Mrs. Martin in front of the family farmhouse. At right is the early winter cheese room. The summer cheese room was adjacent to the water house, circa 1940s.

Deliveries took place on Tuesdays and Thursdays. The first customers were small Portuguese groceries in Fall River and New Bedford.

Manuel Martin, Sr. loading a tabuleiro of cheese, 1930.

Photographs courtesy of Martin family

Lillie Smith elaborates:

It wasn't just the Portuguese farmers. The dairies did it to everyone. In those days, if you did not sell your milk, it was trouble because money was scarce. My father and some other Portuguese farmers tried to start a dairy of their own but it never made enough money to survive.

Seeking a way to be less dependent on the dairy, the Martins decided to process their milk into Portuguese cheese by using an old family recipe. Joseph Martin, a son who grew up in the early business recalls:

My mother knew the recipe. When my great-grandfather was in the Azores, he swore he would never use a hoe, you know, to farm. He would never be a farmer! So his family turned to cheese. In those days, many Portuguese women knew how to take curdled milk to make a spread that looks a little like cottage cheese. My mother knew how to make it from fresh milk, and that is what is special about our cheese.

Manuel Martin tested various molds to form the cheese. With some molds or *cincho* borrowed from Mr. Vieira, Manuel and Maria used a morning's milking and processed it into cheese. Manuel then took the cheese to market in Fall River, and it was well received. From then on, they continued to make cheese, and the new business began. In a few years, cheese production outpaced farming and became the primary family business. As the cheese business grew, the dairy farm expanded. The Martins used the morning milking for cheese and the evening and weekend milking for dairy.

Martin's Cheese employed the whole family in the business of cheese-making and packaging. The work was done entirely by hand and performed by both the men and women. "Milking was done at 6 AM," says Joe Martin. "We let the milk warm before we could use it. Then from about 8 AM to 10 AM, we made cheese." According to Lillie Smith:

We put the cheese in an icebox because we didn't have a refrigerator at first. My father got ice at an ice house down by the Narrows, you know, the Head of Westport. It was up to one of us to keep an eye on the cheese and ice. After we made the cheese, there was a lot of cleaning to do.

Today the government is involved with inspections and laws. Angie-Mae Cane claims:

My father was tougher than the government. We had to clean the cheese room, top to bottom everyday, after each batch was made. You had better have that cheese room clean! He put the fear of God in us. Don't think he wasn't just as fussy about the barn either. He made the boys and girls clean there too.

Cheese delivery took place on Tuesdays and Thursdays. The first customers were mainly small Portuguese groceries in Fall River and New Bedford. Around 1935, the business expanded to Providence. Says David Martin:

My father had a gentleman's agreement with a farmer who also made Portuguese cheese. He sold only east of Dartmouth and my father sold west of Dartmouth. When we started the business, my father dealt mainly with Portuguese markets, neighborhood stores.

David Martin prepares a tabuleiro of cheese for delivery, 1998.

Still a family owned business, Ellen Martin, David's wife, packages fresh cheese for market, 1998.

John K. Robson photographs

266

We delivered to Puritan Markets, Leite's Market, White Food Mart in Fall River, Ambrose Market in East Providence and Eagle Market in Providence itself. There were so many others that I can't even remember.

David's brother Earnest Martin recalls:

After the cheese business was going good, my father expanded the farm to market garden—that's produce and vegetables. We grew turnips, potatoes, kale, carrots and other things. We did not wholesale them out, though. My father went directly to the markets where we sold the cheese and cut out the middlemen. He also had us clean the potatoes and turnips before we put up a bushel. We could get maybe 15 or 25 cents a bushel more.

Another brother, James, remembers that the pace did not slow down in winter months.

We worked in the root cellar, or even behind the stone drag clearing the land of rocks, unless the ground was so damn hard you couldn't budge a stone. We had to constantly clear the land of stones. I was the youngest boy and my older brothers ran the fields. We would drive a big wooden sledge, like a big flat sled, behind a tractor and put stones on it. Back then they used horses. You used a sledge because you could roll the big rocks on it that were too heavy to pick up.

Though many jobs at that time were divided by gender, many of the Martin women worked in nontraditional capacities. Generally, the men loaded the trucks and shipped the cheese to market. Manuel Martin was a stubborn businessman, driven never to yield to lower-than-market prices for his cheese and produce. Joseph Martin describes his father's philosophy:

My father would not budge on price. If he could not sell his vegetables or firewood, he gave them to the poor or the church instead. When we started selling cheese, he would drop off only what the store could sell, maybe a little more. He took back what didn't sell, replacing it with fresh cheese. Nothing went to waste.

Mary Martin Vieira best describes the Martin legacy:

Mama and papa had nothing when they started and we did not have much growing up, but we always had enough food and clothes. We did well, even during the Depression. Papa made it a sin to waste anything. We gave the poor whatever we couldn't sell or use. They made sure we never forgot who we were.

Martin's Cheese is owned and operated in the same tradition today by David Martin, one of the oldest continuously run Portuguese cheese businesses in the country.

Author Stephen Farrell is the great-grandson of Manuel and Maria Martin, and lived briefly on the Martin farm. A graduate of UMass Dartmouth and a graduate student at Bridgewater, he is a teacher at West Side Junior/Senior High School in New Bedford.

Allen Martin, David's son, packs cheese in molds, 1998. The process of making cheese takes anywhere from five to seven hours. The Martins begin their day at 5AM and usually finish making cheese by noon.

The Martin family also breeds and raises dairy cows for market.

John K. Robson photographs

267

Tale of Two Dairies

Gulf Hill Dairy and Model Dairy of Dartmouth

by Christina Connelly

Many Americans remember the milkman's wagon delivering clear glass bottles full of fresh-from-the-farm, four percent butterfat cow's milk. What we now buy at the store in plastic jugs and cardboard cartons once appeared as regularly as the morning newspaper on doorsteps in every neighborhood, in every town, across the country. And even though the milkman made his rounds until fairly recently, we think of it as the "old days." The milk on those doorsteps came not from anonymous, faraway co-ops of dairy farmers but from actual milk-producing farms and milk-distributing dairies in Dartmouth, Westport and Fairhaven; not from Stop & Shop and Shaws but from Silvias, Salvadors, Fernandes, Santos and Lopes. Dairy farms in Dartmouth and Westport are an important part of the Portuguese narrative in this region. Mary Silvia Vermette of Model Dairy and Gil Fernandez of Gulf Hill Dairy tell that story.

Son of a Dairy Farmer

"My grandfather, Frank Fernandes started Gulf Hill Dairy as Gulf Hill Farm in late 1896. He was a real estate developer," relates Gilbert Fernandez. "He was the only local miner to turn a profit. He mined stones and, instead of using them for stone walls, sold them. He carted them from the farm to the south end of New Bedford on low-gears. The stones were used to build the foundation of the Page Mill (now the site of Cove Discount Store). That's why there were no stone walls on Gulf Hill Farm."

From those beginnings, Gulf Hill grew, getting a considerable boost from Gil's father, Joseph, a hard-working teenager. Born in 1880, Joseph was 16 when he started in the milk business, establishing his own delivery route. Gil recalls:

There was no such thing as a dairy in those days. You milked the cows, put the milk in jugs and distributed

Mary Fernandes on Gulf Road in Padanaram, 1902. On Saturdays she would take her horse (Evangeline) and buggy to collect from customers on the milk route.

it. A horse and wagon delivered the milk early in the morning—mostly in the South End. Then on Saturdays, my mother got in her horse and buggy and Evangeline (the horse) drove her to all the customers to collect the money. I was the youngest of four and sometimes I would go with her. To this day, I remember counting the pennies, and to this day, I'm a penny hoarder.

By 1920, my father built the first dairy building on Gulf Road, west of the barn. By that time, there were dairies that bottled the milk. Two years earlier, my father led the movement in New Bedford for pasteurization. Bad milk was the suspected cause of a scarlet fever epidemic during the war. By the early twenties, there were four routes with drivers and the milk was now pasteurized. We were one of the few farms that had the capability to pasteurize. Other farmers would bring their milk to us to be pasteurized, bottled, and distributed by Gulf Hill. This allowed the business to really grow.

Gulf Hill Farm began with about 125 acres. My father kept adding, buying four pieces of property on Bakerville Road and some on Tucker Road (now Hawthorn Country Club). By the end, Gulf Hill owned and operated 500 acres. My father also bought property across the street from the farm where he eventually put up the Certified Barn.

When my father was growing up, he had black and white cattle—Holsteins—because they were efficient and economical. But he always had a love for Guernsey cows. So in the mid-1920s he bought some Guernsey cattle, which was very unusual then. Guernsey cows were considered the thing; they had a butter fat content of four percent, very good for ice cream, a business we started in 1928. We also advertised our Golden Guernsey Milk, which was richer than milk from Holstein cows.

In the 1930s, my father built a barn for a special certified herd of Ayrshire cows, a Scottish breed. Stringent regulations were involved in certifying a herd and we were one of only two certified dairies in New England. My father took great pride in his certified herd. Milk from certified cows was more digestible; it was meant for babies and older

One of the earliest Gulf Hill Delivery trucks, mid-1920s. Gil and his brother delivered milk to Nonquit, Bay View, Salter's Point, Potomska, and the summer colony area. They later expanded to Horseneck Beach.

The main dairy barn, built in the 1920s, was the center of operations.

Below, the Fernandes family in front of Gulf Hill's original homestead.

Bottom, view from the silo looking east alongside Gulf Road.

Photographs courtesy of Fernandes family

269

Gulf Hill's 1941 calendar advertises their special certified milk. The smiling baby is Gilbert's son.

A "Shining" Example of Health and Happiness, this is a Gulf Hill Baby of the Fourth Generation, fed exclusively
- - on - -

GULF HILL
CERTIFIED MILK

RICH, PURE AND PROTECTED
- It is the World's Finest Food -

Produced under Medical Supervision at

GULF HILL FARMS - SO. DARTMOUTH
Dial 8-5888 For Your Health's Sake

Joseph Fernandes (top left) and the certified dairy crew in front of the Certified Barn. At top right is the certified dairy technician, 1940s.

The famous Gulf Hill Bucket, circa 1935. The motorized crank broke off during the '38 hurricane.

GRADE "A" MILK

GULF HILL DAIRY
ICE CREAM

Photographs courtesy of Fernandes family

people with digestive trouble. The certified barn was an operation in itself. People came and watched the cows being milked through a big picture window. The building housing our Certified Barn still stands across the street from the main farm. The Children's Museum building was our main barn, built in the 1920s. It replaced the older structure as the central site of farm operations.

Gil was never forced to be a farmhand, which is unusual for a farm family. He and his brother were involved to a certain extent, cleaning and capping the bottles before those procedures became mechanized and taking on their own delivery route in the summers. In the mid 1920s, he and his brother Raymond delivered milk in Nonquit, Bay View, Salter's Point, Potomska, the whole summer colony area, and later on they expanded to Horseneck Beach. Gil says, "I never did learn how to milk cows. My fingers were too long. I tried, but I was never good at it." He also remembers, at 10, learning to drive a big Autocar delivery truck. But, for the most part, their lives were kept separate from farm and dairy business. This he attributes to his mother's unique, forward-thinking attitude and lifestyle.

Mary Fernandes, born Mary Foster (originally Figueiredo), grew up on a farm on Sconticut Neck Road in Fairhaven. (Her father came from the Azores on a whaling ship.) Mary knew farm life firsthand but wanted to expand her horizons, and later, those of her children.

We did not really become farm children. My mother was a remarkable woman, very modern, very advanced for her time. She left the Catholic Church to become a Christian Scientist, something that was unheard of. She bobbed her hair and took elocution lessons. All four of us children went to prep school, finishing school and college. We had music lessons and dance lessons in the Duff building. She had indoor plumbing installed in the 20s and even hired an interior decorator. She played golf, took riding lessons, built a tennis court in part of our orchard and she started the Gulf Hill Ice Cream Parlors. She was really something.

The family bought the Bates and Kirby Ice Cream Parlor on Pleasant Street in New

Bedford. Gulf Hill Parlors began selling ice cream, cakes, sherbet and then expanded into a restaurant. Gil remembers it being the most popular eating place downtown, especially for lunches. The family also established smaller ice cream outlets that were only open in the summer. These stands dotted the highways throughout the area: Oxford Creamery on Route 6 in Mattapoisett was once a Gulf Hill satellite location. The Gulf Hill Bucket was built in 1930s after Joseph Fernandes' trip to California when he saw novelty structures like huge ice cream buckets and Brown Derbies. Gil points out:

There was nothing like that around here, so when my father built our Bucket on the main farm, it became an attraction. The bucket actually had a motorized working crank, until it broke off during the 1938 hurricane. People would come from all over to see the bucket, and to sample our unusually rich ice cream. I spent many a summer as an ice cream stand operator.

Gulf Hill Parlors was sold in 1951, around the same time Cumberland Farms moved in and began selling cheaper milk without deliveries, thus eliminating a lot of overhead. By this time, 1947, Joseph Fernandes had died, leaving Gil and Raymond to run the business. Raymond died in 1952, and Gil continued the operation until about 1961, when he sold the land to the Lester Insurance Company. By this time, farming had ceased, and grazing stopped in 1965. The main barn then became a restaurant/nightclub called the Twin Silos, which operated for several years. In the 1980s, the land was bought by a trust that later established the Dartmouth Children's Museum.

If the story of Gulf Hill Farm and Gulf Hill Dairy sounds more like an American Dream scenario than a Portuguese-American immigration narrative, perhaps it is. The Gulf Hill Dairy story has little talk of feasts and homelands and traditions, but is rich in Americana. Gulf Hill Dairy stands as an example of the central role farming played in the lives of Portuguese Americans in southeastern Massachusetts. More important, it illustrates the role that Portuguese Americans played in shaping American agriculture and the landscape.

Dairy Farmer's Daughter

Mary Vermette, formerly Mary Silvia of South Dartmouth, sits forward in her high-backed chair and recites a long litany of Portuguese surnames—Silva, Silvia, Freitas, Perry, Motha, Camara, Vieira, Gaspar. Attached to all these names is a dairy farm in Dartmouth or Westport. "There were many, many dairies when I was growing up," she says. Her own people were dairy farmers on both sides, so she has an intimate knowledge of the life, memories that have stayed with her through many years of academic life.

She was, in many ways, a "farm girl," like her mother and grandmother before her. Her mother, Mary Santos Silvia, grew up on the Santos Slocum Road farm, and when, after a two-year romance with Charles, she married into the Silvia family, her farm life continued. As Mary recalls, her mother played a crucial, active role in the day-to-day operations of the farm and dairy, particularly during the war years. Mary remembers her mom and the farm:

She was not one to stay in the house. She used to do the haying, and I would join in. And later, during World War II, it was very hard for people because all the men were at war. My father, being in the dairy business, was not drafted but he was left with no help. So I can still remember; my mother

Seated are Charles G. Silvia and his bride, the former Mary Santos. Standing are Mary's sister Marianna, Charles' brother Antone, and the young ring-bearer Raymond Miranda. The Silvia/Santos marriage was one between two dairy farming families. The newlyweds' combined experience and business acumen kept the family farms going.

Bottom, Mary Vermette (right) and her cousin Cecilia (Pacheco) Russell enjoy a pasture stroll.

Photographs courtesy of Mary Silvia Vermette

had a big thirty-three truck, and she would drive it to make deliveries. And then later on, things got so bad with gas and tires, they had to go by horse and wagon to deliver the milk. My mother would do this herself, and I would go with her sometimes. The dairy could not have run without her. But she was raised on that kind of work and she was very good at it, and very smart in her way. Like many Azoreans, we were agrarian people. Altogether, our family had three and a half farms—two farms on Chase Road bought by my grandfather, Frank Silvia (Joaquim), and a farm on Slocum Road begun by my mother's father, Manuel Santos. Also on Chase Road was a third farm, operated by my great-uncle.

The story of how Mary's people ended up on these farms is, like so many Portuguese immigration narratives, both typical and unique. Both sets of Mary's grandparents came from the Azores, her father's family from Faial, her mother's family from Terceira. Frank Silvia, her paternal grandfather, got work on a farm in New Bedford's south end and boarded in one of the many Portuguese-run boarding houses around Rivet Street and Acushnet Avenue. The woman he married, Maria da Gloria DaRosa, might have been a housekeeper at one of the homes where Frank distributed milk.

Mary's maternal grandparents, the Santos, were married on Terceira, came to the United States and moved to the Newport area, where Manuel worked as a caretaker for the work horses on one of the Vanderbilt estates. The entire time Manuel Ferreira Santos was in Newport, he was known as Manuel Smith, due to miscommunication over the meaning of Ferreira. Loosely translated, Ferreira means blacksmith. As Manuel tried to explain his name in his limited English, the men took this to mean "Smith." The next day, the name Smith appeared on his mailbox and remained there until he left.

Just after Manuel moved back to Dartmouth in 1912 (at the prompting of his brothers), his former boss took a cruise on a new ship, the *Titanic*, putting out from Liverpool. When it sank, Mr. Vanderbilt was among those who lost his life. A generous sum of money was left to all those in his employ. Manuel Santos, no longer an employee, lamented the tragedy at sea but also the missed financial opportunity. With the sum Vanderbilt left each of his employees, he could have bought his farm on Slocum Road outright. As it was, Manuel Santos and Frank Silvia had to obtain mortgages after years of working for other people. Mary recalls that most of the Azoreans who ended up owning their own dairies first worked for old established Yankee farms.

I believe the farm on Brock Avenue that grandfather Silvia worked on was Yankee-owned as most property was in those days. While the Yankees and the new Portuguese immigrants got along, some Azorean farmers were treated less than generously by the people they worked for.

I heard this story from grandfather Salvador (of Salvador Dairy in Dartmouth) when I was growing up. When he and other farmhands on the Yankee farm where they worked sat down at mealtime, it was understood that you took only one potato each. If you violated that rule, you were looked at like a criminal. The farm owner passed the butter around, putting the dish in front of each of them for no more than a second, saying "Do you want butter? No. Do you want butter? No…," not even giving them the chance to say yes. At the end of the rounds, he would put the butter down and say, "Well, no one wants butter." That was the end of that. There were a lot of little stories like that.

Mary laughs as she finishes the story, but she becomes more serious as she tells of a letter she was given by a local historian, written by a captain on Bakerville Road, "lamenting the fact that so many farms were being bought up by these Portuguese." Yet, she points out, the Portuguese got along with everyone because "they stayed in their place. The French didn't try to go build a house in the middle of the Portuguese area either."

None of her own experiences with discrimination dampened the love and pride she has for her heritage. "I've always had a good time with everything: the sweet bread and the *suspires* (meringues), the *sopas*, the feasts. I remember one thing distinctly. They used to send people to Portugal or the Azores to film. Then they'd come back and show the pictures. I saw a film about Mount Brasil on Terceira where my family comes from, and I don't know what happened…I started to cry. That was my Vovó's land."

Mary's father, Charles G. Silvia, transformed the Silvia family's milk-producing farms into a large milk distributing dairy that took product from eight or nine other farms in the area as well as their own. This operation started out as Silvia Brothers Dairy in 1922, then became Model Dairy in the mid-to-late '30s after an amicable split with his brother John. However, no matter how good Charles Silvia was in the business, he always hoped to go to school, become a lawyer, explore different fields.

The great disappointment of his life was that he never finished school. That was why my education was always looked after. He never told me, but he was as proud as he could be that I went to Harvard. But that was the way things were in his day; you did what you had to do.

Christina Connelly of New Bedford holds a master's degree in English from Boston College. She is a contributor, editor, and sales representative for the South Coast Insider.

ASSIMILATION AND FUTURE PERSPECTIVES

BY MARIA DA GLORIA MULCAHY

Image of the Portuguese

"Portuguese Diplomat Comes Bearing Gifts," said the top story in *The Standard-Times* of New Bedford, March 19, 1998. Portuguese Foreign Minister Jaime Matos Gama presented checks for $500,000 to the New Bedford Whaling Museum, $400,000 to the Center for Portuguese studies at UMass Dartmouth and $13,000 to the Great Feast of the Holy Ghost in Fall River. He also promised government support for a new museum in Fall River dedicated to religious and cultural celebrations. "We are clearly trying to increase the visibility of Portuguese immigrants in the United States," said the minister, whose picture accompanied the article.

If local newspapers mirror the communities they serve, then the image of the Portuguese is becoming more visible and positive than in the past. A closer look at the newspaper reveals that persons of Portuguese ancestry are involved in many spheres of local life: Ric Oliveira and Dick White, reporters; Arthur Motta, New Bedford marketing director; George Rogers, New Bedford City Council president; Kenneth Souza, chairman of Acushnet Public Works; Jose Castelo, a prominent realtor and Armand Fernandes, former New Bedford city solicitor, "headed for swift confirmation as the state's first Portuguese-American probate court justice" on the Bristol County Probate and Family Court.

This picture is very different from the image painted in 1923 by Donald Taft in his book, *Two Portuguese Communities in New England*. Attracted by the high infant mortality of Fall River's Portuguese in the early 1920s, Taft undertook what would become the seminal work in studies of assimilation of the Portuguese in the United States. A thorough researcher, Taft examined Portuguese history, local records and conducted interviews with Portuguese families in Fall River, Massachusetts and Portsmouth, Rhode Island. Influenced by the theories of eugenics popular at the time, Taft looked at complexion and eye color, size and shape of heads and other racial characteristics in his attempt to ascertain how much "Negroid blood" flowed through the veins of the Portuguese. By his own admission, his data left "unanswered the fundamental question whether the Portuguese are naturally inferior or their poor showing is chiefly due to tradition and lack of incentive and opportunity." Nevertheless, his conclusions, stated with a candor that would be politically incorrect today, served to delineate the image of the Portuguese in this country until the present.

Mr. Taft's study emphasized the "ignorance and illiteracy of the Portuguese," associated with "lack of interest and meager attainment in education, low wages and economic exploitation, superstition and fatalism, cheap amusements and unrestrained fecundity." Typically, they are unskilled laborers who work in farms or factories, the women leaving their children in the care of others and joining their husbands on the factory floors. Their children leave school "almost invariably at the earliest possible moment" and go to work to help the family. Through their industry and thrift, "they save money and make considerable economic progress as measured by ownership of property."

Mr. Taft probably echoed the feelings of many when he concluded that their cheap labor was needed, but it was unfortunate one had to put up with their alien ways. "But the Portuguese are a permanent element in our two communities," he stated. "Moreover, if they should leave, a substitute labor supply would have to be found." He noted that the Portuguese were recent immigrants and, although their overall condition was dismal, there were some signs of improvement. Namely, their standard of living rose with duration of residence, and infant mortality decreased in the second generation. If it turns out their "backwardness" is not a "result of inborn racial inferiority, but of social handicaps, the future may value them more highly," he speculated. With patriotic caution, he concluded if one were to be optimistic, "much may be done for and by the Portuguese when their handicaps shall have been removed and when they shall be truly of America as well as in America."

Mr. Taft's book follows in the tradition of anti-immigrant sentiment generated by the great influx of immigrants from Eastern, Central and Southern Europe after the turn of the century. The white Anglo-Saxon Protestant majority became fearful that the character of American society would be transformed by these predominantly Catholic and Jewish undesirables, belonging to distinct and inferior races. In 1917, Congress began issuing laws aimed at damming the flow of immigration from these areas. The Johnson Act of 1921 and subsequent revisions established national immigration quotas based on the number of persons of the same national origin already residing in the United States. Since most of the immigration had been from Western and Northern Europe, those from other areas received very low quotas. Portugal received a quota of 503 immigrants per year and, in 1929, it was reduced to 440 by the President's Proclamation Act, Number 1872. By this time, it was evident that United States no longer needed their cheap labor. Although no statistics exist, many Portuguese and their American-born children returned to Portugal during the Depression. The migratory flow from Portugal, from 1911 to 1930, comprised about 120,000 people; this number was reduced to 10,752 between 1931 and 1950.

At the end of World War II, United States again needed labor to help rebuild the economy. In 1952, immigration laws were revised to allow skilled workers into the country, but most Portuguese willing to emigrate did not qualify. Resumption of Portuguese immigration to the United States resulted from the eruption of the Capelinhos volcano on Faial in 1957. Appeals to the American government led to the passage of the Azorean Refugee Acts of 1958-1960 and 4,811 people came to this country. A few years later, the Immigration Act of 1965 abolished the national quota system and Portuguese immigration experienced a tremendous surge. In 1969, Portugal became the seventh largest contributor of immigrants to the United States with 16,528 persons. According to the Justice Department, 106,710 Portuguese immigrants entered the United States between 1971 and 1980. Social and economic improvements in Portugal since the Revolution of 1974 have slowed immigration to a mere trickle. However, in 1990, the U.S. Bureau of The Census estimated there were close to one million persons of Portuguese ancestry living in the United States.

The Portuguese in America: Where Do They Live?

Seventy-five years have passed since the publication of Donald Taft's study and the Portuguese story needs updating. Where are the Portuguese in America today and how much are they "of America?" This writer will rely primarily on data from the 1990 U.S. Census of Population and Housing, especially regarding ancestry and the foreign-born. This data will be supplemented with previous research on the subject, local publications and interviews by the author with Portuguese immigrants. Although the term assimilation is used in the title, the important question may not be how the Portuguese have assimilated, adapted or acculturated, but where they stand with respect to "middle-classness."

According to the 1990 Census, there were 900,000 persons nationwide who identified themselves primarily as Portuguese. Of these, 3/4 were born in the United States and 1/4 were born abroad, primarily in Portugal. These include only individuals who said they were Portuguese, or Portuguese and one other nationality. In Massachusetts, 195,040 persons reported they were simply Portuguese; 46,133 said they were Portuguese and one other nationality; 48,251 described themselves as one other nationality and Portuguese. This last group was excluded from this analysis.

Not all of those 232,583 foreign-born persons were born in Portugal. According to census estimates, only 210,122 were natives of Portugal. Many Portuguese came to the United States by way of Canada, France, Brazil and the former Portuguese colonies, which may explain the discrepancy.

Table 1 shows the Portuguese live primarily on the East and West coasts. Fifty-two percent live in the Northeast and of these, 47 percent are foreign-born. Some 39 percent live in the West where 13 percent are foreign-born.

TABLE 1. PEOPLE OF PORTUGUESE ANCESTRY IN THE U.S., 1990						
REGION	# OF NATIVE BORN	%	# OF FOREIGN BORN	%	TOTAL #	%
Northeast	292,738	63%	171,569	47%	464,307	52%
Midwest	16,472	86%	2,565	14%	19,037	2%
South	50,169	78%	13,830	22%	63,999	7%
West	308,098	87%	44,619	13%	352,717	39%
Total	667,477	74%	232,583	26%	900,060	100%

Source: U.S. Census, 1990

The greater number of foreign-born in the Northeast is not surprising since most post-1965 immigration was directed to the East Coast, primarily Massachusetts, New Jersey, Rhode Island and Connecticut. What is surprising is that the West should exceed the Northeast in the number of American-born Portuguese. Prior to 1900, most Portuguese immigration was directed to the Pacific states; the pattern then changed and most immigrants were coming to New England. This finding is even more striking when you consider only California and Massachusetts (table 2).

TABLE 2. NATIVITY OF PORTUGUESE IN THE U.S. BY STATE OF RESIDENCE, 1990					
STATE	# OF NATIVE BORN	%	# OF FOREIGN BORN	%	TOTAL #
California	233,603	85%	41,889	15%	275,492
Connecticut	20,377	57%	15,146	43%	35,523
Massachusetts	166,981	69%	74,192	31%	241,173
New York	17,070	50%	17,385	50%	34,455
New Jersey	19,721	35%	37,207	65%	56,928
Rhode Island	53,556	70%	23,217	30%	76,773
All Others	156,169	87%	23,547	13%	179,716

Source: U.S. Census, 1990

Table 3 shows that most of the Portuguese in Massachusetts are concentrated in the Southeast region. In Bristol County, the Portuguese make up 32 percent of the total population; Dukes 14 percent; Barnstable and Nantucket six percent; Plymouth four percent. In terms of absolute numbers, Bristol County is again first with over 164,000 persons of Portuguese ancestry, followed by Middlesex and Plymouth.

Tables 4 and 5 show the distribution of the Portuguese within Bristol County. Table 4 shows that 56 percent live in New Bedford and Fall River, 10 percent in Taunton and 44 percent are distributed throughout the suburbs. Dartmouth is the most populous, followed by Somerset, Fairhaven, Westport, Swansea, Acushnet and Seekonk.

Table 5 indicates the Portuguese have their highest concentration in Fall River where they are 50 percent of the total population. New Bedford follows at 45 percent, Dartmouth 42.5 percent; Somerset and Westport, 40 percent. The density of the Portuguese diminishes as one moves away from the major urban centers.

Portuguese migration is family migration, which accounts for the patterns. New immigrants are sponsored by relatives who procure a home and jobs for the new family, often before they arrive here. New immigrants tend to live in the tenement houses of other Portuguese, close to the factories where they would start working soon after arrival. The usual pattern is for the new immigrant family to save money and buy their own tenement house after a few years. Later on, if they succeed, they sell the old three-decker and buy a house in Dartmouth or another suburb. The story of Eduardo Melo, a well known travel agent in New Bedford, illustrates this pattern.

Mr. Melo came to New Bedford with his wife and three children in 1962 from Ponta Delgada, São Miguel. His cousins picked up the family at the airport. Mr. Melo

TABLE 3. POPULATION OF PORTUGUESE ANCESTRY BY COUNTY – TOP TEN		
COUNTY	NUMBER	PERCENT
Bristol	164,049	32.4
Dukes	1,662	14.3
Barnstable	11,030	5.9
Nantucket	340	5.7
Plymouth	19,289	4.4
Middlesex	41,742	3.0
Essex	16,589	2.5
Hampden	9,876	2.2
Norfolk	8,362	1.4
Worcester	7,998	1.1

Source: U.S. Census, 1990

TABLE 4. RANKING ACCORDING TO TOTAL NUMBER OF PORTUGUESE (FIRST AND SECOND ANCESTRY)		
CITY/TOWN	NUMBER	PERCENT
Fall River	46,329	28.0
New Bedford	45,091	27.5
Taunton	16,468	10.0
Dartmouth	11,580	7.1
Somerset	7,014	4.3
Fairhaven	5,754	3.5
Westport	5,326	3.2
Swansea	4,825	2.9
Acushnet	3,537	2.2
Seekonk	2,716	1.7
All others	15,409	9.4
Total for County	164,049	100.0

Source: U.S. Census, 1990

TABLE 5. RANKING BY PERCENTAGE OF COMMUNITY POPULATION (FIRST AND SECOND ANCESTRY)		
CITY/TOWN	TOTAL POP.	TOTAL PORT.	% PORT.
Fall River	92,703	46,329	50.0
New Bedford	99,922	45,091	45.0
Dartmouth	27,244	11,580	42.5
Somerset	17,655	7,014	39.7
Westport	13,852	5,326	38.4
Fairhaven	16,132	5,754	35.6
Taunton	49,832	16,468	33.0
Acushnet	9,554	3,537	32.7
Swansea	15,411	4,825	31.3
Freetown	8,522	2,551	30.0

Source: U.S. Census, 1990

started working right away at a Portuguese daily newspaper on Rivet Street. "The job was waiting for me when I got here," he said. "Some acquaintances in New Bedford promised me I would have a position, taking the place of someone I knew. My relatives had a home ready for us on Rodman Street, a Portuguese neighborhood. We paid rent but it was completely furnished and equipped."

After a few years, the Melos bought a house, lived there for four years, then bought a second house in New Bedford. Nine years later, "After working so hard, I thought I should have a brand new house," said Mr. Melo. "I had a little money, the bank had the rest…and I had the rent from the other two houses to help me pay for the new one." So the family built a brand new home in Dartmouth. Not all families are able to do this, or receive this kind of support, but it is a common pattern.

The move to the suburbs has been intensifying since 1990. Heavily Portuguese neighborhoods such as the North and South Ends of New Bedford have been losing residents along with the character imparted by the immigrants. Older immigrants remain, along with institutions such as churches, clubs and stores, but families with children have, in large part, moved to the suburbs or to less densely populated sections of the city.

Work

"Portuguese immigrants are amongst the most ambitious and energetic of all the immigrant races that have come to the United States. They are seekers of work, and if properly handled and guided are as good workers as are to be had anywhere. In many fields of labor the employers say that they prefer the Portuguese laborers to any other kind," wrote Christian Bannick in 1917. Many would agree with him today.

Sponsoring relatives assist the new arrivals in finding jobs as well as homes so they reflect the occupations of relatives rather than the immigrant's background or previous experience. Grace Anderson, who studied Portuguese immigrants in Canada (1974), found a marked difference in income and occupation between those who found their jobs through mainlanders and those who used Azorean contacts, a finding that reflects different work patterns by region of settlement and community of origin. For example, those who went to California often worked on dairy farms; settlers in the East in factories. This pattern is illustrated by the story of Gracinda and Humberto Fernandes.

The Fernandes, who lived in Cadaval, Portugal, had relatives in Newark and New Bedford. In 1970, their relatives encouraged them to come to the United States. Mr. Fernandes did not want to come, but his wife decided to try. She came to New Bedford as a tourist in 1971, could not get a job and decided to try New Jersey. "A cousin of my husband's, a gardener, helped me get a job as a housekeeper," said Mrs. Fernandes. In New Jersey, she was able to change her immigration status to that of legal resident. Once she got her green card, she returned to Portugal to get her family.

In 1978, Gracinda, Humberto and their two children, Jorge, 11, and Carla, 7, arrived in New Bedford. "We had cousins here, which made it easier to get jobs," said Humberto, who worked as a waiter and bartender in Portugal. He said he did not have a job waiting for him, but he had ideas and prospects. "My intention was to work in fishing, but my cousin knew that Cafe Europa needed a waiter. Since I had done that in Portugal, we talked to the owners and they gave me the job." Four years later, Cafe Europa closed. Humberto then asked a friend who worked in construction to help find him a job. He did. Gracinda used similar networks to find a job in a garment factory.

Humberto and Gracinda Fernandes are typical of continental Portuguese who came to this area in the 1970s. Continental men were more likely to work in construction or fishing than Azoreans, who predominated in the factory jobs. Among women, there were no significant differences between islanders and mainlanders; most worked in the garment industry.

Table 6 indicates that 50 percent of Portuguese immigrants in Massachusetts worked in manufacturing in 1990. American-born Portuguese are much less likely to be working in manufacturing jobs. In 1990, only 20 percent worked in manufacturing, while overall, 25 percent of Bristol County residents worked in this sector. American-born Portuguese have been moving away from the factories and into the service sector, especially into retail business, which has the largest concentration of the three groups (about 20 percent). Portuguese immigrants are more likely to work in construction, fishing, and business and repair services than American-born Portuguese or others.

American-born Portuguese are as likely to work in professional and related services as others in Bristol county (22 percent), whereas only 10 percent of the foreign-born work in this sector. However, these figures may obscure more than they reveal. For example, the table shows that nine percent of the population of Bristol County work in health services; also nine percent of Portuguese in Massachusetts work in health services. However, we do not know which proportion are physicians, nurses or orderlies. Interestingly, American-born Portuguese have the highest proportion (of the three groups in table 6) working in public administration.

Table 6 shows that Portuguese immigrants are factory workers, fishermen, landscapers, construction workers and mechanics, while Americans of Portuguese descent are teachers, middle-managers, plumbers, electricians, salespersons and office workers.

TABLE 6. DISTRIBUTION BY INDUSTRY FOR EMPLOYED PERSONS OVER 16 IN 1990			
INDUSTRY	MASS. PORTUGUESE FOREIGN BORN	MASS. PORTUGUESE BORN IN U.S.	BRISTOL COUNTY TOTAL POP.
Agriculture, forestry and fisheries	2.8	1.6	1.6
Mining	0.1	0.1	0.1
Construction	8.0	6.5	6.4
Manufacturing, nondurable goods	26.3	8.6	10.7
Manufacturing, durable goods	23.2	11.5	14.7
Transportation	1.7	4.0	3.1
Communications & public utilities	0.7	2.4	2.6
Wholesale trade	2.6	4.1	4.5
Retail trade	12.5	19.9	17.5
Finance, insurance and real estate	3.8	6.6	5.6
Business and repair services	4.1	3.8	3.5
Personal services	2.3	2.9	2.2
Entertainment, recreation services	0.3	0.9	1.0
Professional and related services			
Health services	5.0	9.2	9.4
Educational services	3.0	7.4	7.7
Other prof. & related services	2.0	5.2	5.2
Public Administration	1.0	5.2	3.0
			Source: U.S. Census, 1990

The Portuguese appear to own many small retail businesses in New Bedford and Fall River such as grocery stores, bakeries, coffee shops, restaurants, furniture stores, funeral parlors; also travel, insurance and real estate agencies. Until recently, many pharmacies in New Bedford were owned by Portuguese persons but most have fallen prey to giant chains, the last victims being Macedo Pharmacy in New Bedford and Matos Pharmacy in Fall River, absorbed by Stop & Shop.

Previous researchers have noted the absence of Portuguese names in the liberal professions. Suzete Baptista, a dressmaker who came to the United States in 1965 from Matozinhos, Portugal, recalls "there weren't any [Portuguese lawyers or physicians] then. Or if they were Portuguese, they weren't too proud of it. We had to get a translator or try to understand each other through gestures." She believes the situation began to change around 1980. "The Portuguese started hearing their language spoken more and stopped being ashamed of speaking it." Nowadays, one is very likely to find a professional who speaks Portuguese. However, the proportion of Portuguese professionals is still smaller than what would be expected from the total Portuguese population. This is especially true in the most prestigious professions, such as medicine and law.

This situation has been attributed primarily to two factors: the low human capital of the Portuguese as a group and the opportunity structure they found in this area. The Portuguese came to the United States with a very low level of education and professional skill. The factories needed people with a strong work ethic who could easily be trained on the job. As Dorothy Gilbert (1989) pointed out, there was a good fit between what the Portuguese had to offer and what the industry needed. While the factories provided immigrants an opportunity to make a decent living, in the long run, they may have become traps by depriving the second generation of the need to look for alternative and more prestigious jobs. They also offered little opportunity for internal upward mobility. Manufacturing industries have very little room at the top and few factory workers were able to move up or acquire the capital and knowhow necessary to open their own factories. But exceptions do exist.

James Pavao of Fall River is an example. Mr. Pavao owns Whaling Manufacturing, Inc., a garment factory employing about 500 workers. He also opened a similar factory in his native island of São Miguel. Although he is perhaps the most successful, or the most well known, he is not the only one. Gil Borges, owner of Andrea Sportswear in New Bedford, says there are at least six sewing factories in that city owned by Portuguese immigrants who worked in shops that closed. In Fall River there are at least ten. Mr. Borges, who took out loans and invested his life's savings, says it is extremely difficult to turn a profit. As a rule, the new factories are small and cannot benefit from economies of scale. Overhead costs are high, the price of the finished product is low and there is but a limited pool of talent to draw from. Programs aimed at retraining displaced workers have ignored the needle trades, said Mr. Borges. Other shop owners agree. Recent coverage of the Labor Department's investigation into "sweatshops" has also denigrated the image of the industry and made it more difficult to attract workers.

In summary, the industrial structure of this area has been changing drastically. The factories have closed. Dwindling catches and restrictive fishing legislation have forced many Portuguese boat owners to sell their fishing boats and lay off their workers. The traditional jobs of the Portuguese are disappearing. Portuguese immigrant men must travel outside the area to get work. Construction workers often spend weeks away from their families, or travel long distances to work sites in Massachusetts, Rhode Island, Maine, Connecticut and New York. Those who do factory work often have to travel close to Boston. Many women retired when their factories closed. Some of the displaced were recruited to work as chambermaids by Cape Cod hotels, which provide special vans to pick them up in New Bedford. The younger ones found jobs in the service sector as homemakers, health aides, clerks and cleaners.

The children of immigrants view factory work as something to be avoided. A low-grade job in an office, store or restaurant is perceived as superior to a factory job even if it pays only minimum wage. The few garment factories that remain in the area have trouble finding stitchers, pressers and other workers. What this means for the Portuguese is unclear. On the one hand, non-factory jobs require a higher level of education and they give workers a broader view of job opportunity. This could lead to greater occupational mobility. On the other hand, the lower wages of service jobs could hamper the group's overall socioeconomic achievement and reduce the means of providing for the education of subsequent generations.

Income

In 1985, this writer compared the 1979 wage earnings of Portuguese males in Massachusetts and Rhode Island to that of non-Portuguese, native, white males in the same area. The wages of Portuguese immigrants were, on average $5,000 lower than those of non-Portuguese whites, even though the Portuguese worked two weeks longer. American-born Portuguese fared slightly better: $3,000 lower than non-Portuguese whites for the same number of weeks worked. If median values were considered, the contrasts were less, but the differences were still striking. The median annual wage of Portuguese immigrants ($11,005) was only 76 percent of the wage of non-Portuguese whites ($14,505). American-born Portuguese earned 84 percent of the wage of their non-Portuguese counterparts ($12,250). The difference in wages can be attributed to the lower levels of education of the Portuguese, rather than to discrimination. In fact, the Portuguese earned more than white Americans with the same education.

This ability to earn a decent living despite low prestige jobs and low levels of education is even more striking in regard to median household income. In 1989, the median household income for persons of Portuguese birth was $32,500, higher than that of Bristol County ($31,520) or Americans of Portuguese ancestry ($31,293).

This pattern has been consistent across space and time. Grace Anderson (1974) found that the Portuguese did not need the same level of education as their Canadian counterparts to achieve the same median household income. Closer to home, and to our times, Dorothy Gilbert (1989), who studied the Portuguese of Fall River, also found no significant differences between the Portuguese and others in Fall River. They were "as poor as everyone else," she quipped. Actually, it seems they were doing a little better than most. Table 8 shows the percentage of families who lived below the poverty line in 1989.

Table 7. Median Household Income	
Portuguese immigrants	$32,500
Americans of Portuguese ancestry	31,293
Total population of Bristol County	31,520
Total population of Massachusetts	32,952
White population of Massachusetts	38,083
	Source:U.S. Census, 1990

TABLE 8. PERCENTAGE OF FAMILIES BELOW POVERTY LINE, 1989

Portuguese Immigrants in Massachusetts	8.1
Americans of Portuguese ancestry in Massachusetts	8.1
Total population of Fall River	12.3
Total population of New Bedford	14.6
Total population of Massachusetts	8.9
White population of Massachusetts	7.0
Total population of the U.S	10.3
White population of the U.S	8.1
	Source: U.S. Census, 1990

Only 8.1 percent of Portuguese families in Massachusetts lived below the poverty line. In comparison, 12 percent of the population of Fall River and 14 percent of New Bedford were below poverty status. Of the groups compared, only the white population of Massachusetts had a lower rate of poverty.

The Portuguese also appear to do well in terms of home ownership and savings, but few statistics exist to substantiate these perceptions. Gilbert (1989) found the rate of home ownership in Fall River for non-immigrant Portuguese was slightly higher than that of others; lower for those born in Portugal, but immigrants residing here the longest had rates close to that of natives. Financial institutions have been created to cater to Portuguese banking needs, the largest being the Luzo Bank in New Bedford. Banks from Portugal, such as Totta & Açores and Pinto & Sotto Mayor, have also opened branches to capture the immigrants' savings. On a recent visit to Banco Pinto & Sotto Mayor in New Bedford, this writer was shown a stack of deposit slips. Few were lower than ten thousand and some amounted to hundreds of thousands of dollars. How do they do it?

The most frequently heard explanation is that Portuguese families pool the wages of all family members, including the children's, and use the money for the family as a group. Often this is done at the expense of the education and needs of the children. Also their patterns of consumption differ from those of the natives. Immigrants transport patterns from home, where overall consumption is lower. Immigrant families are less likely than Americans to spend money on convenience foods, entertainment and other leisure activities. They are more likely to have a higher rate of savings, having come from societies that offered little or no public assistance in hard times. Saving is a means of insuring future financial safety.

The relative economic success of the Portuguese results from a combination of values toward work, spending and saving, as well as from strategies of utilizing the labor potential of family members to increase family income.

Education

Low education continues to be the curse of the Portuguese. All serious researchers and interested observers consider this finding a salient feature of the Portuguese immigrant profile.

According to the 1980 U.S. Census, 74 percent of foreign-born Portuguese over age 25 had less than a high school education. Analyzing data from the same source, Pereira (1985) found that American-born Portuguese males in Massachusetts and Rhode Island did better. Their median education was 12 years, one year below that of other white natives. The overall pattern for the Portuguese, however, was four years for those born in Portugal and 12 years for those born in the United States. These figures correlate with the number of years education is offered free in each country.

Ten years later, in 1990, the situation was not significantly improved for those born in Portugal and residing in Massachusetts. About 41 percent of women and 40 percent of men over 25 had four or fewer years of schooling. About 16 percent of Bristol County have bachelor's degrees or higher; about three percent of Portuguese immigrants fall in that category. This is not surprising considering they are adult immigrants who came with family responsibilities. The Portuguese government provided only four years of free, compulsory education. Most did not come to America to improve their education, but rather to work so their children would have a chance to go to school.

Unfortunately, the dream did not always materialize. The Portuguese are perceived as not valuing education. However, those who looked more closely found a more complex picture. Gilbert (1989) found that 80 percent of the Portuguese in her study were dissatisfied with their low number of years of education. They also believed education was the most efficacious way of getting a better job. However, for a variety of reasons, their stated values frequently conflict with their behavior patterns. One of the most obvious reasons for their low educational achievement is the humble social origins of the parents. A father who has only four years of education cannot easily help his child through academic hurdles or become a good academic role model. Language barriers, prejudice and the high demand for unskilled labor contribute to the problem.

But there are reasons for optimism. The notorious dropout rate of the Portuguese appears to be going down. More Portuguese children are staying in school beyond age sixteen and going on to college. A cursory look at the list of 1997 graduates of New Bedford High School indicates that 33 percent of the students graduating with "Highest Honors," and 45 percent of those graduating with "Honors," had Portuguese surnames. Table 9 reveals that more and more Portuguese are seeking a college education.

TABLE 9. COLLEGE ENROLLMENT IN 1990, MASS			
	AGE	MALE	FEMALE	TOTAL
Immigrants	18-24	14.2	19.2	16.6
	25+	2.6	2.9	2.8
Natives	18-24	28.4	33.7	31.3
	25+	3.4	5.3	4.3
				Source: 1990 Census of the Population and Housing

In 1990, almost 17 percent of young people, ages 18 to 24, born in Portugal were attending college; 31 percent of American-born Portuguese were enrolled. In both groups, the proportion is higher for females by about five percent. Education is definitely increasing among younger immigrants and American-born Portuguese.

Language

According to the 1990 Census, 133,373 Massachusetts residents (age 5 and over) spoke Portuguese or Portuguese creole at home. In 1990, Portuguese was the third most spoken language in the state, after English and Spanish. In Bristol County, Portuguese is spoken at home by over 15 percent of the same-age-group population. It is the most spoken language after English.

TABLE 10. PERCENTAGE OF PERSONS 5 YEARS AND OVER WHO SPEAK PORTUGUESE OR PORTUGUESE CREOLE AT HOME	
CITY/TOWN	PERCENT
Fall River	29.5
New Bedford	29.2
Dartmouth	19.5
Taunton	15.7
Somerset	11.3
Acushnet	11.2
Bristol County	15.8
	Source: U.S. Census, 1990

In Fall River and New Bedford, Portuguese is spoken at home by over 29 percent of the population, a number that decreases as we leave the cities. A sizable proportion, almost 16 percent of Bristol County, speaks Portuguese.

TABLE 11. PERCENTAGE OF PERSONS WITH ABILITY TO SPEAK ENGLISH				
AGE	ENGLISH ONLY	VERY WELL	WELL	NOT WELL	NOT AT ALL
5-17	2.9	52.7	40.4	3.3	0.7
18-44	7.9	48.1	23.6	15.8	4.5
45+	5.7	17.0	22.0	30.6	24.7
					Source: U.S. Census, 1990

A number of Portuguese weeklies, radio programs, two television channels, several official Portuguese Schools, a Portuguese library, and two major centers for Portuguese studies, at UMass Dartmouth and Brown University, help preserve the language. The television programs, especially RTPI, broadcast directly from Portugal, are playing a major role in the preservation and update of the Portuguese language and culture. United States residents now can tune in daily for current sounds and images of a country that most of them left about 20 to 30 years ago. But how well do they speak English?

TABLE 12. PERCENTAGE OF PERSONS WITH ABILITY TO SPEAK ENGLISH - AGES 5 AND OVER				
ARRIVAL	ENGLISH ONLY	VERY WELL	WELL	NOT WELL	NOT AT ALL
Before 1980	7.3	36.8	24.9	20.3	10.7
1980-1984	3.2	36.3	19.0	23.4	18.1
1985-1990	4.0	25.7	22.5	23.7	24.1
all periods	6.7	35.9	24.2	20.8	12.4
					Source: U.S. Census, 1990

In the 5 to 17 age group, only 4 percent do not speak English well. In the 18 to 44 group, only 4.5 percent cannot speak English at all. About 16 percent do not speak it well, but almost 80 percent speak it at least well. In the older age group 45 and over, ability to speak English decreases. Only about 35 percent speak well or better. As expected, ability to speak English increases with duration of residence, as shown on Table 13. Of those who resided in the United States for ten years, 69 percent spoke English well and about 11 percent did not speak English at all. Overall, only 12.4 percent of foreign-born Portuguese do not speak English at all.

TABLE 13. CITIZENSHIP BY SEX, NATIONAL ORIGIN AND PERIOD OF ARRIVAL MASSACHUSETTS, 1990			
ALL PERIODS			
	MALES	FEMALES	TOTAL
Portuguese	41.2	43.9	42.5
All others	42.7	48.3	45.7
BEFORE 1985			
Portuguese	43.8	46.5	45.1
All others	55.7	59.6	57.8
			Source: U.S. Census, 1990

The children often speak English among themselves, even when their English is not fluent, and Portuguese with their parents. Eventually, the parents ability improves and they begin to speak broken English with the children. Portuguese is reserved for parents and grandparents speaking with each other. Portuguese adults who speak English seem to prefer it to their native language. Frequently, they mix the two languages in the same sentence, speaking what some have termed "Portlish."

Political, religious and social participation

The strongest theoretical influences in studies of immigrants are human capital/status attainment theory and socialization theory. In the first case, theorists argue that once the immigrants attain the same characteristics as the natives in terms of education, job experience, parental occupation, etc., their position within the host society will be the same as that of the natives. Others have said that in order for real transformation to occur, there has to be a process of resocialization leading to the establishment of a new identity, e.g., American vs. Portuguese.

Though these two perspectives do not explain all the outcomes when cultures meet, they were used to guide our analysis because of their heuristic value. In the preceding sections we looked primarily at human capital. Let's now look at the process of resocialization.

In order for this transformation to occur, there must be a process of boundary reduction between members of different ethnic groups, or so it is argued. Milton Gordon (1964 and 1978) stated this would occur through intermarriage and participation in the cliques, institutions and clubs of the host society, on a primary group level.

Due to limited data, our conclusions must be guarded. To a large degree, the process is intrapsychic, but it does have behavioral manifestations. One of the primary requirements to become American is obtaining citizenship. The Portuguese are perceived as slow in acquiring citizenship, and this prevents them from participating in their communities and improving their situation.

The 1990 Census reveals about 43 percent of Massachusetts residents born in Portugal became United States citizens. The equivalent figure for all foreign-born residents was about 46 percent. This difference becomes more striking when we exclude those who have not completed their five-year residency requirement. If we look only at those who were qualified at the time of the census, the percentage of Portuguese immigrants who are citizens only goes up to 45, while that of the foreign-born goes up to almost 58. The Portuguese follow the same pattern in regard to gender as the general foreign-born: More immigrant women than men become citizens. Forty-four percent of Portuguese females were American citizens in 1990 as opposed to 41 percent of the males.

The citizenship picture has been changing in the past twelve years. Isabel Lopes Kochman, who deals with immigration issues out of Senator Tom Norton's office in Fall River, states that since the citizenship exams started being offered in this area in 1985, she has seen "a couple of thousand persons a year" become citizens and "about 98 percent are Portuguese." Maria Tomasia, New Bedford's election commissioner, said she lacks statistics on new citizen voters, but she has noticed a steady increase in their numbers over the past few years.

The increase in naturalization is not solely the result of a change in identity from Portuguese to American. These trends owe much to changes in the welfare law of August 1996, which threatened the well being of the elderly and the most disadvantaged. The Portuguese were shaken from their indifference by the antiterrorism laws which allow the INS to deport noncitizens convicted of a felony. Over the past two years, the community became increasingly aware that hundreds of young Portuguese were being deported, primarily to São Miguel. They are primarily males arrested for involvement with drugs, who came to the United States as children, and grew up speaking English without giving much thought to the fact they were not citizens.

The Portuguese are far from reaching a level of political representation commensurate to their numbers though things appear to be improving. This area now has four Portuguese legislators at the state level, Representatives Antonio Cabral, Robert Correia, Michael Rodrigues,

and Senator Marc Pacheco. At the local level, the Portuguese are still under-represented, but indications are the situation will be more favorable in the future. Table 14 compares the percentage of people in the community with Portuguese surnames who are officials, to the percentage of people of Portuguese ancestry.

Table 14. Political and Social Participation (Portuguese Surnames)				
	Officials	Appointed Officials	School Dept. Heads	Total Pop.
Fall River	25	0	17	50
New Bedford	32	16	37	45
Dartmouth	41	40	40	43
Fairhaven	15	35	33	36
Westport	17	17	17	38
Acushnet	23	32	43	37
* Includes the School Committee				
				Source: U.S. Census, 1990

Only in Dartmouth does the percentage of Portuguese involved in town affairs come close to their representation in the total population. New Bedford, which is half Portuguese, has only 32 percent elected officials and 16 appointed officials. In the school department, however, 37 percent of department heads and principals, including the superintendent, have Portuguese surnames. Fairhaven and Acushnet do fairly well in terms of appointed officials and representation in the school department, but the number of elected officials is considerably lower than expected. Fall River, with 50 percent of the population of Portuguese ancestry in 1990, shows the lowest rate of participation: no current appointed officials and only 25 percent of elected officials. In Westport, participation is less than half of what would be expected. The Portuguese have a higher rate of participation in education with a fairly good show of Portuguese surnames as department heads, principals and teachers. New Bedford, Fairhaven and Somerset have Portuguese school superintendents, and Fall River an assistant superintendent. For a group said not to value education, this is quite remarkable.

General opinion does not always mirror general patterns. It is said that Portuguese do not believe in the vote as a vehicle for social change. However, Rita Marinho studied the political profiles of Portuguese Americans in New Bedford and Providence in the late 1970s and discovered that so-called community leaders espoused this view about their fellow Portuguese, but she found no significant difference in beliefs about the power of the vote between Portuguese and Americans. The low political and social participation of the Portuguese needs to be further explored.

The Portuguese are believed to be a very religious group. In a predominantly Catholic region, they appear to be the most Catholic, due, in part, to the visibility of their religious festivals, which are public celebrations in New Bedford and Fall River. Indeed most of the Portuguese are Roman Catholics and belong to churches where services are conducted in both Portuguese and English. Church participation appears to be declining, but most children are still baptized, make their First Communion, are confirmed, married and receive their last rites within the Church. Christian-Revival churches are also attracting many Portuguese. These new groups are active in their proselytizing and their announcements have become a daily part of radio and television. These churches are frequently headed by pastors of Brazilian origin, or Portuguese who received religious training in Brazil. Some Portuguese are also joining established Protestant churches such as Methodist, Episcopal and Unitarian, but their numbers are very small.

No studies of the marriage patterns of the Portuguese are known to this writer. Casual observation supports the view that the first generation tends to marry predominantly Portuguese. Language and propinquity alone would predict this pattern. However, a growing number of American-born Portuguese marry people of other ancestries, reflected in marriage announcements in local papers.

While all immigrants interviewed by this writer said that individuals should choose their own marriage partners, most preferred their children to marry someone who spoke Portuguese, which is a statement about communication rather than unsuitable ancestry. In choosing a marriage partner, most stated that language is more important than religion. However, non-Catholics were more likely to want their children to marry within their religion and to give religion more importance than nationality. The stereotypical Portuguese family is headed by an authoritarian father who does no housework or child care and is very controlling of all family members, but especially his wife and daughters. The wife is perceived as the mediator, not only between the father and the children, but also between the family and the community at large. Despite this role as intermediary, the wife is said to have little power within the family.

Estellie Smith has done some work to dispel this stereotype, but the image persists. Most people interviewed agreed the male and female spheres were more clearly delineated in Portugal than in the United States, but once here, men are more likely to get involved in housework and the upbringing of the children. Overall, most said that women are usually responsible for the running of the home. Usually, men give their wives their pay to administer and receive an allowance. Women are more likely to cook and clean, but husbands also help. The disciplining of the children is shared. Men take care of the cars and the structural upkeep of the home. Couples together make major decisions. As with any group, generational and class differences follow general patterns.

Conclusions and predictions

The experience of the Portuguese in this area is inextricably bound to the history of Bristol County. The Portuguese have adapted to a new land, new people and new ways of living. They have experienced a large degree of assimilation, but they have also changed the overall image,

mores and traditions of this area. Although they are still a distinct group, with particular characteristics, the trend is to become part of "middle America." The Portuguese are moving from city to suburbs, from manufacturing to the service industries. The movement away from factory work predominates in the American-born and is not always accompanied by a rise in household income. As they move away from their immigrant roots, they discard some of the strategies that helped their ancestors attain economic success, in spite of their humble occupations.

In education, the trend is positive. Younger immigrants are staying in school longer and entering college at a higher rate than in the past. Within a generation, the exceedingly low levels of education of the majority of immigrants should disappear. Also, in Portugal, education has become compulsory up to 16 years. The generations born in this country show educational levels superior to the immigrants, but are still lower than the overall white population of the state. This may be due to their lower social origins. Though it may take a few generations, the Portuguese should be able to catch up.

English fluency should not impede the advancement of the Portuguese as a group. After being here 10 years, only about 30 percent of the immigrants said they could not function well in English. These are primarily older persons who have little opportunity to learn English because their lives take place within a Portuguese social enclave. As for the future of Portuguese as a major language in this area, the outcome is less clear. With fewer immigrants arriving, and those already here becoming more fluent in English, the natural outcome is for Portuguese to fade away. However, this fading away may be slowed down by radio and television programs in Portuguese and by an increase in ethnic pride.

The Portuguese are prouder of their heritage today than they were in the past, in part, due to the socioeconomic advancement of the group and to a reduction in perceived prejudice. As group self-esteem increases and prejudice wanes, participation in community affairs and primary relationships with persons of different ethnic groups should also increase. In the last 10 to 12 years, Portuguese immigrants are becoming American citizens at a fast rate. Although some are becoming citizens to avoid loss of benefits and privileges, many want to participate more actively in the affairs of their communities. This increase in participation is already visible in places such as Dartmouth, which augurs well for the sociopolitical future of the group.

In the past decade, Portugal's image in Europe has greatly improved. Immigrants who go back and forth feel the fresh breeze of change and take a new pride in their heritage. With ethnic pride on the rise, this writer would venture to predict that the U.S. Census of the year 2000 will register an increase in the number of people of Portuguese ancestry in this area as well as an improvement in their overall socioeconomic status.

BIBLIOGRAPHY

AZOREAN DREAMS

"A Profile of the Azorean," in *Issues in Portuguese Bilingual Education*, Donaldo Macedo, ed. National Assessment and Dissemination Center, Cambridge, 1980.

Almeida, Onésimo T. ed. *The Sea Within. A Selection of Azorean Poems*, translated by George Monteiro. Gávea-Brown, Providence, 1983.

Almeida, Onésimo T. *(Sapa)teia Americana*. Lisboa, 1983.

Amaral Pat. *They Ploughed the Seas: Profiles of Azorean Master Mariners*. Valkyrie, St. Petersburg, 1978.

da Silveira, Pedro. *A Ilha e o Mundo (The Island and the World)*. Lisboa, 1952.

Da Vida Quotidiana na L(USA)lândia (Of Everyday Life in L(USA)land). Coimbra, 1975.

de Melo, Dias. *Dark Stones*, translated by Gregory McNab. Gávea-Brown, Providence, 1988.

L(USA)lândia - a Décima Ilha (L(USA)land - the Tenth Island). Angra do Heroísmo, 1987.

Nordhoff, Charles. *Whaling and Fishing*, 1885.

Pap, Leo. *The Portuguese-Americans*. Twayne, Boston, 1981.

Vermette, Mary T. Silvia. *The Image of the Azorean: Portrayals in Nineteenth and Early-Twentieth Century Writings*. Instituto Histórico da Ilha Terceira, Angra do Heroísmo, 1984.

Vorse, Mary Heaton. "Clan Avellar", in Mary Heaton Vorse, *Time and the Town: A Provincetown Chronicle* . Dial, New York, 1942.

Williams, Jerry. *And Yet They Come: Portuguese Immigration from the Azores to the United States*. Center for Migration Studies, New York, 1982.

DOWN ON COLUMBIA STREET

"A plan of a lot of land belonging to Charlton Sherman and situated in the Village of Fall River." Surveyed and plotted August, 1828 by Simeon Borden.

Atlas of Bristol County. F.W. Beers, New York, 1871.

Atlas of Fall River City. George H. Walker, Boston, 1883.

Champlin, Kenneth M. Notes compiled for "People and their Places of Worship: A Neighborhood Interpretive Bus Tour and Interior Tour of Five Churches," Preservation Society of Fall River, May 22, 1983.

Cumbler, John T. *Working Class Community in Industrial America: Work, Leisure, and Struggle in Two Industrial Cities*. Greenwood, CT, 1979.

Herald-News, The. Fall River. March 19, 1955; June 6, 1976; November 1, 1976; June 25, 1984; June 19, 1988; August 24, 1990.

Fall River Street Maps of 1850 and 1854.

New Topographical Atlas of Surveys, Bristol County, Massachusetts. Everts and Richards, 1895.

Our County and Its People, A Descriptive and Biographical Record of Bristol County, Massachusetts. The Boston History Company, Boston, 1899.

"Plan of Land Situated in Fall River & Tiverton." Surveyed for Andrew Robeson, by Josiah Brown. Tappan & Bradford's, Boston, 1850.

THE PORTUGUESE FEAST

Bentley, Duncan, T. *Atlantic Islands: Madeira, the Azores and Cape Verde in Seventeenth Century Commerce and Navigation*. Univ. of Chicago Press, Chicago, 1972.

Fonseca, James W. "The Portuguese Community in New Bedford, Massachusetts," *Proceedings of the Northeast St. Lawrence Valley Geographical Society*, Vol. 16, 1976.

Gallop, Rodney. *Portugal: A Book of Folkways*. Oxford University Press, Cambridge, 1961.

Handler, Mark J. "Azoreans in America: Migration and Change Reconsidered," in *Hidden Minorities: The Persistence of Ethnicity in American Life*, Joan M. Rollins, ed. University Press of America, Washington, D.C., 1981.

Pap, Leo. *The Portuguese-Americans*. Twayne, Boston, 1981.

Salvador, Mari Lyn. *Festas Açorianas: Portuguese Religious Celebrations in the Azores and California*. The Oakland Museum, Oakland, 1981.

Sorenson, E. Richardson. "Visual Records, Human Knowledge and the Future," in *Principles of Visual Anthropology*, Paul Hockings, ed. Mouton Publishers, The Hague, 1975.

CHANGE AND TRADITION IN FOX POINT

Beck, Sam. *Manny Almeida's Ringside Lounge: The Cape Verdeans Struggle for Their Neighborhood*. Gávea-Brown, Providence, 1992.

Cabral, Stephen L. *O Folclore de Outra Vida*. Roger Williams Park Museum Publication Number 6, Providence, 1982.

Cunha, M. Rachel; Pacheco, Susan A.; and Pereira Wolfson, Beth. *The Portuguese in Rhode Island: a History*. The Rhode Island Heritage Commission and the Rhode Island Publications Society, Providence, 1985.

Halter, Marilyn. *Between Race and Ethnicity: Cape Verdean American Immigrants. 1860-1965*. University of Illinois Press, Urbana, 1993.

McKinney, Mary. "The Problem with Plaques," *Fox Point and Its People: A Community Diary*. CETA Summer Youth Employment Program, Fox Point Community Organization, Providence, 1979.

Sutton, Jennifer. "The People Next Door," *Brown Alumni Monthly*, May, 1996.

THE CONSTRUCTION OF IMMIGRANT IDENTITY

Baden, N. *Os Portugueses da America do Norte*, E. Maione Dias, ed. Lisbon, 1987.

Boelhower, W., "The Brave New World of Immigrant Autobiography," *Melus*, Vol. 9, No. 2, (Summer 1982).

da Costa, Pereira; Gomes, D.L.; and Gomes, P. *Introdução a Saudade: Antologia Teorica Aproximação Crítica*. Lello & Irmao Editores, Porto, 1976.

Feldman-Bianco, Bela. *Saudade: Portuguese Soul and Imagery*, a video available at UMassDartmouth.

Serrao, Joel. *A Emigração Portuguesa*. Sondagem Historica, Livros Horizonte Ltda., Lisbon, 4th edition, 1982.

Thompson, E.P. "The Meaning of Memory, Family, Class and Ethnicity in Early Network Television Programs," *Camera Obscura*, vol. 16, (January 1988).

Thompson, E.P. "Time, Work-Discipline and Industrial Capitalism," *Past and Present*, vol. 38, (December 1967).

Vasconcelos, Michaelis de. *A Saudade Portuguesa*. 2nd edition, 1922.

DOWN TO THE SEA FOR FISH

Doel, Priscilla. *Port O' Call: Memories of the Portuguese White Fleet in St. John's, Newfoundland*. Institute of Social and Economic Research, St. Johns, 1992.

Fisheries of the United States, 1976-1997. U.S. Department of Commerce, National Marine Fisheries Service, Washington, D.C.

Halter, Marilyn. *Between Race and Ethnicity: Cape Verdean American Immigrants. 1860-1965*. Univ. of Illinois Press, Urbana, 1993.

Mullins, Dan. *Down to the Sea for Fish*. Reynolds Printing, New Bedford, 1939.

Pap, Leo. *The Portuguese-Americans*. Twayne, Boston, 1981.

Stewardson, Jack. "Fishing Catch Down," *The Standard-Times*, New Bedford, February 9, 1998.

Williams, Jerry. *And Yet They Come: Portuguese Immigration from the Azores to the United States*. Center for Migration Studies, New York, 1982.

Wolforth, Sandra. *The Portuguese in America*. R&E Research, San Francisco, 1978.

LABOR

Bookman, Ann. "Unionization in an Electronics Factory: The Interplay of Gender, Ethnicity and Class," in W*omen and the Politics of Empowerment*, Ann Bookman and Sandra Morgan, eds. Temple Univ. Press, Philadelphia, 1988.

Cumbler, John T. *Working-Class Community in Industrial America: Work, Leisure, and Struggle in Two Industrial Cities*. Greenwood, Westport, 1979.

Georgianna, Daniel and Aaronson, Roberta Hazen . *The Strike of '28*. Spinner Publications, New Bedford, 1993.

Kelly, Richard. *Nine Lives for Labor*. Praeger, New York, 1956.

Standard-Times, The. Aug. 27–Sept. 27, 1934; May, 16 and 19, 1955.

Silvia, Jr., Philip T. "The Position of 'New' Immigrants in the Fall River Textile Industry," *International Migration Review*, Vol.X, No. 2, 1976.

Smith, M. Estellie. "Portuguese Enclaves: The Invisible Minority," in *Social and Cultural Identity*, Thomas K. Fitzgerald, ed., Southern Anthropological Society Proceedings, No. 8. Univ. of Georgia Press, 1974.

Williams, Jerry. *And Yet They Come: Portuguese Immigration from the Azores to the United States*. Center for Migration Studies, New York, 1982.

Strawberries and Cement

Agarwal, Eva. "The Portuguese," In *The Book of Falmouth: A Tricentennial Celebration*, Mary Lou Smith, ed. Falmouth Historical Commission, 1986.

Costa, Raleigh. *Recollections of Teaticket*. Tataket Civic Association, Falmouth.

Early Neighborhood

Boss, Judith A. and Thomas, Joseph D. *New Bedford, A Pictorial History*. Donning, Norfolk, 1983.

Flourio Cabral, Eileen and Vermette, Mary T. Silvia . A program: *Our Lady of Mount Carmel Renovation Dedication*. New Bedford, 1990.

"A Stepping Stone to New World Fortunes," *The Evening Standard*, New Bedford, September 20, 1917.

Huggins, Leon M. "Portuguese Navy Yard," *The Evening Standard*, New Bedford, July 8, 1905.

Huse, Donna, ed. *Spinner: People and Culture in Southeastern Massachusetts, Vol. I*. Spinner Publications, New Bedford, 1980.

Moeller, Elsie S. "The Living Conditions of the Portuguese in New Bedford." Unpublished document from the Federal Writers' Project in the collection of the Library of Congress, 1937.

Ricketson, Daniel. *History of New Bedford*. New Bedford, 1858.

Thomas, Joseph D. and McCabe, Marsha, eds., *Spinner: People and Culture in Southeastern Massachusetts, Vol. IV*. Spinner Publications, New Bedford, 1986.

St. John The Baptist Church, New Bedford, Quasquicentennial 1871-1996. Taylor Publishing, Dallas, 1996.

Vera, Stella. "The Portuguese-American Race: Early Customs in New Bedford." Unpublished document from the Federal Writers' Project in the collection of the Library of Congress, 1937.

Assimilation and Future Perspectives

Al-Khazraji, Emilie and Al-Kharaji, M. *The Portuguese Community of New Bedford, Mass*. Onboard, New Bedford, 1971.

Alpalhao, J.A. and da Rosa, V. P. *Immigration and Beyond: The Portuguese Community of Quebec*. University of Ottawa Press, Ottawa, 1971.

Anderson, Grace. *Networks of Contact: The Portuguese in Toronto*. Wilfred Laurier University Press, Ontario, 1974.

Bannick, Christian John. "Portuguese Immigration to the United States: Its Distribution and Status." A.B. (Stanford University) 1916 thesis, University of California. Reprinted in 1971 by Rand E Research Associates.

Gilbert, Dorothy Ann. *Recent Portuguese Immigrants to Fall River, Mass.: An Analysis of Relative Economic Success*. AMS Press, New York, 1989.

Gordon, Milton. *Assimilation in American Life: The Role of Race, Religion and National Origins*. Oxford University Press, New York, 1964.

Gordon, Milton. "Toward a General Theory of Racial and Ethnic Relations" in *Ethnicity: Theory and Experience*, Nathan Glazer and Daniel P. Moynihan, eds. Harvard University Press, Cambridge, 1975.

Katz, Jamie. "Opportunity, Exclusion and the Immigrant: Textile Workers in New Bedford, Massachusetts, 1890-1930." Unpublished B.A. thesis, Harvard College, Cambridge, Mass., 1974.

Marinho, Rita and Cornwell, Elmer E., Jr. *Os Luso-Americanos no Processo Político Americano: Estudo duma Situação Concreta*. Gabinete de Emigração e Apoio as Comunidades Açoreanas, Angra do Heroismo, 1992.

McGowan, Owen. "Factors Contributing to School Leaving Among Immigrant Children: The Case of the Portuguese in Fall River, Massachusetts." Unpublished Ph.D. Dissertation, Catholic University of America, Washington, DC., 1976.

Moniz, Rita. "The Portuguese of New Bedford, Massachusetts and Providence, Rhode Island: A Comparative Micro-Analysis of Political Attitudes and Behavior." Unpublished Ph.D. Dissertation, Brown Univ., Providence, 1979.

Pereira, Maria da Gloria. *A Posíção Socioeconomic dos Imigrantes Portugueses e seus Descendentes nos Estados de Massachusetts e Rhode Island (U.S.A.)*. Secretaria de Estado da Emigração, Centro de Estudos, Porto, 1985.

Ribeiro, Jose Luis. "Portuguese Immigrants and Education", Portuguese-American Federation, 1982.

Silvia, Philip T. "The Position of 'New' Immigrants in the Fall River Textile Industry", *International Migration Review*, Vol.10, No. 2 (Summer 1976).

Taft, Donald. *Two Portuguese Communities in New England*. AMS Press, New York, 1967.

U.S. Bureau of the Census. "The Foreign-Born Population of the United States." Tape file SSTF1, 1990.

_____. "Ancestry Population of the United States." Tape file SSTF2, 1990.

General

Huse, Donna, ed. *Spinner: People and Culture in Southeastern Massachusetts, Vol. II*. Spinner Publications, New Bedford, 1981.

Huse, Donna, ed. *Spinner: People and Culture in Southeastern Massachusetts, Vol. III*. Spinner Publications, New Bedford, 1984.

McCabe, Marsha and Thomas, Joseph D. *Not Just Anywhere: The Story of WHALE and the Rescue of New Bedford's Waterfront Historic District*. Spinner Publications, New Bedford, 1995.

McCabe, Marsha and Thomas, Joseph D., eds. *Spinner: People and Culture in Southeastern Massachusetts, Vol. V*. Spinner Publications, New Bedford, 1996.

Old Shipping Days in Boston. State Street Trust Company, Boston, 1918.

Tavares, Belmira E. *Portuguese Pioneers in the United States.*. R.E. Printing, Fall River, 1973.

Thomas, Joseph D., ed. *Cranberry Harvest: A History of Cranberry Growing in Massachusetts*. Spinner Publications, New Bedford, 1990.

Thomas, Joseph D. and McCabe, Marsha, eds. *A Picture History of Fairhaven*. Spinner Publications, New Bedford, 1986.

Venables, Bernard. *Baleia! Baleia!* Alfred A Knopf, New York, 1969.

Whitman, Nicholas. *A Window Back: Photography in a Whaling Port*. Spinner Publications, New Bedford. 1994.

About Some of the Oral History Subjects

Maria Candida Pereira and Liduina Linhares, old friends who share warm memories of their childhood in Pico, met again in the U.S. when they worked in the same factory. They continue to work as stitchers in local factories.

Soccer player Pedro Tavares lives in New Jersey and occasionally visits New Bedford.

Jorge Manuel Pereira, "the new immigrant" who came of age in Portugal after the Revolution of '74, graduated from UMass Amherst and works in human resources at St. Luke's Hospital in New Bedford.

Fernanda DeSousa, the little girl who hid "the letter" that eventually propelled her from her beloved Azores to a foreign land, lives in Fall River. A graduate of Lesley College, she has a degree in human development and a certificate in elementary education. She is the director of SStar Family Service Center and the assistant coordinator of the Greater Fall River Tobacco Free Coalition.

Raymond Canto e Castro lives outside the area and is no longer associated with *O Jornal*. Kathleen Castro is the current publisher.

Mary Fonseca, a Massachusetts Senator for 32 years, is now retired and living in Fall River.

Joseph Sousa, the man who returned to Madeira in search of his father's house, is a 1946 graduate of the Swain School in New Bedford. After working for several decades as a commercial artist, he teaches art in his studio, a remodeled barn on his Dartmouth farm.

Teresa Freitas, the woman who found love at the feast, was born in Madeira and settled in New Bedford in 1971. She is an executive with a local firm. Her name has been changed for privacy reasons.

The late Capt. Frank Parsons, the Provincetown fisherman, was the founder of Acushnet Fish Corporation in Fairhaven and Captain Frank's seafood market in New Bedford.

Azorean whaler José Pinheiro is retired but can be found at Luzo Auto Body on County Street in the south end of New Bedford.

José P. Avila, whaling factory worker, is a retired carpenter in New Bedford and lives with his wife. He spends much of his free time making model whaleships.

Emidio Raposo of Dartmouth is retired from Morse Cutting Tool and lives happily with his wife Marianna.

Noe Gouveia, whose boyhood job as a supermarket worker led to a career in the food industry, lives on Cape Cod. He became Secretary/Treasurer of UFCW, Local 328, in 1995.

Spinner Publications, Inc.

Spinner Publications, Inc. is an independent, nonprofit, community-based small press which seeks to record and promote the history and culture of the cities and towns of southeastern New England. We collect oral histories, particularly from older citizens, which tell the story of the individual, the city, the land; stories of families and their work. We are interested in the history of neighborhoods, farms and ethnic groups, and in photographic collections, artwork and documents of historic value. We seek to promote the humanities and arts of the region and collaboration among artists to present local history in an accurate, dramatic and entertaining way. Spinner also develops programs in the community and schools, including art and photography exhibits, a curriculum called *History Spoken Here,* and an archives and display on the history of textile manufacturing.

Spinner books have examined the effects of the Depression, industrialization and urbanization on the region. We have looked at the cranberry, textile and fishing industries, the rescue of a waterfront historic district, the role of women and children in industry. We have visited neighborhoods and farms, and portrayed the Portuguese, Cape Verdean, French-Canadian, Irish, Anglo, Native American and other cultural groups in the region.

In 18 years of publishing, Spinner has achieved numerous awards. Among them is the Commonwealth Award, Massachusetts' highest cultural achievement award, received in 1997-98 "for dedication to excellence in illuminating and celebrating the heritage of Southeastern Massachusetts through a series of high-quality books and publications." In 1985 and 1995, Spinner was awarded a Certificate of Commendation from the American Association of State and Local History. In 1994, Spinner received the Fontera Award from the Labor Education Center at UMass Dartmouth recognizing our "commitment to educating all people...about the meaning of social justice, the integrity of the human spirit and the importance of struggle in the creation of a truly democratic society." The Commonwealth of Massachusetts recognized Spinner with two official citations, including our contribution to the "African Experience in Massachusetts" exhibit.

Books and Calendars still available

- *Spinner: People and Culture in Southeastern Massachusetts, Volume V*
- *A Window Back: Photography in a Whaling Port*
- *Not Just Anywhere: The Story of* WHALE *and the Rescue of New Bedford's Waterfront Historic District*
- *The Strike of '28*
- *This City and Other Poems*
- *The New England Fisherman Calendar*
- *The Best of Spinner Historical Calendar*
- *The Portuguese Heritage Calendar (new)*

To be reprinted

- *Spinner, Volumes I, II, III and IV*
- *Cranberry Harvest: A History of Cranberry Growing in Massachusetts*
- *A Picture History of Fairhaven*

Forthcoming titles include: *Spinner VI*—another volume in our series of short stories, biography, oral history and photography; and *The Heritage Coast Cookbook Series.*

For our latest catalogue, or for information about books-in-print, calendars, forthcoming books, reprints, the Spinner photographic archives, and Spinner programs and activities, please contact us at:

P.O. Box 1801, New Bedford, MA 02741 • 1-508-994-4564 • 1-800-292-6062
http://www.ultranet.com/~spinner • email spinner@ultranet.com